THE
GREAT CULTURAL
REVOLUTION
IN CHINA

THE GREAT CULTURAL REVOLUTION IN CHINA

compiled and edited by the **ASIA RESEARCH CENTRE**

CHARLES E. TUTTLE CO.: PUBLISHERS
Rutland, Vermont & Tokyo, Japan

Representatives
Continental Europe: BOXERBOOKS, INC., *Zurich*
British Isles: PRENTICE-HALL INTERNATIONAL, INC., *London*
Australasia: PAUL FLESCH & CO., PTY. LTD., *Melbourne*
Canada: M. G. HURTIG LTD., *Edmonton*

Published by the Charles E. Tuttle Company, Inc.
of Rutland, Vermont & Tokyo, Japan
with editorial offices at
Suido 1-chome, 2-6, Bunkyo-ku, Tokyo, Japan

© *1968 by Asia Research Centre, 7F, 15 Ventris Road, Honk Kong*

Library of Congress Catalog Card No. 68-15016

First Tuttle edition, 1968
Second printing, 1968

PRINTED IN JAPAN

CONTENTS

Introduction

PART ONE

THE ORIGIN OF THE GREAT CULTURAL REVOLUTION

Chapter

PART TWO

THE GREAT CULTURAL REVOLUTION IN ITS EARLY STAGES

CONTENTS *(Cont'd)*

CONTENTS *(Cont'd)*

*Unless otherwise indicated, all selections in this
book attributed to official sources carry their
original titles.*

ABBREVIATIONS

CCP	Chinese Communist Party
CCP-CC	Chinese Communist Party Central Committee
CPPCC	Chinese People's Political Consultative Conference
CPSU	Communist Party of the Soviet Union
CYL	Communist Youth League
GPCR	Great Proletarian Cultural Revolution
NCNA	New China News Agency
NPC	National People's Congress
PLA	People's Liberation Army
PRC	People's Republic of China
US	United States

† = mark of reference to notes in *Glossary*

INTRODUCTION

Material gathered in this volume traces the origin and spread of a great upheaval now engulfing the whole of China. Supplemented by documents and releases emanating from official sources, this source-book attempts to give a comprehensive picture of events before and after the launching of the Great Proletarian Cultural Revolution in that country and the aftermath of the revolution in its very first stages.

Without comment on the cultural revolution itself, or anything approaching an explanation of factors which have precipitated the current convulsions throughout China, the purpose of putting out this book is to enable scholars of contemporary Chinese affairs to have access to reference material that may help them gain a better insight into what is going on in China today, so they may assess for themselves the consequences of a movement that encompasses all facets of life — political, ideological, cultural, economic and social — in that country.

Because of the ever widening scope and implications of China's Great Cultural Revolution and particularly because of a lack of indications that an end to the current upheaval is in sight, this volume is largely devoted to the early stages of the revolution, before the emergence of the Red Guards.

PART ONE

The Origin of the Great Cultural Revolution

CHAPTER I

Socialist Revolution in the Cultural Spheres

From 1963 until the formal launching of the Great Socialist Cultural Revolution in April 1966, a socialist revolution had been going on in the ideological and cultural spheres in China.

In this chapter we have extracted a number of articles from official sources which provide background material on the revolution in the fields of literature and art, drama, philosophy, education and academic work.

These articles reveal that, as the revolutionary struggle between proletarian ideology and bourgeois or modern revisionist concepts intensified in the cultural spheres, the socialist revolution was pushed into a broader and deeper stage.
— Ed.

1

All our literature and art are for the masses of people, and in the first place for the workers, peasants and soldiers and are for their use.

—Mao Tse-tung

(Talks at the Yenan Forum on Literature and Art, May 1942)

Modern Revisionism in Literature and Art

Extracts reproduced below are taken from different
articles identified individually in parentheses at the end
of each selection.—Ed.

Modern revisionists in the field of art and literature use a whole
battery of arguments to support what they describe as the "central
principle" in aesthetics—"writing honestly." Brandishing this "principle," they denounce as "dishonest" works of art and literature which
describe the people's revolutionary struggles, faith in the revolution,
and communist ideals. They use this "principle," too, to justify
their approval of works which indiscriminately wax eloquent about
bourgeois humanism, bourgeois pacifism and the bourgeois "ideal"
of a life of creature comforts and indulgence in the trivialities of home
life. Only such works, they say, are "honestly" written, and any work
that is "honestly" written must be a good work.

Why have modern revisionist writers come to play around with
this lie that anything honestly written is a good work? It should be
noted that the "honesty" they advocate is in essence the "honesty" of
the bourgeoisie. If we discard examination of the class content of this
"honesty" and accept the thesis that as long as it is honest it is good,
then there would of course be grounds for what they advocate.

Modern revisionists always try to conceal the class nature of their
ideology by trying to make out that it is of "the whole people," "of
all mankind." They do this precisely because they know that their
bourgeois ideas and standpoint are incompatible with the interests of
the revolutionary people. In order to propagate bourgeois humanism
and pacifism in literature, they claim that the misfortune of death, love
between inseparable lovers, and even lovers who are class enemies,
and so on and so forth are the "eternal themes" of literature — themes

that are close to the hearts of, and stir all readers. In order actually to publicise the ideas of bourgeois liberalism, they argue that "men are by nature inclined to freedom." In order to advocate "individual happiness" as the supreme goal in life to which all else must be sacrificed they make great play in literature with the melancholy, the exasperation, the loneliness and despair of men in the course of their pursuit of such "individual happiness," and present these feelings as "characteristically human" and supremely worthy of our sympathy, denouncing every "obstacle" to the attainment of this "individual happiness" as a bitter "cruelty." In order to negate the existence of classes and the class struggle, they urge that what is important in our social life is not the class struggle but the struggle between the "animal" in a man and his "human nature."

From this they go on to demand that we should pay more attention to describing universal "human nature" and that we should not get "over-involved in the class struggle." They want to market their baggage of bourgeois decadence and degeneration in a big way so they argue volubly that to eschew in literary works bold descriptions of relations between the sexes and of the beauty of the human body is to neglect major questions of human nature. It is not difficult to see that what they are trying to do is to pass off their decadent bourgeois trash as something pertaining to "all mankind," that is, as something transcending classes. What is sure is that in the depths of their hearts, there are a host of bourgeois things striving to break loose from all restraints so that they can come out into the open and dominate the stage. That is why modern revisionist writers are so enthusiastic in publicising "honesty in writing," which they wish to use to cover up the bourgeois nature of their ideology. This is undoubtedly one of the "high" aims of this theory of "writing honestly."

By calling things bourgeois "honest" and then asserting that this bourgeois "honesty" is the honesty of "all mankind," modern revisionists claim that they themselves are "honest" and at the same time revile as dishonest those writers who firmly adhere to the proletarian standpoint. This, as the old Chinese saying has it, is "to measure the mind of an upright man by the yardstick of a knave." This is exactly the way modern revisionists treat writers who uphold the proletarian standpoint; they judge such writers' proletarian minds according to their own bourgeois hearts; they denounce as dishonest anything that does not suit their own ideas and standpoint. Thus, when a proletarian writer warmly

4

praises some advanced phenomenon or revolutionary heroes of the new, proletarian age or sharply criticises some decadent phenomenon, the protagonists of "honest writing," basing their judgment on their own negative and scabrous sentiments, assert that this writing is not honest, that the writer is not speaking from the heart but is pretending. According to them, only those writers are honest who, like themselves, depict and lavish their sympathy on fallen women, rogues, nihilists and all sorts of queer characters who stand outside the mainstream of social history. When a proletarian writer, drawing on the logic of the people's life and the logic of the characters of his heroes and heroines, gives a vivid portrayal of lofty communist sentiments, the advocates of "honest writing" again proceeding from their empty, debased and degenerated outlook say: This is not honest because the writer has put on the "coloured spectacles" of the "doctrinaire," and so fails to write what is really in his heart. According to them, only people like themselves who unreservedly publicise individualism, liberalism, and what they call "liberty, equality and fraternity" are honest. It is clear that these means have been adopted by modern revisionists to strangle the development of proletarian literature and to drag proletarian writers onto the wrong path. They say to proletarian writers: Do you want to achieve "honesty in writing"? Then discard those Marxist "coloured spectacles" of yours! Marxist ideas are not the "words of your heart." If you don't forsake Marxist ideas and express "what is in your heart," you will inevitably fall into the abyss of "hypocritical writing." This is another of the "high" aims of the modern revisionists in advertising "writing honestly."

In the ranks of revolutionary writers there are still some people who are going through the process of ideological remoulding, of changing their class stand. They have reached a certain level of revolutionary consciousness and feeling, but at the same time their innermost soul is still petty bourgeois.

On many occasions, proletarian and bourgeois ideas still fight a sharp seesaw battle in their minds. They have not yet completely proletarianised their ideas and sentiments. That is to say, the conflict between old and new ideas is still going on in their minds. In writing about new things, therefore, they are all the more likely to encounter difficulties.

Modern revisionists take advantage of these very difficulties to check their progress. At a time when these writers are energetically studying Marxism, trying to discard their old, non-proletarian ideas and acquire new, proletarian ones, modern revisionists tell them: "You can't give answers to problems by going according to the old class categories!" You must free yourself from "dogmas" and project "your own philosophy of life!" Modern revisionists tell them that the new ideas are "false" and it is not worth one's while to write about them or expend energy in chasing after them; while, on the contrary, the old ideas are "honest," so it would be better to follow the old ways and write about these old ideas "honestly." Obviously, this theory of "writing honestly" is motivated by the vicious aim of negating ideological remoulding and pulling these writers back.

Modern revisionists publicise the need to free oneself from the "fetters" of dogmas even more frenziedly in the field of art and literature than they do in politics. Having freed themselves from these "fetters" what do they then describe as being in tune with their "own philosophy of life"? As we indicated earlier in this article, some of them declare that their only ideal and faith is that everyone should live and have a good time, increase and multiply and concentrate on creature comforts. They have indeed freed themselves from the "fetters" of Marxist "dogma" and "courageously" stated their "own philosophy of life," which, in fact, is nothing but the philosophy of bourgeois philistinism. For them, "honesty" in literature can only be achieved by shaking off Marxism which, they think, necessarily entails formulism and abstract generalisation in writing.

It may be worthwhile to discuss whether the literary theory of modern revisionists can serve writers as a guide to writing honestly. Modern revisionists don't, in actual fact, want socialism; they want capitalism, but they pretend to side with socialism. They are bent on imitating the decadent and declining culture of imperialism, but they want to give the impression that they have not departed from the proletarian stand. They have in fact discarded as "dogma" the revolutionary principles of Marxism-Leninism, but they still want people to believe that their "theory" represents a development of Marxism-Leninism. For this reason, they cannot help but stammer, stutter and talk falteringly. In most cases they cannot and dare not speak their mind out fully. They describe their imitation of reactionary and decadent imperialist literature as the pursuit of a "modern international style"; they describe as a "reform" and a "quest" their abandonment of the fine traditions of revolutionary literature; they dig up out of the dog-eared literary

6

theories of the bourgeoisie the view that "a book bares its writer's soul, it is his means of self-expression" and, proclaiming this view as their own invention, use it to defend their decadence.

We are justified, therefore, in saying that modern revisionist literary theory is a theory of the most dishonest kind. It can only create confusion among writers. Writers who have been caught by it are reduced to ravings which they cannot even understand themselves. If they are really honest, the modern revisionist literary theorists should discard their disguise and frankly admit that their theory is just an echo of modern bourgeois theories, that the "honesty" they advocate is exactly what is advocated by modern bourgeois literary theorists — simply self-expression, a baring of the soul, an escape from reality, a distortion of the truth, vilification of socialism, the lauding of capitalism and a portrayal of individualistic, liberalistic and nihilistic "complex souls," "melancholy states of mind" and "frenzied passions." The literary theory of modern revisionism is in essence the subjective-idealist literary theory of the declining bourgeoisie.

It would be well for those who have been befuddled by modern revisionist ideas in art and literature to take a look at the reactionary literary thought of the imperialist bourgeoisie. There they will find the "pinnacle" reached by those who have endeavoured to shake off the fetters of all "dogmas" and to glorify in every way the "honesty" of the soul.

Some literary "theorists" of the Freudian school, for example, have developed the following argument according to their own logic: an honest literary work is determined by the honesty of the writer's soul; honesty of soul, in its turn, is determined by a welling forth of the subconscious; all reasoning is a fetter on the subconscious and an honest depiction of the world is possible only when the subconscious is not directly affected by conscious thinking. They therefore claim that in order to write honestly, one must describe the world as one feels it as it were, in one's dreams. But even then, to carry the logic further, the dream is still affected by reason, so that the mental state best fitted for artistic creation should be that of a sick man in a coma. But even so, limited consciousness is still present in a state of coma, so in order to shake off the fetters of thought and consciousness completely, the artist should really describe the world as perceived by the mentally deranged. When the artist reaches such a state, his "honesty" is complete, he is free from all fetters of "dogma" and is thus in a position to

7

create miracles of "beauty" at will!

The theory of "writing honestly" advertised by modern revisionists is imbued with the same spirit as the literary theories of the reactionary bourgeoisie. If subjective-idealist literary theory is carried to its logical conclusion, one must inevitably land in the mire of complete reaction such as we have just described. This is well worth pondering over.

It is now quite clear what it is modern revisionists are peddling with this idea of "writing honestly." It is obvious that they raise this cry about "writing honestly" and oppose "hypocrisy" not because they want to solve the common sense problem that genuine feeling is necessary for vivid and effective writing. What they want to do is to prepare the way to discard Marxism and to publicise revisionism. At the same time they try to brand revolutionary Marxist writers as "hypocritical" in the hope that this will force these writers, for fear of being branded "hypocritical," to discard the great ideological weapon of Marxism and join them in "honestly" extolling revisionism. But this is sheer wishful thinking. The broad masses of the people and proletarian writers will never be misled by this.

(From a translation of the article "In the Field of Literature and Art, Modern Revisionists Follow in the Footsteps of the Declining Bourgeoisie," *Hung-ch'i,* No. 21, 1962)

*   *   *

CCP Central Committee's Communique

The Tenth Plenary Session of the Eighth Central Committee points out that throughout the historical period of proletarian revolution and proletarian dictatorship, throughout the historical period of transition from capitalism to communism (which will last scores of years or even longer), there is class struggle between the proletariat and the bourgeoisie and struggle between the socialist road and the capitalist road. The reactionary ruling classes which have been overthrown are not reconciled to their doom. They always attempt to stage a comeback.

Meanwhile, there still exist in society bourgeois influence, the force of habit of old society and the spontaneous tendency towards capitalism among part of the small producers. Therefore, among the people, a small number of persons, making up only a tiny fraction of the total population, who have not yet undergone socialist remoulding, always attempt to depart from the socialist road and turn to the capitalist road whenever there is an opportunity.

Class struggle is inevitable under these circumstances. This is a law of history which has long been elucidated by Marxism-Leninism. We must never forget it. This class struggle is complicated, tortuous, with ups and downs and sometimes it is very sharp. This class struggle inevitably finds expression within the Party.

Pressure from foreign imperialism and the existence of bourgeois influence at home constitute the social source of revisionist ideas in the Party. While waging a struggle against the foreign and domestic class enemies, we must remain vigilant and resolutely oppose in good time various opportunist ideological tendencies in the Party.

The great historic significance of the Eighth Plenary Session of the Eighth Central Committee held in Lushan in August 1959 lies in the fact that it victoriously smashed attacks by Right opportunism, i.e., revisionism, and safeguarded the Party line and the unity of the Party. Both at present and in the future, our Party must sharpen its vigilance and correctly wage a struggle on two fronts, against revisionism and against dogmatism. Only thus can the purity of Marxism-Leninism be always preserved, the unity of the Party constantly strengthened and the fighting power of the Party continuously increased.

(From The Communique of the 10th Plenary Session of the 8th CCP Central Committee, Peking Review, No. 39, 1962)

*   *   *

Role of Modern Revisionists

In this "warfare against the mind and the heart" the modern revisionists play the ignominious role of lackeys of the class enemy. While trying by every means to negate the healthy educational function of art and literature, they make a great to-do about so-called "individual happiness" with the aim of luring young people into a blind pursuit of their individual interests and material comforts.

Take a look at revisionist art and literature and see what they provide for the young people to learn from. They depict great revolutionary wars as meaningless bloodshed, dark and gruesome enterprises; soldiers in action are portrayed as weak-minded, cynical pessimists;

the truth of socialist society is distorted to a fantastic extent. What such so-called art and literature offers to the youth is a philosophy of life characterised by extreme egoism and a nihilistic and pessimistic attitude towards the cause of the revolution and the collective.

Under revisionist influence, the young people gradually degenerate ideologically and they drift further and further away from the spirit and ideals of the revolution, forgetting their duty in the fight to overthrow imperialism and to support the revolution of the peoples throughout the world. When the younger generation gets into such a state, can they be expected to carry on the work of building socialism and communism and to safeguard the fruits of the revolution, the winning of which cost so many lives?

(From "Revolutionary Art and Literature—Their Educative Role," *Peking Review,* No. 27, 1963)

*   *   *

Portrayal of "Middle Characters"

In August 1962, someone formally put forward the idea of "writing about middle characters." On the plea that literature and art should reflect reality and play an educative role and in consideration of the current situation in these fields he found all sorts of "reasons" to stress repeatedly the importance of "writing about middle characters" and downgrade the importance of depicting heroes. He called on writers to concentrate on writing about these so-called "middle characters." His main reasons may be summed up as follows:

1. Positive heroes are a minority among the masses of the people whereas "middle characters" make up the vast majority, so writers should write a great deal about the latter;

2. Literary and artistic works should reflect social contradictions and "contradictions are often concentrated in the middle characters," so writers should concentrate on portraying these;

3. "It is mainly the middle elements that literature and art are called upon to educate;" and one should educate these people by writing about them;

4. In our literary works, too much has been written about heroes and too little about "middle characters." If everyone were to write

10

about heroes, "the path would be too narrow;" to broaden the path, writers should write more about "middle characters."

Many other similar assertions have been made, but these will suffice for the time being. In a word, the purpose of all such talk is simply to push the "portrayal of middle characters" into the central and most important position in our literary and artistic works and this inevitably pushes the task of creating heroes out of that key position.

What sort of people after all are these so-called "middle characters?"

According to the advocate of this theory, they are people from among the masses, and especially the peasant masses, who are midway between good and bad, the positive and the negative, the advanced and the backward, people tainted by the "old things" — "the mental burden which has weighed down on the individual peasant for thousands of years." It is said that "people in this intermediate state constitute the great majority" of the masses and that "broad masses of the people of various social strata are all of this in-between character." Some articles advocating the "portrayal of middle characters" describe them as "selfish people," others characterise them as "backward people who belong to the labouring masses but are not without weaknesses." This puts backward people into the category of "middle characters." Some define "middle characters" as "the middling, colourless masses who are neither good nor bad, and both good and bad," that is, "petty characters" who are phlegmatic and apathetic. As a matter of fact the main advocate of the "portrayal of middle characters" himself sometimes also mixes up "middle characters" with backward people and "petty characters" and fails to draw a clear distinction between them.

In order to explain their concept of "middle characters" they cite certain examples from existing literary works. According to their examples and explanations, their so-called "middle characters" turn out to be those peasants and workers who vacillate between the socialist and capitalist roads, people who do not want or are not enthusiastic about the revolution, people with little or no awakened class consciousness, people weighed down by the "mental burden" of the bourgeoisie or the petty bourgeoisie.

The people are the makers of history and the masters of the new society. To describe the great majority of them as "middling, colourless masses who are neither good nor bad, and both good and bad," that is, "dull masses" who are ignorant and indifferent, "petty characters" who are phlegmatic and apathetic — does this not expose as anti-popular

11

the stand of those who make such assertions?

In recent years, the class struggle between the proletariat and the bourgeoisie, the struggle between the socialist and capitalist roads, has been quite acute on the various political and economic fronts of our country. This struggle cannot but be reflected on the literary and artistic front. The series of theories and proposals centring around the "portrayal of middle characters" have inevitably led to discussions and criticisms. This sharply reflects in literary and artistic circles the class struggle in society and the struggle between the two roads.

All these theories and proposals put out by the advocates of "writing about middle characters" are advantageous to the bourgeoisie and capitalism but are disadvantageous to the proletariat and socialism.

(From a translation of the article "Writing about Middle Characters—A Bourgeois Literary Notion," *Wen-i Pao,* September 30, 1964)

*   *   *

Militant Role of Writers and Artists

The Third National Committee of the All-China Federation of Literary and Art Circles held its second enlarged conference in Peking in May 1963. Its deliberations centred on how to strengthen the literary and art front and enable literature and art to play a fully militant role in the current internal and international situation.

Premier Chou En-lai called on the nation's writers and artists to be revolutionary writers and artists and take an active part in the class struggle both at home and abroad. Writers and artists, he said, should take a firm proletarian stand and have high revolutionary ideals. They should steel and remould themselves in the long and complex class struggles which had to be waged; they should strengthen themselves in proletarian ideology and in the proletarian style of work so as to be able to stand all tests of storm and stress which they might be called upon to meet. He called on them to devote all their efforts to strengthening the revolutionary literary and art front.

The conference reviewed the achievements of China's literary and art workers in various fields since the Third (1960) National Congress of Chinese Writers and Artists. It was agreed that guided by the Party's line that literature and art should serve the workers, peasants and soldiers and the cause of socialism, and by the policy of "letting a hundred flowers blossom and a hundred schools of thought contend," and "weeding through the old to let the new emerge," China's literature and art had made many fresh gains in the past two years and more.

The conference discussed the new situation in the revolutionary struggle both at home and abroad, and all came to understand more clearly what an important militant task rested on the shoulders of literature and art. The conference stressed that the nation's writers and artists should hold still higher the banners of Marxism-Leninism and Mao Tse-tung's thinking and resolutely oppose imperialism, the reactionaries in all countries and modern revisionism as well as their influence in the realm of literature and art.

The conference discussions made it clear that in the sharp class struggles which were now raging in the international arena, all truly revolutionary writers and artists were faced with the following questions: should they take up their position on the anti-imperialist front, safeguard the interests of socialism and support the people of all countries in their revolutionary struggles, or should they fawn upon and capitulate to imperialism, slander socialism and break the people's revolutionary militant will? Should they use works of art and literature to reflect the revolutionary struggles of the masses, eulogise the heroism and collectivism of the masses in their labour and revolutionary struggles and praise the new people and new personalities of the new age, or should they stand aloof from the mass struggle, separate themselves from the common destiny of the people and immerse themselves in descriptions of the "fate of the individual" and the exalting of so-called "personal happiness" treated in isolation, which in effect means publicising the individualist world outlook of the bourgeoisie? Should revolutionary socialist art and literature fly their own colours, with new content and new styles in radical contrast to the various schools of bourgeois literature and art, or should they willingly serve as the rump of Western bourgeois literature and art, join them in their cesspool and hail the decadent as wonderful, as "innovation?"

The socialist art and literature of the world are undergoing rigorous tests. Certain former communist writers, noted the conference, had discarded the banner of proletarian revolution and become fanatical preachers and disseminators of revisionist thought as well as popular figures with imperialism and the bourgeoisie.

This phenomenon of degeneration in the ranks of world socialist literature and art drew the unanimous condemnation of the conference. It pointed out that Chinese writers and artists should pay close attention to the course of the class struggle in the ideological field of world literature and art, and that they should hold high the banners of Marxism-Leninism and Mao Tse-tung's thinking on the literary and art front and wage a resolute struggle against the adverse current of modern revisionism. They should maintain vigilance at all times and resolutely prevent the growth of revisionist and all other forms of bourgeois ideology in Chinese literary and artistic circles, and use their work in literature and art to serve even more effectively the workers, peasants and soldiers, the cause of socialism and the revolutionary struggles of the world's people.

The conference agreed that Chinese writers and artists should identify themselves with the new revolutionary era in order to better serve the workers, peasants and soldiers and socialism with their literature and art. There exists a fundamental difference between Chinese writers and artists on the one hand and modern revisionists on the other in regard to their assessment of the present age.

Analysing the present age from the point of view of the class struggle of the proletariat, Chinese writers and artists hold that it is unprecedentedly favourable for the revolution in all countries. In contrast, the modern revisionists have been declaring loudly that the present age is one of "positive coexistence" and "peaceful growth into socialism." Consequently they see no need for literature and art to portray the revolutionary struggle of the proletariat and the working masses; and declare that the one thing that is needed is to preach supra-class "humanism" and "love for all men." Chinese writers and artists are resolutely opposed to this nonsense of modern revisionism. They are determined to embrace the new revolutionary age wholeheartedly and join the broadest sections of the world's people. Only by so doing can they create works that are needed by the people.

The conference emphasised that to portray the new, people's epoch truthfully, the cardinal point was for literary and art workers to identify themselves with the broad masses of the labouring people, with the workers, peasants and soldiers. To go to the factories, to the villages and army units, to participate to a certain extent in labour and public work at the basic levels and take an active part in the struggles of the masses of workers and peasants was an established system which should be persisted in over a long period; it was a fundamental way in which literary and art workers could integrate themselves with the masses.

(From "National Conference of Writers and Artists," *Peking Review,* No. 22, 1963)

*   *   *

Chou Yang Refutes Modern Revisionism

Revisionism in the academic field is the mouthpiece of revisionism in politics and is a variety of bourgeois ideology. It serves the revisionist political line, provides it with a theoretical basis, and tried to justify it and to sway public opinion. The revisionist thinking of a section of people in Soviet academic circles is growing steadily along with the development of the revisionist political line of the leadership of the CPSU. Supporting the "combat against the personality cult," they have repudiated all Stalin's theoretical writings under the slogan of "eliminating the consequences of the personality cult." To repudiate Stalin completely is in fact to negate Marxism-Leninism, which Stalin defended and developed. On the pretext that times have changed, they brazenly declare Leninist theories to be outmoded. They energetically praise the line and programme formulated at the 20th and 22nd Congresses of the CPSU, lauding them as "a model of creative Marxism-Leninism," "the supreme achievement of contemporary social-scientific thought" and "the Communist Manifesto of the present epoch."

Let us now see how the modern revisionists have tampered with the fundamental principles of Marxism-Leninism in its main aspects: philosophy, the theory of socialism and communism and political economy.

In philosophy, like the old revisionists, the modern revisionists replace materialism by subjective idealism, revolutionary dialectics by vulgar evolutionism and sophistry, and the Marxist-Leninist theory of class struggle by the hypocritical bourgeois theory of "supra-class" human nature.

In political practice, the modern revisionists replace proletarian dialectical materialism by the imperialist and bourgeois philosophy of pragmatism.

Pragmatism, which originated in the United States in the late nineteenth century, is a subjective idealistic philosophy of the bourgeoisie in the era of imperialism. It denies objective reality, objective

15

laws and objective truth. It holds that truth is nothing but an instrument used by man to achieve his immediate purposes in his acts of coping with the environment, and its motto is that "it is true because it is useful." It is an out-and-out philistine philosophy and represents the reactionary outlook on life of the decadent and moribund bourgeoisie. It is the philosophy *par excellence* of US imperialism. The bourgeoisie can no longer act on the basis of knowledge of objective laws and principles of truth in contradistinction from falsehood and of right in contradistinction from wrong, since these laws and principles are diametrically opposed to their interests. They can only observe society and deal with the environment in a pragmatist way and they need a pragmatist philosophy to rationalise their actions. At the same time, pragmatism is a philosophy the imperialists and bourgeois reactionaries use to benumb the revolutionary consciousness of the masses. It causes the masses to consider only superficial appearances and not the laws of social development and the broad prospect for changes on a world scale; it causes the masses to seek only their immediate interests and not to struggle for their complete emancipation.

The representatives of modern revisionism are all worshippers of the United States politically. What they follow in all their policies is the American brand of pragmatist philosophy. Of course, they do not openly admit their belief in pragmatism, for that would interfere with their disguise as revolutionaries.

Lenin gave a good description of the old revisionism.

> To determine its conduct from case to case, to adapt itself to the events of the day and to the chops and changes of petty politics, to forget the basic interests of the proletariat, the main features of the capitalist system as a whole and of capitalist evolution as a whole; to sacrifice these interests for the real or assumed advantages of the moment—such is the policy of revisionism. ("Marxism and Revisionism," *Selected Works*, F.F.P.H., Moscow, 1950, Vol. 1, Part 1, p.94.)

The modern revisionists go even farther. They cater to imperialism, sacrifice the fundamental interests of the proletariat on major questions of principle and bargain away principles as though they were commodities. On the one hand, they yield and surrender to the nuclear blackmail of US imperialism, while on the other they gang up with the US imperialists to conduct nuclear blackmail against the people of the world. Nuclear fetishism and nuclear blackmail are the basis of their theories and policies. The modern revisionists do not believe in the strength of the people and deny that the people are the makers of history. They

16

do not believe that historical development will unquestionably lead to the destruction of nuclear weapons by man and not the other way round. They preach that in the face of nuclear weapons questions of principle cease to exist and that principles are already liquidated. "What is the use of principles, if the head is cut off?" — such is their pragmatist philosophy of survival. Thus the sufferings of the people, the world revolution and the communist ideal can all be totally ignored. This is the way in which the modern revisionists have replaced the revolutionary philosophy of the proletariat by the philistine philosophy of mere vegetative existence.

Since the representatives of modern revisionism are essentially pragmatists in their approach to objective truth and objective laws, it is only natural that they look down upon theory. The modern revisionists regard the basic theories of Marxism-Leninism not as truths which must be adhered to, but as expedient tools and as apologetics which they can wilfully concoct and revise in order to serve their immediate interests.

The modern revisionists have wantonly distorted and revised the Marxist-Leninist teachings on the laws of contradiction, and spread their views about the merging and reconciliation of contradictions.

On the pretext of what they call the characteristics of the transition from socialism to communism, they preach a "new way of putting the question," namely, "the overcoming of opposites through their uniting [merging],"[1] claiming that under socialist conditions "new phenomena" or "new processes" emerge in which "dialectical opposites, contradictions, turn into differences and differences merge into unity."[2] Some of their philosophers even claim that the law of the unity and struggle of opposites is outmoded under socialist conditions.

This theory of the merging or reconciliation of contradictions and the theory that the laws of contradiction are outmoded constitute a radical revision of materialist dialectics.

In the past, some comrades one-sidedly emphasised the "moral and political unity" of socialist society and failed to see that contradictions, classes and class struggle continue to exist in it, and that the struggle against bourgeois ideology within socialist society remains a main task of the dictatorship of the proletariat for a long period after the seizure of power. They only recognised solidarity and unity and denied the existence of internal contradictions in socialist society and the fact that contradictions are the motive force of social progress. They thus denied the universality of contradiction and did away with dialectics, and as a result the "theory of absence of conflict" spread far and wide.

The mistakes in their understanding of contradictions in socialist society paved the way for the modern revisionists of today. The modern revisionists have formulated a theory about the merging or reconciliation of contradictions, in order to provide a philosophical basis for their fallacies concerning "a State of the whole people" and "a Party of the entire people." Moreover, they have extended this theory of the merging or reconciliation of contradictions to the sphere of international struggle, so as to present a philosophical justification for their line of "peaceful coexistence," "peaceful competition" and "peaceful transition." They use the fictitious contradiction between the survival of mankind and nuclear weapons to cover up the class contradictions and national contradictions of real life. They hold that the appearance of nuclear weapons has rendered senseless the principles of class analysis and class struggle. They say that "the atom bomb does not adhere to the class principle." They hold that the contradiction between imperialism and socialism, the contradiction between imperialism and the oppressed nations, the contradiction between the bourgeoisie and the proletariat and the contradictions among imperialist powers and among monopoly-capitalist groups within an imperialist country can and should be reconciled and merged. Such is their conclusion and their political purpose.

Completely discarding historical materialism, the modern revisionists substitute the bourgeois theory of human nature for the Marxist-Leninist teachings on class struggle and proletarian dictatorship, for scientific communism. They have dropped the proletarian banner of revolution and raised the bourgeois banner of the theory of human nature. They have equated the concept of humanism so-called with that of scientific communism and completely merged scientific communism with bourgeois humanism.

They say, "Communist ideology is the most humane ideology,"[3] they talk of humanism as "the highest embodiment of communism," and they assert that "humanism in the broad sense of the word merges with communism,"[4] and that "the communist system means the triumph of humaneness."[5] They harp on such slogans as "Everything for the sake of man and for the benefit of man," "Man is to man a friend, comrade and brother" and "Long live the fraternity of all the peoples and all men on earth." They brag about "peaceful co-existence" as "the most humane, the proletarian method of class struggle in the international

18

arena," and about the plan for universal and complete disarmament as "the highest expression of humanism."

The modern revisionists try to cover up their betrayal of the revolutionary cause of the proletariat by harping on the fashionable slogan of "humanism." They never tire of saying, "Everything for the sake of man." We would like to ask, for what kind of man? They have no love for the revolutionary people or the labouring masses. The ones they do have love for are the leaders of imperialism and reaction. They fear the people and the people's revolution. After World War II, "humanism" as advocated by the bourgeoisie became fashionable for a time. Though there were many different schools of "humanism," most of them reflected the anxiety, fear and despair of the decaying and moribund monopoly capitalists, and served as an opiate to lull the vigilance of the people of the world against the imperialists' nuclear blackmail. The "humanism" advocated by the modern revisionists is intimately tied up with the contemporary humanism of the reactionary bourgeoisie of the West.

The humanism on the lips of the modern revisionists is not only profoundly reactionary when contrasted with scientific communism, it is even reactionary when contrasted with the bourgeois humanism which in the past once played a progressive role.

In the field of the theory of socialism and communism, the modern revisionists have been even more brazen in betraying Marxism-Leninism and the revolution. They have discarded the theory of the dictatorship of the proletariat and the theory of the proletarian party, which form the essence of Marxism-Leninism.

The modern revisionists attempt, on the one hand, to write off class struggle and the proletarian revolution in the capitalist countries and, on the other, to deny that classes and class struggle as well as the possibility of the restoration of capitalism continue to exist in the socialist countries throughout the historical period of the transition from capitalism to communism. They have flagrantly abolished the dictatorship of the proletariat.

The modern revisionists completely ignore the enthusiasm of the labouring masses for collective production in socialist society and are opposed to giving prime importance to political education which heightens the socialist consciousness of the masses. They are infatuated with the much vaunted idea of "individual material incentive," which can only lead people to the pursuit of purely personal interests, whet their desire for personal gain and profit, encourage the growth of bourgeois individualism and damage the socialist economy based on ownership by the whole people and on collective ownership or even cause it to disintegrate.

They also use the quest for profit to stimulate the management of enterprises and confuse socialist with capitalist profit in their attempt to replace the socialist economic principle of planning by the capitalist economic principle of profit, and so pave the way for the liberalisation of the economy and the degeneration of socialist into capitalist economy. It is not surprising, therefore, that the modern revisionists are becoming more and more recipient to the fashions and vogues of bourgeois economic theory.

NOTES

1. P.N. Fedoseyev, "The 22nd Congress of the C.P.S.U. and the Tasks of Scientific Research Work in the Field of Philosophy," *Voprosy Philosophii* (Problems of Philosophy), 1962, No. 3.

2. M.B. Mitin, "The 22nd Congress of the C.P.S.U. and the Tasks of Scientific Work in the Field of Marxist-Leninist Philosophy," *Voprosy Philosophii,* 1962, No. 4.

3. Programme of the Communist Party of the Soviet Union, adopted at the 22nd Congress of the C.P.S.U.

4. *Foundations of Marxist Philosophy* (in Russian), edited by the Institute of Philosophy of the Academy of Sciences of the U.S.S.R., Moscow, 1962, p.548.

5. O.V. Kuusinen and others, *Foundations of Marxism-Leninism* (in Russian), Moscow, 1959, p.751.

(From "The Fighting Task Confronting Workers in Philosophy and the Social Sciences," by Chou Yang, deputy director, Propaganda Department, CCP Central Committee, in *Peking Review,* No. 1, 1964)

Debate on Philosophical Concepts

In the following excerpts from a translation of the article "New Polemic on the Philosophical Front", *Hung-ch'i*, No. 12, 1964, Yang Hsien-chen, a member of the CCP Central Committee and former president of the Higher Party School, is said to have started the great debate on the philosophical concepts of "one divides into two" and "two combine into one."

Yang's heresy, according to an article carried in *Jen-min Jih-pao* of August 14, 1964, consists of the contention that "two combine into one." He is accused of having stressed the inseparable connection of opposites in a permanent unity, thus diverging from the orthodox emphasis upon the division of opposites from the point of their origin and upon their connection in a temporary unity. He is said to have argued that the nature of opposites compels them to seek unity and that the dialectic is "precisely a study of how to identify (unify) opposites, to seek common ground and let differences remain."

In the eyes of his critics, Yang's major sin is gross neglect of the process of uninterrupted struggle held necessary to bring about a unity of opposites. If contradictory elements unite without a struggle, without one vanquishing the other, then the final unity must contain elements of both in what is essentially a compromise. In application to social problems, Yang's theory would lead away from class struggle to class conciliation, with the proletariat not fighting for victory over the bourgeoisie but remaining committed to lasting compromise with it.—Ed.

A new and heated polemic has developed on the philosophical front in China: it concerns the concepts of "one divides into two" (一分爲二) and "two combine into one" (合二而一).

This debate is a struggle between those who are for and those who are against materialist dialectics, a struggle between two world outlooks — the proletarian world outlook and the bourgeois world outlook. Those who maintain that "one divides into two" is the fundamental law of things stand on the side of materialist dialectics; those who maintain that the fundamental law of things is that "two combine into one" stand in direct opposition to materialist dialectics. The two sides draw a clear line of demarcation between themselves and their arguments are directly opposed to each other. This polemic is an ideological reflection of the acute and complex class struggle now being waged both internationally and in China.

Polemic Provoked by Yang Hsien-chen

Our Party has pointed out that everything tends to divide itself into two. And theories are no exception; they also tend to divide. Wherever there is a revolutionary, scientific theory, its antithesis, a counter-revolutionary, anti-scientific theory, is bound to arise in the course of its development. As modern society is divided into classes and as the difference between progressive and backward groups will continue far into the future, the emergence of such antitheses is inevitable.

The Party has further pointed out: The history of the international communist movement demonstrates that like everything else, the international working-class movement tends to divide itself into two. The class struggle between the proletariat and the bourgeoisie is inevitably reflected in the communist ranks. It is inevitable that opportunism of one kind or another should arise in the course of development of the communist movement, that opportunists should engage in splitting activities against Marxism-Leninism and that Marxist-Leninists should wage struggles against opportunism and splittism. It is precisely through such struggles of opposites that Marxism-Leninism and the international working-class movement have developed.

The Party has criticised the so-called "new concept" advanced by modern revisionism with regard to the current international situation, pointing out that this concept implies that in the present-day world antagonistic social contradictions of all kinds are waning, and that contradictory social forces are tending to unite themselves into a single whole.

But, while our Party is strengthening its propaganda on the revolutionary dialectics of "one divides into two," Yang Hsien-chen talks a lot about the concept that "two combine into one," thus setting up another platform opposite to that of the Party.

Yang Hsien-chen's idea of reconciling contradictions and negating

22

struggles was formed a long time ago. In November 1961 when lecturing in the Higher Party School, he said: "The unity of opposites, the unity of contradictions means: the two opposites are inseparably connected." "What we want to learn from dialectics is how to connect two opposite ideas."

Since the Party strengthened its propaganda on the concept of "one divides into two," Yang Hsien-chen has disseminated his idea of reconciling contradictions with even greater zeal. In November 1963, he generalised his idea as "two combine into one," and made this public while lecturing in the Higher Party School.

Repudiation of Yang's Concept

Yang Hsien-chen's concept that "two combine into one" has also evoked a great deal of controversy among the general public. Some people support it; but, many criticise and reject it. Up to the end of August, more than 90 articles on the subject had been published in newspapers and in magazines, both national and local.

Yang Hsien-chen had all along, repeatedly and painstakingly, propagated the idea that "the tendency in everything is for 'two to combine into one.'" He had talked with great zeal about "the inseparable connection" between antitheses, the "inseparability" of things, and asserted that the task of studying the unity of opposites lies solely in seeking "common demands," or "seeking common ground while reserving differences." If things are viewed in the light of his concept that "two combine into one," their internal contradictions disappear and the struggle of opposites within them disappears; the concept that one side of a contradiction must of necessity overcome the other side, that the outcome of struggle is the destruction of the old unity and the emergence of a new unity, and that old things are replaced by the new — all this too disappears. In this way, Marxist-Leninist materialist dialectics is completely negated.

The concept that "one divides into two" is the kernel of the revolutionary philosophy of materialist dialectics, the world outlook of the proletariat. Using this world outlook to apprehend things, the proletariat recognises that contradictions are inherent in everything, that the two sides of a contradiction are in a state both of unity and of struggle, and that contradiction is the motive force in the development of things. While the identity of opposites is relative, their struggle

23

is absolute. Therefore, the task of materialist dialectics has never been to cover up contradictions, but to disclose them, to discover the correct method for resolving them and to accelerate their transformation, in order to bring about the revolutionary transformation of the world. Using the world outlook of materialist dialectics to analyse class societies, the proletariat recognises class contradiction and class struggle; it recognises class struggle as the motive force of social development; it firmly maintains that the proletariat must carry the class struggle through to the end and so bring about the transformation of society.

But, to view relations between the various classes of society in accordance with the concept that "two combine into one" as advocated by Yang Hsien-chen will inevitably lead to obscuring the boundaries between classes, and to repudiating the class struggle, and thus lead to the theory of class conciliation.

Class Struggle in the Ideological Sphere

At the present time, internationally, the revolutionary struggle waged by the people of various countries is developing vigorously against imperialism, headed by the United States, and its lackeys. Inside the international communist movement, a fierce struggle is being waged between Marxism-Leninism and modern revisionism. In our country, the class struggle between the proletariat on the one hand and the bourgeoisie and the remnant feudal forces on the other, as well as the struggle between the socialist and capitalist roads have advanced to a new, deep-going stage. Confronted with this situation in the class struggle internationally and at home the Central Committee of the Party and Comrade Mao Tse-tung place great emphasis on using the concept that "one divides into two" and the Marxist-Leninist theory of the class struggle to combat modern revisionism and to arm our people and have proposed to crush the offensive launched by the bourgeoisie and the remnant feudal forces by carrying out a widespread movement for socialist education in the cities and the countryside.

Yang Hsien-chen's propagation of the concept that "two combine into one" at such a time is precisely and deliberately designed to meet the needs of modern revisionism, and aid the modern revisionists in their propaganda for class peace and class collaboration, and also for the theory of reconciling contradictions. It is at the same time deliberately designed to meet the needs of the bourgeoisie and the remnant

24

feudal forces at home by providing them with so-called theoretical weapons for resisting the movement for socialist education.

It has already become very clear that this new polemic, that concerns the question of who will win over whom on the philosophical front, is a serious class struggle in the realm of ideology.

That such a debate should have arisen on our philosophical front is not difficult to understand. History has shown us that whenever a sharp class struggle develops in the political and economic fields, there is bound to be acute class struggle in the ideological field as well.

Reform of Peking Opera

Excerpts reproduced below are taken from an editorial in *Hung-ch'i*, No. 12, 1964 entitled "A Great Revolution on the Cultural Front"; and a speech made by Lu Ting-i, director of the Propaganda Department of the CCP Central Committee and concurrently Minister of Culture, on June 5 at the opening ceremony of the 1964 Festival of Peking Opera on Contemporary Themes.—Ed.

The reform of Peking opera is a major event. It is not only a cultural revolution but also a social revolution. The reform which began with the 1964 festival of revolutionary Peking opera on contemporary themes held in Peking and the further revolutionary measures that (will follow) in drama, *Chü-i*, film, literature, music, dancing, fine arts and other literary and art fields, are an important component of China's socialist revolution in the field of culture and ideology.

Serving the workers, peasants and soldiers is a direction from which we will never swerve. For socialist literature and art to serve the workers, peasants and soldiers they are required to serve the socialist revolution and socialist construction and to struggle for the elimination of the exploiting classes and their ideological influence. In the field of literature and art, theatrical art is one of the art forms which has a particular mass character. Peking operas have a vast number of devotees and audiences. Therefore, like all other literary and art forms, what kinds of ideology are to be used to educate the masses and what sentiments are to be aroused to influence them is a vital question of principle for Peking opera.

From the literature and art of modern revisionism represented by Khrushchev, its theatre included, we have already seen how the revisionists lavishly disseminate the bourgeois theory of human nature, humanitarianism, pacifism and so on and so forth, how they do their

26

utmost to oppose revolution, attack the dictatorship of the proletariat and besmirch the socialist system: they bring in the rotten and degenerated "novel" art of US imperialism, give publicity to the American way of life and poison the masses in the socialist countries, particularly the younger generation, with all sorts of things that are decadent, debauched and reactionary so as to corrupt them mentally and morally and sap their will power. Modern revisionist literature and art are such that they extinguish and blunt the revolutionary will of the masses, meet the needs of imperialism, serve the imperialist policy of "peaceful evolution" and the cause of restoring capitalism.

With the development of the socialist revolution and socialist construction, it is necessary to further deepen the socialist revolution in the political and ideological fields. It is also necessary for the theatre, as a component part of the superstructure, accordingly to make as its primary task fostering proletarian ideology and eliminating bourgeois ideology, propagating socialism and communism, and serving socialism directly. This makes it imperative for the art of Peking opera to carry out reforms according to the policy of "weeding through the old to let the new emerge." What is meant by "weeding through the old to let the new emerge"? It means to weed through the old, that is, capitalism and feudalism, to let the new, that is, socialism and communism, emerge. Not only should there be new contents compatible with the era of socialism, but also new forms compatible with the era of socialism. Revolutionary operas on contemporary themes depicting contemporary life of struggle with new creations both in form and content must have the main place on the Peking opera stage; they must have the main place on the stages of other theatrical arts as well. Only in this way can our theatre and stage, which is an important ideological position, really become an ideological position of the proletariat.

Since time is on the march, there must be corresponding changes in the content of literature and art. It is inconceivable that a stage dominated by emperors and kings, generals and prime ministers, talented scholars and beauties can serve the militant task of "fostering proletarian ideology and eliminating bourgeois ideology." Though there exist, in varying degrees, progressive ideas in certain traditional plays, they fall far short of the needs of the masses of working people and are far from adequate in educating the people in socialist ideas. As to those bad plays containing feudal dregs, they are harmful and must be resolutely discarded.

In this cultural revolutionary movement, it is an extremely welcome phenomenon that revolutionary Peking operas on contemporary themes are beginning to be staged. Some people have asserted that performing such operas means the withering away and death of Peking opera as an art. Facts show exactly the opposite to be true: Because Peking opera has begun to be revolutionised and popularised, revolutionary Peking operas on contemporary themes have not only won praise from literary and art circles but are welcomed by people from all walks of life; not only the faithful audiences of Peking opera love these revolutionary operas, but those who formerly did not attend Peking operas very often have also become enthusiastic audiences. Thus, by staging revolutionary operas on contemporary themes, the art of Peking opera has gained new vitality and broad, new prospects have been opened.

The socialist cultural revolution is a great and arduous long-term task. Party organisations everywhere and departments in charge of literature and art must attach great importance to this work, give it earnest leadership and help it to go forward in a healthy manner so as to defeat and wipe out bourgeois and feudal forces thoroughly in the ideological sphere in a planned way and step by step, and enable socialist literature and art to play their great role still more effectively in the three great revolutionary movements — the class struggle, the struggle for production, and scientific experimentation.

(From a translation of an editorial in *Hung-ch'i,*
No. 12, 1964)

*   *   *

Class Struggle Reflected in Peking Opera, "Ghost Plays"

A socialist society is a society in which there is class struggle. This is reflected in Peking opera as in other cultural fields. The past 15 years have witnessed ups and downs in Peking opera. All of us can remember that when the bourgeoisie launched a frenzied attack in 1957, there were some people who dug out and staged a number of harmful operas. This was, in fact, part of the wild attack launched by the bourgeoisie and the feudal forces against socialism. Recently, when our country suffered three consecutive years of natural calamities, when the modern revisionists headed by Khrushchev withdrew experts and tore up contracts, when the Indian reactionaries launched armed

28

provocations on our southwest border, when the Chiang Kai-shek bandits under the wing of US imperialism clamoured about "attacking the mainland," when the landlords, rich peasants, counter-revolutionaries and bourgeois Rightists seized the opportunity to carry on their activities in a big way, there again appeared a host of ghost operas and other harmful operas on the Peking opera stage. This happened in Peking and also in other cities. With ghost operas appearing in the cities, the villages, too, had them. Ghost operas helped feudal superstitions to raise their ugly heads. This was again an unbridled attack against socialism by the bourgeoisie and the feudal forces. At that time there were some people in theatrical circles who could not see the situation very clearly. They were fooled by the talk of "no harm in having ghosts." Now, they should learn the lesson from this and become more politically aware.

The modern revisionists are paving the way for the restoration of capitalism, which is the "peaceful evolution" the US imperialists have pinned their hopes on. The emergence of the modern revisionists has made the imperialists beside themselves with joy. They even hope that some day in China too a "peaceful evolution" will take place. The bourgeois Rightists in our country, echoing the imperialists and the modern revisionists, have said that "poverty causes change, change opens the way, the way leads to wealth, and wealth leads to revisionism." They use this incantation to try and make the people believe that the restoration of capitalism in our country will certainly take place. In view of this we should take a firm stand and work hard to guarantee that revisionism shall not appear in succeeding generations, and that capitalism shall never be reinstated in China.

Clearly, if Peking opera themes are restricted to stories about emperors, kings, generals, ministers, scholars and beauties, Peking opera will not be able to conform to the socialist economic base. In that case, serving the workers, peasants and soldiers, and letting a hundred flowers blossom and weeding through the old to let the new emerge would then become just empty talk.

We are never against Peking opera staging good traditional plays such as those adapted from *Romance of the Three Kingdoms, Water Margin, Generals of the Yang Family,* and others. Nor do we oppose the staging of good mythological plays such as *Uproar in Heaven,* or *Monkey Sun Wu-kung Defeats the White-Bone Ghost.* We also advocate new historical plays which are written from a historical materialist point of view and have educational significance, particularly those with themes from modern history since the Opium War. But these alone are not enough. Peking opera needs a new revolutionary flower, that is, plays on such contemporary themes as the revolutionary struggles since the May Fourth Movement, class struggle and production and construction since the liberation.

(From Lu Ting-i's speech at the opening of the 1964 Festival of Peking Opera on Contemporary Themes on June 5, 1964.)

A New Educational System

Extracts from an article appearing in
Peking Review, No. 51, 1965, entitled
"Part-Work, Part-Study System Shows
Its Advantages," and another article
appearing in *Peking Review*, No. 2, 1966,
entitled "A Significant Development in
China's Educational Revolution."—Ed.

The National Conference on Urban Part-Work, Part-Study Education held in Peking in December last year pointed out: experiments in part-work, part-study education are being made currently in all parts of the country. A deep-going revolution is taking place in the sphere of education. To carry out this revolution is a fundamental measure for the consolidation of the dictatorship of the proletariat and for the prevention of the restoration of capitalism. The part-work, part-study schools run on an experimental basis in cities throughout the country at the present time have shown their superiority in promoting the integration of education with productive labour, in bringing up workers who can labour with their hands and who are both socialist-minded and cultured, and in gradually diminishing the differences between mental and physical labour.

Since the Central Committee of the Chinese Communist Party had directed in 1964 that part-work, part-study education should be gradually introduced, the large and medium-sized cities throughout the country and some of the smaller cities had set up a considerable number of work-study schools on a trial basis. The past one year and more, the conference noted, had witnessed the emergence of schools of various types: work-study secondary specialised schools and work-study classes of higher learning, work-study schools and classes equivalent to junior middle schooling, schools which catered to the needs of both town and country and where students did both factory and farm work, and schools which were orientated towards the countryside

31

and recruited their students from cities on the understanding that upon graduation they would go to work in the countryside. Varied in organisational forms, some of these schools were run by factories or enterprises either individually or jointly; some had regular links with factories; some were factory-school-in-ones; some had their own small factories or farms; and some arranged for students to do whatever work was available, having themselves no definite places where physical labour could be done.

Practice in 1964 had shown clearly the superiority of the part-work, part-study educational system. It had enabled education to be closely integrated with productive labour, making full use of the two kinds of classroom (that in the school and that at the place of work) and two kinds of teacher (the school-teacher and the worker-tutor), thus facilitating the all-round moral, intellectual and physical development of the students. Steeled in the class struggle and in the struggle for production in the factories and influenced by working-class ideology, students of such work-study schools had raised their political consciousness very rapidly. These schools had shown their advantages in turning out people who can do physical labour and who are both socialist-minded and cultured.

Facts produced at the conference had shown that, though students in work-study schools spent only half of their time in classroom studies, what they learnt was not less than those studying at full-time schools. Sometimes their knowledge had proved to be even more closely related to life. Participation in labour had much improved the students' physique also. The consensus among workers was that this new system was satisfactory in four respects: the factory was pleased because such students helped production; the school was pleased because through linking theory with practice, the quality of teaching was raised; the parents were pleased because they needed to spend little or no money for their children to obtain a good education; the student was pleased because he could both study and do manual work. In some factories where this type of school was successfully run, the students had become an important force in production as well as bringing about political, cultural and technical changes among the ranks of the workers.

The conference reviewed the situation in part-work, part-study education, the experiments made during the past year, and the experience gained. After further study and discussion of the writings of Marx, Engels and Lenin on education, as well as the directions given by the

32

Party's Central Committee, Chairman Mao Tse-tung and Chairman Liu Shao-chi concerning the Party's policy on education, the meeting made clearer the course to follow, raised general understanding of the new system and reinforced confidence in it.

The conference pointed out that making the work-study educational system a well-thought out and well-organised one would be a long process. It would take several years or even longer to master its laws and accumulate experience, so it would be necessary to persist on the principle of "five years experimentation, ten years popularisation." The main tasks at the present time were to strengthen the leadership, to make unified plans and conduct active experimentation, to consolidate what had been achieved and to raise the level of work. The emphasis of experimentation should be on secondary technical schools and institutions of higher learning. In running work-study schools on a trial basis, it was necessary to persist in the correct direction, to implement in an all-round manner the Party's policy on education so as to enable the students to develop vigorously and actively in character, mind and physique, and to bring up a new type of people who can do physical labour, who possess socialist consciousness, and have a wide general and scientific knowledge, technical ability and working skill. Graduates should be able to engage in both mental and manual labour. They should be able to work as cadres, technicians, ordinary workers or peasants.

The raising of quality and the reform of teaching would play an important role in ensuring the smooth institution of the new educational system. The conference held that the reform of teaching hinged on the revolutionisation of the teachers and the fact that they became physical labourers at the same time. The teachers could really play their part in reforming teaching only by devoting their working time to both teaching and physical labour so as to link theory with practice. The conference urged the teachers and leading personnel of the urban work-study schools to arm themselves with Mao Tse-tung's thinking and to acquire a revolutionary world outlook to be equal to their status as a vanguard in part-work, part-study education.

The conference stated that the establishment of work-study schools orientated to support the countryside was a question of policy. Work-study schools in the cities should train for the countryside large numbers of graduates who were politically progressive, cultured and who had a technical ability. Such schools might be set up in the rural areas,

33

students being recruited from the cities on the understanding that after graduation they would be assigned to work in the countryside; or they might be set up in the cities or suburban areas with their graduates going to work in the countryside.

(From "Part-Work, Part-Study System Shows Its Advantages")

*   *   *

Significant Development in Education

The establishment of a new system of work-study education which combines classroom study with work in the factories and on the farms is a development of far-reaching importance in China's cultural revolution.

Though experiments are still being made in order to best solve the common and specific problems of its many different kinds of schools, the new system has already brought universal education nearer and is showing its value in bringing up a new generation of revolutionaries who are accustomed to both mental and physical labour and who are both "red and expert," i.e., who are both politically conscious and professionally competent.

The new system is contributing greatly to the universalisation of primary education in China. It has also opened up ways for the gradual universalisation of secondary and even higher education in the future. This is in marked contrast to the position in capitalist countries. In order to safeguard the interests of the bourgeoisie and to maintain the differences between mental and manual labour, the bourgeois educational system can only universalise primary or general secondary education at the most. It definitely cannot, nor is it willing to universalise higher and specialised secondary education. The socialist countries, in order to render immediate service to the socialist revolution and socialist construction and to diminish gradually the differences between mental and manual labour, besides universalising primary and general secondary education step by step, must go further and universalise higher and specialised secondary education also.

The gradual modernisation and development of industrial and agricultural production has created a pressing need for a huge technical force both in the cities and the countryside. This is where the new

34

schools fulfil an increasingly important function. Work-study schools set up by factories can produce in a relatively short period large numbers of workers of a new type — workers who are good with their hands and have specialised skills and an adequate level of general education.

In the countryside, the situation is the same. Many graduates from work-study agricultural middle schools have become leaders of production teams, book-keepers, storemen, tractor drivers, irrigation and drainage equipment operators, technicians, health workers, electricians, veterinarians and livestock breeders. Excellent results have also been obtained from the special short courses run by these schools to meet the need for agro-technicians, veterinarians, accountants and other technical personnel. An equally important role is played by the work-study technical middle schools in supplying skilled personnel needed by state farms specialising in agriculture, forestry or livestock breeding, fishing enterprises, hydroelectric and farm machinery stations and other production units.

The graduates are well equipped for the jobs that lie ahead of them as they have already done practical work. While studying, they are an effective productive force, too. Students of some agricultural middle schools, for example, have turned low-yielding land into high-yielding land by scientific farming. Some have raised improved strains of seeds. Some have assisted production teams in disease and pest control and prevention, and in this way they have helped to ensure high yields over large areas of farmland.

(From "A Significant Development in China's Educational Revolution")

CHAPTER II

Revolutionary Movement for Socialist Education

The movement for socialist education developed from the socialist revolution in the political, economic, ideological and organisational fields into a revolutionary movement to re-educate and re-mould Party cadres, the working people and young students.

Socialist education is conducted in both urban and rural areas under the guidance of Mao Tse-tung's thinking — described in this chapter as the source of the revolutionary theory of Marxism-Leninism—in the wake of what is called complicated class and production struggles.

In giving class education to government functionaries and workers alike, no effort is spared to acquaint them with the actual situation in the class struggle, educate them in the revolutionary spirit of Marxism-Leninism and give them a correct political orientation. In the latter aspect, emphasis is laid on a serious study of Mao Tse-tung's written works.

In the following articles, reproduced in full or in part, the long-term task of socialist education—its role in upholding proletarian and eradicating bourgeois ideology — is described as requiring decades to accomplish.

This protracted period is deemed necessary in these articles in order to stem modern revisionists' influences and thwart their attempts to promote bourgeois humanism and class conciliation, to combat capitalist forces and prevent any "peaceful evolution" into capitalism, to supervise cadres and prevent any of them from degenerating and to educate and remould the great majority of intellectuals. — Ed.

The new social system has only just been established and requires time for its consolidation. It must not be assumed that the new system can be completely consolidated the moment it is established, for that is impossible. It has to be consolidated step by step. To achieve its ultimate consolidation, it is necessary... to carry on constant and arduous socialist revolutionary struggles and socialist education on the political and ideological fronts.

—Mao Tse-tung

(Speech at the Chinese Communist Party's National Conference on Propaganda Work, March 12, 1957)

Significance of Socialist Education

Excerpts from Premier Chou En-lai's Report on the Work of the Government to the 1st session of the 3rd NPC on December 21-22, 1964, a *Jen-min Jih-pao* editorial greeting the 16th anniversary of the founding of the People's Republic of China on October 1, 1965, and *Jen-min Jih-pao's* 1966 New Year's Day message.—Ed.

The socialist education movement now going on in the countryside and in the cities has a great revolutionary and historical significance. In this movement we should firmly rely on the working class, the poor and lower-middle peasants, the revolutionary cadres, the revolutionary intellectuals and other revolutionaries, carry out a cleaning up and "capital construction" in the political, economic, ideological and organisational fields in accordance with the socialist principle of thoroughgoing revolution, and conduct a profound class education and socialist education among the masses of the people. We should further develop the socialist revolution on the ideological and cultural fronts in order step by step to realise the goal of having intellectuals who are at the same time manual workers and manual workers who are also intellectuals. This movement has far-reaching significance for the consolidation of our socialist positions and of the dictatorship of the proletariat, for the destruction of the social foundations of revisionism, for the consolidation of socialist ownership by the whole people and by the collective, and for the development of production and the building of a powerful socialist country.

(From Premier Chou En-lai's Report on the Work of the Government to the 1st session of the 3rd NPC on December 21-22, 1964)

*   *   *

The socialist education movement is the key link in all work. It gives impetus not only to progress on agriculture and industry, but in culture as well.

The socialist revolution is the great · motive force propelling our society forward. We shall persist in taking class struggle and the struggle between the socialist and capitalist roads as the key link, promote proletarian ideology and eliminate bourgeois ideology, and unceasingly extend the positions of socialism so as to carry the revolution through to the end.

(From a translation of *Jen-min Jih-pao's* editorial greeting the 16th anniversary of the founding of the People's Republic of China on October 1, 1965)

* * *

A series of great debates and reforms have been carried out in philosophy, history, literature, art and education, spreading Marxism-Leninism and Mao Tse-tung's thinking, repudiating revisionism, upholding proletarian thinking and uprooting the ideas of the bourgeoisie and the landlord class. Many of those working in the social science field have gained a deeper understanding of Marxism-Leninism and Mao Tse-tung's thinking. Many writers and artists have more clearly recognised their direction of serving proletarian politics, serving the workers, peasants and soldiers and serving the economic base of socialism. While continuing to reform the full-time schools, educational workers started to put the system of part-farming, part-study and part-work, part-study into practice experimentally. The intellectuals have gone to rural areas, factories and army units to integrate themselves with the workers, peasants and soldiers; this has helped them to remould their thinking and greatly heighten their socialist consciousness.

(From a translation of *Jen-min Jih-pao's* 1966 New Year's Day message)

Socialist Education for Cadres

Extracts from an editorial appearing in the
July 10, 1963 combined issue of *Hung-ch'i* under
the title "Cadres' Participation in Collective
Productive Labour is a Matter of Fundamental
Importance to the Socialist System."—Ed.

What are the advantages of cadres taking part in collective productive labour according to the systems established?

The articles published in this issue of *Hung-ch'i* and other related materials tell us:

1. By working together with the masses, our cadres prove by actual deeds that they are also part of the working people; in consequence, the masses will look on them as their close friends, talk with them without reservation and become very close to them.

2. By taking a regular part in labour, cadres will be able to retain the true qualities of working people, foster a hard-working and plain-living style of doing things and resist the influence of bourgeois ideology.

3. Participation of rural cadres in labour will help strengthen their class consciousness and class feeling, and help them to carry out still better the Party's class line in the countryside by relying on the poor peasants and the lower middle peasants.

4. By taking an active part in labour and setting a good example themselves, cadres can greatly stimulate the labour enthusiasm of the masses and encourage their initiative in production.

5. Active participation in labour by cadres increases the material wealth of society, lightens the burden of the producers, consolidates the collective economy and the economy owned by the whole people, and promotes the development of production. Having sweated in productive toil themselves, cadres

41

will show still greater concern for the fruits of labour and become good and frugal housekeepers of the socialist economy.

6. Cadres' participation in labour will bring about changes in customs and habits, and help create a new social attitude which regards labour as honourable and not taking part in labour as shameful. In these circumstances, anyone who is able to work but will not take part in labour will feel in the wrong and ashamed.

7. With the example of the cadres taking part in labour before them, the younger generation will grow up soundly, advancing along the road of industry, frugality and ardent love for the collective.

8. Participation in labour by cadres at the basic levels will enable them to become still more familiar with the situation in production and further enrich their knowledge of production. Those cadres who do not know much about production techniques, should take veteran peasants or workers as their teachers, learn the production techniques from them and gain experience in production, so as to be able to give more concrete and down-to-earth guidance in production.

9. Regular participation in labour will make it more convenient for cadres to carry out scientific experiments in the course of production. By painstaking study, they will be able to temper and turn themselves into functionaries who are politically advanced and professionally proficient.

10. While working together with the masses, cadres have the opportunity to give timely explanations of the Party's policies and lines and implement them better and to hear the opinions of the masses and understand the actual situation. This will further promote democratic life and help to solve correctly questions arising in the course of work.

Important Aspect of Class Struggle

To indulge in idleness and despise labour or to labour honestly? To have a contempt for labour or ardently love labour! — This question is an important aspect of the class struggle on the political, economic and ideological fronts in the period of socialism. If our cadres do not have a sufficient understanding of this question and have a relatively low level of political consciousness, if they do not take an active part in labour in accordance with the systems established by the Party and the State, and if they do not set an example among the masses of working honestly and loving labour; we will then be unable to enhance the labour enthusiasm of the masses effectively, uphold socialist labour discipline effectively or organise properly the ranks of the revolutionary classes to exercise strict supervision over all exploiters and parasites in the matter of labour. If this state of affairs should last long, the reactionary elements of the exploiting classes, the landlords, rich peasants, counter-revolutionaries and bad elements, would take advantage of the opportunities resulting from the divorce of certain cadres from labour and from the masses and use every means to corrupt and demoralise them. These elements would turn degenerated and corrupt cadres into their agents or plant their men in certain organisations, so that they could usurp the leadership in some of our units and change the character of certain Party and State bodies and economic and people's organisations. Should this go on unchecked, a grave situation extremely disadvantageous to the proletariat and socialism and a grave danger of a counter-revolutionary comeback could arise in the struggles between the proletariat and the bourgeoisie and between socialism and capitalism.

Effective System to Strengthen Proletarian Dictatorship

Aiming at pushing forward the socialist revolution and socialist construction and at realising the great ideal of Communism in China, all our people and all members of our Party are faced with a serious task, namely, the task of further consolidating and strengthening the revolutionary dictatorship of the proletariat and the revolutionary party of the proletariat in our country. We must wage a serious struggle against all tendencies that attempt to weaken the revolutionary proletarian dictatorship and revolutionary proletarian party of our country, even though such tendencies exist only in embryo. We must wage a serious struggle against those tendencies that may cause our revolutionary proletarian dictatorship and our revolutionary proletarian party to change their character, when those tendencies are still only in their embryonic stage.

In this regard, implementation of the practice of cadres taking part in collective productive labour is a question of vital importance. Our

43

Government and Party organisations at all levels are duty bound to keep close to the working masses; they have no right to divorce themselves from the masses. Our Government and Party organisations at the grass-roots levels must be entrusted to those advanced elements who are active in labour. Our Government cadres and Party secretaries at the grass-roots levels must be people who are not only the most advanced politically but also the keenest in productive labour. They should strive to become master hands in production and model farm workers. So long as the broad masses of our cadres, particularly the cadres working at the grass-roots levels, take an active part in the collective productive labour of our socialist economy in accordance with Party and State regulations, our cadres and our Government and Party organisations at all levels will certainly be able to maintain the closest contacts with the working masses, we will certainly be able to smash and even root out the reactionary forces of all types trying vainly to erode and undermine the revolutionary proletarian dictatorship and the revolutionary proletarian party of our country.

The System of Cadres' Participation in Labour

Reproduced from a translation
of an editorial in *Jen-min Jih-pao*
of August 28, 1964.—Ed.

The system whereby cadres at all levels take part in collective productive labour has been put into practice throughout China's vast countryside. In many places outstanding achievements have been made in this respect, greatly facilitating the class struggle in the rural areas to foster proletarian ideology and liquidate bourgeois ideology. Whether or not cadres take part in collective productive labour is in itself a serious and sharp class struggle. A host of facts show that only by persistently taking part in collective productive labour can cadres resolutely carry on with the socialist revolution.

A Question of Class Stand

A large number of facts such as the following have taught our cadres a profound lesson: those ex-landlords, rich peasants, counter-revolutionaries and undesirable elements who have not yet been re-moulded as well as bourgeois elements and people with a rather serious spontaneous capitalist tendency have the greatest fear of cadres taking part in labour; they do everything they can to prevent cadres from taking part in labour and try to lure them away from it. Contrary to this, the former poor and lower-middle peasants and the over-whelming majority of those commune members who actively participate in collective labour most heartily welcome cadres taking part in labour; they help the cadres do this in every way and are against cadres divorcing themselves from labour.

These sharply contrasting attitudes should heighten our vigilance and are well worth pondering. Why do people of different classes have diametrically opposed attitudes towards cadres taking part in collective productive labour? The reason is that, as an old saying goes, "All ingenuity comes from diligence and all evil stems from laziness." Ardent love for labour is a virtue of the proletariat and all working people whereas indulgence in an easy life and aversion to labour is a most pernicious force of habit left over by the exploiting classes. The more industrious a person is, the more will he be able to bring the vigorous revolutionary spirit into play, the better will he know how to cherish the fruits of labour of the masses of the people, and the more will he be able to keep his ideology healthy. Once a person gets lazy, seeks personal satisfaction, loafs around, turns little things to his profit and even does evil and wicked things, he is liable to make all sorts of mistakes. How is one going to live if he does not work? It is inevitable that he will seize or steal the fruits of labour of others and wallow in the mire with the erstwhile exploiters and parasites. A cadre who does not take part in labour will, consciously or unconsciously, inevitably defend the interests of those who gain without working or gain more by working less, and become their agents. Only those cadres who persistently and diligently engage in production along with the working people can defend the latter's interests and become their staunch leaders in carrying on the socialist revolution and construction. The difference between the industrious and the lazy is indeed tremendous! The two are heading in opposite directions: one towards the bright future of the proletarian revolution and the other towards the stinking quagmire of the declining exploiting classes.

From this it is clear that whether or not a cadre takes part in labour and whether or not he ardently loves it is in essence a question of what class stand he takes. If a cadre does not take part in labour and is not very keen on labour, he cannot possibly stand firmly on the side of the overwhelming majority of the working people and resolutely oppose acts and ideas of exploitation characterised by unearned gains, and he is liable to be corrupted by the ideas of the exploiting classes, and thus a "peaceful evolution" down the capitalist road will be effected in his case. Only by conscientiously and persistently taking part in labour together with the working people, fostering and reinforcing his ardent love for labour, will it be possible for a cadre to take deep root in the class ranks of the former poor and lower-middle peasants; only in this way can he be fearless in any kind of storm and always remain firm. Only in this way can cadres from working families always maintain and constantly bring into play the innate fine qualities of hard work, plain living, industry and courage, and maintain a firm class stand on all occasions; only in this way can cadres from non-working families really remould themselves through labour and become members of the working people and really acquire the class sentiments of the proletariat.

Participation in Labour Facilitates Class Struggle

The living facts in the movement for socialist education also have profoundly educated the cadres: Where the cadres at every level persistently take part in collective productive labour with the masses there the movement for socialist education will be developed more effectively, and comparatively profound changes will take place in the political situation in the countryside.

During the movement for socialist education, cadres at every level have raised their class consciousness and fostered their class sentiments by persistently working together with the masses of commune members, and this helps them the better to comprehend and rectify their mistakes and shortcomings in being divorced from the masses and to improve their working style and method. Thus the viewpoint of relying on the former poor and lower-middle peasants will be further clarified, the nucleus of leadership at every level and class ranks will unite more closely, and the predominance of the former poor and lower-middle peasants will be established more firmly. Under these circumstances, the well-to-do middle peasants will generally rally more closely around the Party branch and the former poor and lower-middle peasants, and will participate in collective production with greater enthusiasm; the class enemy will be further disintegrated, the handful of diehard landlords, rich peasants, counter-revolutionaries and undesirable elements further isolated and all freaks and monsters in the countryside will draw in their horns.

Where cadres persistently take part in labour, there the old ideas and habit of despising physical labour and labouring people left over by history will be dealt a serious blow, and the new idea and habit of loving collective productive labour and the collective economy will develop rapidly. As a result, the enthusiasm of the mass of the commune members for collective production is higher, cadres at every level find their leadership in production more effective, and new improvements are made in the management of the collective economy. Therefore, cadres take part in collective productive labour not only because it is beneficial to their leadership in the struggle for production, but primarily because it enables them to lead the class struggle better. Only when good leadership has been given to the class struggle can the struggle for production and scientific experiment be really effectively promoted.

Theory of Proletarian Dictatorship

In helping cadres at every level sum up their experiences in participating in collective productive labour through living facts, restudy of the directives of the Party's Central Committee and Comrade Mao Tse-tung on cadres' participation in collective productive labour must be organised for them to understand further the great significance of the fact that only by persistently taking part in productive labour can they persist in the revolution.

Our Party has always advocated the practice of cadres' participation in productive labour. In recent years, with the deepening of the socialist revolution, the Central Committee of the Communist Party and Comrade Mao Tse-tung have given closer attention to cadres' participation in productive labour and have issued several directives and stipulated a necessary system on this score. The "Directive Concerning Participation in Physical Labour by Leading Functionaries at All Levels" issued by the Central Committee of the Communist Party in May 1957 points out that participation by leading cadres at all levels in physical labour and the gradual integration of mental and physical labour are a development of the fine tradition of Party cadres taking part in productive labour during the Revolutionary Civil Wars and the War of Resistance against Japan. It also declares that some comrades, under the ideological influence of the exploiting classes of the old society, have forgotten this fine tradition of the past. They look down upon physical labour and have formed a habit of seeking fame, gain and position. They are reluctant to go back to their production work once they have left it. This tendency is extremely dangerous, and the Party must wage a resolute struggle against it. The directive also points out in particular that whether or not Communist Party members take part in physical labour is a momentous test for them to see if they are capable of striving

48

to fulfil the general task of the Party under new historical conditions.

In his May 1963 note on "The Seven Well-Written Documents of Chekiang Province Concerning Cadres' Participation in Physical Labour," Comrade Mao Tse-tung pointed out still more explicitly the great significance of cadres' participation in labour in the class struggle, linking it up with the task of consolidating the people's democratic dictatorship and preventing a counter-revolutionary comeback. Comrade Mao Tse-tung, in summing up the practical experience in the dictatorship of the proletariat, has put forward a series of theories and policies; one of the main contents is as follows: "It is necessary to maintain the system of cadres' participation in collective productive labour. The cadres of our Party and State are ordinary workers and not overlords sitting on the backs of the people. By taking part in collective productive labour, the cadres maintain extensive, constant and close ties with the working people. This is a major measure of fundamental importance for a socialist system; it helps to overcome bureaucracy and to prevent revisionism and dogmatism." This is a major development in the Marxist-Leninist theory on the dictatorship of the proletariat.

Part of the Socialist Revolution

The nature and task of our Party and State as well as those of the socialist revolution all determine that cadres must take part in productive labour to create material wealth in accordance with a definite system. The Communist Party is the vanguard of the proletariat and represents the supreme interests of all working people. The working people are the masters of our socialist State; the leading cadres of our Party and State at all levels are both revolutionaries and ordinary workers.

Socialist revolution means the abolition of all systems of exploitation and the enforcement of the principle of "He who does not work neither shall he eat." The period of socialism is one of transition to communism, during which the differences between physical and mental labour should by no means be widened, but should be reduced step by step so as to create the conditions for the gradual elimination of those differences. If the cadres, instead of participating in labour, live far better than the ordinary working people, they will easily degenerate. Whether or not cadres at all levels participate as ordinary labourers in productive labour with the working people, therefore, involves the important questions of whether or not the socialist revolution can be

49

carried through to the end and whether or not revolutionary cadres will assuredly never fade in colour. Cadres' participation in labour is in itself an extremely important part of the socialist revolution.

Cadres' participation in labour, which is a revolution, has made a very good start in our country. But a full account must be taken of the enormously difficult nature of the revolution. In various parts of the country many facts show that only after undergoing repeated processes of acquiring both positive and negative experiences and lessons can a cadre take part in labour regularly and combine it closely with revolutionary work. Genuine revolutionary consciousness can be firmly established only after the process of practice, knowledge, more practice and more knowledge is repeated many times, and after one ideological struggle after another. Such an ideological revolution must be carried forward through the self-education of the cadres themselves. But, just as all mass movements for socialist revolution in all other fields cannot take place spontaneously, so the revolutionary consciousness of the masses of cadres in participation in collective productive labour cannot grow spontaneously. This growth requires repeated education and guidance by the Party organisations at various levels and the guarantee of an appropriate system.

In the countryside, the cadres' participation in labour is both a very important link binding them closely with the class army of the former poor and lower-middle peasants and the most effective weapon for resisting ideological corrosion by all exploiting classes. Its even more profound and far-reaching significance lies in the fact that it sets an example for the younger generation to follow and points up the path for the healthy development of successors to the revolutionary cause. The cadres at different levels and the successors to the revolutionary cause for generations to come must all look at labour from the proletarian viewpoint of class struggle and persist in participating in collective productive labour according to a system and on the basis of continuously raising their class consciousness. When this is achieved, there will be a reliable guarantee in the most important respect that our revolutionary ranks will be always staunch and our revolutionary cause will advance from victory to victory. The cadres' participation in labour is a revolution of profound significance and far-reaching influence — politically, ideologically and economically — a revolution which must be carried through to the end, if the socialist revolution on all fronts is to be brought forward to its conclusion.

Socialist Education for Workers

Extracts from a translation of an article published in *Hung-ch'i,* No. 1, 1964, entitled "Strengthen the Socialist Education of the Workers." The author, Ku Ta-ch'un, is a member of the Secretariat of the All-China Federation of Trade Unions.—Ed.

The question of educating the workers in socialism is fundamental to assuring victory for the socialist revolution and socialist construction. The great historic mission of the proletariat is to eradicate capitalism and build communism. But not all the working class are aware of this at the start. It is only after they have accepted Marxist-Leninist theory and gained an understanding of the nature of capitalism that they come to understand this mission.

It is necessary to educate the workers in socialism throughout the entire historical period of the proletarian dictatorship. In a socialist society, the class struggle continues even though the economic system has been transformed. Especially at a time when imperialism still exists in the world, the reactionary classes at home, though overthrown, will never be reconciled to defeat; they will constantly gang up with the imperialists to challenge the proletariat to tests of strength and time and again try to stage a comeback. To achieve this aim they first of all contend with the working class for ideological positions, propagating reactionary political ideas, trying to poison and corrupt the working class and the rest of the revolutionary people with their rotten bourgeois way of life so as to pave the way ideologically for a counter-revolutionary comeback.

Catering to this need of the reactionary classes, and serving the imperialist policy of "peaceful evolution," the modern revisionists, in order to blunt the class consciousness and revolutionary fighting will of the working class, sing the praises of class collaboration, bourgeois humanitarianism and pacifism; put the theory of the spontaneous advance of the workers on a pedestal and one-sidedly stress the value of individual material incentives. They try to coexist with the class enemy in the political and ideological spheres and bring about a gradual economic degeneration into capitalism. In this complex class struggle any weakening of proletarian ideology means a growth of bourgeois ideology. To defeat the bourgeoisie in the class struggle during the transition period, the working class must master the laws governing the class struggle, consolidate and extend its own ideological positions, eliminate the ideological influences of the bourgeois and feudal forces and avoid corruption by modern revisionist ideas.

In 1952, on the eve of embarking on planned economic development, the Chinese people, led by the Communist Party, launched two mass movements — one against corruption, waste and bureaucratism, and the other against capitalist bribery of government workers, tax evasion, cheating on government contracts, theft of state property, and stealing economic information from government sources. Known as the Three-Anti (*San Fan*) and Five-Anti (*Wu Fan*) Movements, they were designed to consolidate the fruits of the revolution, ensure the smooth progress of national construction and repulse the attacks of the bourgeoisie. The broad masses of workers took an active part in the struggle against corrupt elements and law-breaking capitalists.

At that time some workers were still befuddled by the absurd talk of the capitalists to the effect that "it is the capitalists that keep the workers fed." Discussions were therefore held among the workers on "who keeps whom fed?" Through these discussions they came to see how capitalists exploit workers and with this understanding of the ugly nature of the bourgeoisie, were able to draw a clearer line of demarcation between the working class and the bourgeoisie. With the workers' class consciousness enhanced, a movement to increase production and practise economy was launched. And this provided favourable conditions for large-scale economic construction.

By 1957, guided by the Communist Party's general line for the transition period, China had, in the main, successfully completed the socialist transformation of agriculture, handicrafts and capitalist industry and commerce. Following this great victory on the economic front, the socialist revolution was carried forward on the political and ideological fronts as well. It was at this time that, under the influence of the international counter-current of anti-communism and the ideological tide of modern revisionism, the bourgeois Rightists at home launched a fierce attack on the Communist Party and the people. The Party led the people throughout the country in an anti-Rightist struggle, smashed the onslaught of the bourgeois Rightists and greatly strengthened the workers' understanding of the class struggle. They realised that the overthrown classes will try to stage a comeback whenever an opportunity presents itself and that the question of "who will win?" on the political and ideological fronts will be settled only after a long period of repeated struggles.

In conjunction with the struggle against the bourgeois Rightists, the people throughout the country unfolded a rectification campaign for self-education and self-remoulding. In this campaign, the workers held forums on "whom are we working for?" They analysed the difference between the proletarian and bourgeois world outlooks and developed a socialist attitude towards labour. This was followed by education in the Party's general line for building socialism.[1] It further boosted the morale of the workers. They strode forward bravely, holding high the red banner of the general line. This laid the ideological foundation which enabled the workers to overcome successfully the difficulties brought on by three consecutive years of natural calamities.

At the present time, a socialist education movement is gradually unfolding throughout the country. Closely integrated with the movement to increase production and practise economy, it is a revolutionary movement to re-educate the people — a movement of urgent practical significance as well as far-reaching historical significance. This is so because it will fortify the workers' viewpoint on the class struggle, help them learn to master the method of class analysis and enable them better to resist corruption by bourgeois ideas and the influence of revisionist thinking. It will also inspire them with the spirit of working hard to build the country diligently and thriftily and in a self-reliant way.

Socialist education is conducted in China's factories and mines with Mao Tse-tung's thinking as the guide and class education as the key. Through socialist education, whether given over a period regularly or in a concentrated way (in the form of mass campaigns), the workers get to understand the nature of classes and the class struggle, which is the moving power of history; they get to understand that there are classes and class struggles in a socialist society.

Aspects of Socialist Education

Socialist education should begin with class education so that the workers can gradually learn to base themselves on the viewpoint of the class struggle and master the method of class analysis.

This viewpoint and this method are the basic viewpoint and method of Marxism-Leninism; they concern the basic stand of the working class. To enable the workers to maintain a firm political stand in any upheaval, stand any test in the material conditions of life and have a clear-cut class stand, it is necessary to educate them in actual class struggle by presenting the facts, by reasoning things out and by examples culled from their personal experience.

China is building socialism in an environment of peace, but also amidst complicated class struggles. In giving a class education to the workers, therefore, it is necessary in the first place to bring out the concrete facts of the class struggle both at home and abroad and expose the ugly features of the class enemy, so that the workers can get an understanding of the actual situation in the class struggle.

Presentation of the facts must go hand in hand with reasoned discussion. People may hold different views even about the same fact and it is not possible to distinguish right from wrong without the people themselves arguing the matter out. The key to successful discussion is to give democracy full scope — to encourage the participants to raise questions and present their dissenting views fully, make one's criticism sound like "a gentle breeze and fine drizzle" and convince people by sound arguments. And all this in accordance with the formula of "unity — criticism — unity"[2] with a view to enhancing the people's understanding and achieving unanimity. Comrade Mao Tse-tung has pointed out that "it is not only futile but very harmful to use crude and summary methods to deal with ideological questions among the people, with questions relating to the spiritual life of man. You may ban the expression of wrong ideas, but the ideas will still be there... That is why only by employing methods of discussion, criticism and reasoning that we can really foster correct ideas, overcome wrong ideas, and really settle issues."[3]

In presenting the facts and reasoning things out, it is necessary to educate the people through their own experience in struggle. When one analyses the actual situation in the class struggle and compares the lot of the working class in the new society with that in the old, the veteran

54

workers will naturally be reminded of their own experiences in life and struggle. That is why in the socialist education movement the workers repeatedly recall their sufferings in the old society and contrast them with the happiness in the new, and use their personal experience to analyse the root sources of class oppression and exploitation. In this way the majority will gradually raise the level of their class consciousness and dedicate themselves more devotedly to the revolutionary cause. Practice has shown that the method of recalling the past and contrasting it with the present is a reliable way of enhancing the class consciousness of the workers.

Of late, factories and mines have made use of workers' family histories, the histories of their enterprises and of revolutionary struggles in general to educate the younger generation of workers. Workers relate the history of their families in their own small groups, in their workshops and in the homes of veteran workers. The bitterness of the past is vividly recalled in this way and the sons and daughters of veteran workers learn a deep lesson. In some cases young workers are enlisted to help the veterans write their family histories. This writing is in itself a process in which the younger workers receive a further class education. In this way the basic Marxist-Leninist viewpoint is applied to actual examples of the workers' class struggle and young workers learn in practice as well as in theory that it is only by bearing the past constantly in mind that one learns to cherish the present and defend the fruits of the revolution and that socialism can be built successfully only through class struggle and all-round and continuous socialist revolution. That is why it is necessary to hand the revolutionary tradition of the proletariat down generation after generation.

Educating the workers in collectivism is another aspect of socialist education for our workers.

Individualism, which seeks satisfaction for oneself at the cost of others, lies at the heart of the bourgeois world outlook. In contradistinction, the proletariat places the collective interests above all else. The fate, happiness and future of each and every member of the proletariat are inseparably bound up with those of the whole class. Their immediate and individual interests are closely linked with the long-term and collective interests. The livelihood of the workers has improved under the care and solicitude of the State and the collective. They vividly describe the dialectical relationship between a worker's individual interests and those of the collective under socialism in the following words: "The tributaries are filled when there is water in the main stream and they dry up when there is no water in the main stream."

Education in collectivism is designed so that the workers learn to uphold collectivism and oppose individualism from the working-class viewpoint, in their class interests and from the point of view of the proletarian world outlook and ethics; it is designed to help the workers understand that they are fighting not for personal interests pure and simple, but for the liberation of the proletariat of the whole world. Armed with this collective spirit the workers will be able to take a correct stand in handling matters involving the relationship between the State, the collective and the individual, work for socialism selflessly, and public spiritedly leave the easier jobs to others while tackling the difficult ones themselves.

A highly developed collective spirit and strict organisational discipline are innate qualities of the working class determined by its economic position in large-scale production and fostered through bitter class struggle over a long period of time. Under socialism, the means of production are in the hands of the people and the aim of production is to satisfy the needs of all. These new relations of production give greater scope to the collective spirit of the working class. But, for a fairly long period, the ranks of the working class will have to be replenished by the petty producers who will inevitably bring their liberalistic habits along with them. Lenin pointed out: "The historic task of the proletariat is to assimilate, re-school, re-educate all the elements of the old society that the latter bequeaths it in the shape of offshoots of the petty bourgeoisie."[4] In order that the working class shall influence the petty producers and not be influenced by them, it is necessary to strengthen collectivist education through labour emulation, gradually overcome the liberalistic habits of the petty producers and steel every member of the working class into a disciplined, class-conscious proletarian fighter.

Industrial and mining workers are currently engaged in a big campaign to compare with, learn from and catch up with the advanced and help those who are lagging behind. This constitutes at once a production movement designed to increase output and practise economy and an educational movement designed to enhance the communist consciousness of the workers and foster their collectivist outlook. Through these activities, whole regions, enterprises and individual workers support, unite, and co-operate with each other, with the more advanced helping those lagging behind and the latter doing their best

56

to catch up with the former. This helps the workers to realise that a socialist enterprise is a collective in which there is both division of labour and co-operation and that the whole country is also a big collective. It also helps the workers to give due consideration to the overall situation and consciously subordinate their immediate individual interests to the long-term collective interests.

To foster a steadily stronger collectivist spirit among the workers, it is also necessary to show them typical examples from real life. Outstanding people constantly come to the fore in every field in the course of the revolution and construction. They are either people who show staunchness in the struggle against the enemy or people who excel in production or in scientific research. These people have become the pace setters and staunch core of the masses because, in the first place, they are armed with collectivist thinking. Their living example must be used to educate the workers. The masses, inspired by the fine example, will emulate them.

Education in the revolutionary tradition of plain living and hard struggle forms still another important aspect of socialist education. This tradition of industry and thrift, simple living and hard struggle has been formed by the Chinese working class and labouring people in the course of their protracted revolutionary struggles. It is a concentrated reflection of the Chinese people's revolutionary courage in daring to struggle and seize victory; it reflects the revolutionary initiative and steadfastness of the Chinese working class. It is necessary for the broad mass of workers, on the basis of their heightened class consciousness, to promote the spirit of building a prosperous country by their own energetic efforts, and foster the tradition of simple living and hard struggle in building the country with industry and thrift.

In order to make the policy of building socialism by self-reliance the guide to conscious action on the part of every worker, it is essential to regard education in the revolutionary tradition of simple living and hard struggle as an important part of socialist education. The mass of workers should be encouraged to learn from the staunch militant spirit the veteran Red Armymen showed when they crossed the snow-clad mountains and marshes on their Long March, and from the "Yenan style" of overcoming difficulties in a spirit of self-reliance. They should be encouraged to bring their sense of responsibility as masters of their country into full play and value every bit of the property of socialist enterprises. Given the spirit of running all enterprises with industry and thrift, it becomes possible to carry out the policy of self-reliance more effectively, increase the prosperity of our country and bring about a vigorous political situation in which everyone highly values the collective, the state and socialism. Given such a fine style of work, enterprises will become outstanding collectives in production and staunch bulwarks of socialism which bring up generation after generation of new people with a communist consciousness and high moral standards as well as professional skill.

This style of simple living and hard struggle and building the country with industry and thrift has been developed in constant struggle against corruption by bourgeois ideas and the influence of the habits of the old society. It cannot be fostered if the workers are exposed to these influences without combating them. This is why in educating the younger generation of workers in the revolutionary tradition of simple living and hard struggle they should be encouraged to take over this style of work as a revolutionary tradition and an important step in developing a proletarian world outlook.

The bourgeoisie, in trying to find a market for its ideology, often begins by corrupting the people's way of life, for decadent living inevitably leads to political degeneration. In order to be able to resist bourgeois ideological influence, recognise bourgeois ideas even if they are camouflaged and avoid temptation and corruption by the rotten bourgeois way of life, it is essential for the rising generation of workers to understand, from the height of their understanding of classes and class struggle, the great significance of simple living and hard struggle and of building the country with industry and thrift, and regard the upholding of the working-class tradition of plain living and hard struggle and of industry and thrift as fundamental in carrying the proletarian revolution through to the end.

To sum up: to strengthen socialist education among the mass of workers means to educate them in the revolutionary spirit of Marxism-Leninism, to give them a firm class stand and correct political orientation, revolutionary, collectivist ideas, and a style of plain living and hard struggle.

The source of the revolutionary spirit is invincible Marxist-Leninist theory and Mao Tse-tung's thinking which is the integration of the universal truth of Marxism-Leninism with the concrete practice of the Chinese revolution and construction. Mao Tse-tung's thinking is the basic guarantee of victory for the Chinese people in revolution and construction. Socialist education must be guided by Mao Tse-tung's thinking. To help the workers grasp the essence of Mao Tse-tung's thinking, it is necessary to organise them to make a serious study of Comrade Mao Tse-tung's writings. This is an important part of political and ideological work and a fundamental task of socialist education. Only by persistently educating the workers in Mao Tse-tung's thinking will they be able to have a better understanding of the basic principles of Marxism-Leninism in the light of their knowledge of the actual revolutionary struggle; only in this way, will they be able to keep the revolutionary spirit of the proletariat alive, gain a clear understanding of the situation and orient themselves correctly in the current class struggle both at home and abroad.

Effective Steps for Conducting Socialist Education

The experience of many years shows that in order to educate the workers in socialism effectively, it is essential to handle the following relations correctly:

In the first place, it is necessary to handle correctly the relation between ideological and political work on the one hand and economic work on the other. Ideological and political work serves the economic base and guarantees the success of economic and technical work. It must proceed from production, be conducted in close connection with it and aim at guaranteeing the fulfilment of production targets. Otherwise it would be divorced from reality as well as the masses and weakened to such an extent as to be ineffectual. Ideology and politics are in command; they are the soul of all work. Once ideological and political work is relaxed, economic and technical work will inevitably go astray. As Comrade Mao Tse-tung put it: "Political work is the life-blood of all economic work. This is particularly true at a time when the economic system of a society is undergoing a fundamental change."[5]

If a socialist enterprise is to run production well, it is essential for its administration to give full consideration to people. This means first of all to do ideological work. When this work is well done and the people's political consciousness is enhanced, their wisdom and talent can be given maximum scope. This is why production in a socialist enterprise can be constantly developed only when the workers' political consciousness is constantly heightened and their revolutionary initiative brought into fuller play. If an industrial or mining enterprise relies solely on "material incentive" to stimulate its workers' initiative without doing persistent ideological and political work, the result will be a progressive lessening of the revolutionary and production initiative of the workers and the unbridled growth of bourgeois individualism.

Secondly, socialist education must be integrated with revolutionary practice. It is quite aimless and fruitless if it is divorced from the practical tasks of socialist revolution and socialist construction. The working class is a militant class and it is precisely the aim of socialist education to arm the workers for struggle. Experience shows that the more complex the struggle, the more urgently the workers need the theory of Marxism-Leninism as a guide to action. Socialist education, therefore, must not be conducted in an abstract way, but in relation to the class struggle and struggle for production. A characteristic feature of the workers' study of Marxist-Leninist theory is that they learn amidst struggle and for the purpose of carrying on the struggle. It is also a characteristic feature of socialist education that it is given in the midst of struggle and designed for carrying on the struggle. Comrade Mao Tse-tung pointed out that "In the class struggle and the struggle against nature, the working class remoulds the whole society, and at the same time remoulds itself." Guided by Comrade Mao Tse-tung's teachings, the Chinese working class is closely integrating its activities in remoulding the objective world with the remoulding of their subjective world and closely linking practice with study.

Thirdly, it is necessary to integrate theoretical training with ideological education by living example. The Party's line, principles and policies are the products of the integration of the universal truth of Marxism-Leninism with the concrete practice of the Chinese revolution; they are the embodiment of Mao Tse-tung's thinking. A fundamental requirement in socialist education is that the workers must not only understand the universal truth, but also its actual application to the practice of the Chinese revolution. They must not only understand the Party's principles and policies in various periods, but must also follow them as a guide in their own action. In carrying on socialist education, therefore, it is necessary to go among the masses, study their ideological trends, master the laws governing their thinking, and then use the Party's principles and policies as a guide in answering the specific questions raised by the masses in the course of their actual struggles and in solving the practical problems troubling their minds. To

60

discover living examples of how workers think, it is necessary to integrate education with production. It is necessary to gain a knowledge of each individual's mental and emotional state, character and temperament in the process of production as well as the interconnection between their outlook on the one hand and their material conditions of production and living conditions on the other. Different cases should be handled differently on the basis of specific analysis; ideological and political work should be carried out with a well-defined objective in mind.

Fourthly, it is necessary to integrate enlightenment from above with self-education of the masses, with the main emphasis on the latter. Mass self-education is the Party's mass line applied to ideological education. Socialist education cannot be penetrating and really solve ideological problems without bringing the workers' own initiative into play and relying on their voluntary action. In relying on the workers to educate themselves, reliance should be placed mainly on the skilled veteran workers and outstanding workers who have a firm class stand. The rich experience of the veteran workers in production and life, their class consciousness and organisational discipline must play a big role in educating the younger generation of workers. In this educating process, the sense of responsibility of the veteran workers themselves should be heightened so that they can maintain their advance and become the mainstay of the socialist cause.

The method of the masses educating themselves is a democratic method of persuasion, a method of criticism and self-criticism.

In relying on the masses to educate themselves, good use should be made of those forms that the masses prefer. Cultural activities and the propaganda media in factories and mines should be used as keen instruments for educating the workers and attacking the enemy. The struggle against the bourgeoisie and feudal remnants in the ideological sphere is a very complicated one. Bourgeois and feudal ideas find profound and elegant expression in the arts, literature and religion and the younger generation of workers often come under their influence. In carrying on self-education, therefore, it is necessary to use various artistic and literary forms in order to resist corruption by bourgeois ideas and propagate the new culture.

61

Long-term Task of Socialist Education

To spread proletarian ideology and root out bourgeois ideology is a long-term struggle. Class education of the workers is a strategic task for the entire period of socialism; it cannot be fulfilled in a short time, say eight or ten years; it is an activity of a whole historic period. Only by upholding the red banner of Mao Tse-tung's thinking and bringing their proletarian revolutionary spirit into play, will the Chinese working class be able through the class struggle to consolidate the dictatorship of the proletariat and accelerate socialist construction; only thus will they be able to carry the revolution through to the end and finally fulfil the historic task of the proletariat.

NOTES

1. This refers to the general line of "going all out and aiming high to achieve greater, faster, better and more economical results in building socialism" proclaimed by the CCP in 1958.

2. This means: starting with a desire for unity and achieving it on a new basis through criticism.

3. *On the Correct Handling of Contradictions Among the People.*

4. "The Faction of Supporters of Otzovism and God-Building," *Collected Works,* Foreign Languages Publishing House, Moscow, 1963, Vol. 16.

5. Editor's Note to "A Serious Lesson, *Socialist Upsurge in China's Countryside.*"

Socialist Education for Young People

Extracts from a translation of a report on the work of the Communist Youth League delivered by Hu Yao-pang, secretary-general of the CYL Central Committee, at the 9th Congress of the CYL, June 11, 1964.—Ed.

The development of socialism is by no means all plain sailing. The period of socialism is a historical period of transition from capitalist society to communist society; it is a period of the dictatorship of the proletariat. What distinguishes this period is that classes and class struggle still exist, that the struggle between the road of socialism and the road of capitalism remains, that the question of "who will win" is still unsolved, that there is still a danger of capitalism making a comeback, that there remain the antitheses between workers and peasants, between town and country, between manual and mental labour. It appears that this period of transition will take five or ten generations or even longer to complete itself.

In his great work *On the Correct Handling of Contradictions Among the People,* Chairman Mao gave an all-round and systematic analysis of classes, contradictions and class struggle in a socialist society after the nationalisation of industry and the collectivisation of agriculture has, in the main, been completed, that is, after socialism has won the basic victory on the economic front. This is a new development of Marxism-Leninism: Chairman Mao teaches us that class struggle will continue through the whole historical period of socialism.

Complexity of Class Struggle

This struggle is protracted, tortuous, complex and, sometimes, even very acute. This is because the exploiting classes, though overthrown, are not reconciled to their fate of being eliminated and always seek to stage a comeback; because the influence of bourgeois ideology and culture and force of habits of the old society will continue to exist over a long period and, in some respects, will be stronger than ours; because the spontaneous tendency towards capitalism still exists among the petty bourgeoisie whose remoulding is a long-term task; and because a number of degenerates and new bourgeois elements will also appear within the ranks of the working class and the personnel of the State organs as a result of the influence of the bourgeoisie and the corrosive role it plays. The complexity of the class struggle is further increased by the fact that the forces of capitalism and other reactionary forces at home invariably collude with and are connected with the international capitalist forces.

In his work *On the Correct Handling of Contradictions Among the People,* Chairman Mao also teaches us that contradictions in a socialist society are of two types, that is, contradictions among the people and contradictions between ourselves and the enemy, and that many contradictions of the former type exist. These two types of contradictions can, under certain conditions, be transformed into each other. A dictatorial method must be adopted in dealing with the enemy. To resolve contradictions among the people the method of "unity-criticism-unity" must be used; this means to start off with a desire for unity and resolve contradictions through criticism or struggle so as to achieve a new unity on a new basis. By acting in accordance with this teaching of Chairman Mao, the working class will be able to unite the whole people, constituting more than 90 per cent of the country's population, isolate the enemy, comprising only a few per cent of the population, and consolidate the dictatorship of the proletariat.

There are various classes and strata among the whole people constituting more than 90 per cent of the population. We should rely on the workers and the poor and lower-middle peasants, unite the middle peasants, all working people and other classes, strata and social groups who approve, support and take part in the cause of socialist construction and oppose all the social forces and social groups who resist socialist revolution and harbour hostility to socialist construction and sabotage it. This is the Party's strategic line throughout the period of socialism.

Social Foundation of Modern Revisionism

Since classes and class struggle, the three antitheses and the two different types of contradictions continue to exist in a socialist society, it has not one but two possibilities of development, not one, but two possible futures. A socialist country will be able to abolish classes step by step, narrow down the existing antitheses and pass over into communism in the end if it persists in carrying out its Marxist-Leninist line and policies, consolidates the dictatorship of the proletariat, correctly handles the two different types of contradictions, carries the socialist revolution on the political, economic as well as ideological fronts through to the end and strengthens and develops its socialist economy. Otherwise, the bourgeois forces will get out of hand, new bourgeois elements and new rich peasants will emerge and the three antitheses will be more accentuated. The new bourgeois elements and new rich peasants are the social foundation of modern revisionism. Once the revisionist forces occupy a dominant position, a socialist society will evolve into capitalism. It is precisely in anticipation of this situation that imperialism has never for a single moment forgotten to implement towards the socialist countries a strategy of achieving victory by peaceful means.

The "peaceful evolution" of socialism into capitalism has long since been realised in Yugoslavia. Khrushchev is the biggest revisionist of today and under his revisionist leadership the fruits of socialism, which were gained at the cost of tremendous sacrifices by the great Soviet people, are being increasingly lost, the capitalist forces are becoming rampant and youths are being subjected to serious corruption by capitalism. This situation cannot but arouse our greatest vigilance.

Struggle To Win Over Youth

The struggle between the proletariat and the bourgeoisie to win over the youth is an important aspect of the class struggle in the period of socialism. The proletariat demands that youth should revolutionise itself and take over from their elders not only in the struggle for production but also in the class struggle, and shatter all possibility of a capitalist comeback. On the other hand, all the enemies of the revolution are doing all they can to drag the youth on to a non-revolutionary or counter-revolutionary path. The former US Secretary of State Dulles and the former US Assistant Secretary of State for Far Eastern

Affairs Hilsman openly revealed that US imperialism placed its hopes of staging a counter-revolutionary comeback in China on the degeneration of China's younger generation and that at no time were they forgetting to achieve the so-called "peaceful evolution" through the instrumentality of the youth of the third and fourth generations. This struggle to win over the youth will have a bearing on the issue of who will win, the proletariat or the bourgeoisie and on whether or not the revolution can be carried through to the end.

In our socialist, New China, all favourable conditions exist for training our youth to be heirs to the revolution of the proletariat. We have the correct, Marxist-Leninist leadership of the Chinese Communist Party headed by our great Chairman Mao. We have in the main completed the socialist transformation in the ownership of the means of production; we are carrying on large-scale socialist construction and carrying out the socialist revolution politically and ideologically in a thoroughgoing way. Proletarian ideology holds a leading position in many fields of social ideology. The whole country and the whole Party has taken up the cause of educating the youth in the spirit of our revolutionary traditions. People can see in the youth of our country a spirit of warm love for the Party, and for socialism, and of bitter hatred for imperialism and all reactionaries, and for revisionism, and a spirit of bold enterprise in the people's cause and dedication to the revolution. The great communist fighter Lei Feng[1] is one of the most outstanding representatives of contemporary youth in our country.

At the same time, we must also bear in mind that young people, coming from different classes and strata of society, still bear the impress of various class ideologies. Since they have been brought up under conditions of peace and stability, it is easy for them to lapse into a false sense of peace and tranquillity and to look for a life of ease and security. Because they have not been through the severe test of revolutionary struggle, they lack a thorough understanding of the complexity and exacting demands of revolution. Thus it is that, under the corrupt influence of bourgeois ideology, a certain number of new bourgeois elements and revisionists will inevitably crop up among the young people. It is wrong and dangerous to think that youth, "born in the new society and brought up under the red flag," is "born red" and can automatically be heirs to the revolutionary cause without revolutionary Marxist-Leninist education, steeling in practical revolutionary struggle and conscious ideological remoulding.

Class Education for Youth

At the Tenth Plenum of the Eighth Central Committee of the Communist Party, Chairman Mao, our beloved leader and teacher, pointed out with great emphasis that it is necessary to strengthen the class education of youth to ensure that the revolution in our country will not be perverted in generations to come. This historic directive of Chairman Mao charts the course of the work of our Communist Youth League throughout the period of socialism and illumines the way ahead for the hundreds of millions of youth in our country.

It is a great strategic task of the proletarian dictatorship and also a fundamental aim of the work of our Communist Youth League to hold aloft the red banner of the great thinking of Mao Tse-tung, so as to help turn the young people of the coming generations in our country into proletarian revolutionaries.

Opposed Lines in Youth Work

In order to ensure that the young people of the coming generations will always be revolutionaries and not be corrupted, it is necessary to wage a continuous struggle to eliminate bourgeois ideology and foster proletarian ideology throughout the socialist period. At the Second Session of the Eighth National Congress of the Chinese Communist Party, Comrade Liu Shao-ch'i pointed out that "to build a socialist and communist society, we must not only wipe out all the old systems of exploitation and oppression of man by man, but also utterly eliminate obsolete ideas and habits which are derived from and serve these old systems; we must eliminate bourgeois ideology and foster proletarian ideology, that is to say, eventually eliminate all vestiges of the exploiting classes and exploiting systems from the minds of the people." Two diametrically opposed lines exist in youth work. Which one is followed determines whether that work will foster proletarian ideology and eliminate bourgeois ideology or foster bourgeois ideology and eliminate proletarian ideology.

One is based on the standpoint of proletarian class education, to arm youth with a Marxist-Leninist class viewpoint, a mass viewpoint, a labour viewpoint, a dialectical-materialist viewpoint, in other words, with the communist world outlook and Mao Tse-tung's thinking, so as to help turn young people into proletarian revolutionaries. This is the Marxist-Leninist line in youth work.

The other is based on the standpoint of class reconciliation and the liquidation of the revolution, to corrupt the revolutionary will of the young people with the deceptive pacifism and humanism of the bourgeoisie and bourgeois individualism, to do everything possible to draw the young people away from the revolution and even lead them on to the path of opposing the revolution. This is the modern revisionist line in youth work. The modern dogmatists, who trail behind the modern revisionists in response to their baton, also implement this line in their youth work.

The question of which line to follow is a vital question which decides whether the youth can carry on the cause of the proletarian revolution; it is a vital question which concerns the future of the socialist state. It is a serious fighting task of our Communist Youth League to persist in the Marxist-Leninist revolutionary line and to combat resolutely the fallacious line of the modern revisionists and modern dogmatists in youth work.

Importance of Class Education

One of the fundamental differences between the modern revisionists and us is on the question whether to arm youth with Marxist-Leninist teaching on class struggle or to corrupt youth with the nonsense of class collaboration, which means capitulation to the bourgeoisie.

The teaching of class struggle is the essence of Marxism-Leninism, and proletarian class education is the basis of the communist education of the youth. This class education is particularly important to young people who grow up in the new society. Lenin has clearly stated: "It [the youth] can learn Communism only by linking up every step in its studies, training and education with the continuous struggle the proletarians and the toilers are waging against the old exploiting society."

The primary question in class education is to distinguish between the enemy and ourselves. We must not only be able to recognise US imperialism, the Chiang Kai-shek bandits and other open enemies of all kinds, as well as remnant and emerging capitalist forces; we must also be able to recognise those hidden enemies who persist in their reactionary stand, oppose the socialist revolution and sabotage socialist construction. The working class, representing the advanced forces of production, is the best organised and the most disciplined, far-sighted

68

and thoroughly revolutionary class; it is the leading class in our country. Only under its leadership can the socialist revolution and socialist construction in our country win victory. The poor peasants and lower-middle peasants are the most reliable allies of the working class in the countryside; they are the force on which we depend in carrying on revolution and construction.

Not everyone clearly understands this vital question of whom to rely upon in socialist revolution and socialist construction. Some, for instance, hold the view that in developing industry and engaging in other kinds of construction reliance should be placed mainly on experts, technology and intellectuals. This viewpoint is wrong. Intellectuals are needed for socialist construction, but they invariably belong to a certain social class and serve its interests. They can play a positive role in revolution and construction only when they accept the leadership of the working class, serve the workers and peasants, and identify themselves with them. There are also people who maintain that following agricultural collectivisation, we should mainly rely on the middle peasants, and who talk about "relying on the poor peasants in the land reform and on the middle peasants in production." This viewpoint is wrong too. In the countryside, the well-to-do middle peasants are always wavering and irresolute in taking the socialist road; some of them represent the spontaneous forces of capitalism. Only those who were farmhands, poor peasants and lower-middle peasants during the land reform and before co-operative farming was introduced, form the majority of the peasants; they suffered most in the old society, go in for revolution most resolutely, and are firm against all exploiting systems and exploiting classes. That is why we should rely upon them not only in the revolutionary struggle and in the fight against the forces of capitalism but also during the whole course of socialist construction.

Reliance on Working People

By relying on the ranks of these revolutionary classes — the working class and the poor and lower-middle peasants — and closely uniting with the middle peasants and the rest of the working people, we are in a position to crush all the activities of the landlords, rich peasants, counter-revolutionaries, bad elements and Rightists aimed at sabotaging and staging a comeback, and transform the majority of them into new men; to battle the urban and rural capitalist forces and prevent any evolution into

69

capitalism; to supervise cadres and prevent any of them from degenerating; to unite with, educate and remould the great majority of the intellectuals and get them to serve socialism; and to effectively educate the young people to take a firm class stand and carry on the glorious traditions of the revolution. Firm reliance on the ranks of these revolutionary classes is the basic guarantee against revisionism and a capitalist restoration, the basic guarantee for successfully completing the socialist revolution and socialist construction.

Our young people must take a staunch proletarian stand, that is, they must be firmly wedded to the idea of relying permanently on the working class and the poor peasants and lower-middle peasants, and always identify themselves with them. Young people can become staunch revolutionaries only when they rely firmly on the working class and the poor peasants and lower-middle peasants, resolutely stand by the people who make up more than 90 per cent of the population, and loyally represent their interests. Should they stand on the side of the small number of people who form only a few per cent of the population and represent the latter's interests, they would be on the road of non-revolution or counter-revolution. A correct solution of the question of which side to stand on and whom to rely upon means for young people the solution of the basic question of revolutionisation.

Repudiation of Class Struggle

The modern revisionists do their best to spread the fallacy about "the state of the whole people" and the "party of the entire people" and negate classes and class struggle, invoking a hypocritical "love of humanity" to obscure the understanding of young people regarding the line of demarcation between the enemy and ourselves, and asserting that "man is to man a friend, comrade and brother" and so on and so forth. Chairman Mao Tse-tung put it well: "There is absolutely no such thing in the world as love, or hatred, without reason or cause. As for the so-called 'love of humanity,' there has been no such all-inclusive love since humanity was divided into classes... We cannot love enemies, we cannot love social evils, our aim is to destroy them." Let us ponder this over: How can there be love between the murderous and plundering imperialists and the oppressed nations and peoples, between the exploiting and exploited classes? And how can the workers and peasants of a socialist country become "friends, comrades and brothers" of speculators and racketeers and thieves of the State treasury, etc.? In performing this sleight of hand the sole aim of the modern revisionists is to pacify the millions of angry people, enslaved and oppressed, with the "love of humanity," and prevent them from rising in resistance, to try to cover up the classes and class contradictions that actually exist in Soviet society and to disarm the young people in the face of the stern class struggle and get them, when they have been bereft of class vigilance, to become captives of the bourgeoisie.

Attitude towards Manual Labour

Another major difference between us and the modern revisionists is on the question of whether to educate young people in an ardent love of labour and of identification with the workers and peasants or to scorn manual labour and divorce themselves from the workers and peasants.

Chairman Mao said: "...the establishment of our socialist system has opened the road leading to the ideal state of the future, but we must work hard, very hard indeed, if we are to make that ideal a reality." The attitude to be taken towards labour for socialist construction is an important yardstick for determining whether the young people have a revolutionary consciousness and whether it is high or low.

All the wealth of the world is created by labour. Nothing can be produced without manual labour. The steady advance of science and technology helps to raise the productivity of labour greatly and lighten its intensity and continuously reduce heavy manual labour to light manual or mental labour, thus creating conditions for the integration of manual and mental labour in the new society, and that is why it is necessary to strive for the modernisation of science and technology. But manual labour will never disappear. With the new developments of science and technology and the extension of man's mastery over nature, new kinds of heavy manual labour will appear again in certain branches and spheres of production. The attitude of looking down on manual labour and of seeking to make gains without doing any work is the common characteristic of all exploiters and the source of all evils.

Manual labour is not only a necessary means of creating wealth and transforming the objective world but also an extremely important condition for carrying out our ideological remoulding and permanently ensuring against degeneration. Only those who ardently love labour and always stand together with the workers and peasants and share their

71

weal and woe can be staunch revolutionaries to the end and immune to degeneration under all circumstances. It must be noted that the idea of loving leisure and hating labour, of holding manual labour in contempt — an idea consistently spread by the exploiting classes — has a deep-rooted influence and so a long struggle is needed before this poison can be removed from society. Revolutionary young people should set an example of ardently loving labour and make themselves pioneers in changing old social habits and customs and implementing new ones.

Making Intellectuals Workers and
Working People Intellectuals

The difference between manual and mental labour remains in a socialist society. The Marxist-Leninist approach to this problem is to strive to reduce this difference, instead of aggravating it. We stand for making intellectuals workers, and the worker and peasant masses intellectuals, both for the same purpose: to enable them to work still better in their socialist labour. Making intellectuals workers means that they should become closely linked with the worker-peasant masses, serve them wholeheartedly, respect manual labour and manual workers, learn from the workers and peasants and become one with them in thought and feeling. Chairman Mao Tse-tung has said: "The ultimate line of demarcation between the revolutionary intellectuals on the one hand and non-revolutionary and counter-revolutionary intellectuals on the other lies in whether they are willing to, and actually do, become one with the masses of workers and peasants." The fundamental road leading to the revolutionisation of educated youth is for them to make themselves working people, to identify themselves with the workers and peasants and to turn themselves into socialist-minded, cultured workers.

Modern revisionists look down upon manual labour. They are opposed to intellectuals becoming workers, alleging that for intellectuals to engage in manual labour is simply a waste of talent and that for cadres to take part in labour means a lowering of efficiency. Modern revisionists buy over a part of the intellectuals by offering them high positions and fat salaries; they thus make them lord it over the labouring people, and turn them into props supporting their revisionist policies. They use this as a bait to make their young people despise manual labour and avoid becoming one with the workers and peasants, while setting as their goal the acquiring of handsome salaries and special privileges. What

72

the modern revisionists in effect uphold is the very thing practised by the exploiting classes — the principle that "those who work with their minds govern others; while those who toil with their hands are governed by others."

Love for the Collective

Yet another major difference between us and the modern revisionists is on the question of whether to educate the youth in the great collectivist spirit of the proletariat or to corrupt them with bourgeois individualism.

In the history of mankind the cause of the proletariat is an unprecedentedly great and arduous one. Its accomplishment calls for the endeavours of millions of people filled with the revolutionary spirit of defying all difficulties and being undaunted by any sacrifice. For such people, the long-cherished goal is not the happiness of one person or one family only, but a happy and prosperous life to be shared by all the working people on earth. They bear the whole world in mind and their outlook is worldwide; they regard dedication to the emancipation of mankind as the highest honour and the greatest happiness. They always give first place to the interests of the people; they have an ardent love for the collective, a deep concern for their comrades; they never work for their own interest but always for that of others. In time of emergency, they come forward without hesitation and sacrifice themselves in the interests of the public. Conscientiously they subject themselves to the collective, and subordinate everything to the needs of the revolution. They always work with a will, and are always keen in creating and making innovations. Yet they live simply, are modest, and never show off. A man like this is a man who upholds the loftiest morals of mankind, a great fighter for communism.

Yet another major difference between us and the modern revisionists is on the question of whether to educate youth to cherish the great ideals of Communism and to carry the revolution to the end, or whether to try hard to propagate the "philosophy of survival" with its emphasis on living regardless of purpose, and use intimidation and deceit to make youth forsake their great revolutionary ideals.

"Goulash" Instead of Revolution

The modern revisionists are cowed by imperialist pressure. They are scared out of their wits by the imperialist policy of nuclear blackmail.

73

From fearing the war, they pass to being afraid of revolution. From giving up the revolution themselves, they pass to opposing other people making revolutions. They have substituted bourgeois individual enjoyment and national egoism for the Communist ideal of emancipating all the oppressed peoples. They frighten the youth: "A single spark can touch off a world war!" "Youth are the first victims of a war." "At all costs, no revolution!" Khrushchev loudly declared that goulash is something worthwhile fighting for. The modern revisionists attack our struggle for the revolution as a policy of "suffering on earth to win 'a place in paradise.'" They have even shamelessly said: "Just because in China a chicken isn't eaten doesn't mean that it's easier for someone in Africa." The modern revisionists dare not harm a single hair of imperialism and capitalism. They just want to survive, they don't want revolution. They have utterly cast away Communist ideals. If this is not downright selfish philistinism seeking nothing but to live and to keep clear of death, what is it?

But it should be pointed out that the patent rights for the invention of such a philistine philosophy do not belong to the modern revisionists. Ever since the birth of the Communist movement, there have been scum in the revolutionary ranks who stop at nothing in enticing people to give up their great goals for immediate interests. The old-line revisionists said long ago: It would be better for the young people to spend their money on sausages rather than on buying the *Communist Manifesto*. More than 60 years ago, leaders of the Economists in Russia also raised the cry: An increase of a kopeck on every ruble of wages is more practicable and valuable than any kind of socialism or politics. But neither the lure of "sausages" nor of a "kopeck increase" could stop tens of thousands of young people in those days from choosing the revolutionary road, so how can such talk about "goulash" today halt the advance of the revolutionary ranks which are mighty now as never before?

Harm of Revisionist Line

Comrades! From the foregoing we can see clearly that the Marxist-Leninist line in our youth work is aimed at bringing up our young people as staunch and reliable heirs to the proletarian revolution, and enable them to uphold the revolutionary red banner from generation to generation, till the complete victory of Communism. The aim of the modern revisionist line in youth work, on the contrary, is to turn young people

74

into captives of the bourgeoisie and tools to be used by the modern revisionist groups in implementing their rule. This constitutes part of the whole fallacious line of the modern revisionists who are throwing the revolutionary cause of the proletariat overboard and are effecting a capitalist comeback. The appearance in the socialist camp of this modern revisionist line which denies and opposes revolution is an extremely pernicious thing poisoning the minds of thousands upon thousands of young people. But a bad thing can be turned to good account. If we thoroughly expose this revisionist line which does such great harm to the young people and turn it into a teacher by negative example, it will be of great help in educating all cadres who are doing youth work and all our revolutionary youth, making them more awake and alert, and able to rally still more conscientiously under the banner of Marxism-Leninism to struggle still more resolutely to implement the proletarian line for revolutionisation.

The Role of Youth in the Three
Great Revolutionary Movements

How do we carry out the Marxist-Leninist line in our youth work? Our experience can be summed up in a nutshell: Under the guidance of Mao Tse-tung's thinking, firmly adhere to the integration of revolutionary education and revolutionary practice, mobilise the broad masses of youth to play their role, steel themselves and mature in the three great revolutionary movements — in class struggle, in the struggle for production and in scientific experiment.

Chairman Mao Tse-tung has stressed the great importance of these movements. He has pointed out that while they are great revolutionary movements facilitating the building of a strong socialist country, they are also reliable guarantees against bureaucracy, revisionism and dogmatism — thus making our position for ever invincible — and also reliable guarantees that the proletariat unite with the broad masses of the working people to put democratic dictatorship into practice. Fiery revolutionary struggles are the best crucible for steeling revolutionaries. Our revolutionary predecessors were tempered in the stress and strain of mass revolutionary struggles. If young people want to join the new generation of revolutionaries, they too must go and steel themselves in the stress and strain of socialist, mass revolutionary struggles.

How should the Communist Youth League do its work in helping young people play a positive role in these three great revolutionary movements and in getting a revolutionary education?

First, it must lead the youth in joining the class struggle and in actively participating in the movement for socialist education.

The socialist education movement now being unfolded all over the country is a profound development of our socialist revolution; it is capital construction in the political, economic, ideological and organisational fields in a socialist country, and another great movement for re-educating and remoulding men on a large scale. It is also the best school for class education among the youth. In this movement, face-to-face struggles are waged against our class enemies and their criminal activities exposed; by recalling the miseries of the past and considering the happiness of today, the poor and lower-middle peasants compare the old and new societies to bring out their sharp contrasts; serious bourgeois ideas and acts are criticised, and the danger of taking the capitalist road shown up. Experience shows that in places where such education is earnestly carried out among the youth through the socialist education movement, the revolutionisation of their ideology has been greatly promoted. Organisations of the League should, first and foremost, effectively mobilise the youth among the workers and the poor and lower-middle peasants, help them raise their level of class consciousness and rely on them to rally the other young people. These organisations should give guidance to the mass of young people in conscientiously studying the directives and various policies concerning the socialist education movement issued by the Party's Central Committee, help them master the correct handling of contradictions among the people and the correct handling of the relations between the State, the collective and individuals, develop production, consolidate the socialist economy and the system of the people's communes, and smash the attacks of the capitalist and feudal forces.

In unfolding the socialist education movement, we should make extensive use of the histories of villages, people's communes, factories and families to educate the young people. Experience has proved that educating the young in these "four histories" is a good way of helping them carry forward the work of keeping the "family records" of the proletariat going and of educating young people by relying on the working class and the poor and lower-middle peasants; it is a new development in implementing the mass line in class education. In order to

76

help the young keep the "family records" of the proletariat going generation after generation, education in the "four histories," in the history of class struggle and in revolutionary tradition should be made compulsory political subjects for the youth and children of our country.

In the socialist education movement, the Communist Youth League must win over, educate, and remould the youth who come from the families of landlords, rich peasants and other exploiting classes and it must do this work earnestly. These young people did not take a direct part in exploitation, so they are not exploiters. However, as they grew up in homes of the exploiting classes, they have been influenced by those families in varying degrees and in this respect they are different from the sons and daughters of the working people. We should organise them to take an active part in the socialist education movement, teach them to turn against the classes they were born into, resolutely go over to the side of the working class and the poor and lower-middle peasants, and take the road of socialism. Although they were not able to choose their class origin, they can certainly chart their own future. They can certainly take their destinies into their own hands and they have bright prospects before them so long as they take the Party's teachings to heart and strive to remould themselves.

Re-education of Youth in the Cultural Field

A mass of facts that came to light in the course of the socialist education movement in various parts of the country reveal that in competing with us to win the youth the class enemy often tries to make a breakthrough on the front of cultural life. If proletarian ideology does not take over the field of cultural life, bourgeois ideology is bound to take over and turn it into one for activities aimed at restoring capitalism. In co-operation with the departments concerned the League organisations should build up fields of study and recreational activities for the youth in an energetic and systematic way, lead them to read revolutionary books and papers, sing revolutionary songs, stage revolutionary dramas, and promote various kinds of cultural, recreational and sports activities which are healthy, colourful and rich in content so as to satisfy the various likes and interests of young people in their spare time and develop their noble revolutionary sentiments.

The Communist Youth League must constantly teach the youth to maintain revolutionary vigilance, defend their socialist motherland

and safeguard the dictatorship of the proletariat. Huang Chi-kuang, Lo Sheng-chiao, An Yeh-min, Tu Feng-jui, Lo Kuang-hsieh, Samuil Mukhamed, Ouyang Hai and many, many other great revolutionary fighters who were trained in the People's Liberation Army and who are loyal to the motherland and to the people, are noble examples who should be emulated by the youth of the whole country. The young officers and men of the People's Liberation Army must keep their weapons at the ready, continuously raise their ideological level, master the skill of destroying the enemy, and strive to have more "five good" soldiers and "four good" companies. The youth of the whole country must take an active part in militia training, study the military arts hard and be ready at all times to defend the motherland arms in hand. U.S. imperialism is determined to be the sworn enemy of the Chinese people. It still occupies our territory of Taiwan and repeatedly carries out provocations against us. We must completely shatter US imperialism's criminal, aggressive acts. We must liberate Taiwan! We will never lay down our arms so long as imperialism exists externally and class struggle exists internally.

Secondly, the Communist Youth League must guide the youth to take part in the struggle for production so that they will become the shock force in the socialist construction of our motherland.

Today we are no longer working for landlords or capitalists, nor merely to support our families. We are working for the great cause of the working class, for the well-being of the people and also to give more powerful support to the revolutionary struggles of the peoples of other lands. The various jobs which have to be done in every sphere of work are all indispensable to the cause of socialism. Every revolutionary youth should ardently love ordinary labour, cheerfully accept the work he is assigned to, consciously take up the difficult tasks, and in his ordinary daily work show revolutionary will and the spirit of revolutionary heroism.

Revolutionary emulation movements to learn from the People's Liberation Army, the oil workers of Tach'ing and the peasants of Tachai, and to "compare with the advanced, learn from and overtake them, and help the less advanced," are taking place throughout the country. These have greatly stimulated the revolutionary spirit of the broad masses of the people and the youth; they have pushed the movement for more production and economy steadily to a new high, opening up broad perspectives for rapid growth of the productive forces in our country.

The Communist Youth League must mobilise the broad masses of the youth to take part in the movement "to compare, learn, overtake and help" for more production and economy, to take an active part in the drive for technical innovations and the technical revolution, and to introduce all kinds of organisational forms and lively working methods to bring the labour enthusiasm of the youth into full play.

In our country's socialist construction, the most outstanding and most important task is to modernise agriculture. At the present time hundreds of millions of peasants in our country are changing the face of nature and working to modernise agriculture. It is a golden opportunity for the youth of our country to win honour in socialist construction. Together with the middle-aged and by relying on themselves and working hard, the young people in the countryside must strive to develop agricultural production, forestry, stockbreeding, side-occupations and fishery, and so build a new socialist countryside.

In recent years, large numbers of educated youth have been taking part in agricultural production. This is an important measure to reinforce agricultural construction and to carry through the cultural and technical revolutions in the countryside. It is also an important means for revolutionising the educated youth of our country. It is also a new development in the period of socialist construction of the glorious tradition of the educated youth of our country joining with the workers and peasants.

Cultured Labourers with Socialist Consciousness

The educational policy of our country is to train our young people into cultured labourers with a socialist consciousness. In the future, and for a relatively long period to come, apart from those who will go on with their studies or take up work in industry, commerce and the service trades, the majority of middle school graduates will take up work in agricultural production. This is a need created by the development of the national economy, and is also the main way for young people to join in socialist construction. All students in school should study conscientiously and well, no matter whether they will later on continue with their studies or go straight to work in industry or agriculture. Study hard, love labour; have a "red heart" and so be prepared for two eventualities. This is the right attitude for educated young people to have in relation to the question of whether they will carry on with school

79

studies or go out to work.

The Communist Youth League must make great efforts to mobilise educated youth politically to take part in agricultural labour, and actively co-operate with the departments concerned to make proper arrangements for them so that they can settle down and work. League organisations should show keen concern for those educated youth who go to the countryside or up into the mountain areas; they must pay attention to using this force effectively, to develop their strong points, to support their reasonable proposals and demands and to enable them to settle down happily in the countryside.

We are confident that the transformation of our countryside will be speeded up with the co-operation between peasants with rich experience in the struggle for production and the educated young people who have some knowledge in science and culture, along with all kinds of aid from the working class and the State.

Movement for Scientific Experiment

Thirdly, the Communist Youth League must lead the young people to take part in scientific experiments, work hard to raise their cultural, and scientific and technical levels.

Young people are most sensitive to new things and most willing to learn; they are the least conservative in thinking, and besides, many young people have a certain store of scientific and cultural knowledge. They are a most active and lively force in the mass movement for scientific experiment. This is a revolutionary movement to search for objective laws in a scientific way in order to make our transformation of nature more effective. League organisations must foster on a wide scale the interest of the youth in the study of science and technology, and so enable them to play a fuller role in the mass movement for scientific experiment.

In organising young people to take an active part in mass scientific experimental activities, we must advocate the fusing of a revolutionary spirit with a scientific attitude. Youth should be encouraged and taught to develop a bold, creative spirit, to break down superstitious beliefs and to emancipate their minds, refusing either to be tied down by old conventions and prejudices, or to give up in face of difficulties or temporary setbacks. Science is a down-to-earth business and must be approached in a serious and strict way. We must respect practice, respect the

80

experience of the masses, and respect those truths that have really been tested and proved. Only by integrating the revolutionary spirit of daring to think, daring to speak and daring to do with a scientific attitude of seeking truth from the facts will we be able to discover objective laws and achieve results of real value.

In order to bring about a continuous rise in the cultural and scientific levels of young workers and farmers, League organisations must take a keen interest in the spare-time education of young people, actively co-operate with the cultural and educational departments, and on the basis of summed-up experience go on to organise young people to resolutely carry on with long-term spare-time studies and build up, step by step, in the cities and countryside a relatively complete system of spare-time education.

The young scientists and technicians of our country are a new emerging force trained by the Party and the State. Young scientists and technicians should aim high and have lofty ambitions and make outstanding contributions in accordance with the scientific plans of the State.

Heirs to Proletarian Revolution

Without a revolutionary theory there can be no revolutionary movement. The three great revolutionary movements of the class struggle, the struggle for production and of scientific experiment in our country are guided by great Marxism-Leninism and the great thinking of Mao Tse-tung. In order to guide the youth to undergo tempering conscientiously in these three great revolutionary movements and to train them to become staunch, reliable heirs to the cause of the proletarian revolution, the movement to study Marxism-Leninism and the works of Chairman Mao must be pressed ahead so as to lead the broad masses of the youth to work hard and master the teachings of Mao Tse-tung.

Comrade Mao Tse-tung is a great Marxist-Leninist of the contemporary era. Integrating the universal truth of Marxism-Leninism with the concrete practice of the Chinese revolution and construction in the course of the great struggle of the Chinese people, Comrade Mao Tse-tung has creatively developed Marxism-Leninism. The thinking of Mao Tse-tung is the Chinese people's guide in carrying on their revolution and socialist construction; it is a powerful ideological weapon against imperialism, modern revisionism and modern dogmatism, and

81

Chairman Mao's works are the best textbooks for revolutionising the youth of our country. In recent years, the movement for studying the works of Chairman Mao which has been growing daily among the young people of our country is an ideological revolutionary movement of the youth of China who want to make progress, who want to master Marxism-Leninism.

It can be confidently expected that the development of the movement for the study of Chairman Mao's works will have an extremely far-reaching effect in furthering the revolutionisation of the youth of our country. It will raise greatly the revolutionary consciousness of our youth, and make our youth red and expert revolutionary fighters filled with a vigorous revolutionary spirit and good at mastering objective laws.

NOTES

1. Lei Feng, a young squad leader of a transport unit in the PLA, lost his life in an accident in 1962 while on duty. He was then only 22. Mao Tse-tung in March 1963 issued a call for learning from Lei Feng, because he was a model CYL member and a "five-good" soldier. In his diary, Lei Feng wrote these words: "I live so that others may live better."

Heirs to the Socialist Revolution

Reproduced from an article carried in *Peking Review*, No. 30, 1964, entitled "Bringing Up Heirs for the Revolution."—Ed.

The matter of bringing up worthy heirs to the proletarian revolution — of raising new generations who will steadfastly carry the socialist revolution through to the end, occupies an important part of the attention of the Chinese people today. Since early July, *Jen-min Jih-pao* and many other papers and magazines have been giving frontpage prominence to editorials, features and news reports on this subject and they promise further discussion, more stories and information on it in the future.

Raised with special authority by Chairman Mao Tse-tung, this question is one of the utmost historical importance. It is a question, in the final analysis, of how to ensure that the revolution, won by the older generation at the cost of such sacrifices, will be carried on victoriously to the end by the generations to come; that the destiny of our country will continue to be held secure in the hands of true proletarian revolutionaries; that our sons and grandsons and their successors will continue to advance, generation after generation, along the Marxist-Leninist, and not the revisionist, path, that is, advance steadily towards the goal of Communism, and not to retreat to make room for a capitalist restoration.

The period of socialism, the period which China is now going through, is a historical period of transition from capitalist to Communist society. Classes and class struggle continue to exist in this period and the question of "who will win?" is still not finally resolved. It appears that this period of transition will take five to ten generations or even longer to complete itself.

The struggle to win over the youth is an important aspect of the class struggle in this period of socialism. The enemies of the revolution of every kind are doing all they can to influence the youth and drag them on to non-revolutionary or counter-revolutionary paths. There is no lack of statements by such reactionaries as the former US Secretary of State Dulles or the former US Assistant Secretary of State for Far Eastern Affairs Hilsman to show that US imperialism pins its hopes on the degeneration of China's younger generation and counts on China's youth of the third or fourth generations to bring about a so-called "peaceful evolution" in our country — back to capitalism.

The question of educating and training our revolutionary heirs is therefore regarded as a most important matter that concerns the long-term advance of the cause of socialism and Communism, not only in the next 100 years, but in the further future.

The following are *résumés* of three news features carried in the Chinese press in the past fortnight. They give an idea of how this task is being tackled.

Eyes on the Future

During the course of the socialist education movement last year in the Taiyangsheng (Sunrise) People's Commune, in Kaiping *hsien* of Liaoning Province, a number of facts came to light which alerted the Party branch of the Hotun Brigade that the class enemy had not been inactive. They had set their dark hands on the youth — doing their utmost to poison their youthful minds and corrupt them. This drove home the urgency of the task of training up a staunch revolutionary younger generation.

Early this year, the Hotun Party branch mapped out a 10-year plan for the development of agriculture in its area. This is a well-thought-out plan that does not forget to include a housing project to take care of the population increase. With a determined spirit of self-reliance, they put forward the slogan "Plant trees first and build houses next." The project envisages, among other things, that beginning this year 20,000 trees will be planted each spring and autumn of every year for five years in succession. That will be about enough to solve the question of lumber ten years hence.

While formulating the plan, members of the Party branch already felt the need for a contingent of young people to help mobilise and organise the commune members to put the plan into execution. So they took a special look at the situation as regards membership: they had altogether 19 Party members in the brigade and seven of these formed the Party committee, the average age of whose members was 41. Who would take over the work of leadership here ten years hence, 20 years hence?

They approached this question with special care, because they had learnt a sharp lesson in 1961. At that time they had picked a young man to train, but because their method was wrong, and their choice not right, the youngster had grown self-conceited, isolated himself from the masses and later sank so low as to make some even more serious mistakes. So this time they made a close study one by one of all the brigade's 242 young men and women, weighing their merits and short-comings again and again until finally they came out with a list of 14 young activists, nine men and five women, all, with the exception of one, being Youth League members. Of the 14 selected, 12 came from poor peasant families; and one from a lower-middle peasant and one from a middle peasant family (he was a dependant of a revolutionary martyr). In cultural level, 12 had six years of primary schooling, one had finished junior middle school and one had a college education. All 14 have shown that they have these good qualities: they have a firm proletarian stand in struggle against the enemy; they are resolute in carrying out the Party's policies and directives and are conscientious both in work and study; they subordinate their own interests to those of the collective, show a deep concern for the collective and the life of the masses, have a good style of work, a high prestige among the masses and are active in all political movements.

The Party branch has also worked out a whole set of measures to help raise the general ideological and political level of these 14 young people. Each of them has been put under the wing of a veteran cadre for advice and training.

This painstaking work is already yielding results. Six of the 14 are now considered to have acquired the qualifications required for Party membership. Following their good examples, more and more young people have become activists of the brigade, and the brigade now finds in its young activists a powerful force for socialist construction.

Training Revolutionary Cadres

Shortly after liberation, the Shihchingshan Power Plant in sub-urban Peking was assigned the dual task of "first, sending out electricity and second, sending out men." Following out these instructions, in the last 15 years the plant has given the state 13 groups of leading cadres, a total of more than 300, for appointment to posts in other places. These include a dozen or so factory directors, and many shop foremen and secretaries of Party branches and committees. All were trained on the job and over the years, the plant has evolved a whole set of measures for cultivating young people.

The Shihchingshan Power Plant is an old works with a long revolutionary tradition. One of its characteristic features is that it has a relatively large number of old workers who with their intimate knowledge of the past are better placed to realize how good the present is. These veterans play an important part in the Party's programme of bringing up the new generation of revolutionary workers.

The plant makes a regular practice of giving all new workers three months' special training before they get down to work. During this period, veteran revolutionaries and old workers help them to raise their level of class consciousness by educating them in the ideas of the revolution, collectivism and the stand of serving the people, with particular emphasis on class education and education in the revolutionary traditions.

When this training period is over, old workers are assigned to take responsibility for training one or two of the newcomers in their work. They help the latter mainly in three ways: by helping them raise their political and ideological level; by teaching them production techniques; by fostering in them a style of simple living and hard work. From among these new workers, advanced elements are picked out and then "young shoots" are chosen from among these advanced elements to be cultivated into full-grown "trees," that is, men and women who will staunchly carry forward the revolution.

This work of training and cultivation is a painstaking process. In general, it involves giving these "young shoots" steadily more responsible jobs in production or additional work such as being secretary of Youth League or Party branch. Here, on the job, they are taught how to do political and ideological work well and how to master the mass line in their method of work. Whenever special political movements are organised, they are given the chance to steel themselves in the class struggle through concrete work. And when veteran cadres are absent, they are asked to stand in and do the work of the veterans so that when they finally take over, they are fully equal to their tasks.

Li Hsi-ming, now secretary of the plant's Party committee, is a case in point. An underground Party worker prior to the liberation, when he was 24 he was picked out as a promising "shoot" by the plant's Party committee after a close study of his records. At 26, he became a deputy secretary of the Party committee, and with the help of the secretary, learnt to handle things in the plant. During this time, he made a diligent study of Chairman Mao's works and the policies of the Party. He regularly went down to do a spell of physical labour at basic units where the work was toughest, and helped to solve key problems in production. When the secretary was transferred to another place, he was promoted to his present post. In the seven years as secretary, he has consistently maintained his close ties with the mass of workers and his fine working style of making strict demands on himself. In the Party committee, he always listens carefully to the opinion of other members and sticks to the principle of collective leadership. In this way, he rallies the entire leading body of the plant in close unity, and sees to it that the Party's policies are carried out both in the letter and spirit.

Li Hsi-ming and the rest of the young cadres raised in the plant have won general acclaim as worthy heirs to the revolution and emulators of their revolutionary predecessors.

Keeping Power in Proletarian Hands

An anti-chemical company of the Chinese People's Liberation Army forces stationed in Canton has distinguished itself for its good work in promoting soldiers to be officers. Of the company's nine officers, seven have come from its own rank and file. In the last few years, it has altogether promoted 23 men to officer rank. Many of them have been sent to reinforce the leading cadres of other PLA companies.

The Party branch of this company bases its work on a series of directives issued by the Military Committee of the CCP Central Committee and the General Political Department of the PLA concerning the training of young revolutionaries and on the idea of upholding the "four firsts", which are the PLA's basic experiences in political work. A deep understanding of the great significance of paying attention to the human factor has enabled it to see that this work concerns the big question of fostering and maintaining the revolutionary spirit of the PLA and ensuring that the power is always in proletarian revolutionary hands. Consequently, the entire Party branch has taken up this work most seriously and worked out a concrete plan for fostering young revolutionary officers.

The company keeps two sets of records, one for picking squad commanders from the ranks and the other, higher officers from among the squad commanders. The Party branch examines every rank-and-filer who has completed one year's service, picks out those who have a good class origin, and are politically progressive, conscientious in work, capable and close to the masses, and then re-examines the selected ones, one by one in detailed discussions. Detailed personal accounts of candidates so chosen are then entered into the records.

Private Wei Kuang-chai was selected in this way. Of poor peasant origin, he became a squad commander in 1961. Wei's records, put briefly, are: Accepted as a member of the Communist Youth League before completing one year's service; accepted as a Communist Party member in September 1960; elected a "5-good" soldier over a number of years and twice elected the company's "Good Party Member." In 1961, he became a "Good Squad Commander" and in January this year was promoted a platoon commander with the rank of second lieutenant.

Officers above the rank of squad leader are chosen with even greater care. The Party branch first examines one by one those squad commanders who have served two years, selects those who are the firmest in their revolutionary stand and are exemplary in all respects, and then submits the name list for the higher authorities' approval before the names are entered into the record. Second Lieutenant Chu Kuang-shou who was promoted a platoon commander in May last year, was one such good squad leader. Under his leadership, his platoon got excellent marks twice in marksmanship tests, and won a place on the "4-good" platoon list at first-round choosing.

The two records keep detailed accounts of every trainee including, among other things, his class background, political ideology, military training and knowledge, organising ability and state of health. The Party branch takes this task of training new revolutionary cadres as a part of its regular work and links this with the work of developing "5-good" soldiers and "4-good" platoons.

All candidates are given guidance in studying Chairman Mao Tse-tung's works so that they are armed with Mao Tse-tung's thinking and can become Party members, proletarian fighters and all-round developed "5-good" soldiers before they are promoted to be officers. They are given ample opportunities to do political and ideological work and to master military techniques so that once they become officers they can carry out their duties loyally with confidence and efficiency.

88

PART TWO

The Great Cultural Revolution in Its Early Stages

CHAPTER I

Campaign against 'Anti-Party Elements' and 'Persons in Power' behind Them

Although the campaign launched on April 14, 1966 at the meeting of the NPC Standing Committee is called the socialist cultural revolution, it was conceived to extend well beyond the intellectual domain. It is directed largely at Party officials and has affected members of the Central Committee and Government ministers.

The first volley against the historian Wu Han and the writer and journalist Teng T'o was fired by Yao Wen-yüan, chief editor of Chieh-fang Jih-pao, organ of the CCP Shanghai Municipal Committee. After this official start, the campaign of criticism and denunciation has spread to include other historians and writers, Party secretaries, university professors, film producers, playwrights, musicians and propagandists, involving even the Minister of Culture.

These people are attacked in many cases for "terrible crimes"

89

allegedly dating as far back as the thirties. They are accused of being part of a well-conceived conspiracy to restore the dictatorship of the bourgeoisie and of being an "anti-Party and anti-socialist black line" opposed to Mao Tse-tung's teachings.—Ed.

All erroneous ideas, all poisonous weeds, all ghosts and monsters, must be subjected to criticism; in no circumstance should they be allowed to spread unchecked.

—Mao Tse-tung

(Speech at the Chinese Communist Party's National Conference on Propaganda Work, March 12, 1957)

Destroy the "Gangster Inn" Run by Teng T'o, Wu Han and Liao Mo-sha

Excerpts from Yao Wen-yüan's article under the title "On 'Three-Family Village'—The Reactionary Nature of Evening Chats at Yenshan and Notes from Three-Family Village,"[1] carried in *Chinese Literature*, No. 7, 1966. The author, then chief editor of *Chieh-fang Jih-pao* of Shanghai and a member of the CCP Shanghai Municipal Committee, wrote the article "A Review of the New Historical Play, *Hai Jui Dismissed from Office*," which was carried in *Wen-hui Pao* of Shanghai on November 10, 1965. The article criticises Wu Han, then a vice-mayor of Shanghai and author of the play, for having written what Yao branded as a "poisonous weed." Yao's article was later reproduced in *Chieh-fang-chün Pao*, organ of the Military Commission of the CCP Central Committee. In October this year, Yao was named a member of the "Cultural Revolution Group" under the CCP Central Committee.—Ed.

On April 16, 1966 the fortnightly *Ch'ien Hsien* [*Frontline*] and *Pei-ching Jih-pao* [*Peking Daily*] published some material under the title "A Criticism of Three-Family Village and *Evening Chats at Yenshan*" with an editorial note. The note says:

Our magazine and paper published these articles without timely criticism; this is wrong. The reason is that we did not put proletarian politics in command and that our minds were influenced by bourgeois and feudal ideas, and hence in this serious struggle we lost our stand or vigilance.

This is a gross lie. The author of *Evening Chats at Yenshan* is Teng T'o, while *Notes from Three-Family Village* represents a "gangster inn" run jointly by Teng T'o, Liao Mo-sha and Wu Han. Teng T'o was the editor-in-chief of *Ch'ien Hsien*, and he controlled and monopolised the leading posts in the ideological and cultural work of Peking Municipality. He and his cronies of Three-Family Village made *Ch'ien Hsien, Pei-ching Jih-pao, Pei-ching Wan-pao*, etc. instruments for opposing the Party and socialism, pursued a rabid anti-Party, anti-socialist, Right opportunist, i.e., revisionist, line and served as spokesmen of the reactionary classes and the Right opportunists in their attacks on our Party. Could this be just a case of "loss of vigilance" and of publication "without timely criticism?" After letting loose so many vicious blasts against the Party and socialism, how can they claim that their minds are only a little "influenced" by bourgeois ideas? We must thoroughly expose this huge swindle.

Everyone still remembers that at the start of the criticism of Wu Han's drama, *Hai Jui Dismissed from Office,* Teng T'o feigned a correct posture. After hectic plotting, he used the pen-name Hsiang Yang-sheng and wrote a long article, "From *Hai Jui Dismissed from Office* to the Theory of Inheriting Old Ethical Values," which appeared simultaneously in the *Pei-ching Jih-pao* and *Ch'ien Hsien.* This article, which was designed to save Wu Han under the guise of "criticising" him, was a thoroughly anti-Party and anti-Marxist poisonous weed.

Does the prominence given by both the *Pei-ching Jih-pao* and *Ch'ien Hsien* to Teng T'o's article "criticising" Wu Han merely show a "loss of vigilance?" Merely a "relaxation of the class struggle on the cultural and academic front?" No, not at all. Their vigilance is very high. They spared no effort in their class struggle against the Party and the people. When they saw that the problem of Wu Han could no longer be glossed over, Teng T'o hastily came out with a fake criticism; but one who had always acted a negative role could not act a positive role convincingly, and so left a great many holes. Then, as soon as it became clear that even Teng T'o could not be saved, they hastily wrote another fake criticism in the name of the editorial departments, stubbornly fighting back to prevent the struggle from going deeper. But this sham was even more obvious, and there were even more holes. They are trying to deceive people by this talk of not putting proletarian politics in command and not making a timely criticism, hoping by their bogus criticism of Teng T'o and Three-Family Village to fool the readers and the Party into believing that they are on the side of truth.

How can they clear up the problem by taking such an attitude? How can they "unfold serious criticism?" The editorial note says that Wu Han "time and again... spoke on behalf of the Right opportunists who were dismissed from office." This was something which they first tried to cover up but which they now have to admit because it was exposed earlier on. The editorial note also says that Liao Mo-sha was "a protagonist consciously opposing the Party, socialism and Mao

Tse-tung's thought." But the reference to Teng T'o towards the end simply says that he "glorified dead men and stubbornly advocated learning from them... He propagated a large number of feudal and bourgeois ideas, opposing Marxism-Leninism and Mao Tse-tung's thought." No mention, however, is made of his anti-Party, anti-socialist activities, which makes the whole thing hard to believe. Do the countless poisonous weeds in the 150-odd articles of *Evening Chats at Yenshan* and in *Notes from Three-Family Village* just advocate "learning from dead men?" Do they just propagate feudal and bourgeois ideas? Do they represent only an ideological mistake and not a political problem? Is it logical and credible that two out of the three "brothers" in Three-Family Village are anti-Party and anti-socialist, while the third who actually did most of the writing merely advocates "learning from dead men?" Starting with a great flourish and then petering out and making a fake criticism in the hope of slipping by, they are simply putting on a show of criticism to resist the instructions of the Central Committee of the Party. Isn't this clear enough?

The material under the title "What Did *Evening Chats at Yenshan* Actually Advocate?" compiled to support the editorial note covers two whole pages of the *Pei-ching Jih-pao,* and yet it too tries to gloss over the sharp political questions. The sub-titles of the various sections read: "Distorting the Party's Directive 'Let a Hundred Flowers Blossom and a Hundred Schools of Thought Contend,' Advocating Complete Freedom for Bourgeois Ideas;" "Idealising All Aspects of the Feudal Social System;" "Using Corpses from Old Feudal Times to Resurrect the Bourgeoisie;" "Propagating the Exploiting Classes' Decadent Philosophy of Life;" and "Using Ancient Things to Satirise the Present and Attacks by Innuendo." Sub-titles reveal the tendency and judgment of editors. This method of editing suggests to the reader that *Evening Chats at Yenshan* contained little or nothing which was opposed to the Central Committee of the Party and Chairman Mao or which supported the Right opportunists, and was different in character from *Hai Jui Dismissed from Office.* Prominence is given in the first section to the distortion of the Party's policy of "let a hundred flowers blossom and a hundred schools of thought contend," while "Using Ancient Things to Satirise the Present" is put at the end with a few mild comments and one or two examples for the sake of appearances. Anyone with a discerning eye can see at a glance what the editors are up to.

When we investigate the matter, however, we find that it is not at all as they present it. A great mass of political comments, which grossly slandered the Central Committee of the Party and Chairman Mao, supported the Right opportunists and attacked the General Line and the cause of socialism, are either left out or abridged, while some of the most obviously vicious comments using ancient things to satirise the present and oppose the Party and socialism have been included in other sections in a deliberate attempt to make them stand out less; and there is not a single word about the pernicious nation-wide influence of *Evening Chats at Yenshan*. On the other hand, excerpts which did not touch on vital problems are presented with a great fanfare. There is an attempt to turn big issues into small ones and slip through. In particular, the editors have concealed the fact that the mass of articles attacking the Party written by Teng T'o, Wu Han and Liao Mo-sha during this period were not produced independently of each other but were produced by the partnership of Three-Family Village under direction, according to plan and with clear co-ordination. Wu Han was in the van and Liao Mo-sha followed close behind, but of these three warriors the real "commanding general," the manager and boss of the Three-Family Village gangster inn was none other than Teng T'o himself.

Comrade Mao Tse-tung has taught us: "We must firmly uphold the truth, and truth requires a clear-cut stand." *(A Talk to the Editorial Staff of the "Shansi-Suiyuan Daily")* In a sharp and complex class struggle, all sorts of disguises are bound to be encountered. Only when we hold high and in prominence the revolutionary banner of Mao Tse-tung's thought, adhere to principle, persist in the truth, and speak out clearly without mincing our words to expose the true nature of things, can we avoid being taken in by disguises. Since *Ch'ien Hsien* and the *Pei-ching Jih-pao* have suddenly raised the problem of *Evening Chats at Yenshan* and *Notes from Three-Family Village* but are concealing the truth, it is obviously the duty of all revolutionaries to make a thorough exposure of the reactionary character of these writings. Despite the jumble of trash in them, once we make an analysis we can see that they consistently follow a single black anti-Party and anti-socialist line, just as "Hai Jui Scolds the Emperor" and *Hai Jui Dismissed from Office* do, and some dark clouds have been raised up over China's political skies in the last few years. It is now time to reveal the inside story of this big Three-Family Village gangster inn more fully.

Evening Chats at Yenshan and Notes from Three-Family Village Came on the Stage

Evening Chats at Yenshan and *Notes from Three-Family Village* came on the stage close on the heels of *Hai Jui Dismissed from Office.* They formed a deliberate, planned and organised major attack on the Party and socialism, master-minded in detail by Three-Family Village. One look at the time-table will give us a clear picture of what happened.

Hai Jui Dismissed from Office was published in *Pei-ching Wen-i [Peking Literature and Art]* in January 1961. Today, the reactionary nature of this drama has become increasingly evident. It directed its spear-head precisely against the Lushan meeting and against the Central Committee of the Party headed by Comrade Mao Tse-tung, with a view to reversing the decisions of that meeting. The clamorous message of the drama was that the dismissal of the "upright official Hai Jui," in other words of the Right opportunists, was "unfair" and that the Right opportunists should come back to administer "court affairs," that is, to carry out their revisionist programme. It was then the urgent desire of the author to support a Right opportunist comeback and resumption of office so as to bring about the restoration of capitalism. This was also the common desire of the "brothers" of Three-Family Village.

The drama was praised and supported by certain people as soon as it was published; and the "brothers" of Three-Family Village went wild with joy in the belief that their vanguard had won the first round. Rubbing his hands with glee, Liao Mo-sha wrote in the *Pei-ching Wan-pao* on January 2, 1961, "After the winter drums have sounded, the spring grass begins to grow... An all-out effort will begin in spring." This was early spring for Three-Family Village. Then, on February 16 Liao Mo-sha wrote an open letter to Wu Han, "congratulating" him on "breaking through the door and dashing out... in order to encourage people to greater efforts." He suggested "a division of labour and co-operation" between "history" and "drama." On February 18 Wu Han in his role as vanguard replied to his "elder brother," "May I suggest to you, brother, that you too break through the door and dash out?" And he added boastfully, "You say I have broken through the door and dashed out; you have hit the nail on the head. That is precisely what I have done. This door must be broken through." What an aggressive posture, what brave airs! It really looked as if he meant

95

to fight it out. He believed that the time for the offensive had arrived and that with the production of *Hai Jui Dismissed from Office* the winter drums had sounded and the gang should ready themselves for "an all-out effort."

On February 25, 1961, one week after the shout, "This door must be broken through!", Wu Han in an article "Meetings of 'Immortals' and a Hundred Schools of Thought Contending" burst out with the statement, "We must have a series of meetings of 'Immortals' at different levels right down to the grass roots... Since the men at the grass roots are doing practical work and are in touch with reality, their problems are more concrete, striking and concentrated." He called on all those at the grass roots level "with misgivings in their hearts" to go into action. He shouted about "clearing away all obstacles along the forward path of contention by a hundred schools of thought." And he boasted smugly, "Perhaps I can be rated as an intellectual, having studied for more than forty years, taught in universities for some twenty years, and written several books." Thus he considered that, with his capital and the backing of the bosses behind the scenes, the time had come for the anti-Communist bourgeois intellectuals to take the stage and show their prowess.

In March 1961, amid this great fanfare and in the "dramatic" atmosphere of night and cloud raised by *Hai Jui Dismissed from Office,* immediately after Wu Han had "cleared the path" with his staff, the commanding general took the stage. With *Evening Chats at Yenshan,* he "broke through the door and dashed out" "at the suggestion of friends." Teng T'o said he had been "compelled to mount horse," but this is wrong. Rather, he was "begged to mount horse." After the vanguard had cleared the way, and with another "brother" wielding the whip for him, wasn't it time for the commanding general to mount horse?

Close on the heels of Wu Han's preface to *Hai Jui Dismissed from Office* came *Notes from Three-Family Village.* In August 1961, when the reactionary classes in the country were intensifying their attacks, Wu Han made a special point in his introduction to the same book, "This drama lays stress on the uprightness and tenacity of Hai Jui, who was undaunted by force, undismayed by failure and determined to make a fresh start after defeat." He actively incited and supported the Right opportunists who had been "dismissed from office" to renew their attacks on the Party. In this preface he gloated over the way in which his friends were helping to plan his campaign and claimed that his effort was "a modest spur to induce others to come forward with valuable contributions," to "induce" many other poisonous weeds to come out. Then on October 5, 1961, in an article entitled "Show Concern for All Things" in the column *Evening Chats at Yenshan,* Teng T'o quoted the couplet:

> Sounds of wind, rain and the reading of books all fill my ears;
> Family, state and world affairs, I show concern for them all.

He declared with deep feeling that this "fully reflected the political ideals of the scholars of the Tunglin party at that time," and that "this couplet has a really profound significance." The Tunglin party was an "opposition party" within the landlord class during the Ming dynasty. The reason why Teng T'o so much admired their "political ideals" was that the term "opposition party" resounded in his mind. Apparently, he felt that all the "sounds of wind and rain," all the ill winds and pestilential rains of the time, had induced such a state of restlessness that he must take a step further to live up to his "political ideals," "show concern for all things," and launch even more open attacks on the Party and on socialism. Only a few days later, on October 10, 1961, the "Three-Family Village" signboard was publicly hung up in *Ch'ien Hsien,* edited by Teng T'o, and this underground factory was turned into an open partnership. The three partners concentrated their fire, and in its first issues extremely vicious attacks, like "Great Empty Talk" and other articles, were launched against the leadership of the Central Committee of the Party.

The appearance of *Evening Chats at Yenshan* and *Notes from Three-Family Village* signified another offensive against the Party, which was planned, organised and under direction, following up on *Hai Jui Dismissed from Office.* Only by linking up the writings of the Three Families can we get to the bottom of this gangster inn's secrets.

Black Waves and Gusts of Ill Wind

Teng T'o explained how the topics for *Evening Chats at Yenshan* were chosen when he said, "I often thought of, saw or heard of things which struck me as problems, and these at once provided topics." Since Teng T'o was in a position of leadership, what things did he see? What people did he hear talking? His remarks disclose that these evening chats were written to deal with "problems" from real life over which he felt dissatisfaction. Some of the vicious anti-Party and anti-socialist stuff was first heard and then written up by him. In all cases, the points of departure and themes of these essays were important current political issues intimately bound up with reality, and were by no means just the "idealising of the ancients." This clue, provided by the author himself, helps us to see clearly that *Evening Chats at Yenshan* and *Notes from Three-Family Village* are shot through and through with the same black anti-Party, anti-popular and anti-socialist line as that followed in "Hai Jui Scolds the Emperor" and *Hai Jui Dismissed from Office,* namely, slanderous attacks on the Central Committee of the Party headed by Comrade Mao Tse-tung; attacks on the General Line of the Party; all-out support for the attacks of the Right opportunists who had been "dismissed from office" in an attempt to reverse earlier correct decisions concerning them; and support for the frenzied attacks of the feudal and capitalist forces. In step with the changes in the situation of the class struggle at home and abroad and with the different "problems" thought of, seen and heard of, they selected different lines of attack and there was a division of labour, in which they complemented and responded to each other, in whipping up a succession of black waves and gusts of ill wind.

The Ninth Plenary Session of the Eighth Central Committee of the Party, held in January 1961, pointed out:

> ...a very small number of unregenerate landlord and bourgeois elements, accounting for only a few per cent of the population... invariably try to stage a come-back... They have taken advantage of the difficulties caused by the natural calamities and of some shortcomings in the work at the primary levels to carry out sabotage.[2]

These elements stirred up an anti-Party and anti-socialist ill wind, did their utmost to slander and vilify the socialist cause of the Party and the people and abused the Central Committee of the Party in a futile attempt to overthrow the Party's General Line. Serving the political ends of the bourgeois and landlord class elements who were attempting a come-back, *Evening Chats at Yenshan,* which appeared soon after the plenary session, exploited certain economic difficulties caused by the grave natural calamities to concentrate on stirring up an evil flurry of attacks on the General Line and on bolstering up the restorationist activities of the landlord and capitalist classes.

On March 26, 1961, Teng T'o raised the slogan, "Welcome the 'miscellaneous scholars.'" Who were these "miscellaneous scholars?"

98

According to him, they were those "with a wide range of knowledge" and knowing "an assortment of bits of everything." He said: "The noted scholars of yore could all, more or less, be classified as miscellaneous scholars." He added the warning to the Party: "It will be a great loss to us if we now fail to acknowledge the great significance of the wide range of knowledge of the 'miscellaneous scholars' for all kinds of work of leadership and for scientific research work."

From these words of Teng T'o's it is quite clear that the "miscellaneous scholars" were none other than the unregenerate elements and intellectuals of the bourgeois and landlord classes, a handful of characters of dubious political background, as well as such reactionaries as the "scholars" of the landlord and bourgeois classes. The motley collection of the dead—emperors, generals and ministers, scum of all sorts, feudal die-hards, and charlatans like geomancers—all of whom Teng T'o wrote about with great awe in his articles, have their memorial tablets in the ancestral temple of the "miscellaneous scholars." Using their "knowledge" as their capital, such characters are trying desperately to intrigue themselves or climb into leading positions at different levels and change the nature of the dictatorship of the proletariat. In demanding that we recognise the "great significance" of the "miscellaneous scholars" for the "work of leadership," Teng T'o was, in effect, demanding that the Party open the door to those "miscellaneous scholars" who had taken the capitalist road and allow them to lead in "all kinds of work of leadership" and in "scientific research work" — in other words, in the academic and ideological fields—and so to prepare public opinion for the restoration of capitalism. He styled himself a first-rate "miscellaneous scholar." At that time some bourgeois elements were eagerly urging the "leadership" to "respect" their "wide range of knowledge" of how to carry out capitalist exploitation. They wanted to use this "knowledge" of theirs to change socialist enterprises into capitalist enterprises. The slogan "Welcome the 'miscellaneous scholars'" raised by Three-Family Village in support of the seizure of leadership by members of the exploiting classes must not be regarded as mere empty talk. Did not the "miscellaneous scholars" of Three-Family Village actually control a number of leading positions?

On April 13, 1961 Teng T'o demanded in his essay "Guide Rather than Block" that "everything" should be "actively guided to facilitate its smooth development." "Blocking the path of the movement and development of things" is "doomed to failure." "Everything," please

99

note, including those dark, reactionary things that are anti-Party and anti-socialist. If we are to persist in the socialist road, we have to block the road to the restoration of capitalism; if we are to support all new-born, revolutionary things, we have to strike down all decadent, counter-revolutionary things. As the saying goes: "There is no construction without destruction, no flowing without damming and no motion without rest." To clear the way for the tide of revolution, we must dam the tide of reaction.

By demanding that instead of blocking we should "facilitate the smooth development" of "everything," including anti-socialist things, was not Teng T'o clearly demanding that we should practise bourgeois liberalisation and bend and surrender to the ill winds which were blowing at the time, the winds of "going it alone" (i.e., the restoration of individual economy) and of the extension of plots for private use and of free markets, the increase of small enterprises with sole responsibility for their own profits or losses, and the fixing of output quotas based on the household? "Guiding" meant paving the way, and these men styled themselves "the vanguard paving the way"—for the capitalist forces. Three-Family Village counted on the "failure" of socialism and the "certain triumph" of the black wind of capitalist restoration, and thought they could now openly throw themselves into the arms of the reactionary forces for the development of capitalism!

On April 30, 1961, in an essay "The Theory of Treasuring Labour Power," Teng T'o levelled a direct attack on us for not "treasuring labour power." Mentioning the dictatorship of the proletariat and that of the landlord class in the same breath, he argued that "as far back as the periods of the Spring and Autumn Annals and the Warring States and thereabout," the exploiting classes "discovered certain objective laws governing the increase and decrease of labour power... through the experience of their rule" and were able to calculate the limits on "the labour power to be used in different kinds of capital construction." Teng T'o demanded that "we should draw new enlightenment from the experience of the ancients, and take care to do more in every way to treasure our labour power."

What Teng T'o was saying, in other words, was this: It is "beyond your capacity" to carry on through self-reliance. This is "excessively forced." Call a halt at once. Give it up quickly and use the old methods of the "miscellaneous scholars" of the landlord class! Was this not clearly co-ordinated with the vicious attacks of US imperialism and modern revisionism? Had we followed this line, not only would we have had no Taching, no Tachai, no atom bombs, but we would have been reduced to an imperialist colony.

It is by no means accidental that both before and after the publication of this article, Teng T'o ranted in favour of learning from the Khrushchev revisionist clique. In his essay "The Way to Make Friends and Entertain Guests," he advocated "learning from" and "uniting with" countries "stronger than our own" and said, "We should be pleased if a friend is stronger than we are." In the essay "From Three to Ten Thousand," he swore, "If a man with a swelled head thinks he can learn a subject with ease and kicks his teacher out, he will never learn anything." This was a vicious attack on our struggle against modern revisionism and a demand that we ask the revisionists in and let the wolves into the house. In his series of indirect accusations, "reviling the locust tree while pointing to the mulberry," Teng T'o sings exactly the same tune as the Right opportunists, slandering the Party line for socialist construction as "forced" and claiming that China's only "way out" is to "learn from" the Soviet revisionist clique and practise revisionism in China.

In stirring up this evil wind, Three-Family Village raised a hullabaloo and cleared the way for the release of all kinds of monsters from confinement, collaborating from within with sinister forces from without. In league with the reactionaries in China and abroad and with the modern revisionists, it made dastardly attacks on the Party's General Line for socialist construction, the great leap forward and the people's communes, and painted modern revisionism in glowing colours in a vain attempt to create public opinion favourable to a come-back by the Right opportunists.

In June and July 1961 Three-Family Village let loose another vicious blast. July 1 was the fortieth anniversary of the founding of the Communist Party of China. Holding high the red banner of the General Line, the great, glorious and correct Chinese Communist Party headed by Comrade Mao Tse-tung was leading the Chinese people forward triumphantly along the socialist road amidst sharp struggles against reactionaries in China and abroad and against serious natural calamities. Not reconciled to their defeat, the domestic reactionary forces and the Right opportunists who had been dismissed from office were trying harder than ever to have the previous decisions reversed, in an attempt to negate the repudiation of the Right opportunists at the Lushan meeting and the fruits of the various other major political struggles since liberation. It was at this moment that the "brothers" of Three-Family Village shot poisoned arrows thick and fast at the Central Committee of the Party in support of the Right opportunists.

On June 7, 1961 Wu Han described another "trumped-up case" in an insidious article ostensibly written in memory of Yu Chien. He glorified Yu Chien who had been dismissed from office, calling him "unbending and simple," and a man whose "spirit will live for ever." He made a point of stating that Yu Chien had been "rehabilitated," that "Yu Chien's political enemies failed one after another," and that he was moreover appointed "Secretary of War (Minister of National Defence)." "Rehabilitate" is a modern term which no emperor would ever have used. By using it, Wu Han betrayed what was in his mind, namely, that the proletarian revolutionaries would fail one after another and the Right opportunists would soon be rehabilitated.

On June 22, 1961, shortly after Wu Han's article on Yu Chien, Teng T'o published "The Case of Chen Chiang and Wang Keng." It was so blatantly vicious that the author's heart misgave him and he dared not include it in the collected volumes of Evening Chats at Yen-shan. We can find it, however, in the Evening Chats column in the Pei-ching Wan-pao. The author claims to have picked this "anecdote" up from some old books because it was so "thought-provoking." The article threw out hints about a "deliberately exaggerated and trumped-up case," but the revelation comes in the last paragraph, which reads:

> By the reign of Empress Dowager Ming Su, the Sung government was growing daily more corrupt. There was no intelligent and capable prime minister at the top with responsible assistants to take charge of personnel and administration, while the local officials lower down did exactly as they pleased.

As a result, he wrote, "this case was inflated and complicated." This was venomous slander, directed against our Party and expressed in the counter-revolutionary language of landlords, rich peasants, counter-revolutionaries, bad elements and Rightists. The ostensible attack on Empress Dowager Ming Su and on the prime minister was a malevolent denigration of the Central Committee of the Party, while the statement that "local officials lower down did exactly as they pleased" was a malicious denunciation of Party cadres at various levels, a charge that the Right opportunists and other anti-Party elements had been unjustly treated. He even used the modern term "inflated." What sort of thought was provoked? Was it not the thought that would pave the way for reversing the previous decisions on the Right opportunists and other anti-Party elements? Was it not the thought that would release monsters to attack socialism and the dictatorship of the proletariat? What is particularly interesting is the fact that Teng T'o pinned his hope of reversing the previous decisions on an "intelligent and capable prime minister" coming forward and seizing the leadership. To those with discerning eyes, it is as clear as daylight what kind of people he was appealing to for the seizure of power. This is the true voice of the commanding general of Three-Family Village. He refrained from including this article in the collection, but the harder one tries to conceal a thing, the more it attracts attention.

At the same time, in another article "The Prosperity and Decline of Two Temples," Teng T'o gave full vent to his feelings about the fate of two temples. One had had many worshippers and was "famed far and near," while the other was "in decline" and "ignored all along." For fear that others might not understand his meaning, he urged readers to apply this to "similar situations," implying that we had cold-shouldered the Right opportunists and stopped paying tribute to them. Teng T'o expressed strong dissatisfaction over the fate of being "ignored all along" that had overtaken those anti-Party, anti-socialist clay idols who had fallen from their political pedestals, the Right opportunists and other anti-Party elements who were utterly spurned by the Party and the people. He wanted the Party to "esteem" them highly again, to put these clay idols "in decline" back in their shrines.

Immediately afterwards, Wu Han in his introduction to *Hai Jui Dismissed from Office* cried even more openly, "Although Hai Jui lost his post, he did not give in or lose heart." He shouted about the need to be "undismayed by failure and determined to make a fresh start after defeat." This was the common cry of Three-Family Village at the time, and certainly not an isolated phenomenon. They not only incited the Right opportunists to try again, but also redoubled their own efforts.

On July 25, 1962 Three-Family Village came out with a most venomous anti-Communist article, entitled "Special Treatment for 'Amnesia.' " They vilified responsible Party members as suffering from "amnesia," which made them "quickly forget what they have seen and said... go back on their own word, fail to keep faith," and become quite "capricious." They proposed "hitting the patient over the head with a special club to induce a state of 'shock.' " They were not only using

103

exactly the same language as the Right opportunists to slander the Central Committee of the Party which they hated; they actually wanted to finish off the proletarian revolutionary fighters with one blow. What poison! Were they not hoping to render revolutionaries unconscious or kill them so that revisionism could seize power? This article was a stark revelation of their deep class hatred for the Party, an attack on our Party made completely from the stand of the landlords, rich peasants, counter-revolutionaries, bad elements and Rightists.

The series of facts listed above definitely proves that *Hai Jui Dismissed from Office* not only represented Wu Han's personal political attitude but was a prelude to the anti-Party, anti-socialist political activities of the Three-Family Village clique in support of the Right opportunists who had been "dismissed from office." The members of this small clique, who pinned their hope on the seizure of power in the Party and government by the anti-Party, anti-socialist elements, stirred up an adverse current. "Like mayflies trying to topple the giant tree, they ridiculously overrated themselves" — the slanderous attacks by this handful of anti-Party, anti-socialist elements could not damage the great prestige of our Party in the least, but only revealed their own criminal features, aroused the people's anger, and ended up in their repudiation by the Party and the people.

The Three-Family Village offensive was at its most frenzied from the start of publication of *Notes from Three-Family Village* until March 1962, when the Third Session of the Second National People's Congress met. In the first place, during this period, the imperialists, reactionaries and modern revisionists abroad had intensified their anti-China chorus, which was very noisy for a time. At the 22nd Congress of the CPSU in October 1961, the leadership of the CPSU systematised the revisionist line which it had been gradually developing since the 20th Congress, and pushed further ahead with its revisionist political line for splitting the international communist movement and restoring capitalism. In China, the reactionary classes and their political agents, aiming to come back to power, took advantage of the three consecutive years of serious natural calamities we had suffered to launch a still wilder all-out attack in the political, economic and cultural fields in a futile attempt to overthrow the Party leadership and the dictatorship of the proletariat at the very time when we were implementing the policy of "readjustment, consolidation, filling out and raising of standards."

The Counter-Current and the Mainstream

Two articles typified how Three-Family Village sized up the situation during this period. The first, "On Waves" by Wu Han, appeared on January 1, 1962. With irrepressible fanaticism he hailed the "wave" that had been pounding society "during the past half year and more." He joyously declared that "this is a really big tidal wave," advertising the counter-current against the Party leadership and the dictatorship of the proletariat as one of its achievements. He predicted that this "tidal wave" would grow "bigger and bigger." Blinded by inordinate ambition, Wu Han believed that the gang he belonged to would win and the adverse current of revisionism would become the mainstream. Shortly afterwards, on February 4, in his article "This Year's Spring Festival" which later he dared not include in the collection *Evening Chats*, Teng T'o wrote even more explicitly, "The bitter cold of the north wind will soon come to an end. In its stead a warm east wind will blow and a thaw will soon set in on this earth." Was not "thaw" one of the terms in the out-and-out counter-revolutionary vocabulary used by the Khrushchev revisionist clique against Stalin? Blinded by inordinate ambition, this gang now predicted that by 1962 socialist New China would "soon come to an end," that the dictatorship of the proletariat would be toppled by the anti-socialist adverse "tidal wave" and "in its stead" there would be a Right-opportunist or revisionist regime, that Three-Family Village would gain greater influence and would be able to do whatever it wanted. Comrades, you can see how eagerly this group wished China to have a revisionist "thaw!"

It was with this estimate of the situation that Three-Family Village launched its wild all-out offensive.

On November 10, 1961 Teng T'o came out with his article "Great Empty Talk" in *Notes from Three-Family Village*. In ostensibly criticising a child's poem, he indirectly condemned the statement that "the East wind is our benefactor and the West wind is our enemy" as "empty talk," "jargon," "cliches" and "pomposity." This was a flagrant denigration of the Marxist-Leninist scientific thesis that "the East wind prevails over the West wind" as "empty talk."

Teng T'o said, "In certain special situations such great empty talk is inevitable," hinting to readers that what he was condemning was not the child's poem but our Party's ideological weapon for carrying on the struggle and educating the masses in "special situations," that is, in the international and domestic class struggle. What was Teng T'o's purpose? It was to slander the great thought of Mao Tse-tung, which leads us forward, as "empty talk," to get us to abandon Mao Tse-tung's thought in our political life, and to give up the Marxist-Leninist line. He went so far as to make the arrogant demand that our Party should "say less and take a rest when the time comes for talking." If Mao Tse-tung's thought were laid to rest, would it not become possible for revisionist ideas to run rampant?

In close co-ordination with the above, Three-Family Village brought out a series of articles attacking Mao Tse-tung's thought and maligning revolutionaries. *Evening Chats at Yenshan* came out with the article "Give It Up and You Will Be on Firm Ground." Its central idea was that the Party should "give up" the General Line for socialist construction, and it ridiculed those who would not give it up for being "blind" and "looking for trouble." It demanded that the Party should "boldly give it up" so as to come down to "firm ground," i.e., the ground of capitalism. On November 25 Liao Mo-sha also published two articles, "Wherein Lies Confucius' Greatness?" and "Jokes About Being Afraid of Ghosts." In the first he sang the praises of Confucius for being "rather 'democratic' and welcoming criticisms of his theories," implying that the Party should encourage bourgeois democracy and thus allow the reactionary elements to come forward and attack Mao Tse-tung's thought. In the second he vindictively slandered Mao Tse-tung's thought and vilified revolutionary Marxist-Leninists as "braggarts... who claim that they are not afraid of ghosts but are actually frightened out of their wits by them." He tried to show them up as "utterly ridiculous."

> Only heroes can quell tigers and leopards,
> And wild bears never daunt the brave.

This couplet sums up the fearless heroism of the great Chinese people. Such heroism prevails over all evil trends. Liao Mo-sha even planned to edit a collection of *Stories About Being Afraid of Ghosts*. Was this not open collaboration with the reactionaries, both in China and abroad, and the modern revisionists to defame the Chinese people who are not afraid of ghosts, to defame our Party and the revolutionaries who persist in following Mao Tse-tung's thought?

The day after the appearance of these two articles, "Two Foreign Fables" was published in the *Evening Chats at Yenshan* column as a

106

further attack on so-called bragging. It claimed that "even now one can always and everywhere find such braggarts," and clamoured viciously, "We must not let these charlatans off lightly." Do you want revolution? Do you want to keep the interests of the country and those of the world at heart? Do you want to rely on your own efforts to overcome difficulties? All this is "bragging" and "boasting." Three-Family Village will settle accounts with you. When this article was included in the collection, the author deleted the sentence, "Instead of being overcome, difficulties will daily grow in number and seriousness." See how maliciously these men ridiculed our Party's policy of self-reliance in overcoming difficulties! They even thought that the difficulties would grow in number.

A little later, Wu Han in his article "Chao Kuo and Ma Su" made use of two historical tales about what he called "talking big to impress people" and "boasting" in order to satirise the present and urge us to "review now" the "lessons of failure," the "lessons of harming oneself and others and ruining the country." Obviously, Wu Han imagined that the great Chinese people had "come to grief," that the General Line had "failed," and that the Right opportunists would soon come to power. The gust of foul wind which started with Teng T'o's "Great Empty Talk" was closely co-ordinated with the clamour for the advent of the Right opportunists to power.

A subsequent series of articles also "breaking through the door and dashing out" directed the attack even more crudely against the Central Committee of the Party headed by Comrade Mao Tse-tung. In an exceptionally savage attack they shifted the emphasis from political to organisational problems.

In an article "Is Wisdom Reliable?" published on February 22, 1962, Teng T'o urged the "emperor" to "seek advice from all sides." He emphasised that "one need not plan everything oneself" and said with ulterior motives that "when a man plans everything himself, flatterers will seize the chance to say things to please him." By this he certainly did not mean that those in leading positions should listen modestly to opinions from below; what he wanted was the acceptance by the Central Committee of the Party of the revisionist line which he and his like supported. They insolently warned the Party, "One will eventually suffer heavy reverses" if "one makes all decisions oneself in the hope of achieving success with original ideas," without accepting "good advice" from "below," in other words from Three-Family Village.

107

On February 25, 1962, only three days later, there appeared another article, "The Royal Way and the Tyrant's Way." Now the Marxist theory of the State teaches us that both the "royal way" and the "tyrant's way" are ways of dictatorship by the landlord class, forms of counter-revolutionary violence. However royal in appearance, all landlord rule was nevertheless essentially tyrannical. "Benevolent government," so-called, was merely a mask for sanguinary counter-revolutionary violence. As Lu Hsun sharply pointed out, "Though the Chinese royal way appears to be the opposite of the tyrant's way, in actual fact they are complementary. The tyrant's way invariably precedes and succeeds the royal way."[3]

Teng T'o, however, extolled the "royal way," saying that "after all, even in ancient times the royal way was much better than the tyrant's way." Why did he eulogise the dictatorship of the landlord class in this most absurd manner? He did so with the aim of making us accept the "lesson" he had fabricated: "Thus people can see at a glance how those who wanted to be tyrants made enemies everywhere and became very unpopular." He even translated this into "our language" (the language of Three-Family Village), saying that "by the tyrant's way... we mean the arrogant, subjectivist and arbitrary way of thinking and style of work of one bent on acting wilfully."

If we compare the language used, it is evident that when *Evening Chats at Yenshan* slandered those who "wanted to be tyrants," "made enemies everywhere," "became unpopular" and were "bent on acting wilfully," their target was the revolutionary line of our dictatorship of the proletariat, and they were parroting the reactionaries in China and abroad. This was certainly not merely a question of "idealising the feudal social system," as the article in the *Pei-ching Jih-pao* claimed.

Instances of Three-Family Village's direct attacks on the Central Committee of the Party, on Chairman Mao and the General Line are too numerous to quote. But it is clear even from some of the evil blasts after the publication of *Hai Jui Dismissed from Office* how shocking the secrets of Three-Family Village are, what virulent class hatred this handful of men have for the Party and the cause of socialism, and what lavish praise and support they have given the Right opportunists, i.e., the revisionists. They hoped that China would change its colour from red to black. Their "gangster inn" is an important den of restorers of capitalism, a nest of poisonous snakes which we must expose thoroughly and destroy completely. Our fighting task today is to step forward

108

and destroy Three-Family Village and carry the revolution through to
the end!

Doing Everything Possible to Promote
"Peaceful Evolution"

In addition to writings openly opposing the Party, the people and
socialism, *Evening Chats at Yenshan* and *Notes from Three-Family Village*
contained most poisonous weeds in the form of so-called "academic
discussion," "textual research" and "relaxation." Under the cover
of "learning useful knowledge, both ancient and modern," they launched
all-round attacks on socialism. They did not merely "idealise the feudal
social system" and "glorify dead men," but had their own practical
political objectives. On the one hand, in co-ordination with the black
line of shameless opposition to the Party, the people and socialism,
they used the cover of "history," "knowledge" and "things of interest"
to dull the revolutionary vigilance of the people, hoodwink more readers
and extend their influence. On the other hand, they employed what
is called "the gentle method of decapitation" to conduct all-round attacks on the proletarian line consistently upheld by the Party and Comrade Mao Tse-tung in all fields, and used the ideas of the landlord and
bourgeois classes to corrode the revolutionary cadres and revolutionary
people in every way in order to promote "peaceful evolution." Whoever is addicted to and obsessed by all this will degenerate and become
a new bourgeois element. The dual tactics of Three-Family Village
consisted of using sharp poisonous arrows and all kinds of sugar-coated
bullets.

Stratagems in Retreat

In September 1962 the Tenth Plenary Session of the Eighth Central
Committee of the Chinese Communist Party was convened. At this
meeting Comrade Mao Tse-tung issued the great call to the whole
Party and the people throughout the country never to forget class
struggle. The meeting raised high the great red banner of Mao Tse-
tung's thought and sounded the clarion call for resolute struggle against
the forces of capitalism and feudalism seeking restoration. It pointed
out, "This class struggle inevitably finds expression within the Party."
Deeply alarmed, the monsters and freaks of all descriptions trembled
with fright. Seeing bad weather ahead, Three-Family Village began

109

to beat a retreat, with its commanding general withdrawing first. Soon afterwards, in his "Announcement to Readers" in the fifth volume of *Evening Chats at Yenshan* in October 1962, Teng T'o said, "I am discontinuing *Evening Chats at Yenshan* because I have recently turned my attention to other things in my spare time."

The last essay in *Evening Chats at Yenshan* published on September 2, 1962 was entitled "Thirty-Six Stratagems." "Of all the thirty-six stratagems, to depart is best." This remark indicated that he was about to slink away. However, in collecting these "chats" in one volume, the author, fearing that this might leave a trace of his slinking away, placed this particular essay in the middle of the volume instead of at the end in disregard of the order of publication. This article says with a deep implication:

> "To depart is best" was not the only stratagem Tan Tao-chi then employed; without employing other stratagems he could not have succeeded in getting away, much as he wanted to. It was thanks to several co-ordinated stratagems he employed, such as those of deceptive military deployment and sowing discord among the enemy... that he succeeded in making good his retreat.

After the Tenth Plenary Session of the Eighth Central Committee of the Party, Three-Family Village, besides continuing its attacks, did indeed employ "several co-ordinated stratagems" with the intention of "making good its retreat" once the revolutionary people started their counter-attack. This is why they have staged numerous other fascinating performances. Let us see some of their stratagems:

1. Making the following hypocritical announcement in the fifth volume of *Evening Chats at Yenshan:*

> For some time I have been compelled to "mount horse" in writing Evening Chats and I now dismount in order not to feel dissatisfied with myself any more. It will not be too late to write again when there is really something to write about in future and when I feel the urge to do so.

Here Teng T'o was trying on the one hand to explain that he had not made deliberate attacks and that both in "mounting" and "dismounting" he was acting under compulsion and, on the other hand, to give a hint that "in future" when the situation became favourable, he would write again and start all over again.

2. Retaining their position, namely, the column of *Notes from Three-Family Village,* and continuing their attacks while writing a number of articles like the "Ode to Petroleum" as a gesture of approval for

"Comrade Mao Tse-tung's policy of self-reliance" in order to cover their retreat.

3. Encouraging papers elsewhere, which, inspired by *Evening Chats at Yenshan,* had opened up "special columns for miscellaneous essays, to carry on for a long time to come" so as to retain more positions.

4. Taking down the signboard *Notes from Three-Family Village* in July 1964, lest the criticism of Liao Mo-sha's article "There Is No Harm in Ghost Plays," which was unfolded from 1963 to 1964, should expose Three-Family Village as a whole.

5. Letting Liao Mo-sha write a sham self-criticism in which he ascribed "the cause of my mistake" to "the bourgeois world outlook" which "still dominates my mind," and to his being "forgetful of the fact that classes, class contradictions and class struggle still exist in our socialist society." Please note that Wu Han repeated this almost word for word in his own "self-criticism" at a later date! Liao Mo-sha added that he had "unconsciously lent a helping hand to the bourgeois and feudal forces in their frenzied attacks on the Party and socialism." Since Liao Mo-sha was a mere "helping hand" to Meng Chao, there would, of course, be no need to make an inquiry into Three-Family Village. What a wonderful stratagem!

6. After the criticism of *Hai Jui Dismissed from Office* began, Teng T'o hastily wrote a "critical" article under the pseudonym Hsiang Yang-sheng, saying that the "guiding thought" and the "basic idea" of the play was "to propagate the moral code of the feudal ruling class" and solely "to propagate historical idealism." In doing so, on the one hand, he tried to cover up the political motive and the politically reactionary nature of the drama, thus trying to save Wu Han and to lead the discussion into a blind alley. On the other hand, he implied that such an entity as Three-Family Village did not exist and that he had "broken away from" Wu Han. Towards the end of his article, he added a line of reminder to Wu Han: "It is also my hope that Comrade Wu Han will continue to write if he has anything to say..., to make an analysis and a study of things in a truth-seeking way." Here he was instructing Wu Han on how to make his next move.

7. Wu Han responded immediately to his call and wrote more than one article to show his "gratitude" to Hsiang Yang-sheng, while continuing his furious attacks in the name of "self-criticism." Emboldened by the backing he had received, Wu Han proceeded to lavish praise on himself and, taking over for his own use the weapon employed by

Liao Mo-sha in the latter's "self-criticism," he said, "Correct thinking has not established a dominant position in my mind" and, "in a word, I have forgotten the class struggle!" Hsiang Yang-sheng's "criticism," he added, "has helped me realise my mistakes." As if this would enable him to get away!

8. Finally, seeing that the situation was getting pretty hot for them, they suddenly "criticised" Teng T'o in the name of the editorial departments and used every stratagem for slinking off to cover their retreat.

Can all these "co-ordinated stratagems" enable them to "make good their retreat?" They have played a great many tricks and indeed have gone to extreme lengths in cheating people. But they have seriously underestimated the ability of the revolutionary people to see things in their true light and the determination of the proletariat to carry on with the revolution. Can they lock up their secrets? Can they slip away? Led and educated by the Central Committee of the Chinese Communist Party and Comrade Mao Tse-tung, the broad masses of the revolutionary people are determined to eradicate this black anti-Party and anti-socialist line. These persons think their different stratagems very clever. Actually the things they have done are stupid and only serve to expose them. They have not only common reactionary political ideas but also a common programme of action; theirs is an anti-Party, anti-popular, anti-socialist clique of a handful of individuals. Is this not crystal clear?

In March 1962, when the frenzied attacks by Three-Family Village reached their zenith, Teng T'o published a poem entitled "Black Swan" in the *Pei-ching Jih-pao*. One verse reads: "When the spring breeze brings dreams and the lake waters send forth their warmth, I alone have foresight!" How he exulted in his keen "foresight!" But his "foresight" has failed this time. It is the revolutionary people who have grasped Mao Tse-tung's thought that have real foresight. Look, are not the secrets of Three-Family Village being gradually exposed by the broad masses of the people?

Thoroughly Uproot Three-Family Village and Eliminate the Poison It Has Spread

One cannot help asking why is it that such wild, venomous and unscrupulous activities opposing the Party and socialism on the part of Three-Family Village could have gone on for several years? Could it be that the only reason lay in "not putting proletarian politics in command?" What was put in command if not proletarian politics?

Since the criticism of *Hai Jui Dismissed from Office* began, people have been exposing its reactionary nature, its political motive which was to lend support to the Right opportunists, and Wu Han's ugly history of opposition to the Communist Party, the people and the revolution. But it is only when we view *Hai Jui Dismissed from Office* in the context of all the activities of Three-Family Village and ascertain the latter's role in the acute class struggles of the last few years that we are able to get down to the very roots of these big poisonous weeds, uproot them thoroughly and destroy this big inn of gangsters.

Comrade Mao Tse-tung has said, "Everything reactionary is the same; if you don't hit it, it won't fall."[4] The fact that since the criticism of *Hai Jui Dismissed from Office* the Three-Family Village clique has tried to make a stand at every step and carried on the fight while beating a retreat again confirms this universal truth. In no circumstances will the reactionary classes and their representatives retire from the stage of history of their own free will. Only when the broad masses of workers, peasants and soldiers rise up and wage arduous struggles step by step will the proletariat be able gradually to wrest back positions from these "miscellaneous scholars."

The tentacles of the Three-Family Village clique have reached into many departments. *Evening Chats at Yenshan* has exerted a bad influence throughout the country. Under the signboard of "knowledge" and a "fine style," it attracted a number of people who lacked political discrimination. It did not lack admirers and followers in journalistic, educational, literary and art, and academic circles. Teng T'o himself has boasted, "The viewpoints and theses in many of the articles are approved by friends." "Letters sent to me by readers from afar have increased." "In order to satisfy readers' requests, some newspapers in other places have also adopted the same form and published special columns for miscellaneous essays which impart knowledge." A number of articles were also written to echo certain viewpoints of *Evening Chats at Yenshan*. On September 9, 1961 the *Peiching Jih-pao* advertised the publication of these essays in boldface characters, bragging that "the author has grasped certain contemporary questions," and that they are "both rich in ideological content and useful in enriching knowledge." The paper tried by every possible means to spread the pernicious effects of these essays among the people. As a result, they did much to corrode people's minds and spread their poison far and wide. It is imperative for the broad masses of workers, peasants and soldiers to come forward and thoroughly expose in all their aspects the evils done by *Evening Chats at Yenshan* and *Notes from Three-Family Village* and conduct still more penetrating criticism. Only in this way can their bad effects be liquidated.

The course of events from the criticism of *Hai Jui Dismissed from Office* to that of Three-Family Village has been one of stirring class struggle. It is a great revolution in the political, ideological and cultural fields. Faced with so arduous and militant a task, we must dare to make revolution.

Comrade Mao Tse-tung's words encourage us: " 'He who is not afraid of death by a thousand cuts dares to unhorse the emperor' — this is the indomitable spirit needed in our struggle to build socialism and communism."[5] Today we very much need to give play to this principled and critical spirit which proceeds from the interests of the cause of communism. All those who oppose Mao Tse-tung's thought, obstruct the advance of the socialist revolution, or are hostile to the interests of the revolutionary people of China and the world should be exposed, criticised and knocked down, whether they are "masters" or "authorities," a Three-Family or a Four-Family Village, and no matter how famous they are, what influential positions they hold, by whom they are directed or supported, or how numerous their flatterers are. On questions of principle, it is either the East Wind or the West Wind which must prevail. For the sake of the socialist revolution, of the defence of Mao Tse-tung's thought and of the cause of communism, we must have the courage to think, to speak out, to break through, to act and to make revolution.

> The Golden Monkey wrathfully swung his massive cudgel,
> And the jade-like firmament was cleared of dust.

No matter how much poisonous fog or blinding dust has been spread by Three-Family Village, it will certainly be thoroughly cleared away by the spirited struggle of the millions of workers, peasants and soldiers who are armed with the "massive cudgel" of Mao Tse-tung's thought. The brilliant light of Mao Tse-tung's thought will penetrate all the dark corners and show up all the monsters and goblins in their true colours.

114

NOTES

1. This article was first published simultaneously in two Shanghai newspapers, *Chieh-fang Jih-pao* and *Wen-hui Pao,* on May 10, 1966.

2. Communique of the 9th Plenary Session of the 8th Central Committee of the Communist Party of China, January, 1961.

3. *Collected Works of Lu Hsün,* Chinese edition, People's Literature Publishing House, Peking, 1963, Vol. 6, p. 10.

4. "The Situation and Our Policy After the Victory in the War of Resistance Against Japan," *Selected Works of Mao Tse-tung.*

5. Speech at the Chinese Communist Party's National Conference on Propaganda Work, March 12, 1957.

115

Major Charges against 'Monsters and Demons' or 'Black Gangsters'

"Monsters and demons" or "black gangsters" named in this section, in alphabetical order, refer to those persons accused of either carrying out "anti-Party and anti-socialist" activities or deviating from the "correct" Mao Tse-tung line for literature and art. They were attacked, in many cases more than once, in newspapers, periodicals and other mass media controlled by the CCP Central Committee's Propaganda Department.

This book was set in November 1966. Since then, certain "persons in power" said to be behind those who were publicly branded as "anti-Party elements" have been subjected to severe criticism in wall posters reportedly put up by "revolutionary teachers and students" of secondary schools in Peking.

These personalities at the CCP Central Committee level, including P'eng Chen, Lu T'ing-i and Lo Jui-ch'ing, have been removed from part or all of the offices they held.

Charges against those films, stage plays and books branded as "poisonous weeds" are also based on reports carried in China's national and provincial newspapers and other publications, as well as Chinese mainland broadcasts.—Ed.

Chang Ch'ing-chi (張青季)

Former deputy director, Public Health and Physical Culture Department, CCP Peking Municipal Committee; chairman, Peking Municipal Physical Culture and Sports Committee; vice-chairman and Standing Committee member, All-China Sports Federation; chairman, China Basketball Association.

Chang Ch'ing-chi was labelled a "black gangster of the sports world" in the *Ti-yü Pao* of Peking, August 8, 1966, for following the black line of the anti-Party, anti-socialist counter-revolutionary clique of the former Peking Municipal Party Committee. He was accused of cherishing deep-seated hatred for the thought of Mao Tse-tung, attacking the general line, the great leap forward and the people's commune, and actively promoting the revisionist line of "peaceful evolution," in a vain attempt to lead Peking's sports workers into the revisionist quagmire and turn them into bourgeois successors, with the object of staging a counter-revolutionary come-back.

Chang and his fellow "gangsters" were said to have put up a stubborn resistance against the cultural revolution, using the Department of Physical Culture of Peking Normal College as a stronghold, and vainly tried to suppress the revolutionary mass movement.

He was also accused of having employed extremely dirty means to obstruct the broad masses of sports workers and athletes from studying and applying Mao Tse-tung's works. Furthermore, he was said to have openly attacked Lin Piao's directive concerning the creative study and application of Mao Tse-tung's works.

In the field of sports, Chang was alleged to have vigorously publicised the idea of "skill first" and opposed the Party policy of putting politics in command, bringing forth the fallacy that "the United States of America had succeeded in raising its sports level without talking about putting politics in command."

Chang Ching-chih (張敬之)

Former editor, Department of Literature and Art,
Anhwei Jih-pao, Hofei.

Chang Ching-chih was criticised, in the July 20, 1966 issue of *Anhwei Jih-pao* for having written anti-Party articles in 1961, in support of the then deputy chief editor of *Anhwei Jih-pao,* Lin Hung.

Chang Ju-chang (張如章)

Former procurator-general, People's Procuratorate, Inner Mongolia Autonomous Region; former CCP Committee secretary and concurrently political commissar of the "four clean-up" work team of Tumote.

Chang Ju-chang was branded as "the ringleader of a counter-revolutionary black gang" which committed the crimes of promoting the line of revisionism and national splittism during the "four clean-up"† movement of the Tumote Banner in the Inner Mongolia Autonomous Region.

117

Radio Huhehot, in a broadcast on September 6, 1966, charged that Chang, in collaboration with a number of counter-revolutionary elements, perpetrated a multitude of criminal activities in splitting national solidarity and restoring capitalism.

Chang's black gang, the broadcast said, openly opposed Chairman Mao's teachings on giving prominence to politics and class struggle. Under the pretext of resisting drought, they ordered discontinuation of the "four clean-up" movement, saying that "when there are contradictions between production and the movement, the latter must give way to the former."

Chang's black gang also opposed the study of Mao Tse-tung's works as called upon by Comrade Lin Piao. They derided those who read Mao Tse-tung's works as bookworms.

In regard to class struggle, Chang's black gang deliberately directed their attack on so-called great Han nationalism instead of on those in power in the Party who took the capitalist road. In this connection, they ruthlessly carried out persecution against the revolutionary comrades of Han nationality. They even slandered some leading comrades of the CCP Inner Mongolia Regional Committee, who directed the "four clean-up" movement in the Tushih area in 1964, as being imbued with great Han nationalism.

"There is ample evidence," the broadcast concluded, "that Chang's black gang have adopted all possible means to resist the higher authorities, deceive those who are under them, oppress the masses and openly defy the leadership of the Party in an attempt to promote their line of counter-revolutionary revisionism and national splittism, as well as to restore capitalism and feudalism."

Chang Tung-yüeh (張東月)

Former leading official of Sinkiang University.

Radio Urumchi broadcast on September 21, 1966 that revolutionary students and teachers of various nationalities at Sinkiang University exposed at a mass meeting the crimes committed by Chang Tung-yüeh.

"The thorough exposure of Chang's counter-revolutionary crimes is a victory for the Great Proletarian Cultural Revolution in the Sinkiang-Uighur Autonomous Region and a victory for Mao Tse-tung's thought.

"The Party Committee of the Sinkiang-Uighur Autonomous Region has decided to strip this anti-Party element of all his positions in the Party.

"Open denunciation at the mass meeting revealed that as early as the winter of 1951, when Chang took up a leading position at Sinkiang College—now Sinkiang University—he already began to commit a series of grave errors. The Party organ and students and teachers criticised and helped him to amend his ways, but he showed no sign of repentance.

"He persisted in his reactionary stand and openly carried out criminal intrigues against the Party, socialism, and Mao Tse-tung's thought. He tried all he could to prevent the students, teachers and staff of the University from studying Chairman Mao's works. For a long time, Chang waved 'red flags' to oppose the red flag and, in the name of spreading Mao Tse-tung's thought, wrote articles and reports unscrupulously distorting Mao Tse-tung's thought."

Chang Wen-sung (張文松)

Director, Department of Culture and Education,
CCP Peking Municipal Committee.

Chang Wen-sung was labelled by the *Pei-ching Jih-pao* of June 21, 1966 as the "hard-core of the anti-Party black gang." As a member of the Standing Committee and head of the Education Department of the former CCP Peking Municipal Committee, he was accused of:
— Carrying out the bourgeois revisionist line of education and going all out to oppose and undermine the educational line laid down by the Communist Party and Mao Tse-tung;
— Taking an active part in the activities of the anti-Party black gang, suppressing mass exposure and criticism of anti-Party and anti-socialist elements, diverting the attention of the masses, resisting, obstructing and undermining the development of the cultural revolution.

Chao Chien-ch'iu (趙劍秋)

Former deputy director, Shantung Provincial Institute
of Shantung Opera.

Kuang-ming Jih-pao on June 21, 1966 denounced Chao Chien-ch'iu as an exponent of bourgeois and landlord classes. In 1961, Chao rewrote one of the traditional Shantung operas, "Hsu Lung Beats

119

the Emperor," into a new opera, "Sun An Petitions the Emperor." In 1962, Chao wrote the screenplay of "Sun An Petitions the Emperor" which was later produced under the direction of Ch'en Wan-li.

Chao's opera was branded as a poisoned arrow shot at the Party in co-ordination with Wu Han's "Hai Jui Dismissed from Office" and Chou Hsin-fang's "Hai Jui's Memorial to the Emperor."

The article concluded: "Chao Chien-ch'iu and the like are enemies without guns in our revolutionary ranks..."

Chao Li (趙利)

> Director, Cultural Revolution Development Team, Chengtu University; deputy secretary of the University's Party Committee, and director of the Marxist-Leninist study class.

Chao Li was dismissed from his posts on June 23, 1966 by the CCP Chengtu Municipal Committee with the approval of the CCP Szechwan Provincial Committee and the Southwest Bureau of the CCP Central Committee.

A Radio Chengtu broadcast on June 24, 1966 alleged that Chao attempted to obstruct and disrupt the cultural revolution by discrediting the big-character posters put up by the revolutionary students and faculty members of Chengtu University which criticised the Party Committee of the University.

Chao is further alleged to have denigrated the revolutionary students and faculty members as "demons and monsters," "anti-Party and anti-socialist elements," and "gangsters of the Three-Family Village," and engaged in activities contrary to the great socialist cultural revolution launched by the CCP Central Committee and Mao Tse-tung.

Chao P'an (趙潘)

> Former deputy secretary general, CCP Committee, Inner Mongolia Autonomous Region.

Chao P'an was denounced, in a rally held in Huhehot on September 6, 1966, as the "supreme commander" of the counter-revolutionary black gang headed by Chang Ju-chang (listed elsewhere in this section—Ed.), which had committed serious crimes of opposing the Party, socialism and Mao Tse-tung's thought and of damaging the unification of the motherland and the solidarity of national minorities in China.

Ch'en Ch'i-t'ung (陳其通)

Deputy director of both the Cultural and Propaganda
Sections, PLA General Political Department.

Ch'en Ch'i-t'ung was condemned by the *Jen-min Jih-pao* of June 17, 1966 for his work, "A Searching Anatomy," in which he emphasised the "esthetic enjoyment" a work of art and literature should give the public to the neglect of its political content.

Ch'en is also condemned for the high praise he gave the film, "The Pressgang," which was said to serve the interests of the landlord class and the bourgeoisie better than it did the interests of the proletariat.

"A Searching Anatomy," according to the paper, represented a hodgepodge of Ch'en Ch'i-t'ung's feudal, capitalist and revisionist ideas about art and literature. It was a concentrated expression of his anti-Party and anti-socialist views on art and literature. His proposed reactionary programme for drama was completely contrary to the Party's and Mao Tse-tung's line on art and literature. It was altogether a big poisonous weed utterly in contravention with the resolutions adopted at the 1960 enlarged session of the Military Affairs Committee conference, specifying tasks for literary and art workers of the armed forces. It had seriously undermined the militant traditions of revolutionary literary and art workers of the PLA.

The *Kuang-ming Jih-pao* of Peking, August 30, 1966, also denounced Ch'en as a rightist, revisionist, bourgeois individualist schemer, and a member of Chou Yang's "black gang."

He was said to have openly attacked Mao Tse-tung and his doctrine and criticised those who showed reverence of Mao Tse-tung.

Ch'en was condemned for his anti-Party, anti-socialist stand in directing cultural activities within the army. He opposed the policy that culture should serve the workers, peasants and soldiers, and wrote some plays derogatory to political workers in the army.

He was criticised during the anti-rightist campaign in 1958 and sent to the rural areas for "tempering" and reform, but apparently he came out of it unscathed and unrepentant.

121

Ch'en Ching-po (陳景伯)

Former second secretary, Kirin University's Party Committee.

Radio Changchun on August 15, 1966 carried the following item denouncing Ch'en Ching-po as an anti-Party and anti-socialist element.

The revolutionary teachers, students and staff workers of Kirin University had brought to light many facts which proved that for a long time Ch'en stubbornly clung to the side of bourgeois reactionaries and tried to distort, boycott and oppose Mao Tse-tung's thought.

Ch'en openly negated the universal truth of Mao Tse-tung's thought by saying that Mao's instructions should be considered in the light of different situations and carried out in different ways.

He stubbornly opposed the students' practice of treating Mao Tse-tung's works as the guideline for all work. He said: "It is impossible to expect a book or a few words to enlighten all people and to solve all contradictions."

His book, "Reminiscences of a Guerrilla in the War Against Japanese Aggression," propagated the reactionary bourgeois theory of human nature by saying that people, either rich or poor, all have a conscience. During the 1957 anti-rightist campaign, he said: "In the past, the Party held the stick of dogmatism in one hand and a label in the other: anyone who disobeyed would be beaten with the stick and receive a label."

He strongly opposed the putting of proletarian politics in command, and openly took a stand against Mao Tse-tung's teachings that politics is the supreme commander and the soul. He said: "The putting of politics in command must not be overdone; or the word 'command' will lose its real meaning."

The CCP Kirin Provincial Committee had decided to dismiss him from all posts both in and outside the Party.

Ch'en Huang-mei (陳荒煤)

Former vice-minister, Ministry of Culture; Former director, Film Bureau, ministry of Culture; former member of the Editorial Board, *Wen-i Pao*.

Ch'en Huang-mei was attacked in the *Chung-kuo Ch'ing-nien Pao* of Peking on June 9, 1966 for disseminating revisionist, bourgeois theories of film making, reviving nearly one hundred films of the thirties, and catering to bourgeois tastes in films under the pretext of making films for export.

He was accused of opposing Mao Tse-tung's directive of placing literature and art in the service of workers, peasants and soldiers and of proletarian politics.

The newspaper noted that during the period when Hsia Yen, former Vice Minister of Culture, and Ch'en Huang-mei held sway over the Film Bureau of the Ministry of Culture, all films of some weight were big poisonous weeds. These included, according to the newspaper, "Early Spring in February" and "The Lin Family Shop" produced by Peking Film Studio; "Sisters of the Stage," "Nightless City," "Red Sun" and "A-shih-ma" by Shanghai Film Studio; "Sailing A Thousand *Li* against the Wind" by Chuchiang Film Studio; "The Peach-Blossom Fan," by Sian Film Sudio; and "Laying Siege to A City" by Ch'ang-ch'un Film Studio.

The newspaper recalled that when the anti-rightist struggle was launched in 1957, Peking Film Studio made these films: "Shanghai Girl," "Foam of Life," "Visiting A Relative" and "Fantasy of the Ming Tomb Reservoir." Some of them were poisonous weeds and some made serious mistakes, the newspaper said.

The release of an abundance of monsters and demons began in 1962, the newspaper asserted. Among them there were "Dancing Butterflies," "Hsiao Erh Hei's Wedding," "Early Spring in February," etc. In addition, there were films which had not been finished or had been abandoned — such as "Rapids of the Red River," "Rolling Waves," "Happy Is the Whole Family" and "Ulan O-te." Apart from the poisonous weeds which had been released, among the films which the studio planned to shoot were "Story of Chi Kung," "Mrs. Yu Nee Chao," "Bridge of Husband and Wife," "Chirping Birds and Fragrant Flowers," "Love Tree," "Swallow Li San," "Li Hui-niang," "Hsieh Yao-huan" and "Li Hsiu-ch'eng, Pricne of Loyalty." The list of selected titles included also "Mother As a Slave" and "Lovers Without Love," films peddling revisionist ideas. At that time, "a collective group for handling fairy tales" was also set up to propagate the poisonous ingredients of feudal superstition.

123

Ch'en I-hsin (陳一新)

Former member, Standing Committee, CCP Hupeh
Provincial Committee; vice governor of Hupeh; secretary,
Party group for political science and law.

Ch'en I-hsin's infamous conduct was denounced in the *Hung-wei Pao* of Canton of September 13, 1966. The following charges were laid against him:

— Rabidly attacking the Party's general line, the great leap forward, the people's commune, the proletarian dictatorship, and the socialist system.

— Resisting the leadership of the Hupeh Provincial Party Committee, refusing to take orders from the Party and regarding his own department as an "independent kingdom."

— Opposing Mao Tse-tung's theory of "one divides into two" and advocating the theory of "two combine into one."

Ch'en Kuang-yüan (陳光遠)

Former chief editor, *Tsinghai Jih-pao*, Sining.

Ch'en Kuang-yüan was dismissed from the post of chief editor of *Tsinghai Jih-pao* and ordered to undergo self-criticism by a decision of the Tsinghai Provincial Party Committee on June 11, 1966 for his grave error in publishing the editorial, "Great Offensive, Great Counter-attack, and Great Revolution" in the paper on June 3.

A statement made by the editorial board of *Tsinghai Jih-pao* on June 13 supported the decision of the Party organ, saying that the editorial mentioned above was a big poisonous weed against Mao Tse-tung's thinking, the Party, and socialism. The statement pointed out that the editorial deliberately creates confusion with Leftist phrases and seductive slogans, playing a role of undermining the great socialist cultural revolution. It put forward a reactionary slogan that ran counter to the line of the revolution laid down by the Party Central Committee and Chairman Mao, encourages a horde of monsters to carry on their wanton attacks against the Party, stirred up gusts of ill winds, vilified the socialist system and the dictatorship of the proletariat, and laid the ideological groundwork for the restoration of capitalism.

The editorial also opposed Party leadership over the cultural revolution and vilified the movement, saying that it had bookworm odour, and that it was in the style of a woman with bound feet.

The statement criticised Ch'en for his unwillingness to undergo extensive self-examination and accept the criticism of the people as directed by the Provincial Party Committee. Instead, he had gone so far as to adopt a bad bourgeois attitude of suppression of the criticism of workers, peasants and soldiers, in a futile attempt to strike back at those who criticised him.

Ch'en Leng (陳冷)

Deputy director and deputy Party secretary, Institute of Philosophy, Chinese Academy of Sciences.

Hupeh Jih-pao on June 12, 1966 exposed Ch'en Leng's crime of opposing Mao Tse-tung's thought and of undermining the great socialist cultural revolution.

Ch'en Po-lin (陳博霖)

Chief editor, *Chengtu Wan-pao*, Szechwan.

Szechwan Jih-pao carried an article on June 9, 1966 which laid bare the crime committed by Ch'en Po-lin for his management of a "gangster inn" for "Evening Chats at Yenshan" by Teng T'o.

Like all other "gangster inns" at different localities, the one under Ch'en's management made reactionary remarks to let loose poisoned arrows in co-ordination with other "gangster inns" to maliciously attack Mao Tse-tung's thought, the CCP Central Committee, the three red flags of the Party, and proletarian dictatorship.

Ch'en Ta-yü (陳大羽)

Deputy director, Propaganda Department, CCP Kweichow Provincial Committee.

Ch'en Ta-yü was described as a "bourgeois theoretic authority" who had wormed his way into the Party, in the *Kweichow Jih-pao* of Kweiyang, August 31, 1966.

The article said that Ch'en, in collaboration with Wang Hsiao-ch'uan (listed elsewhere in this section—Ed.), director of the Propaganda Department of the CCP Kweichow Provincial Committee,

125

made use of five Party work conferences to frenziedly oppose the Party, socialism and Mao Tse-tung's thought and promote the revisionist black line, committing "extremely serious counter-revolutionary crimes."

Ch'en Teng-k'o (陳登科)

Chairman, Anhwei Provincial Federation of Literary and Art Circles.

Ch'en Teng-k'o, according to a Hofei Radio broadcast on September 5, 1966, was an accomplice of Liu Hsiu-shan (listed elsewhere in this section—Ed.), who was denounced at a meeting held in Hofei on the day before for his "counter-revolutionary crimes."

Ch'i Hsia (漆俠)

Assistant professor, Department of History, Hopei University; author of four books, namely "The History of Peasant Wars in Ch'in and Han Dynasties," "The Peasant Uprising in the Late Period of the Sui Dynasty," "Emperor T'ai Tsung of T'ang" and "Wang An-shih's Land Reform."

Ch'i Hsia, according to the *Hopei Jih-pao* of June 15, 1966, was criticised by all teachers and students of Hopei University who had written thousands and thousands of big-character posters to expose his anti-Party, anti-socialist crimes.

An article, entitled *"Hopei Jih-pao* and *Tientsin Jih-pao* Expose Ch'i Hsia's Anti-Marxist Histor:cal Viewpoint" carried in *Kuang-ming Jih-pao* of Peking, May 18, 1966 said that for more than ten years since the liberation, Ch'i had been following Wu Han and Chien Po-tsan, and persisting in an anti-Marxist historical stand.

Chien Po-tsan (翦伯贊)

Former member, CCP Peking Municipal Committee; former member, Propaganda Department, CCP Central Committee.

In an article carried in *Hung-ch'i* No. 15, 1966 entitled "The True Features of Chien Po-tsan, an Anti-Communist Intellectual," Chien Po-tsan was accused of being the leader of the reactionary academic "authorities" of the bourgeoisie, and an important member of the former Propaganda Department of the CCP Central Committee.

Chien was also accused of having—under the guise of a Party member and a veteran Marxist historian—shot one poisoned arrow after another at the Party, socialism and the thought of Mao Tse-tung.

He was identified in the article as an erstwhile underling of Chiang Kai-shek, a saboteur of agrarian reform, an anti-Party vanguard and a big bourgeois Rightist opposing the revolutionisation of historical science, favouring the restoration of capitalism, echoing modern revisionism and resisting the Great Proletarian Cultural Revolution.

Chin Cheng-i (金正儀)

> Former member, Editorial Board, and director, Political, Cultural and Educational Department, *Anhwei Jih-pao,* Hofei.

An article carried in *Anhwei Jih-pao* of June 20, 1966 accused Chin Cheng-i of having written articles in *Anhwei Jih-pao* in 1961 supporting the views of the then deputy chief editor, Lin Hung (listed elsewhere in this section—Ed.), and viciously slandering the Communist Party.

Ch'in Mu (秦牧)

> Former assistant chief editor, *Yang-ch'eng Wan-pao;* vice-chairman, Kwangtung branch, Union of Chinese Writers.

Ch'in Mu was roundly condemned in the *Yang-ch'eng Wan-pao* of Canton, June 10, 1966 for his views on art and literature, which were said to be contrary to Mao Tse-tung's thinking on art and literature.

The Chinese Communist line for art and literature is that art and literature must serve the workers, peasants and soldiers and that artists and writers must become one with the workers, peasants and soldiers.

Ch'in Mu, however, thinks that the source of creative writing is knowledge of life. He did not think that writers must mix with workers, peasants and soldiers in order to know life.

For his non-conformist views, Ch'in was branded as an anti-Party, anti-socialist element.

In another article carried in the same paper on June 8, 1966, Ch'in Mu's book, "Collecting Shells in the Sea of Art," was called a "big poisonous weed" and a "rattlesnake."

Ch'in was accused of trying to obliterate the fighting character and political role of the revolutionary literature of the proletariat, opposing Mao Tse-tung's thinking on art and literature, propagating reactionary literary theories, and trying to poison the younger generation with bourgeois ideas.

In two other articles appearing in the same paper on June 17 and July 5 respectively, Ch'in was upbraided for having said that Communist cadres cared only for themselves and were arrogant and ruthless, that Communists "were made of bad stuff," and that the new society was "icy cold."

He was described as an anti-Communist writer who served the "US-Chiang reactionaries."

Chou Hsin-fang (周信芳)

> Noted Peking opera actor; former member, Shanghai Municipal People's Council; chairman, 2nd Council, Shanghai Branch, Union of Chinese Stage Artists; vice-chairman, Shanghai Municipal Federation of Literary and Art Circles; co-author of the play, "Hai Jui's Memorial to the Emperor."

Chou Hsin-fang and T'ao Hsiung, vice-president of the Shanghai Academy of Peking Opera, were held responsible for the production of the play, "Hai Jui's Memorial to the Emperor," which was accused in a *Chieh-fang Jih-pao* article published on May 26, 1966 of being one of the "poisoned arrows" shot at the Party by the Right opportunists.

In writing the play, Chou and T'ao were alleged to have launched frenzied attacks on the CCP Central Committee and Chairman Mao by making such remarks as: "As the main pillar is not upright, so the secondary columns are all out of place," "the discipline is poor," "a slip of the tongue incurs criminal charges," "a hell of a like," "public opinion is far from favourable!" "the most vicious, exceedingly abusive and heartless despot," "because of natural calamities and foreign pressure the people are leading a miserable life," "every household has used up its food supplies," "poverty everywhere," "families are broken up," "there are many homeless people," "civil affairs are in a state of disorder."

The article noted that the play included many scenes which suggested to the audience that they must wage a "legitimate struggle" against

128

the Party. It accused Chou Hsin-fang and T'ao Hsiung of having played a leading part in the anti-Party and anti-socialist chorus conducted by Right opportunists and revisionists, and of having used the play as a weapon to attack the Communist Party.

Chou Huan (周桓)

Former Secretary, CCP Liaoning Provincial Committee; secretary, Secretariat, CCP Liaoning Provincial Committee.

Radio Shenyang broadcast on June 23, 1966 a report saying that revolutionary cadres of the Liaoning Provincial Party Committee and the Lioaning Provincial People's Council held a meeting on that day to condemn the terrible anti-Party and anti-socialist crimes of Chou Huan and acclaim the exposure of his misdeeds as an important victory for the great cultural revolution and a new victory for Mao Tse-tung's thought.

Chou was accused of:

— Taking the reactionary bourgeois stand and openly opposing the socialist literature serving proletarian politics, workers, peasants and soldiers;

— Showing deep-seated hatred for and viciously attacking Mao Tse-tung's thought, opposing the study of Mao's works by the masses, and disparaging literary works that propagate Mao's thought;

— Being a representative of the bourgeoisie who wormed his way into the Party, a "commander-in-chief" of the anti-Party and anti-socialist black gang in Liaoning province,... a "time-bomb" planted in the Party, and a poisonous snake;

— Expressing dissatisfaction during the Liaoning Provincial Drama Festival in May 1964 over certain plays praising Mao Tse-tung's thought and openly instigating all monsters and demons to oppose Mao Tse-tung's thought.

Chou Jen-yu (周仁有)

Former member, Editorial Board, and director, Department of Literature and Art, *Anhwei Jih-pao,* Hofei.

Chou Jen-yu was accused of having written many anti-Party, anti-socialist articles in *Anhwei Jih-pao* in 1961, supporting the views of the then deputy chief editor Lin Hung (listed elsewhere in this section—Ed.), and viciously slandering the Communist Party.

Chou Wan-ch'eng (周萬誠)

> Producer, Chuchiang Film Studio, Canton; script writer and producer of the film, "Sailing a Thousand *Li* against the Wind."

Chou Wan-ch'eng, as script writer and producer of the film, "Sailing a Thousand *Li* against the Wind," was the target of a press campaign involving *Chieh-fang-chün Pao, Kuang-ming Jih-pao, Ta-kung Pao* and *Jen-min Jih-pao* on June 14, 1966.

The film was branded in these papers as "a big poisonous weed" with an extremely reactionary content. It was said to have distorted historical facts, vilified Mao Tse-tung's ideas on people's war, made dastardly attacks on the people's troops and at the same time extolled to the skies the Kuomintang reactionary troops.

The film was alleged to have entirely met the requirements of reactionaries at home and abroad, encouraged and mobilised them to stage a come-back, in a futile attempt to subvert the proletarian dictatorship.

Chou Yang (周揚)

> Alternate member, CCP Central Committee, ex-deputy director, Propaganda Department, CCP Central Committee; former vice-chairman, All-China Federation of Literary and Art Circles; former vice-chairman, Union of Chinese Writers.

A representative of the bourgeoisie who had wormed his way into the Communist Party, was the way Chou Yang was denounced as the ringleader of the black line against the Party, socialism and Mao Tse-tung's teachings in literary and art circles.

Charges laid against Chou for carrying out a counter-revolutionary revisionist programme for literature and art were given in a lengthy article in *Peking Review,* No. 34, 1966. There, Chou was accused of:

— Opposing the spread of Mao Tse-tung's thought in a futile attempt to remove the very soul of proletarian literature and art.

— Flagrantly opposing the orientation of literature and art to serve the workers, peasants and soldiers as set by Mao Tse-tung, and advocating revisionist "literature and art of the whole people."

— Distorting the Party policy of "let a hundred flowers blossom and a hundred schools of thought contend," and energetically working for bourgeois liberalisation.

— Promoting a wide range of bourgeois, reactionary concepts of literature and art and opposing the Marxist conception of literature and art.

— Frantically advocating the worship of things foreign and the restoration of the ancient, and obstinately resisting socialist transformation of literature and art.

— Opposing proletarian literary and art criticism and attacking the struggle on the literary and art front to foster proletarian and eradicate bourgeois ideology.

— Disseminating the fallacy that class struggle had died down, advocating the "three-famous" principle† favouring a policy of "three-highs"† and scheming to bring about "peaceful evolution" throughout the ranks of literary and art workers.

— Opposing Party leadership in literary and art work, in a futile attempt to usurp leadership and bring about the restoration of capitalism.

At a meeting held in July by the Propaganda Department of the CCP Central Committee, Chou Yang was denounced as a "political fraud, an anti-Party schemer and a counter-revolutionary revisionist consistently waving a 'red flag' to oppose the red flag."

He was accused of having begun his conspiratorial activities as a political opportunist as early as the thirties and of having brought out a complete counter-revolutionary revisionist programme for "literature and art of the whole people."

Chou Yang's "literature of the whole people" was said to be an imitation of the Soviet "revisionist whole-people Party" and the "whole-people State." Further it was called a "free market for the bourgeois, the feudal class, and revisionist literature and art," according to *Jen-min Jih-pao* of August 30, 1966.

In that article, Chou was attacked for having said that Mao Tsetung's "Talks at the Yenan Forum on Literature and Art" was out-of-date and for promoting a literature that would serve the needs of all classes, including the bourgeoisie. This was contrary to the Communist doctrine that literature and art must serve only the workers, peasants and soldiers.

131

In another article, in the *Chieh-fang-chün Pao* of August 22, 1966, Chou Yang was accused of having championed the "Wang Ming capitulationist, revisionist line"† in literature and art in the thirties.

In opposition to Lu Hsün, who upheld Mao Tse-tung's "correct line" and put forward the slogan of "Mass literature of national revolutionary war," Chou Yang advanced the slogan of "literature for national defence," which was said to have served Wang Ming's capitulationism.

The article also accused Chou and his gang of trying, as late as in 1957, to vindicate the Wang Ming line and rehabilitate Wang Ming.

In the great socialist revolution which began in 1963 or even earlier in the cultural spheres, Chou Yang was said to have resisted or boycotted Mao Tse-tung's directives to literary and art circles in June 1964, according to Tung Feng, author of an article carried in *Jen-min Jih-pao* of October 27, 1966.

Mao Tse-tung took a leading part in several important struggles on the cultural and literary and art front after the liberation, the article continued, including

— The criticism against the film, "Story of Wu Hsün," in 1950.
— The criticism against the book, "Study of Dream of the Red Chamber," and against Hu Shih and others, in 1954.
— The struggle against the Hu Feng clique in 1955.
— The "anti-rightist" struggle in 1957.

In all these struggles Chou Yang was said to have taken a stand opposed to that of Mao Tse-tung.

When in Honan in December 1958, according to the *Kung-jen Jih-pao* of Peking, October 28, 1966, Chou Yang maliciously attacked local dramas written on modern revolutionary themes while encouraging local theatrical companies to produce traditional plays.

Encouraged by Chou Yang, reactionary bourgeois "authorities" in Honan also attacked one of the companies which specialised in contemporary revolutionary drama and even tried to have it dissolved, the article concluded.

Chou Yu (周游)

Former president, Peking Publishing House; former chief editor, *Pei-ching Jih-pao*.

Pei-ching Jih-pao of June 13, 1966 attacked Peking Publishing House for having published, under the management of Chou Yu, a number of "poisonous weeds" cultivated by the "Three-Family Village black gang."

These "poisonous weeds" included Teng T'o's "Evening Chats at Yen-shan," Liao Mo-sha's "A Fen of Time," Wu Han's "Hai Jui Dismissed from Office" and "Study," and a number of other works, mostly of a historical character.

The Peking Publishing House was also alleged to have played an ignominious role in covering the retreat of the "Three-Family Village."

Ch'ü Pai-yin (瞿白音)

Deputy director, Shanghai Municipal Bureau of Cinema; member, Shanghai Municipal Federation of Literary and Art Circles.

Ta-chung Tien-ying (Popular Cinema), No. 6, 1966 carried an article entitled "Ch'ü Pai-yin's Monologue on the Question of Innovation of Films."

The article accused Ch'ü of frantically attacking the thought of Mao Tse-tung, the socialist system and the leadership of the Party. In the name of "getting rid of old sayings," he was said to have smeared Mao Tse-tung's thought as "devoid of new meaning" and "buried under historical dust."

Ch'ü was also alleged to have instigated the demons and monsters of art and literary circles to oppose the thought of Mao Tse-tung. In his monologue, he called on the bourgeois elements in film circles to muster up their "courage," "uphold truth and charge into the enemy's positions" and struggle against the "old sayings."

In his monologue, Ch'ü put forward a whole set of bourgeois programmes for art and literature. In the name of "demolishing the three gods (god of theme, god of structure, and god of conflict)," he attacked them as "frames and rules" hampering the creation of artists. He advocated, therefore, the establishment of "three new things (new thought, new image and new artistic structure of ideas)." He adored films of capitalist countries which write off class struggle, white-wash the capitalist system, and express base feelings of small people. He praised the thirties as an "era of vigorous innovation," and said during that period "works with new ideas, new images, and new artistic structure rushed to the screen like the surging tide in spring."

The article pointed out that Ch'ü's anti-Party talent won the recognition of Hsia Yen and others. Early in 1962, they summoned him to

133

Peking and secretly discussed with him the release of an anti-Communist article under the guise of commemorating the 20th anniversary of the publication of Mao Tse-tung's "Talks at the Yenan Forum on Literature and Art." That article later turned out to be the now published monologue which contained the opinions of Hsia Yen, Ch'en Huang-mei, and Yüan Wen-chu who exchanged ideas over a number of meetings. The draft was personally revised by Hsia Yen who added to it a cloak of some revolutionary phrases. After its publication, Ch'ü Pai-yin called a number of forums under the name of the Shanghai branch of the China Cinema Workers Association. It was the "collective creation" of the counter-revolutionary black gang in the film circles headed by Hsia Yen, Yang Han-sheng, Ch'en Huang-mei and Yüan Wen-chu.

Chu Shao-t'ien (朱少天)

First secretary, Party Committee, Wuhan University; vice-president, Central-South Institute of Finance and Economics.

Radio Wuhan on June 13, 1966 denounced Chu Shao-t'ien in a broadcast.

Chu and certain bourgeois "authorities," after usurping the leadership posts at Wuhan University, were said to have turned the school into a stubborn fortress for restoring capitalism, committing anti-Party and anti-socialist crimes.

Chu was also denounced for frenziedly opposing the thought of Mao Tse-tung, viciously assailing the correct leadership of the Party Central Committee and the Hupeh Provincial Party Committee.

He was said to have refused to take heed of repeated criticism and warnings against him by the Provincial Party Committee, and refused to execute its directives and decisions.

Obeying orders in name, Chu was alleged to have disobeyed them in fact, deceiving higher authorities and taking high-handed action against those below him. He was also charged with resorting to political, organisational and other means to persecute leftists, exclude them, and conduct illegal struggle and political persecution against revolutionary teachers.

The proletarian revolutionary leftists of Wuhan had waged a violent struggle against the black gang, according to the broadcast. In opposition to Chu, some revolutionary teachers of the Department of Mathematics of Wuhan University had refused to yield since 1958. They had persisted in running the "Wuhan Steel Works Experimental Class" which was based on the part-work and part-study system. Chu and his followers, however, took the experimental class as a thorn in their sides, so that they attached labels on the revolutionary teachers and persecuted them politically.

Chung Lin (鍾林)

Former chief editor, *Kwangsi Jih-pao*.

Chung Lin was denounced in the *Hung-wei Pao* of September 24, 1966 for his opposing the Party, socialism and the thought of Mao Tse-tung.

Specifically, Chung was accused of resisting Mao Tse-tung's directive on the management of *Kwangsi Jih-pao,* changing the orientation of the paper, opposing the propagation of Mao's teachings, disparagingly speaking of Mao's writings, holding poor peasants in contempt, advocating "three freedoms and one contract"† and attacking the socialist system, discriminating against workers, peasants and soldiers but favouring bourgeois writers, resisting Party leadership, and regarding *Kwangsi Jih-pao* as his own "independent domain."

Fan Chin (范瑾)

Member, Standing Committee, CCP Peking Municipal Committee; vice-mayor of Peking; vice-chairman, All-China Journalists' Association; director, Editorial Board, *Pei-ching Jih-pao* and *Pei-ching Wan-pao.*

Fan Chin was dismissed from the post of director of the former Editorial Board of *Pei-ching Jih-pao* and *Pei-ching Wan-pao,* in accordance with a decision of the reorganised Peking Municipal Party Committee on May 25, 1966.

A report released by NCNA on June 6, 1966 charged that under the guidance of Fan Chin, *Pei-ching Jih-pao* and *Pei-ching Wan-pao* had degenerated into instruments of some of the principal members of the former Peking Municipal Party Committee for carrying out their revisionist line and the restoration of capitalism, instruments of the counter-revolutionary "Three-Family Village" black gang for opposing the Party and socialism.

These newspapers were said to have spread a good deal of poison and frantically attacked the Chinese Communist Party and the socialist system. They shielded the bourgeois Right while dealing blows at the proletarian Left; deceived the people and suppressed the criticisms of a great many readers; waved a "red banner" to oppose the red banner and donned the cloak of Marxism-Leninism and of Mao Tse-tung's thought to oppose Marxism-Leninism and Mao's teachings.

Fang Huang (方惶)

Film Director, Chuchiang Film Studio, Canton.

Fang Huang was the director of the film, "Sailing A Thousand *Li* agaist the Wind," produced by Chuchiang Film Studio in 1963. Charges laid against Fang are similar to those directed against Chou Wan-ch'eng (listed elsewhere in this section—Ed.).

Ho Lu-ting (賀綠汀)

President, Shanghai Institute of Music; member, National Committee of All-China Federation of Literary and Art Circles; vice president, Central College of Music of Ministry of Culture; member, Board of Directors, Shanghai Branch, Sino-Soviet Friendship Association; delegate to World Peace Conference; deputy for Shanghai to 1st NPC; composed "The East Is Red" and the "Guerrilla Song" during the Sino-Japanese War, and organised the Chungking Symphony Orchestra.

Chieh-fang-chün Pao on June 7, 1966 openly denounced Ho Lu-ting as a stubborn reactionary representative of the bourgeoisie. He was said to have entrenched himself in such posts as president of Shanghai Institute of Music, vice-chairman of the Association of Musical Workers, chairman of Shanghai municipal branch of the Association of Musical Workers under the guise of being a veteran musician and Party member.

Ho was alleged to have consistently engaged in counter-revolutionary activities, especially in the years when China encountered temporary economic difficulties. He was accused of having responded to the anti-Chinese chorus raised by orges of all kinds abroad. He was also accused of having maintained close contact with landlords, rich peasants, bad elements, and teamed up with art and literary "authorities" and "venerable masters" of the thirties to launch frenzied attacks on the Party.

136

Ho Ting-hua (何定華)

Vice-president, Wuhan University; former deputy director, United Front Work Department, CCP Hupeh Provincial Committee; member, Hupeh Provincial People's Council.

Ho Ting-hua and Chu Shao-t'ien (listed elsewhere in this section—Ed.), former first secretary of the Party Committee of Wuhan University, were charged in a *Hupeh Jih-pao* editorial of June 13, 1966 with being the leaders of an anti-Party, anti-socialist "black gang" of the University.

For the past five years, the editorial said, Chu and Ho, two bourgeois representatives within the Party, have usurped Party and administrative leadership of the University, acted as faithful vassals of the bourgeoisie, and paved the way for the restoration of capitalism.

Both had greatly vilified the great educational revolution in 1958, opposed the part-work, part-study education system, arbitrarily destroyed the University-run factory, and even carried out political persecution of an experimental part-work part-study class run by the Mathematics Department, in the fond hope of strangling it.

The editorial further accused Chu and Ho of nursing bitter hatred for Mao Tse-tung's thinking on education, Party educational policies and activists in the educational revolution, and having done everything possible to discriminate against and do away with them.

Ho Yao (何耀)

Researcher, Office of Investigation and Research, CCP Committee, Inner Mongolia Autonomous Region; former Standing Committee member, Party organ of the "four clean-up" work team of Tumote, Inner Mongolia.

Ho Yao was accused of being an active member of the counterrevolutionary black gang headed by Chang Ju-chang (listed elsewhere in this section — Ed.), which committed the crimes of promoting the line of revisionism and national splittism in the Inner Mongolia Autonomous Region.

Hou Wai-lu (侯外廬)

Well-known historian, philosopher and writer; member, Department of Philosophy and Social Sciences, Chinese Academy of Sciences; deputy director, Second Institute of History (Medieval), Chinese Academy of Sciences; member, Committee of Departments, Chinese Academy of Sciences; deputy director, Institute of Historical Research; member, Editorial Board, *Li-shih Yen-chiu* [Historical Research.]

Hung Ch'i No. 10, 1966 carried an article entitled "Firmly Eradicate Hou Wai-lu's Three Big Poisonous Weeds Dealing with T'ang Hsien-tsu's Plays."

The article said: "Hou Wai-lu is a bourgeois reactionary 'authority' of learning among the historians. Having wormed his way into the Party and donned the Marxist mantle, he outrageously spread poison over a long period of time. His three articles on T'ang Hsien-tsu's plays published in 1961 are three big poisonous weeds against the Party, socialism and the thought of Mao Tse-tung. He lauded T'ang Hsien-tsu, calling the latter's 'prominent and progressive thought' a kind of 'fighting spirit' for 'chopping the world and reforming realities.' "

On dark reality Hou said: "Nothing can be said of the ways of Heaven because men of renown are being slaughtered by the nameless persons."

In his writings, Hou viciously attacked the general line, the great leap forward and the people's commune, assailed the CCP Central Committee, and glorified the Right opportunists who had been "relieved of offices."

In the name of analysing the ideological character of T'ang Hsien-tsu's "four dreams," Hou reviled the "restraint on people's freedom" and "lack of equality" in "realistic world." He cursed the socialist system as a "world of sins" without freedom, equality and happiness. He urged the people to act in the same way as T'ang Hsien-tsu — to "show resolve in reforming realities with drastic measures."

Obviously, Hou sought to publicise and extol, through the mouth of T'ang Hsien-tsu, a "utopian world" that ran diametrically opposed to the socialist system.

In 1961 when "US imperialism, reactionaries of all countries and modern revisionists" conducted an uproarious anti-China chorus, Hou put forward such fallacies as "the Utopia" of abundance to disintegrate the revolutionary morale of the people. In this "Utopia," according

138

to Hou, "there is neither poverty nor misery nor bullying. People lead a happy and comfortable life; there is no class struggle, and the land is as happy as paradise on earth." Hou has precisely echoed the tunes of the bourgeoisie and modern revisionism. It is clear to people that "liberty, equality and fraternity" and "humanitarianism" — which the reactionary bourgeoisie and modern revisionists publicise and extol as above classes — are in the final analysis political tools for implementing class oppression and benumbing the thinking of the revolutionary people, the article said.

Hou was denounced in the *Jen-min Jih-pao* of November 22, 1966 for having urged people to "censure the emperor," defended the "Right opportunists" and advocated "taking vengeance" against the Communist Party.

In April 1959, Hou was said to have released "The Ideal of Universal Harmony Throughout the Ages in China," a book which maliciously slandered the people's commune.

In October of the same year, he released "General Review of Progressive Philosophical Thoughts in 16th-Century China in Philosophical Questions," a publication controlled by Khrushchev revisionism of the Soviet Union. He cried injustice for the "persecution" to which Wang T'ing-hsiang, a "Minister of the Army" of 400 years ago, was "subjected." He said such nonsensical things as that this "Minister of the Army" had "a sense of justice towards the people."

In another article carried in the same paper on November 22, 1966, Hou was shown to be an anti-Communist old hand who "flattered Chiang Kai-shek and adored American imperialism."

Some of Hou's writings and utterances, produced and made during the war against Japan, were quoted in the article to show how he had always been against the Communist Party and its Chairman, Mao Tse-tung.

Hsia Yen (夏衍)

Former vice-minister of Culture; vice-chairman, All-China Federation of Literary and Art Circles.

Hsia Yen's book, "Collected Works on Motion Pictures," was attacked in the *Kuang-ming Jih-pao* of March 11, 1966 for having deviated from the Party line on literature and art, particularly in regard to the direction of serving the workers, peasants and soldiers.

In the article, Hsia was accused of having made a series of grave mistakes, including a tendency to contradict the teachings of Mao Tse-tung and to spread bourgeois ideas.

Hsia's bourgeois views are said to run counter in every way to the direction set by the Communist Party of making literature and art serve the workers, peasants and soldiers.

According to an article in *Kuang-ming Jih-pao* of March 12, 1966, Hsia Yen's play, "Sai Chin Hua," attacked the *I Ho T'uan* Movement [The Boxers, whose name is connected with the uprising of 1900]— with the objective of disparaging the revolutionary tradition of the Chinese people against imperialism.

Although this play runs counter to the spirit of the age, the article said Hsia has never admitted that it was a serious political error. He continued to defend and publicise it in 1956.

Hsia was also criticised by Ho Ch'i-fang, Director of the Institute of Literature, in the *Jen-min Jih-pao* of April 1, 1966 for portraying the old democratic revolution of China in favourable light in the film circles and for embracing bourgeois ideas in his works.

In another article carried in *Chieh-fang-chün Pao* of December 10, 1966, Hsia was attacked for his "extreme hostility toward the thought of Mao Tse-tung and rabid opposition to its propagation." He was said to have made vicious attacks against the Communist Party in opposition to the Mao Tse-tung line for literature and art.

Hsia was said to have gathered around him "capitulationists and renegades" and made preparations for bringing about a "capitalist restoration."

He criticised Communist films, saying that they contained nothing but "revolutionary classics" and "the way of war" (i.e., glorification of war and destruction), the article said.

In another article published in *Kuang-ming Jih-pao* of Peking, December 10, 1966, Hsia was denounced for faithfully carrying out Chou Yang's counter-revolutionary, revisionist line and for engaging in "criminal activities" against the Party, socialism and the thought of Mao Tse-tung.

He was alleged to have appealed to film makers to "depart from the scripture" of the thought of Mao Tse-tung and "rebel against the way" of Communist militancy and to free the film industry from the fetters of Communism.

In a *Kung-jen Jih-pao* Editorial Note of December 10, 1966, Hsia

Yen—named the ringleader of Chou Yang's counter-revolutionary, revisionist group and the patriarch of monsters and demons in the film world—was condemned for taking advantage of his powers over film production to resist the Mao Tse-tung line for literature and art.

He was accused of being instrumental in encouraging the showing of such bad films as "Sailing a Thousand *Li* against the Wind," "Early Spring in February" and "The Peach Blossom Fan" to corrupt the minds of the audience with the ultimate object of clearing the way for the restoration of capitalism in China.

Hsieh Chin (謝晉)

Co-writer and director of the film, "Senior Li, Junior Li, and Old Li."

This film was produced by Shanghai T'ienma Motion Picture Studio in 1962. *Kung-jen Jih-pao* on June 15, 1966 criticised the film as an anti-Party and anti-socialist poisonous weed.

The film depicted how trade union chairman, Senior Li, organised mass sports activities in a meat processing factory. He ran into difficulties because Old Li, workshop director, stubbornly opposed and sabotaged sports activities, while Junior Li, sports enthusiast, took part in sports only for personal fame and honour.

The film emphasised on contradictions among these three characters, and cleverly turned the contradications into jokes which aroused the "common anger" of the working masses.

The authors of this film used jokes to ridicule Party leadership and propagate revisionism. They waved "red flags" to oppose the red flag and hoisted the signboard of "serving the workers" to vilify and abuse the working class.

Hsü Ch'ang-lin (徐昌霖)

Playwright and director, T'ienma Film Studio, Shanghai.

Jen-min Jih-pao carried on August 17, 1966 a full-page report on a symposium held by workers of Peking, Shanghai, Sian and Tientsin to criticise the film "Football Fans," calling it a "poisoned arrow shot at the socialist system and a poisonous melon grown on the anti-Party black plant of literature and art."

Hsü Ch'ang-lin who wrote and directed this film produced by

141

T'ienma Studio in Shanghai in 1962 was denounced at the symposium as "a hireling of the Chiang dynasty and a faithful lackey of the literary and art black gang of the thirties." Prior to liberation, he was reported to have produced many reactionary films, such as "Good Family Reputation," in praise of US-Chiang special agents, and was editor of the "reactionary newspaper, *Chunghua Times*."

"Football Fans" was one of Hsü's anti-Party and anti-socialist productions highly appreciated by Hsia Yen and Ch'ü Pai-yin. The film was criticised immediately after its completion by the CCP Shanghai Municipal Committee, on the ground that it vilified the working class, attacked the proletarian dictatorship, and prepared public opinion in favour of restoration of capitalism.

A *Chieh-fang-chün Pao* editorial note of August 17, 1966 said: "The playwright and director of the film adopted a thoroughly reactionary bourgeois stand, viciously attacked the socialist society, wantonly vilified the masses, tried in every possible way to popularise the bourgeois modes of living, and vigorously spread revisionist ideas. This is an out-and-out counter-revolutionary film of revisionism."

Hsü Shao-p'ei (徐少培)

> Former secretary, Party Committee, Kiangsi Agriculture Institute.

Hsü Shao-p'ei was wrathfully condemned by the broad masses of workers, peasants, soldiers, revolutionary intellectuals and revolutionary cadres for his crimes in suppressing the mass revolutionary movement and undermining the Great Proletarian Cultural Revolution, according to a Nanchang Radio broadcast on August 31, 1966.

Hsü was dismissed from all his posts both in and outside the Party in the latter part of August, 1966.

Hu Ts'ai (胡采)

> Former deputy secretary-general, Northwest Federation of Literary and Art Circles; editor, *Hsi-pei Wen-i* (Northwest Literature and Art); director, Cultural Bureau of Sian; vice-chairman, Sian branch, Union of Chinese Writers.

Radio Sian broadcast on October 27, 1966 a summary of an article in *Shensi Jih-pao* entitled "Thoroughly Criticise the Towering Crimes of Counter-revolutionary Revisionist Element Hu Ts'ai."

The article called him a "loyal follower of Chou Yang." By making use of the positions he had usurped, Hu had carried out criminal activities against the Party, socialism and Mao Tse-tung's thought.

Under the guise of being a Party member and a literary theorist, Hu vigorously advocated and peddled Chou Yang's counter-revolutionary revisionist programme for literature and art by making reports, delivering speeches at symposia and writing editorials and articles. He also opposed Party leadership over literature and art in an attempt to prevent writers and historians from being influenced by Mao Tse-tung's thought.

The article concluded: "We must thoroughly expose that out-and-out revisionist element, hit him hard, pull him down and completely discredit him."

Hua Chia (華嘉)

Former deputy director, Propaganda Department, CCP Canton Municipal Committee; former Party secretary and concurrently director, Canton Municipal Bureau of Culture.

Hua Chia was denounced in a report carried in *Hung-wei Pao* of Canton, October 10, 1966. The report was based on an article published in *Kuangchou Jih-pao,* organ of the Canton Municipal Party Committee. Hua was accused of:

— Virulently attacking the great Party, energetically opposing the study of Mao Tse-tung's works;

— Rabidly opposing the Mao Tse-tung line for literature and art, and energetically promoting a counter-revolutionary, revisionist line;

— Advocating bourgeois liberalisation and carrying out capitalist restoration in the domain of culture.

Hua Chia was said to have condemned Party cadres, calling them "policemen" who kept investigating the ideological state of artists everywhere and "upsetting the mood of artists." He was also alleged to have exploited the revisionist notion of personal fame and material incentives to corrupt the minds of the artists, and called the political-ideological work "brain-washing."

Huang Chou (黄胄)

A well-known painter.

Huang Chou was denounced in a *Jen-min Jih-pao* article of September 12, 1966. The article called him a faithful executor of Teng T'o's anti-Party, anti-socialist programme for art. He was said to have frequently illustrated Teng T'o's "black" poems to hurl vicious denunciation and slanders at the Party and socialism. The article levelled these charges against Huang:

— Among his paintings the one with the caption "Visiting the Fair" described the "joyous" atmosphere of the "free market" which stemmed from the reactionary practice of "three freedoms and one contract."†

— His "Sending Sons To Surrender" on the quelling of the Tibetan "rebellion" slandered the just struggle of the People's Liberation Army to liberate a million serfs who had for centuries been tortured by the serf-owners.

— He had painted numerous pieces to project the ugly image of idlers, loafers and philanderers in place of the hard-working and plain-living, brave and healthy labouring people and revolutionary fighters of national minorities in the socialist society. He had portrayed the life of abandon, degeneration and even hysterical moral state of the exploiting class to counteract the lofty, magnanimous and soaring revolutionary sentiments of the proletariat.

— This "cultural traitor" was reported to have completed in one evening at Teng T'o's home the painting "A Hundred Mules" to please his master. Instead of carrying public grains for the revolution, the "mules" created by Huang Chou appeared to be transporting "black" merchandise for the counter-revolutionaries.

— A member of the *San Min Chu I* Youth Corps of the Kuomintang, Huang took an active part in the expansion of reactionary organisations and anti-Communist propaganda activities, and nursed deep-seated hatred for the Party and socialism. Once a very popular painter, Huang proved a faithful running dog of the "Three-Family Village gangster inn," and a "cultural traitor."

Huang Shou (黄壽)

Deputy director, Propaganda Department, CCP Chekiang Provincial Committee; Party secretary, Chekiang Provincial Writers Association; vice-president, Hangchow University, 1958-1964; editor, *Jen-min Jih-pao,* 1957.

Huang Shou was the target of criticism in a series of meetings held by the revolutionary teachers and students of Hangchow University in July, 1966. The crimes committed by Huang, according to the *Chekiang Jih-pao* of Hangchow, July 28, 1966, were as follows:

— When Huang was vice-president of Hangchow University between 1958 and 1964, he openly declared that it was not helpful to talk exclusively about Mao Tse-tung's thought and ruthlessly shelved the project of conducting classes on Mao's teachings;

— At the same time, he made every effort to peddle the "black merchandise" of the bourgeois line for literature and art of the thirties; in collusion with the monsters inside and outside the university, he opposed the Party's educational policy and promoted the revisionist line of education;

— In 1957, when he was in charge of the publication of *Jen-min Jih-pao,* he let out many anti-Party, anti-socialist poisonous weeds written by rightists;

— According to recent investigation, way back in 1939, he promoted support for public enemy Chiang Kai-shek in the columns of the weekly, *I Pao;*

— Judging from his words and deeds in the past, Huang Shou is an out-and-out bourgeois representative who had wormed his way into the Communist Party.

Jen Ch'ing (任清)

Former deputy director, Hupeh Provincial Cultural Bureau; vice-chairman, Hupeh branch, Chinese People's Association for Cultural Relations with Foreign Countries.

Radio Wuhan broadcast on October 12, 1966 that more than 1,500 people representing staff and workers of cultural and technical units in Hupeh Province and Wuhan, and institutes of higher learning held on October 12 a denunciation meeting to condemn Jen Ch'ing, a bourgeois rightist, for his persistent opposition to Party leadership over literature and art.

Jen was said to have frequently criticised and opposed Mao Tse-tung's ideas on literature and art and taken Chou Yang's counter-revolutionary revisionist literary and art programme of "literature and art of the whole people." He did his best to undermine the development of plays on modern revolutionary themes and promote traditional dramas eulogising "emperors, kings, generals, and prime ministers, scholars and beauties."

Pai Lien, chief of the Cultural Revolution Group of cultural and technical units in Wuhan, solemnly announced at the rally that the "Hupeh Party Provincial Committee has decided, with the approval of the Central-South Bureau of the CCP Central Committee, to remove Jen Ch'ing from all his posts both in and outside the Party and to label him as a bourgeois rightist."

Jen Shen (任深)

Former deputy secretary, Party Committee, Tsinghai University, and concurrently vice-president, Tsinghai University.

Radio Sining broadcast on August 26, 1966 an open denunciation of Jen Shen by the revolutionary teachers, students and staff of Tsinghai University. The CCP Tsinghai Provincial Committee on August 5 decided to remove Jen from all posts within and outside the Party.

Like Chou Yang, Teng T'o, and other counter-revolutionary revisionist elements, Jen was said to have directly aimed his attack at Mao Tse-tung's thought. With deep hatred for the movement to creatively study and apply Mao's works which had been gradually carried out at Tsinghai University since 1963, Jen had spared no efforts to slander the study movement as typically "philistine," "over-simplified" and "pragmatic."

Waving "red flags" to oppose the red flag, Jen for many years had been playing double-dealing tactics to viciously vilify the great thought of Mao Tse-tung, frenziedly promote the revisionist line on education, team up with bourgeois "scholars" and "authorities," oppose the Party's class line, and create all kinds of obstacles against students from families of workers and peasants, in a vain attempt to convert Tsinghai University into a stronghold for cultivating successors of the bourgeoisie and to realise the criminal plot of restoration of capitalism.

146

Juan Ti-min (阮廸民)

Director, Propaganda Department, CCP Kansu Provincial Committee.

Radio Lanchow on July 28, 1966 broadcast extracts from reports carried in *Kansu Jih-pao*, openly denouncing Juan Ti-min and his partner, Wu Ch'ien (吳前), deputy director, Kansu Provincial Party Committee's Propaganda Department, for their anti-Party and anti-socialist crimes.

At a mass meeting on August 1, 1966, revolutionary staff of the political and legal organisations of Kansu Province disclosed in their speeches that for over ten years, Juan and Wu had used their positions in the press, radio, cultural and educational fields to launch frenzied attacks on the Party, socialism and Mao Tse-tung's thought.

Speakers angrily denounced as nonsense the absurd ideas of the Juan-Wu gang that "class struggle is in the main finished" and "how can capitalism emerge?" They spread these views because they wanted to wage a bourgeois struggle against the proletariat, under the cloak of denying the class struggle to clear the way for a restoration of capitalism. "These wolves in sheep's clothing have sung precisely the same tune as the Khrushchev revisionist clique and the class enemies in China. They have also insulted the general line, the great leap forward, and the people's commune as a violation of objective laws."

K'ang Cho (康濯)

Former vice-chairman, Hopeh Provincial Federation of Literary and Art Circles; vice-chairman, Hunan branch, Union of Chinese Writers.

K'ang Cho was accused in the *Yang-ch'eng Wan-pao* of Canton, July 7, 1966 of being a Khrushchev revisionist who attacked the Communist Party's rural policies and wanted to restore capitalism in agriculture.

At a Dairen conference known as "Forum on Short Novels About the Countryside" held in August 1962, K'ang was said to have openly attacked Mao Tse-tung's line for rural economy and put forward a revisionist line of his own.

In his novels, K'ang portrayed the abject poverty of the rural population and blamed the Communist rural policies for the misery of the people.

K'ang was criticised, in the *Hunan Jih-pao* of June 8, 1966, for having served as a vanguard of the anti-Party and anti-socialist clique

147

led by Shao Ch'üan-lin (listed elsewhere in this section—Ed.).

He was also charged with:

— Holding that since China suffered from natural disasters and
was attacked by enemies at home and abroad, socialism would
be finished soon and the time for the restoration of capitalism
had come;

— Opposing Mao Tse-tung's teachings on a series of fundamental problems;

— Maliciously attacking the Party as lacking Marxism-Leninism
and laws of socialist construction, and slandering the Party's
general line and great leap forward as nothing but day-dreaming;

— Instigating the writers to write more about shortcomings,
errors, lessons by negative example, the painful world, and
blood-soaked tragedies;

— Cherishing the illusion that the Communist Party would give
up the struggle between the proletariat and the bourgeoisie
and between socialism and capitalism in the course of the great
socialist construction;

— Advocating that peasants should work by themselves individually, saying that to do so would not be a repetition of the
past but rather an act with a new overture for building
socialism in a better way.

K'o Lin (柯麟)

Former first secretary, CCP Committee, Chungshan
Medical College, Canton, and concurrently president of
the College; relieved of all his posts both in and outside
the Party by a decision of the CCP Kwangtung Provincial
Committee made in the latter part of June, 1966.

K'o Lin and Liu Chih-ming, deputy secretary of the Party Committee and concurrently vice-president of the Chungshan Medical
College, were leaders of an "anti-Party, anti-socialist black gang"
entrenched in the college, according to the *Yang-ch'eng Wan-pao* of
Canton, July 3, 1966.

K'o and his gang were accused of having stubbornly opposed the
Party's educational line, educational and other related policies, particularly the policies of setting up part-farming and part-study special
classes and of teachers' and students' participation in physical labour.
They were said to have stubbornly opposed the decision made by the CCP

148

Kwangtung Provincial Committee to send 60 per cent of the college's 1966 graduates to rural clinics in the communes, and viciously assailed the Party organ's decision to transfer one-third of the personnel of the medical college to the countryside to cure the sick.

K'o and his gang were further accused of taking a discriminating stand towards students from families of workers and peasants and doing everything they could to exclude such students, in a futile attempt to turn the college into a cradle for training successors to the bourgeoisie. In education, they placed professional studies on top of politics. They slandered the movement for studying and applying Chairman Mao's works as "bringing calamities."

The K'o Lin black gang was also charged with having brutally attacked the Left while shielding and condoning the Right.

Ku Chi-kuang (谷齊光)

Vice-president, Kiangsi University, Nanchang.

Radio Nanchang on June 19, 1966 carried an open denunciation of Ku Chi-kuang. The broadcast said:

Revolutionary teachers, students of Kiangsi University and Kiangsi Normal College, indignantly condemned the terrible crimes of Ku Chi-kuang, manager of the Kiangsi branch of the "Three-Family Village gangster inn." At the instigation of Wu Han, Ku had let loose since 1961 a large number of anti-Party and anti-socialist poisoned arrows, frenziedly attacked the dictatorship of the proletariat, viciously slandered the three red banners,[†] and tried to have the verdict reversed on the rightists who were dismissed from office.

Ku did everything in his power to harm the young people and advocated "peaceful evolution," in an attempt to restore capitalism.

"In dealing with poisonous snakes like Ku Chi-kuang who wormed his way into the Party, we, the revolutionary masses, must wage a tit-for-tat struggle to overthrow him. We should use the broom of the proletariat to sweep him into the historical garbage can."

K'uang Ya-ming (匡亞明)

Former first secretary, Party organ of Nanking University; former president, Nanking University.

K'uang Ya-ming was denounced in a *Jen-min Jih-pao* article of June

149

16, 1966 for his anti-Party, anti-socialist crimes. Reports from Nanking tell how revolutionary teachers and students of Nanking University "struggled" against K'uang, who had been stripped of his principal and concurrent posts in the University.

Hu Wei, 2nd secretary of the CCP Committee of Nanking University, presided over a "denunciation meeting" against K'uang and spoke at the meeting.

K'uang was reported to have organised some sort of counter-attack to save himself, but was completely overwhelmed by the "revolutionary teachers and students" of Nanking University.

K'uang was accused in a Nanking Radio broadcast on June 12, 1966 of having suppressed the revolutionary mass movement in the University by ruthless and treacherous means.

He was alleged to have (1) attempted to lead the great cultural revolution into a blind alley by confounding the nature of the revolution and placing emphasis on the principle of seeking truth from facts; (2) tried to put up a defence for embracing an anti-Party and anti-socialist black line in the University; (3) slandered the revolutionary teachers and students who put up a big-character poster to expose his ugly bourgeois royalist features as reactionaries, and ordered that they be disqualified from probationary Party membership; (4) physically insulted some of the faculty members and students of the Liyang branch of Nanking University who had criticised him, and described them as "Little Three-Family Village," or "black gang."

Kuo Hsiao-chang (郭小章)

A writer and author of the book, "A Lecture on Contradiction."

Radio Chengchow on July 19, 1966 broadcast an open denunciation of Kuo Hsiao-chang. The charges laid against Kuo appeared on the July 20 issue of *Honan Jih-pao*.

Under the bannerline "Raise High the Great Red Banner of Mao Tse-tung's Thought, Open Fire on Anti-Party and Anti-Socialist Element Kuo Hsiao-chang," the paper stated that former Korean War veterans of a certain People's Liberation Army unit held a symposium to denounce Kuo for his monstrous crime of vilifying the Resist-America and Aid-Korea War.

In his book, "A Lecture on Contradiction," anti-Party and

150

anti-socialist element Kuo actually opposed Mao Tse-tung's thought by calling it a thought in name only. On the question of war and peace, he condemned the Chinese veterans as preachers of war and maliciously attacked the Communist Party, the PLA and the people.

Kuo said: "In the prosecution of that war, nobody defeated nobody. The war ended in a draw, an equal match. As a result, both sides had to enter into peaceful negotiations to sign an armistice agreement. One is a preacher of war if one fails to see peace but sees only war, and measures everything in terms of war. Then there will be no end to war."

Kuo Hsiao-t'ang (郭曉棠)

> Former vice-president, Chengchow University, and concurrently Standing Committee member, Chengchow University's Party Committee; relieved of all his posts in the latter part of July, 1966.

Kuo Hsiao-t'ang was described, in an article in *Honan Jih-pao* (reproduced in *Yang-ch'eng Wan-pao* of Canton, August 7, 1966), as an anti-Party, anti-socialist vanguard opposed to Mao Tse-tung's thought.

He and his "boss" Wang P'ei-yü (listed elsewhere in this section—Ed.) planned, organised and took a leading part in the suppression of the revolutionary movement of students in Chengchow University in June, 1966.

Li Ch'ing (黎清)

> Former deputy secretary, Party Committee, Kirin Engineering College.

Radio Changchun broadcast on September 12, 1966 open charges levelled against Li Ch'ing, former deputy secretary of the Party Committee attached to Kirin Engineering College. The CCP Kirin Provincial Committee had decided to remove him from all posts he held both in and outside the Party.

The denunciation of Li was made known at a mass meeting attended by revolutionary teachers, students and staff workers of Kirin Engineering College. "A host of evidence shows that Li Ch'ing has for many years stubbornly taken a bourgeois reactionary stand against the Party and Chairman Mao's thought. He was opposed to the study of Chairman Mao's works and slandered the Party and the socialist system.

"In December 1965, when the students and teachers of the school launched a movement to study Chairman Mao's works, Li urged the students to read stories about knights-errant. He has opposed letting proletarian politics take command over professional work by openly refuting Chairman Mao's teaching that politics is the commander and soul of all work.

"In his lectures on dialectics, Li openly negated the existence of classes and class struggle in a socialist State and propagated his reactionary idea of 'peaceful evolution.'

"After he was removed from the post of third secretary of the Party Committee of Ch'angch'un Geological College in 1960, he wrote a large number of diabolical poems and essays viciously attacking the Party and socialism and insulting Chairman Mao.

"During the Great Proletarian Cultural Revolution, he worked out a set of rules to prevent the revolutionary teachers and students from exposing his counter-revolutionary crimes. The rules limited them to raising questions relating only to educational thinking, the education system, and the method of giving tests. But, under the fire of the revolutionary teachers and students, Li Ch'ing, the man of power in the Party who took the road of capitalism, has finally been dragged out."

Li Ching-min (李景民)

Vice chairman, Shanghai Municipal Federation of Literary and Art Circles; deputy director and concurrently chief editor, Shanghai Editorial Board, Chunghua Book Company.

Li Ching-min was alleged to be an out-and-out counter-revolutionary revisionist in a signed article in *Chieh-fang Jih-pao* of June 25, 1966. The article accused Li of:

— Having spoken for the "Three-Family Village" black gang and stirred up bitter enmity against the Party;

— Having used the Shanghai Editorial Board of the Chunghua Book Company as his base to recruit a group of monsters and demons, suppress revolutionary elements, make trouble, express erroneous views and make a mess of the Board's work;

— Having played a leading role and ganged up with other evil elements in supporting bourgeois rightist elements;

— Having influenced the Shanghai Editorial Board of the Chung-hua Book Company to impose bourgeois dictatorship on the proletariat, thus turning it into a reactionary bulwark against the Party and socialism;

— Having written the article, "Tu Fu Returns Home," to spread the idea that the people are longing for the return of the emperor (obviously referring to Chiang Kai-shek and hoping he will come back to restore the kingdom of the Chiang family).

Li Fan-fu (李凡夫)

> Vice-governor, Anhwei Province; deputy director, Propaganda Department, CCP CC South China Bureau, 1951; deputy director, Propaganda Department, CCP CC Central-South Bureau, 1953; deputy director, United Front Work Department, CCP CC Central-South Bureau, 1953.

Radio Hofei broadcast a report on July 5, 1966 on open charges laid against Li Fan-fu by cadres and students of the Intermediate Party School of CCP Anhwei Provincial Committee at a denunciation meeting. The report said in part:

Li utilised, between 1962 and 1964, the platform of the Intermediate Party School to spread poisonous influence and frenziedly oppose the Party leadership, the socialist system and Mao Tse-tung's thought. He called the "Quotations from Chairman Mao Tse-tung" phrases quoted out of context.

Li also incited the people to "oppose the three red flags" which he said were "material manifestations" of the great thought of Mao Tse-tung. By doing his utmost to oppose, attack, slander, and undermine these red flags, he was actually opposing the Party leadership, the proletarian dictatorship, the socialist system, and Mao Tse-tung's thought.

Li Kuei (李貴)

> Former first secretary, CCP Huhehot Municipal Committee, Inner Mongolia.

Radio Huhehot on August 2, 1966 carried a report on open charges laid against Li Kuei who was removed from office in late July after a reorganisation of the CCP Huhehot Municipal Committee in accordance with the instruction of the North China Bureau of the CCP Central Committee.

153

The report said that in meetings of denunciation held at Huhehot, the masses of all nationalities laid bare a host of facts which proved that Li was a bourgeois representative who wormed his way into the Party, an out-and-out revisionist, and a pioneer in opposing the Party, socialism, and Mao Tse-tung's thought. He was said to have committed no end of evils to restore capitalism and feudalism.

The *Nei-meng-ku Jih-pao* on August 5, 1966 devoted more than a page to articles denouncing Li Kuei. The articles were classified under five different headings:

— Regularly opposing Mao Tse-tung's thought and distorting its essence;

— Viciously attacking Party leadership and vilifying the socialist system;

— Waving the flag of opposing great Han chauvinism, but undermining the great unification of the motherland by fanning the flames of national splittism;

— Befriending decadent elements during the Socialist Education Movement;

— Following the revisionist line.

The report said that Li's criminal activities were co-ordinated with revisionism and imperialism on the international front and with the big anti-China chorus. They were also co-ordinated in an attempt to restore the former status of landlords, rich peasants, counter-revolutionaries, bad elements, and rightists at home.

Li Lin (李林)

Former vice-president, Chengchow University, and concurrently Standing Committee member, Chengchow University's Party Committee; relieved of all his posts in the latter part of July, 1966.

Li Lin was accused in an article in *Honan Jih-pao* (reproduced in *Yang-ch'eng Wan-pao* of Canton, August 7, 1966) of being the principal accomplice of Wang P'ei-yü, former acting president and secretary of Chengchow University's Party Committee, in the suppression of the revolutionary movement of students in Chengchow University in June, 1966.

Li P'ing-hsin (李平心)

History professor, East China Normal College, Shanghai.

Radio Shanghai broadcast on June 23, 1966 excerpts of talks by workers published in the June 20 issue of Shanghai *Wen-hui Pao*:

"Li P'ing-hsin holds mistaken view that there are two criteria for evaluation of historical figures. He is openly opposed to using present-day proletarian yardstick to measure historical figures. We workers have always used the viewpoint of class analysis and class struggle as taught by Chairman Mao to judge all persons and things.

"Li has tried all possible ways to write biographies of kings, emperors, generals, and prime ministers. His writings are poisoned arrows shot at the people."

The same issue of *Wen-hui Pao* also carried an article enumerating new anti-Party and anti-socialist crimes by Li. Entitled "Corruptible Officers Are the Instrument for the Return of Counter-revolution," the article pointed out: "Wu Han and his gang and Li P'ing-hsin are supporting one another in their new attacks on the Party and are openly opposed to the socialist cultural revolution. Li was the spearhead of the bourgeois concept of history directly aimed at refuting Mao Tse-tung's theory of class struggle to back up his vicious attacks on proletarian dictatorship. The time has come for the liquidation of Li's debts to the people."

Li Shu (黎樹)

Chief editor, *Historical Studies*.

Li Shu was attacked in the *Jen-min Jih-pao* of October 23, 1966 for having advanced two slogans which are contrary to the doctrine of Mao Tse-tung.

One of the slogans called on historians to oppose "formulism" (公式主義), or viewing history exclusively from the so-called "class viewpoint," and to stress the importance of historical data.

The other called for "construction before destruction," which was said to have been designed to compel Marxist historians to abandon their criticism of bourgeois historical science.

Li Ta (李達)

President, Wuhan University; a veteran Communist who left the Party during the "Great Revolution" (1927) and then rejoined it in 1949.

Li Ta was severely taken to task in the *Hupeh Jih-pao* of July 11, 1966 for having "rabidly attacked the thought of Mao Tse-tung and promoted revisionist erroneous views" and opposed the Party's leadership over institutions of higher learning.

Li was condemned for:

— Vigorously preaching the fallacies of "peaceful co-existence," "peaceful competition" and "peaceful transition"—singing the same tune as Khrushchev.

— Opposing the creative study and application of Mao's writings by workers, peasants and soldiers.

— Frenziedly attacking the general line, the great leap forward and the people's commune.

— Doing his utmost to vilify the educational revolution and implement the bourgeois line on education, advocating expertness and not "redness."

Chieh-fang-chün Pao of Peking on September 6, 1966 published a comprehensive report summarising press criticisms against Li Ta. Li's principal crime, according to the report, was his contemptuous remarks about Mao Tse-tung's philosophical treatises, "On Contradiction" and "On Practice," which he said were superficial and not necessarily true.

Li was also critical of Mao Tse-tung's theory about classes and class struggle in a socialist society, declaring that there was an essential character common to all classes and that antagonistic contradictions no longer existed in a socialist society.

Li Ts'ui (李崔)

Radio Huhehot broadcast on Sept. 11, 1966 open charges laid against the black gang headed by Li Ts'ui, at a mass meeting attended by more than 1,200 revolutionary people of various nationalities from organisations directly affiliated to the Hu-lan-pei-erh League and Hai-la-erh municipality.

The Li Ts'ui black gang "has been desperately spreading great Han chauvinism in an attempt to undermine the solidarity of different nationalities. The black gang's objective is the restoration of capitalism and opposition to the leadership of the Party and Chairman Mao."

The black gang "attempts to oppose Mao Tse-tung's thought and undermine class struggle, emphasising so-called national solidarity and unity of the great family as key solutions to all problems. All this is nonsense. Can it be true that poor and lower-middle peasants and herdsmen can be united with the landlords, rich peasants, and herdowners? Can it be true that we should call the reactionaries our brothers? This is a theory of class conciliation which can never deceive us."

Li Ya-ch'ün (李亞群)

Deputy director, Propaganda Department, CCP Szechwan Provincial Committee, and concurrently secretary-general of the Party Branch, Szechwan Provincial Federation of Literary and Art Circles.

Radio Chengtu openly denounced Li Ya-ch'ün in a broadcast on July 6, 1966.

Li was said to be the chief criminal advocating the black revisionist line on literature and art in the province. He was labelled a representative of the bourgeoisie who had wormed his way into the Party and usurped leadership over Szechwan's literary and art circles for the past ten years, during which period he had persistently opposed the great thought of Mao Tse-tung and his line on literature and art.

Particularly during 1961-62 when China's national economy ran into temporary difficulties resulting from the abrupt suspension of economic aid by the Khrushchev revisionist clique and from three consecutive years of natural calamities, Li joined the anti-China chorus organised by the imperialists, modern revisionists, and the reactionaries of all countries, chanting in unison with all the class enemies at home to pave the way for the restoration of capitalism, the broadcast said.

Since the 1930's Li had been attacking the correct line of directing the writers and artists to serve the masses of workers, peasants and soldiers, claiming that writers should have the right to select their own themes and write about things they like best. He deplored the idea that writers and artists should participate in physical labour, opposing the Party directive on the elimination of the difference between mental and physical labour and attempting to lead the writers and artists down the revisionist road so as to enlist them in the bourgeois camp — a privileged class

157

that remains aloof from the masses of working people — to lay a social foundation for the restoration of capitalism.

Liao Mo-sha (廖沫沙)

Former director, United Front Work Department,
CCP Peking Municipal Committee.

Liao Mo-sha was accused in the *Jen-min Jih-pao* of June 24, 1966 of the following crimes:

— He and his "brothers" of the "Three-Family Village," acting in behalf of their back-stage big boss, launched a rabid attack against the Communist Party, socialism and Mao Tse-tung's thought.

— Before the war he viciously attacked Lu Hsün, whom Mao Tse-tung once called "the greatest and most courageous standard-bearer of the new cultural army."

— In "Visit to Hsienyang," he attacked by parody the Communists in the Shensi-Kansu-Ninghsia Border Region, saying that terrorism and corruption dominated the region. In another story he sang the praises of the Nationalist rule.

— In a historical novel, "Drifting Away from Yin" (which was ostensibly a story about Emperor Chou Hsin of Yin Dynasty), he blamed Chiang Kai-shek for having let Mao Tse-tung return to Yenan from Chungking, and prophesied a popular uprising against the Communists.

— He persistently attacked the Communists after the liberation.

Lin Chi-fu

Radio Foochow on August 28, 1966 broadcast the editorial of *Fukien Jih-pao* entitled "Severely Punish the Counter-revolutionary Criminal Who Undermines the Cultural Revolution."

The editorial disclosed that Lin Chi-fu, a typical diabolical counter-revolutionary criminal, had committed a towering crime in daring to make murderous attacks on people with a knife and frenziedly undermining the Great Proletarian Cultural Revolution. The Foochow Municipal People's Court, according to the demands of the broad masses, held a meeting and pronounced a death sentence, to be carried out immediately.

Lin was said to have all along been a good-for-nothing bad element. He had been sentenced to a period of reform through labour. After his release, he did not show the slightest indication of remorse. He had the strongest class hatred for the Party and the people. On August 27, 1966, he carried out his vicious counter-attacks against the revolutionary masses, and inflicted stab wounds on 13 persons.

This sinister counter-revolutionary act, according to the editorial, showed clearly that the Great Proletarian Cultural Revolution was an extremely sharp and violent class struggle and that the class enemies invariably attempted to put up a desperate struggle.

All stubborn survivors of the old world, however, would be swept away by the avalanche of the revolution. All demons and monsters attempting to stem this avalanche would receive devastating blows, the editorial said.

Lin Hung (林鴻)

Former deputy chief editor, *Anhwei Jih-pao*, Hofei.

Lin Hung was accused, in the *Anhwei Jih-pao* of July 20, 1966, of having written many anti-Party essays for *Anhwei Jih-pao* and *Hofei Wan-pao* in the past few years.

The paper cited the following instances:

— In the autumn of 1961 when China encountered temporary economic difficulties, Lin wrote an article, under the pretext of reviewing three novels by the US bourgeois writer O. Henry, to attack socialism and vilify the general line and the great leap forward;

— On January 20, 1963, he wrote an article entitled "Material Pleasure and Moral Corruption," using ancient things to satirise the present and denigrating leading Party cadres as leading luxurious lives like the feudal emperors of history and seeking material pleasure;

— On March 5, 1963, Lin wrote another article slandering the general line for building socialism and the great leap forward as a failure;

— On April 23, 1962, he wrote an article in *Hofei Wan-pao* directing the spearhead of his attack against Mao Tse-tung, saying that "No leader is a sage" and "A leader also has erroneous views."

159

Lin Mo-han (林默涵)

Former deputy director, Department of Propaganda, CCP Central Committee; ex-vice-minister of Culture; member, Board of Directors, Union of Chinese Writers; member, Planning Commission of Committee of Cultural and Educational Affairs, Government Administrative Council.

Lin Mo-han was labelled No. 1 accomplice of Chou Yang, arch chieftain of the counter-revolutionary revisionist clique in literary and art circles, in the *Kung-jen Jih-pao* of Peking on September 23, 1966. Lin was denounced for the following "counter-revolutionary and revisionist" crimes:

— Rabid opposition to the thought of Mao Tse-tung.
— Resistance to Mao Tse-tung's line for literature and art while promoting a revisionist line for literature and art.
— Hostility to the three red banners, and attacks on the proletarian dictatorship.
— Frantic sabotage of the great cultural revolution.

Lin Shan (林杉)

Former superintendent, Ch'angch'un Film Studio, Changchun; writer of screenplays under the pen name Lin Mo-ch'en (林漠晨); member, Secretariat, Union of Chinese Cinema Workers.

Lin Shan, as the screenplay writer of the film, "Folks of Two Families," was accused by two soldiers in their letter to the editors of *Chieh-fang-chün Pao* published on August 5, 1966, of making use of the film to vilify the poor and lower-middle peasants, viciously attack the Party and socialism, and give support and encouragement to the landlords, rich peasants, counter-revolutionaries, bad elements, and rightists.

The letter listed ten big crimes connected with the film, summarised as follows:

— Spreading poison and preparing public opinion in favour of a capitalist restoration;
— Implying that the practice of "individual farming" would soon reappear in China;
— Encouraging landlords and rich peasants to counter-attack out of revenge;

160

- Slandering the system of co-operatives;
- Attacking the Party's overall purchasing and selling policy;
- Ignoring Party leadership and obliterating political and ideological work;
- Undermining the noble class feelings of poor and lower-middle peasants;
- Spreading the revisionist viewpoint that struggles cannot solve problems, while the "appeal" of human sentiment can;
- Seeking to shift the target of the people's struggle;
- Attempting to lure youth into the quagmire of bourgeois individualism, with the object of bringing about a "peaceful evolution."

Lin T'an-ch'iu (林坦秋)

> Deputy director, Propaganda Department, CCP Chekiang Provincial Committee; Party secretary, Provincial Writers Association; former vice-president, Hangchow University.

Radio Hangchow broadcast on July 7, 1966 summaries of articles carried in *Chekiang Jih-pao,* denouncing Lin T'an-ch'iu's erroneous reactionary views and sternly condemning the black gang of the "Three-Family Village's" Chekiang branch headed by Lin for its plot to undermine the Party's ties with the people.

The articles were written by worker-peasant masses and revolutionary teachers and students, and published under the bannerline: "Raise High the Great Red Banner of Mao Tse-tung's Thought, Open Fire on the Anti-Party and Anti-Socialist Black Line."

Lin Yang (林楊)

> Former director, Propaganda Department, Party Committee of Inner Mongolia University, Huhehot, and concurrently director of the University's Department of History and Political Science.

Lin Yang was suspended from his Party and other posts by the Party Committee of the Inner Mongolia Autonomous Region on August 29, 1966.

According to a Huhehot Radio broadcast on September 4, 1966, Lin was accused, together with two other Party secretaries of Inner Mongolia University, of taking an active part in opposing and undermining the Great Proletarian Cultural Revolution, coercing the revolutionary students to become counter-revolutionary, and creating "a host of counter-revolutionary incidents."

Liu Chih-hsia (劉知俠)

Vice-chairman, Shantung Provincial Federation of Literary and Art Circles.

Liu Chih-hsia was condemned in the *Kuang-min Jih-pao* of Peking, November 20, 1966 for having released a number of poisoned arrows directed at the Party and socialism.

In "Covering One of the Combat Areas" which was released in 1957 in conjunction with attacks launched by bourgeois rightists, and "Flying Over the Grass," which was published in 1959 when "Right opportunists" ran amuck, which were described as two particularly vicious poisoned arrows, Liu was said to have recorded the merits of the counter-revolution and compiled biographic data on renegades.

For instance, in "Covering One of the Combat Areas," Liu was alleged to have spared no effort in eulogising a faithful lackey of the Kuomintang in the person of Chung Shih, a reactionary army officer, by disguising him as a benign Buddha.

Liu's "Flying Over the Grass" portrayed Chang Li, a renegade of the revolution and a squad leader of the Kuomintang army who surrendered, as an elusive "hero" of the "revolution" of great prowess. In addition, it defended Chang Li's ignominious crimes of defection, claiming that he did so for "catering to the needs of revolution" and that because the Party and the masses "wrongly laid the blame on him," he was compelled to take desperate steps by force of circumstance.

Liu Chih-ming (劉志明)

Former deputy secretary, Party Committee, Chungshan Medical College, Canton, and concurrently vice-president of the college; relieved of all posts inside and outside the Party by a decision of the CCP Kwangtung Provincial Committee made in the latter part of June, 1966.

Liu Chih-ming was the "No. 2 boss" of an anti-Party, anti-socialist black gang of Chungshan Medical College in Canton, the "No. 1 boss" of the gang being K'o Lin, former first Party secretary and concurrently

162

president of the Chungshan Medical College. The charges against Liu are identical to those levelled against K'o.

Liu Hsiu-shan (劉秀山)

Alternate Member, CCP Anhwei Provincial Committee; vice-chairman, Anhwei Provincial Federation of Literary and Art Circles.

Liu Hsiu-shan, author of "On Mount Taipei," was labelled a counter-revolutionary and a "vicious enemy hiding in the Party" by the comrades of the Anhwei Provincial Federation of Literary and Art Circles at a denunciation meeting held in Hofei on September 4, 1966, according to a Radio Hofei broadcast on September 5, 1966.

Liu was alleged to have colluded with Ch'en Teng-k'o, chairman of the Anhwei Provincial Federation of Literary and Art Circles, and Na Sha in forming an anti-Party black gang, enlisting capitulationists and renegades into his service and covering up bad elements and bad things.

After the launching of the Great Proletarian Cultural Revolution, Liu was said to have done all sorts of misdeeds to achieve his goal of undermining the revolution.

His book, "On Mount Taipei," was branded a "big poisonous weed" because it described the People's Liberation Army as "a mob of unorganised, undisciplined, and cowardly people."

Liu Pi-shih (劉畢時)

Secretary, Party Committee, Shantung Teachers College.

Liu Pi-shih and Liu Ming-fan, former vice-president of Shantung Teachers College, were denounced at a meeting held by students and faculty members of the college on June 19, 1966 for their counter-revolutionary crimes of suppressing the revolutionary masses, according to a Radio Tsinan broadcast on June 20.

Consequently, both were removed from all their posts inside and outside the Party by a decision of the CCP Shantung Provincial Committee announced on June 20.

They were branded as "representatives of the bourgeoisie" who had wormed their way into the Party, with the vain hope of turning the

Shantung Teachers College into a counter-revolutionary bulwark of revisionism.

Liu Tan (劉丹)

Vice president, Chekiang University; first deputy
secretary, CCP Party Committee, Chekiang University.

Liu Tan was removed from all his posts by a decision of the CCP Chekiang Provincial Committee on June 22, 1966. The *Chekiang Jih-pao* of June 24 exposed the anti-Party, anti-socialist crimes committed by Liu as follows:

— Attacking and resisting the revolutionary masses;
— Labelling the revolutionary students and teachers of Chekiang University, who put up the first "big-character poster" of criticism against him, as counter-revolutionaries, and restricting them from attending meetings or writing articles in a vain attempt to seal the lips of the revolutionary masses;
— Refusing to carry out the instructions of the CCP Central Committee and Chairman Mao, turning a deaf ear to the instructions of the provincial party organ, adopting double-dealing methods, and even taking direct actions to resist the instructions.

Liu Tzu-chien (劉子建)

Former deputy secretary, Yencheng *Hsien* Party
Committee, Kiangsu province.

Hsin-hua Jih-pao of Nanking, on September 15, 1966 carried an article, "Strike Down Once for All Counter-revolutionary Revisionist Liu Tzu-chien."

The article accused Liu of being an out-and-out revisionist who had wormed his way into the Party. A representative of the bourgeoisie, Liu had long persisted in maintaining a reactionary stand. Since the Great Proletarian Cultural Revolution began, he had stubbornly attempted to maintain his reactionary attitude, the article said.

Lo Jui-ch'ing (羅瑞卿)

> Member, CCP-CC; member, Secretariat, CCP-CC;
> vice-premier; vice minister of National Defence; mem-
> ber, National Defence Council, and chief of general staff,
> the Chinese People's Liberation Army.

While Lo Jui-ch'ing was not pub'icly disgraced in the early phase of the cultural revolution, he was replaced on July 9, 1966 by Yeh Chien-ying as secretary of the CCP Central Committee's Secretariat and by Yang Ch'eng-wu on August 1 the same year as Acting Chief of General Staff of the People's Liberation Army.

For more than six months prior to his removal from all the offices he held, Lo was never mentioned in State functions or important army conferences.

The *Chieh-fang-chün Pao* of August 1, 1966 linked Lo with "important members of the counter-revolutionary, anti-Party, anti-socialist clique" in the People's Liberation Army, where "important posts" were said to have been usurped by "bourgeois representatives."

The army newspaper accused this group of bourgeois agents of seeking to "substitute a bourgeois military line for Chairman Mao's proletarian military line."

Lo Ting (洛汀)

> Deputy director, Liaoning Provincial Cultural
> Department; vice-chairman, Liaoning branch, Union of
> Chinese Drama Workers; president, Liaoning People's
> Theatre of Arts.

Lo Ting was branded "one of the anti-Party and anti-socialist representatives in the field of art and literature in Liaoning" by Radio Shenyang on June 15, 1966. He was accused in the broadcast of having played an important role in the writing and directing of the play, "Laying Siege to the City," a "big poisonous weed" which had provoked nation-wide criticism.

The play was said to have adopted a bourgeois reactionary stand, viciously distorting the history of the people's war of liberation, glorifying the Kuomintang reactionaries, vilifying the PLA, popularising bourgeois and revisionist "Treatise on Human Nature," and opposing Mao Tse-tung's theory of classes, class contradiction, and class struggle.

Lo was also charged with having talked rubbish about bourgeois "liberty," opposed Party leadership, and resisted the literary and art orientation of serving the workers, peasants and soldiers.

Lu P'ing (陸平)

> Secretary, Peking University's Party Committee and concurrently President of the University.

Lu P'ing and a "small number of bourgeois royalists" were attacked by *Jen-min Jih-pao* of June 5, 1966 for using Peking University as "a base of operations for some of the former leaders of the CCP Peking Municipal Committee" to fight with the proletariat for the mind of the students.

Lu and his friends were accused of carrying out a bourgeois line of education, trying to foster revisionist seedlings and transplant them in other parts of the country, adopting discriminatory measures against worker-peasant students who resisted the revisionist line and even brutally struggling against them.

They were also said to have desperately rejected and sabotaged the socialist education movement.

Lu T'ao (盧濤)

> Party secretary and concurrently vice-principal, Party School; deputy director, Propaganda Department, CCP Fukien Provincial Party Committee.

Radio Foochow on August 29, 1966 broadcast an editorial of *Fukien Jih-pao* under the title "Hold High the Great Red Banner of Mao Tse-tung's Thought and Thoroughly Expose and Repudiate the Anti-Party and Anti-socialist Crimes of Lu T'ao."

The editorial said in part:

"The broad masses of workers, peasants, soldiers, revolutionary cadres, and revolutionary intellectuals are by word of mouth and articles condemning the terrible crimes of Lu T'ao in opposing the Party, socialism, and Mao Tse-tung's thought.

"All these people expressed their determination to hit hard at, pull down, and completely discredit him until he can never recover."

Lu was also accused of "peddling Yang Hsien-chen's (theoretician, former vice-president of Higher Party School — Ed.) black goods of 'two combine in one' and of eulogising famed authors in an attempt to win over the proletarian successors."

166

Lu Ti (陸地)

> Former deputy director, CCP Kwangsi Chuang Autonomous Regional Committee; committee member, Canton Branch of the Union of Chinese Writers: deputy director, Cultural and Educational Department of CCP Kwangsi Provincial Committee; deputy director, Propaganda Department, CCP Kwangsi Chuang Autonomous Regional Committee; member, All-China Federation of Literary and Art Circles.

Radio Nanning on June 27, 1966 broadcast the decision of the CCP Kwangsi Chuang Autonomous Regional Committee to remove Lu Ti from all his posts. A notice dated June 18 on this decision was also broadcast followed by a *Kwangsi Jih-pao* editorial note, which said that since Lu's works, "Those Who Uphold the Idea of Bending the Fingers Inward Are the Losers" and "My Old Friends," were branded as "poisonous weeds" in the paper on June 15, a large number of workers, peasants, soldiers, revolutionary cadres and intellectuals had been greatly enraged at Lu's anti-Party and anti-socialist crimes.

Lu T'ing-i (陸定一)

> Member, CCP Central Committee; alternate member, Political Bureau, CCP Central Committee; secretary, Secretariat, CCP Central Committee; vice-premier, State Council; former Minister of Culture; former director, Propaganda Department, CCP Central Committee.

The disclosure by NCNA, in a report on July 10, 1966, that T'ao Chu, then first secretary of the Central-South Bureau of the CCP Central Committee, had assumed the duties as director of the CCP Central Committee's Propaganda Department, meant that Lu T'ing-i, who formerly headed the Propaganda Department, was in disgrace.

Lu presumably lost the post of the Chinese Communist Party's Propaganda Director after Chou Yang and Lin Mo-han, his two former deputies in the Propaganda Department, as well as Hsia Yen, former Vice Minister of Culture, were strongly taken to task for carrying out a "counter-revolutionary programme for literature and art" that was opposed to the Mao Tse-tung line for literature and art.

In "Talks at the Yenan Forum on Literature and Art," Mao Tse-tung defined the role of literature and art in the struggle between the proletarian and bourgeois lines in the cultural sphere. In that document, he specifically drove home the point that proletarian literature

167

and art should serve the workers, peasants and soldiers.

No official explanation was given for the way Lu T'ing-i was removed from the top office he held at the Ministry of Culture. But, at the plenary session of the 1966 Physics Colloquium held on the morning of July 30, 1966, delegates heard a report delivered by Hsiao Wang-tung, referred to in the NCNA report, as "Acting Minister of Culture."

One explanation for Lu's downfall is that the CCP Central Committee's Propaganda Department under Lu failed to carry out Mao Tse-tung's instructions on the conduct of the Great Proletarian Cultural Revolution. The Propaganda Department has direct control of *Hung-ch'i*, theoretical journal of the CCP Central Committee, and *Jen-min Jih-pao*, official organ of the same committee. Until the beginning of June, 1966, *Hung-ch'i* took a cold attitude towards the cultural revolution movement, while *Jen-min Jih-pao* was far behind *Chieh-fang-chün Pao*, the army newspaper, in conducting the cultural revolution campaign.

Ouyang Shan (歐陽山)

> Chairman, Kwangtung Provincial Federation of Literary and Art Circles; chairman, Kwangtung Branch, Union of Chinese Writers.

Ouyang Shan was denounced in the *Hung-wei Pao* of Canton, September 17, 1966 for his revisionist stand, his opposition to Mao Tse-tung's literary and art thinking, and his refusal to be reformed. He was said to have tried to turn the Union of Chinese Writers into a "Petofi Club."†

Ouyang was denounced in the *Hung-wei Pao* of Canton, September 22, 1966 for four of his stories and his "Views on the Work of Full-Time Writers," which was called a counter-revolutionary, revisionist programme for art and literature.

Four articles from contributors to the September 11, 1966 issue of *Hung-wei Pao* of Canton denounced Ouyang for his anti-Party, anti-socialist "poisonous weeds" — novels and stories which disseminated revisionist views and attacked the Communist Party and the socialist system.

Pai Jen (白刄)

Playwright and producer of the play, "Laying Siege to the City."

Pai Jen, playwright and producer of the play, "Laying Siege to the City," was notorious for writing bad plays, according to a broadcast by Radio Shenyang on June 15, 1966.

The play, which had also been adapted for a film bearing the same title, had been branded a "big poisonous weed" and widely criticised in the press.

P'eng Chen (彭真)

Member, CCP Central Committee; member, Political Bureau, CCP Central Committee; secretary, Secretariat, CCP Central Committee; vice-chairman, Standing Committee, NPC; vice-chairman, National Committee, CPPCC; mayor, Peking municipality; former first secretary, CCP Peking Municipal Committee.

Out of public view since March 29, 1966, P'eng Chen was removed from his office in the CCP Peking Municipal Committee following the reorganisation of the municipal Party organ in early June of that year.

On June 4, 1966, it was officially announced that Li Hsüeh-feng, first secretary of the North China Bureau of the CCP Central Committee, had been appointed concurrently first secretary of the reorganised CCP Peking Municipal Committee.

Without naming P'eng Chen, the No. 9, 1966 issue of *Hung-ch'i* charged the CCP Peking Municipal Committee, of which P'eng was the former head, with resisting the Great Proletarian Cultural Revolution and seeking to turn the dictatorship of the proletariat into bourgeois dictatorship.

The theoretical journal of the Central Committee also attacked the former municipal Party organ for discarding the Mao Tse-tung theory of class and class struggle, pursuing a course promoting China's "peaceful evolution" into revisionism, and swaying public opinion in favour of the restoration of capitalism.

P'eng Hsiao-ch'ien (彭笑干)

Vice governor of Honan concurrently in charge of agriculture.

P'eng Hsiao-ch'ien, described as a representative of the reactionary landlord class and an anti-Communist, anti-people old hand, had worked for the Chinese Communists for more than 20 years.

Like other Communist officials "rooted out" in the current cultural revolution, P'eng was accused in the October 4, 1966 issue of *Hung-wei Pao* of Canton of having opposed the thought of Mao Tse-tung, attacked Party leadership, tried to usurp leadership power, opposed the socialist system, and striven to regain the paradise lost by the landlord class.

P'eng favoured setting aside more private plots, promoting the free market, beating the gong to clear the way for the restoration of capitalism, and even endorsing the idea of "peaceful evolution" as opposed to class struggle.

P'eng K'ang (彭康)

Former president, Ch'iao T'ung University, Shanghai; former chairman, Shensi Provincial Scientific and Technical Association, 1963; former president, Sian Ch'iao T'ung University and former secretary of the University's Party Committee, 1964.

P'eng K'ang ws labelled an "anti-Party, anti-socialist criminal" in an announcement of the decision of the CCP Shensi Provincial Committee by Radio Urumchi on June 19, 1966.

The broadcast charged that P'eng and a handful of anti-Party and anti-socialist elements had made a vain attempt to resist and sabotage the cultural revolution of the proletariat led by the CCP Central Committee and Chairman Mao, and had conceived a series of counter-revolutionary plots.

P'eng P'ei-yün (彭珮雲)

A cadre of the University Work Department, CCP Peking Municipal Committee and concurrently assistant secretary of Peking University's Party Committee.

P'eng P'ei-yün and Lu P'ing were denounced by *Jen-min Jih-pao* of June 6, 1966 for having run Peking University in a bourgeois, reactionary way.

Calling for the overthrow of the rule of bourgeois "scholar-tyrants," four graduates of the Department of Law, Peking University, charged that Mao Tse-tung's writings had never been systematically taught in the University during their five-year stay in that school. What was taught included civil and penal codes of the Soviet Union, laws of bourgeois countries, history of Chinese and foreign laws, etc.

P'eng was labelled an element of the "Three-Family Village black gang" in a big-character poster put up in Peking University on May 25, 1966 by seven members of the Department of Philosophy of the University. In that poster, P'eng, Sung Shuo and Lu P'ing were all accused of trying to obstruct the mass struggle against Teng T'o and his friends and of being Khrushchev revisionists.

Sha Ting (沙汀)

Former chairman, Szechuan Provincial Federation of Literary and Art Circles; assistant secretary, Party group of the Federation; chief editor, *Szechwan Wen-hsüeh* [Szechwan Literature].

Jen-min Jih-pao on October 17, 1966 carried an extract from *Szechwan Jih-pao* and *Chengtu Wan-pao,* denouncing Sha Ting on the following grounds:

Sha was one of counter-revolutionary revisionist Chou Yang's able fighters. He was also a fervent trumpeter and faithful executor of Chou Yang's line on bourgeois and revisionist art and literature in Szechwan Province.

Consistently opposing Mao Tse-tung's art and literary line and resisting Party leadership, Sha had aligned himself with a number of anti-Party elements in controlling Szechwan's art and literary circles and in perpetrating numerous anti-Party, anti-socialist misdeeds. For instance, in his speeches at gatherings of literary and art workers in Chengtu on two separate occasions — September 1961 and June 1962 — he spared no efforts in systematically propagating Chou Yang's revisionist programme for art and literature and viciously attacking Mao Tse-tung's "Talks at the Yenan Forum on Literature and Art."

In 1957, Sha published his first novel, "Groping for Fish," which viciously attacked the agricultural co-operativisation movement. In 1958, he released another novel, "Storm," which vilified poor and lower-middle peasants led by the Party and rural cadres, depicting the latter as simple-minded persons ignorant of policy matters and resorted to "telling lies" when class struggle became acute.

Sha also did everything possible to abet the reactionary arrogance of class enemies in a futile attempt to fan a counter-revolutionary evil wind and whip up a counter-current, with the object of reviving capitalism in China.

Shao Ch'üan-lin (邵荃麟)

> A literary writer and theorist; vice-chairman, Union of Chinese Writers; secretary, Party group, Union of Chinese Writers; sponsor of Dairen meeting of artists and writers in August 1962; former assistant chief editor of the Communist-operated San Lien Book Store, Hong Kong, 1948.

According to the *Hunan Jih-pao* of June 8, 1966, the Dairen meeting sponsored by Shao Ch'üan-lin was aimed at opposing the Party, socialism, and Mao Tse-tung's thinking.

The *Jen-min Jih-pao* of December 27, 1964 also criticised Shao for presenting his view of "portraying middle people" in literature, thereby doing his best to belittle the importance of depicting heroic characters.

Shih Ling-ho (石凌鶴)

> Director, Kiangsi Provincial Bureau of Cultural Affairs; former chairman, Kiangsi Provincial Federation of Literary and Art Circles; vice-chairman, Kiangsi Provincial Union of Literary Workers and Artists.

Shih Ling-ho was denounced at a meeting of workers, peasants, revolutionary cadres and intellectuals in Nanchang on June 20, 1966 for his anti-Party, anti-socialist crimes.

Charges laid against Shih, according to a Radio Nanchang broadcast on June 20, 1966, included:

— Harping on the same "black line" as Wu Han, T'ien Han and Meng Chao by having the feudal and bourgeois demons dominate art, in this way clearing the way for a capitalist revival;

— Shooting poisoned arrows directly at the CCP Central Committee and Chairman Mao and attempting to overthrow Party leadership;

— Peddling feudalist and capitalist "black merchandise";

— Waving a "red flag" to oppose the red flag.

172

Sun Shu-p'ing (孫叔平)

Director, Kiangsu Institute of Philosophy and Social Sciences.

Sun Shu-p'ing was denounced in the *Jen-min Jih-pao* of October 23, 1966 for his book, "Outline of Historical Materialism," which was said to uphold Khrushchev's revisionist views.

Sun was accused of having said in his book that "peaceful co-existence" was the essence of Marxism-Leninism and that it was possible to defeat capitalism through "peaceful competition."

Even after the publication of "Long Live Leninism" in *Hung-ch'i* in 1960, Sun still persisted in his "preposterous theory of peaceful transition."

Sun Yeh-fang (孫冶方)

Former director, Economics Institute, Chinese Academy of Sciences.

Sun Yeh-fang's "revisionist fallacies" were denounced in articles appearing in *Jen-min Jih-pao* of August 9, 1966. He was attacked for advocating "putting profit or money in command" and for opposing Mao Tse-tung's thought. In another article in the same paper on the day before, he was accused of taking the bourgeois stand against the proletariat, attacking the general line, the great leap forward and the people's commune, and of advocating a revisionist economic programme.

Sun stood against centralised Party and State control over the national economy and advocated independent operation by enterprises, according to an article appearing in *Hung-ch'i,* No. 10, 1966.

In the same article, Sun was charged with having denied politics is the lifeline of economic work, for having glossed over class contradictions and for denying the existence of class struggle. He was said to have favoured autonomy of enterprises, a free market, fixing the output quota on the basis of households.

Sung Chen-t'ing (宋振庭)

Former member, Standing Committee, CCP Kirin Provincial Committee, with concurrent duties as director of its Propaganda Department.

Sung Chen-t'ing was dismissed from all posts he held both in and outside the Party by a resolution of the CCP Kirin Provincial Committee adopted on September 2, 1966, it was announced on Radio Changchun on the same day.

In the radio announcement, Sung was said to be an element of the anti-Party, anti-socialist black gang usurping various leading positions in education, culture and propaganda in Kirin Province for the past 16 years.

After the dismissal, meetings were held by the masses in Changchun to continue exposing and criticising Sung's anti-Party crimes. It was pointed out that for many years Sung had used his power to carry out criminal and unbridled activities against the Party, socialism and Mao Tse-tung's thought, in a vain attempt to pave the way for the restoration of capitalism. His "black" influence was alleged to have spread out far and wide among the circles of press, publication, education, literature and art in the province, the broadcast said.

Among the charges laid against Sung were:

— He slandered the poor and lower-middle peasants as being lazy, poor and backward who could not even support themselves;

— He spread the fallacious view that the danger of war no longer existed;

— He cursed the socialist system as being inferior even to the political system under the reign of Emperor K'ang Hsi of Ch'ing Dynasty.

Sung Shuo (宋硕)

Deputy director, University Work Department, CCP Peking Municipal Committee.

Sung Shuo, together with Lu P'ing and P'eng P'ei-yün, was accused in a big-character poster put up by seven members of the Department of Philosophy, Peking University, of trying to obstruct the mass struggle against Teng T'o and his friends, according to the *Jen-min Jih-pao* of June 2, 1966.

The poster, carrying the headline "What Have Sung Shuo, Lu P'ing and P'eng P'ei-yün Done in the Cultural Revolution," also accused Sung, Lu and P'eng of being Khrushchev revisionists.

Labelled an element of the "Three-Family Village black gang," Sung was denounced by the *Yang-ch'eng Wan-pao* of Canton, June 3, 1966 for his anti-Party programme.

174

In a long speech at a meeting of more than one thousand political instructors and some political cadres of institutions of higher learning in Peking, Sung was said to have presented an anti-Party and anti-socialist platform aimed at turning the political criticism against Teng T'o and his friends into an academic debate.

In the article, Sung was also charged with attempting to turn the tide of the cultural revolution, distorting the policy of encouraging contending voices, promoting bourgeois liberalisation, and urging "monsters and demons" to strike back at the mounting cultural revolution.

Sung Yü-hsi (宋玉璽)

Member, Standing Committee, CCP Honan Provincial
Committee and director of its Propaganda Department.

Sung Yü-hsi was openly denounced at a mass meeting attended by thousands of Party members and government functionaries on September 7, according to *Hung-wei Pao* of Canton, September 27, 1966.

Sung's anti-Party and anti-socialist crimes included:

— Rabidly opposing the study of Mao Tse-tung's writings and consistently refusing to publicise Mao Tse-tung's thought;

— Suppressing Lin Piao's inscription for the exhibition hall of Comrade Chao Yü-lu's deeds;

— Doing his utmost to oppose art and literature serving the workers, peasants, and soldiers, and energetically executing the Chou Yang revisionist programme for art and literature;

— Resisting Mao Tse-tung's directive on education and public health work.

— Actively rallying under his banner those who would surrender to him, accommodating renegades, cultivating demons and monsters, and enforcing the "three-famous principle"† and the "three-high policy"† for the purpose of corrupting the younger generation;

— Obstructing and sabotaging the Great Proletarian Cultural Revolution.

T'ang Mo (唐漠)

Playwright and film director.

As co-writer of the film, "Folks of Two Families," T'ang Mo shared the criticism made by two soldiers in their letter to the editors of *Chieh-fang-chün Pao,* published on August 5, 1966.

T'ao Hsiung (陶雄)

Dramatist; vice-president, Shanghai Academy of Peking Opera; deputy secretary-general, Shanghai Branch, Union of Chinese Stage Artists; deputy director, Shanghai Peking Opera Theatre; author of the article, "Great Changes in Peking Opera" and co-author of the play, "Hai Jui's Memorial to the Emperor."

As the co-author of the play, "Hai Jui's Memorial to the Emperor," which was branded as an "anti-Party, anti-socialist poisonous weed," T'ao Hsiung faced the same charges as those laid against Chou Hsin-fang (listed elsewhere in this section—Ed.).

T'ao Pai (陶白)

Deputy director, Propaganda Department, CCP Kiangsu Provincial Committee; deputy director, Cultural and Educational Department, CCP Kiangsu Provincial Committee; author of the article, "Run Party School Well."

T'ao Pai was accused in the *Hsin-hua Jih-pao* of June 14, 1966, of having forced newspapers and journals in Kiangsu Province to publish scores of his reactionary articles which insidiously vilified the Communist Party and Mao Tse-tung's ideology.

T'ao was also accused of:

— Having echoed the anti-Chinese chorus of imperialism, modern revisionism and reactionaries of all countries;

— Having collaborated with class enemies in attempting to restore capitalism;

— Having slandered the Party's struggle against Right opportunists as without factual basis.

Teng T'o (鄧拓)

Alternate secretary, Secretariat of the North China Bureau of the CCP Central Committee; secretary, Secretariat of the CCP Peking Municipal Committee; former editor, *Ch'ien Hsien,* theoretical organ of the Municipal Party Committee; former editor, *Jen-min Jih-pao.*

Teng T'o, accused of being the keeper of the "Three-family gangster inn" which he, Wu Han and Liao Mo-sha had established, was attacked in an article appearing in *Chieh-fang-chün Pao* of May 8, 1966 for assailing the Chinese Communist Party and socialism.

Teng and his "black gangsters" were said to have been attacking the Communist Party since 1961, when China was in serious difficulties caused by natural calamities and aggravated by the recall of Russian experts and suspension of Soviet aid.

In the Editor's Note of an article published in *Chung-kuo Ch'ing-nien Pao* of Peking, May 14, 1966, Teng and his "black gang" were condemned for writing articles, making reports, exchanging correspondence and holding talks to corrupt and harm youths, in an attempt to promote "peaceful evolution" among them and to pave the way for capitalist restoration.

Teng was denounced in an article appearing in *Jen-min Jih-pao* of May 17, 1966 for having defended Khrushchev revisionism in a report which he made at a meeting of political teachers and cadres on August 22, 1963.

In his report Teng was alleged to have said that Khrushchev had merely made a minor mistake and that his service to the international communist movement far outweighed his error.

The "Theory of Protecting Labour Power" written by Teng T'o in 1961 was described in an article published in *Ching-chi Yen-chiu,* No. 6, June 20, 1966 as a malicious slander against the Chinese Communist Party and the three red banners, i.e., the general line, the great leap forward and the people's commune.

Teng was accused in an article appearing in *Chung-kuo Ch'ing-nien Pao* of Peking, May 19, 1966 of attacking the Party, socialism, Marxism-Leninism, and the thought of Mao Tse-tung in a speech he made at an enlarged meeting of the Editorial Committee for "Booklet Series on Chinese History," "Booklet Series on History of Foreign Countries," and "Booklet Series on Geography" on October 13, 1962.

An article carried in *Chieh-fang Jih-pao* of Shanghai, May 21, 1966 traced the name "Three-Family Village" to a poem by Lu Yu, a Sung poet, about a high official who lost his post and was spending his last days in "Three-Family Village."

This article was yet another attack on Teng T'o and his "black gang" as counter-revolutionaries and revisionists.

In an article carried in *Ching-chi Yen-chiu*, No. 5, 1966, Teng was attacked for having poured out his deep hatred for the Party and socialism and for having hurled frantic accusations against the people's commune, even calling for the resumption of private farming.

Teng was said to have directed the spearhead of his attack at the commune's three-level ownership policy which has the production team as the base of production. He was said to have parroted Khrushchev's words in vilifying the commune movement as a "failure," declaring cynically that the commune "provides the people with only a pot of boiled water" and that "the boiled water is most delicious."

T'ien Han (田漢)

Chairman, Union of Chinese Drama Workers; vice-chairman, All-China Federation of Literary and Art Circles; author of the stage play, "Hsieh Yao-huan."

T'ien Han was accused in an article published in *Jen-min Jih-pao* of February 1, 1966 of insinuating in his stage play, "Hsieh Yao-huan," that the socialist society is beyond remedy and expressing the foreboding that the socialist boat will overturn.

In another article carried in the same paper on February 24, 1966, T'ien was charged with joining the reactionary front by idealising the practice of "speaking for the people" — in this way drawing an analogy between the socialist society and society ruled by the exploiting class.

As a leader in theatrical circles, T'ien was denounced in yet another *Jen-min Jih-pao* article of March 8, 1966 for being a representative of bourgeois literary and art dogma, instead of implementing the literary and art line of the Communist Party.

T'ien was alleged in an article published in *Hsi-chü Pao*, No. 3, 1966 to have abhorred plays eulogising the three red banners and depicting the new life of the socialist society. By pouring cold water on plays which glorify the heroic images of workers, peasants and soldiers, he was said to have alienated life from militant struggles and

178

led drama astray.

An article carried in *Kuang-ming Jih-pao* on May 5, 1966 provided examples of what T'ien Han said or wrote in the past ten years against "proletarian plays on contemporary revolutionary themes" — to prove that T'ien is a "representative of the bourgeois, revisionist line for art and literature."

T'ien was said to have opposed staging of plays on contemporary themes as early as 1956-57, when "bourgeois rightists" launched their first attack against the Communist Party's general and specific policies.

In an article appearing in *Yang-ch'eng Wan-pao* of Canton on July 28, 1966, T'ien Han was denounced as a "schemer" and "careerist" who "perpetrated anti-Party and anti-socialist crimes" under the pretext of "speaking for the people."

In an article in *Chieh-fang-chün Pao* of December 4, 1966, T'ien was accused of having sold himself and others to Chiang Kai-shek, betrayed the Communist Party, written anti-Communist plays for the Nationalist Government, taken part in the attack on Lu Hsün, etc.

T'ien Hsin (田信)

Former deputy secretary, Party Committee of Inner Mongolia University, Huhehot.

T'ien Hsin was suspended from his Party and other posts by the Party Committee of the Inner Mongolia Autonomous Region on August 29, 1966.

According to a Radio Huhehot announcement, T'ien was accused, together with two other Party secretaries of Inner Mongolia University, of opposing and undermining the Great Proletarian Cultural Revolution, coercing revolutionary students to become counter-revolutionary, and creating "a host of counter-revolutionary incidents."

T'ien Wei (田蔚)

Former director, Kwangtung People's Radio Station and concurrently director of Kwangtung Provincial Broadcasting Enterprise Administration Bureau.

T'ien Wei was accused by the *Yang-ch'eng Wan-pao* of Canton, July 2, 1966 of resisting the campaign against the Teng T'o black gang by refusing to relay actively broadcasts of the campaign.

179

Her anti-Party, anti-socialist crimes had been brought to light by employees and cadres of Kwangtung People's Radio Station.

She was also said to have falsely accused revolutionary elements of being "rightists" and "schemers" who tried to usurp leadership powers.

She even conducted illegal interrogation of those who wrote and put up big-character posters against her and had them shadowed.

Ts'ao Ti-ch'iu (曹荻秋)

Mayor of Shanghai and first secretary of the CCP Shanghai Municipal Committee.

Ts'ao Ti-ch'iu was denounced on November 22, 1966 for pursuing a bourgeois line at a rally of "revolutionary students, teachers and employees and workers," according to a report published in a newspaper called *The Revolutionary Uprising*.

Ts'ao and other members of the Municipal Party Committee were accused of leading the city committee into "carrying out a bourgeois reactionary line and suppressing the Left and shielding the Right during the whole course of the cultural revolution."

Ts'eng Tun (曾惇)

Former member, Standing Committee, CCP Hupeh Provincial Committee and director of its Propaganda Department.

Ts'eng Tun was denounced as a bourgeois rightist and faithful follower of the revisionist line of literature and art in a *Hupeh Jih-pao* article reproduced in *Hung-wei Pao* of Canton, September 5, 1966. Charges against him were:

— Persistently opposing the Party, socialism and the thought of Mao Tse-tung;

— Promoting bourgeois educational policies and viciously assailing the Party's general line for building socialism, the great leap forward and the people's commune;

— Serving as a faithful lackey of the Chou Yang black gang, backstage boss of the "Three-Family Village black gangsters" at Wuhan University, commander-in-chief of the Ch'eng Yun black gang in Wuhan's art and literary circles, and chief representative and ringleader in the Hupeh area of the group carrying

180

out the black, anti-Party and anti-socialist line of the former director of CCP Central Committee's Propaganda Department;

— Carrying out a whole series of counter-revolutionary activities in an attempt to take hold of the superstructure of the socialist economic base in the ideological sphere, swaying public opinion and making ideological and organisational preparations for the restoration of capitalism;

— Consistently and frenziedly opposing the mass movement for creative study and application of Mao Tse-tung's writings, doing everything possible to stall the implementation of the Provincial Party Committee's directive concerning the compilation of "Quotations from Chairman Mao Tse-tung," while observing to the letter "rules and regulations" restricting the publication of Mao's works.

Tung Pien (董邊)

Former director and chief editor, *Chung-kuo Fu-nü* [*Women of China*].

Tung Pien, who entrenched herself for a long time in *Chung-kuo Fu-nü's* propaganda bastion, opposed the red flag while waving the "red flag," claimed all revolutionary staff and workers of the monthly publication. Her crimes, according to Chinese mainland broadcasts, were listed below:

Tung resisted the leadership of the All-China Federation of Women and ruthlessly suppressed the opinions of the editorial department of *Chung-kuo Fu-nü*. She cheated the higher level and hid things from the lower level. Despite the repeated criticisms of the Federation, she kept spreading bourgeois and feudal influences through the periodical.

In the current great socialist cultural revolution, Tung adopted an extremely hostile attitude and refused to carry out the Party centre's directives. As late as May 1966, she continued to stand against publicising the cultural revolution in the periodical.

Wan Sheng-nan (萬盛南)

Lecturer, Department of History, Hofei Teachers College, Anhwei.

Wan Sheng-nan, according to the *Anhwei Jih-pao* of June 5, 1966, was a "loyal disciple" of Wu Han. Under the pretext of giving history lectures at the Hofei Teachers College, Wan "sold counter-revolutionary black merchandise."

Wan was alleged to have let out a great number of pernicious arrows in succession to viciously slander the Communist Party and the great thinking of Mao Tse-tung, in the hope of removing the cornerstone of socialism to pave the way for the restoration of capitalism.

He was said to have termed the works of Mao Tse-tung the "Sixth Classics" of China, saying that it was not a "must" to study such books. He was further alleged to have heaped praises on landlords, feudal officials and bad elements who once trampled on the people, spreading pernicious ideas of feudalism and capitalism through the media of newspapers, periodicals and classrooms.

Wang Chia-liu (汪家鏐)

> Former deputy secretary, CYL Peking Municipal Committee.

Wang Chia-liu was dismissed from the post of deputy secretary of the CYL Peking Municipal Committee on June 15, 1966 in accordance with a decision of the Peking Municipal Party Committee and the CYL Central Committee.

An article in *Chung-kuo Ch'ing-nien Pao* of Peking, June 23, 1966 entitled "Whoever Opposes the Thought of Mao Tse-tung Is a Counter-revolutionary," accused Wang and other leading members of the Peking municipal Party organ of having tried in every possible way to boycott and sabotage mass campaigns for study of Mao Tse-tung's works.

Wang and her colleagues were also accused of making a special effort to peddle the "black goods" of the "Three Family Village." After "Evening Talks at Yenshan" appeared in newspapers, she was said to have lost no time in openly recommending the series to cadres of CYL branches of all secondary schools in Peking.

Wang Chin-ting (王錦定)

> Director, Political Department for Culture and Education, CCP Tientsin Municipal Committee.

Radio Tientsin on August 2, 1966 broadcast a *Hopeh Jih-pao* report exposing the anti-Party crimes of Wang Chin-ting by revolutionary teachers, students and cadres of Tientsin.

The report said that Wang had tried in every possible way to sabotage the current cultural revolution of the proletariat. After the Teng T'o black gang was brought to light, he issued a directive forbidding the students in Tientsin to hold rallies to condemn the "Three-Family Village."

In 1964 when the students took part in a mass movement to study Mao Tse-tung's works, Wang—under the pretext of reducing students' heavy study assignments—forbade study of Mao Tse-tung's writings. At a Tientsin municipal conference on educational work last year, Wang said: "The students have studied many of Chairman Mao's articles in their political classes. The problem now is that we have to standardise political study and reduce the heavy study assignments. Students should, at the most, study two or three of Chairman Mao's articles during each school term."

As a result of Wang's ruling, many sections in charge of the study of Mao Tse-tung's works were dissolved.

Wang Hsiao-ch'uan (汪小川)

> Standing Committee member, CCP Kweichow Provincial Committee; director of the Committee's Propaganda Department; chief editor, *Kweichow Jih-pao*; vice-chairman, Study Committee of the 2nd CPPCC Kweichow Provincial Committee; director, Propaganda Department, CCP Kweichow Provincial Committee; elected in 1960 one of 39 members of the presidium of the 2nd CCP Kweichow Provincial Congress.

According to a Chinese mainland broadcast on June 5, 1966, Wang Hsiao-ch'uan published a series of nine short historical stories and other articles in Kweichow newspapers. Besides publishing a report on the investigation of rural areas, Wang later wrote the play, "Three-Generation Family." All these are anti-Party and anti-socialist "poisonous weeds."

Another broadcast heard on June 6, 1966 denounced Wang's anti-Party and anti-socialist crimes. Big-character posters, blackboard bulletins, wall news sheets, radio stations in the province, according to the broadcast, all concentrated their "firepower" on Wang.

183

Wang K'uang (王匡)

Former member, CCP Kwangtung Provincial Committee and deputy director of its Propaganda Department.

Wang K'uang was accused of having opposed the giving of political lessons for the purpose of thought reform, according to the *Hung-wei Pao* of Canton, October 21, 1966.

Wang was also accused of having opposed the linking of teaching and learning with practice, in the hope of separating teachers from practice and proletarian politics.

He was denounced in another *Hung-wei Pao* article of October 17, 1966 for his friendship with Ch'in Mu, a Kwangtung writer who was earlier denounced for anti-Party crimes.

According to the article, Wang had a high opinion of Ch'in Mu's literary works, and it was Wang who sponsored Ch'in's application for membership in the Communist Party.

Wang was under attack in one of the big-character posters put up at the offices of *Hung-wei Pao*. He was said to have told the chief editor of *Yang-ch'eng Wan-pao* (predecessor of *Hung-wei Pao*) to use his own brain and not just echo everything from Peking.

In another big-character poster that attacked Wang for his decadent bourgeois views on music, he was alleged to have showed the utmost contempt for songs praising the thought of Mao Tse-tung and others reflecting the achievements of workers, peasants and soldiers.

Wang P'ei-yü (王培育)

Former secretary, Party Committee, Chengchow University, and concurrently acting president of the University.

Wang P'ei-yü's alleged "counter-revolutionary crimes" were brought to light by the revolutionary teachers and students of Chengchow University who put up thousands upon thousands of "big-character posters" criticising the University's Party Committee and the handful of anti-Party, anti-socialist elements headed by Wang, since June 2, according to the *Yang-ch'eng Wan-pao* of Canton, August 7, 1966.

Wang was said to have employed every possible means to suppress the revolutionary movement of the students, including the launching of a "counter-attack" against those who criticised the Party Committee, the banning of meetings at the lower levels and the dismissal of four secretaries of the University's CYL branch. He was also accused of ignoring the directives issued by the CCP Honan Provincial Committee concerning the great cultural revolution and of refusing to implement these directives.

Wang Ting-tsao (王仃造)

Book publisher.

Wang Ting-tsao was criticised by members of Chingshui People's Commune, Machin *Hsien,* Chinghai, for his anti-Party crimes, according to a Sining Radio broadcast on July 27, 1966.

It was alleged that "Ho Cha Erh," a book compiled and published by Wang, was a poisonous weed opposing Mao Tse-tung's thought which had influenced the broad masses of Tibetans.

Members of the commune participating in denunciation meetings held in the latter part of July pledged to "wipe out completely" the anti-Party, anti-socialist black gang headed by Wang.

Wang Yüan-chien (王愿堅)

Wang Yüan-chien, a writer hailed by Chou Yang as the "most successful writer of rare accomplishment," was a class enemy who had wormed his way into the Party and the PLA, according to a *Jen-min Jih-pao* article of October 17, 1966.

Under the guise of "depicting revolutionary wars" and "portraying veteran cadres," Wang had for more than ten years perpetrated anti-Party and anti-socialist misdeeds. In the 1955 high-tide of agricultural co-operativisation, he published a novel, "Three Slips of Paper," assailing the Party's rural policies and undermining its flesh-and-blood ties with peasants. As an advance guard of the bourgeois rightists in 1958 in launching rabid attacks against the Party, he outrageously spoke of the Party's "stringent control at each level." He even openly clamoured for withdrawal of Party control in the fields of art and literature.

In 1958, Wang released another novel, "Rest," obliquely attacking the Great Leap Forward by saying: "We not only have fallen heroes but also martyrs of exhaustion." In his many works, he wilfully distorted the history of China's revolutionary struggles, depicting the Long March as something miserable and tragic. He depicted the revolutionary wars as "a bottomless sea of sufferings," in which heroic fighters of

185

the Red Army and the revolutionary people struggled desperately in the abyss of impending doom.

In Wang's works, there was practically nothing about the tremendous power of Mao Tse-tung's thought, nothing about the just cause of revolutionary wars and the prospects of inevitable victories. Instead, he did everything possible to render service to the "conciliatory line and approaches" espoused by Khrushchev revisionism, propagating bourgeois "human love" and disparagingly speaking of revolutionary wars as wrecking "individual happiness."

All these show that Wang on all counts was a "capable trumpeter" for Chou Yang's line on revisionist art and literature.

Wei Tung-ming (魏東明)

Former vice-president, University of Hunan.

Wei Tung-ming was denounced in an article by Ma Hsing-wu published in *Hunan Jih-pao* and reproduced in *Hung-wei Pao* of Canton on October 9, 1966. He was accused of having committed the following "crimes":

— Rabidly attacking the great thought of Mao Tse-tung by saying that "all men err, so does Chairman Mao..."

Specifically, Wei was opposed to Mao's ideas on literature and art and praised "literary works for national defense" which "have spread to other parts of the country from Yenan... and have become a new form of literature and art throughout the country."

— Playing the role of organiser and vanguard of bourgeois rightists in attacking the Party's "contending" policy, and in obstructing the Party's rectification campaign launched in 1957;

— Malignantly attacking the Party and the great socialist system, reversing the judgments passed on the Right opportunists and encouraging them to rise again;

— Remaining hostile to the mass movement and attempting to wreck the Great Proletarian Cultural Revolution.

Wu Han (吳晗)

Ex-member, CCP Peking Municipal Committee and former vice-mayor of Peking; historian specialising in Ming history who taught in Tsinghua University before the war and in Associated Southwest Universities in Kunming during the war; former president, Peking Television University; author of the historical play, "Hai Jui Dismissed from Office," and articles, including "Hai Jui Scolds the Emperor," "On Hai Jui," and "Self-Criticism on Hai Jui Dismissed from Office."

Wu Han's anti-Party and anti-socialist reactionary character was exposed in an article appearing in *Yang-ch'eng Wan-pao* of Canton, May 3, 1966, which summarises the academic discussion on his "Hai Jui Dismissed from Office" by leading newspapers and periodicals.

Wu was labelled a political opportunist who had consistently and for a long time opposed Communism, the people and the revolution.

Wu and the staff of Peking Television University were attacked in a *Jen-min Jih-pao* article of June 11, 1966 for misleading students of the University with regard to the nature of the socialist cultural revolution and attempting to substitute revisionist "liberalisation" for the Chinese Communist Party policy of proletarian revolution.

In a lengthy article carried in *Hung-ch'i*, No. 6, 1966, "Javelin-Throwing" — a collection of satirical essays written by Wu Han in the forties—was criticised for providing Right opportunists with a reactionary programme for the restoration of capitalism and for the overthrow of proletarian dictatorship.

According to the *Hung-ch'i* article, this book tears down Wu Han's mask as a "democratic fighter" and exposes him as an evil character fawning on the United States and hostile to the cause of Communism. The book claimed that Wu had, since the liberation, forged and publicised his own "revolutionary history of the forties" as a principal political weapon against the Communist Party and socialism.

Wu Han's book "Javelin-Throwing" was alleged to have assisted the Kuomintang reactionaries to continue their rule and to have promoted the third road espoused by American imperialism. This anti-Party, anti-Communist and anti-revolutionary book, the *Hung-ch'i* article claimed, threw an ideological javelin at the policies of the Party at a time, 1959, when China was striving to build socialism by implementing the Party's general line, the great leap forward and the people's commune.

Wu Han's counter-revolutionary face was further unveiled in an

187

article published by the *Jen-min Jih-pao* on May 20, 1966. The article contained material which belied Wu's claim that his grandfather was a tenant farmer and his father, an ordinary "public servant." It also attempted to show Wu Han's close ties with the late Dr. Hu Shih and other prominent Kuomintang officials.

Wu Ta-jen (吳大任)

Vice-president, Nank'ai University.

Radio Tientsin broadcast on August 1, 1966 a report on the denunciation of Wu Ta-jen by the revolutionary teachers and students of Nank'ai University.

The report said there was an abundance of evidence that Wu was an active element in promoting the bourgeois educational line. Born in a family of reactionary and bureaucratic landlords, he had all along opposed Communism and the masses politically.

Opposing Mao Tse-tung's line for educational work, Wu blatantly advocated the idea that the primary task of institutes of higher learning was to cultivate specialised personnel. To prevent the teachers and students of the university from studying Mao Tse-tung's works or taking part in political movements and productive labour, he forced them to teach and learn basic knowledge, fundamental theory and fundamental technology under strict rules.

Pretending to be solicitous about the future of the students, Wu spared no efforts to disseminate the bourgeois notion of seeking fame and personal gain among the students in an attempt to alienate them from politics, reality and labour, and to take the road of turning themselves into experts without being "red" ideologically.

Wu T'ien-shih (吳天石)

Director, Kiangsu Provincial Education Department.

Radio Nanking on July 8, 1966 broadcast the summary of an article, "It Is Necessary to Thoroughly Criticise the Reactionary Educational Thinking of Wu T'ien-shih." The article, published in *Hsinhua Jih-pao* of Nanking, contained these charges:

Over the past few years, Wu had written several books and many articles containing feudal, capitalist and revisionist poison. The book,

"A Talk on the Spirit and Methods of Learning by Ancient Chinese Scholars," which he wrote in co-operation with Ma Ying-kuo in particular was a representative masterpiece of his reactionary thought and a big poisonous weed.

Wu was said to have tried hard to follow Confucius and Mencius in words and to imitate ancient people in deeds. He advocated individualism, contrary to Mao Tse-tung's teachings on serving the people wholeheartedly. He favoured studying books first, in opposition to Chairman Mao's instructions of learning from practice. He endeavoured to reform proletarian educational undertaking and corrupt the younger generation and teachers with the world outlook of landlords and the bourgeoisie.

Yang Han-sheng (楊翰笙)

Former vice-chairman, All-China Federation of Literary and Art Cirlces; former secretary of its Party Committee.

In an article carried in *Chieh-fang-chün Pao* of December 27, 1966 entitled "The Counter-revolutionary Features of Yang Han-sheng," Yang was called a big rightist who had used the label of a "leftist writer" to swindle others.

Yang was alleged to have attacked Lu Hsün, the noted leftist writer who firmly implemented the correct Mao Tse-tung line. He was accused of having deliberately disparaged the thought of Mao Tse-tung as merely a question of "language" and "power of expression."

Yang was also charged with having openly denigrated the portrayal of heroic characters of the workers, peasants and soldiers and defended writers and artists who were imbued with the bourgeois world outlook.

Called a "black" secretary of the Federation of Literary and Art Circles, Yang was denounced in the article for having frequently held discussion and writing sessions with the object of turning the Federation into a "Petofi Club."

The *Kung-jen Jih-pao* of December 27, 1966 called for a resolute effort to thoroughly refute the bourgeois reactionary line and thoroughly smash the "Petofi Club" set up by Chou Yang [former deputy director, CCP CC Propaganda Department], Yang Han-sheng and the like.

As one of Chou Yang's right-hand men, Yang was a notorious counter-revolutionary revisionist, according to the paper. In the thirties,

Yang was a sworn partner of Chou Yang and company and a faithful executor of the Wang Ming opportunist line.

He was said to have lauded Chiang Kai-shek's virtues and actively co-ordinated with the anti-Communist and anti-people "politics" of Kuomintang reactionaries. After the liberation, he became the vanguard of the anti-Party and anti-socialist group, frenziedly opposing the great thought of Mao Tse-tung, resisting the Mao Tse-tung line for literature and art and disparaging Party leadership over literature and art. He was charged with having done his best to advocate literature and art of the thirties and the literary works of Soviet revisionism, in this way beating the gong to clear the way for restoring capitalism in China.

Yang Shu (楊述)

Former director, Propaganda Department, CCP Peking Municipal Committee; chief, Political Section, Department of Philosophy and Social Science, Chinese Academy of Sciences.

Yang Shu was labelled in *Chung-kuo Ch'ing-nien,* No. 12, 1966, as "one of the anti-Party, anti-socialist monsters and demons," and an outstanding member of the "anti-Party black gang of the 'Three-Family Village.' "

Yang was accused by seven editors of the periodical of:
— Viciously attacking Mao Tse-tung and his thought;
— Opposing the general line and slandering the great leap forward;
— Frenziedly opposing proletarian dictatorship and cursing the proletarian Left as hypocrites;
— Untiringly lauding the Right opportunists for their "moral courage" in opposing the Communist Party;
— Poisoning the minds of youths and promoting the plot of "peaceful evolution."

Yao Yu-chuang (姚佑莊)

Acting deputy director, Committee for Agriculture, Inner Mongolia Autonomous Region; president, Inner Mongolia branch, Academy of Agricultural Sciences; former leader of the "four clean-up" work team of Tumote, Inner Mongolia.

Yao Yu-chuang was accused of being an active member of the counter-revolutionary black gang headed by Chang Ju-chang, which committed the crimes of promoting the line of revisionism and national splittism in the Inner Mongolia Autonomous Region.

Yü Hsiu (余修)

Vice-governor, Shantung Province; director, Department of Culture & Education, CCP Shantung Provincial Committee.

Yü Hsiu was denounced by the broad masses of workers, peasants and soldiers in Shantung Province as the "manager of the Shantung provincial branch of the 'Three-Family Village' gangster inn," according to a Tsinan Radio broadcast on May 27, 1966.

The anti-Party, anti-socialist crimes committed by Yü, according to the broadcast, included:

— Having written articles and made speeches to curse and vilify Mao Tse-tung's thought and slander the Party as being undemocratic;

— Having deliberately sown seeds of discord in the relations between the Party and the people in a vain attempt to undermine the socialist system and overthrow the proletarian dictatorship, thus paving the way for the restoration of capitalism;

— Having made malicious attacks against the people's commune;

— Having expressed the opinion that anti-Party and anti-socialist bourgeois intellectuals should be dealt with in a democratic way and that the practice of dictatorship over landlords, rich peasants, reactionaries, bad elements and rightists should be discontinued.

Yü Ling (于伶)

Vice-chairman, Shanghai Branch, Union of Chinese Writers; vice-chairman, Shanghai Municipal Federation of Literary and Art Circles; co-writer of the screenplay, "Senior Li, Junior Li, and Old Li."

Kung-jen Jih-pao on June 15, 1966 accused Yü Ling of being one of the four co-authors of the film "Senior Li, Junior Li, and Old Li," which had come under attack. He was further accused of having used extremely vicious means to assail the socialist system, slander the working class, distort the Party's policy on physical culture and deride the mass sports movement.

191

The article says: "We must resolutely struggle against this poisonous weed and pull it up by the roots."

Yü Pei-ch'en (于北辰)

> Former deputy secretary, Party Committee, Inner Mongolia University, Huhehot, and concurrently vice-president of the University.

Yü Pei-ch'en was removed from all his Party and non-Party posts in accordance with a decision of the Party Committee of the Inner Mongolia Autonomous Region made on August 29, 1966, according to a Huhehot Radio broadcast.

Yeh and two other Party secretaries of the Party Committee of Inner Mongolia University were alleged to have actively opposed and undermined the Great Proletarian Cultural Revolution, coerced revolutionary students to become counter-revolutionary, and created "a host of counter-revolutionary · incidents."

After the incidents, Yü and others were said to have distorted facts and confused issues to cover up their errors, and when their errors were finally brought to light, they made false self-examinations in an attempt to continue their deception of the masses.

Yu Yung-nien (俞永年)

> Acting deputy director of Industry and Communications, Political Department, Inner Mongolia Autonomous Region; former Standing Committee member, Party organ of the "four clean-up" work team of Tumote, Inner Mongolia.

Yu Yung-nien was accused of being an active member of the counter-revolutionary black gang headed by Chang Ju-chang, which committed the crimes of promoting the line of revisionism and national splittism in the Inner Mongolia Autonomous Region.

Yüan Hsiao-p'ing (袁小平)

> Former deputy director, Ch'angch'un Film Studio.

Radio Changchun broadcast on September 18, 1966 a news report carried in *Kirin Jih-pao* which said that "revolutionary employees of Ch'angch'un Film Studio have dragged out another anti-Party and anti-socialist element, Yüan Hsiao-p'ing, former deputy director of the Studio."

"A host of evidence shows that Yüan is a representative of the bourgeoisie who has wormed his way into the Party and also an out-and-out counter-revolutionary revisionist. He is a faithful lackey of Chou Yang, ringleader of the black line in literary and art circles.

"From 1956 to 1959, when class enemies launched a frenzied attack on the Party, Yüan blatantly opposed the Party's absolute leadership over the film industry by clamouring that 'putting politics first' does not necessarily mean that everything must be placed under politics.

"Advocating the idea that 'putting politics and Mao Tse-tung's thought first' might affect the development of creative art, Yüan in 1956 worked out a draft proposal on free expression in making films. But the proposal which is dominated by revisionism advocates bourgeois liberalisation in film production and promotes material enjoyment as well. As a result, he was transferred to take up physical labour in August 1960. When he returned to the studio in September 1961, he showed no sign of repentance. He opposed giving publicity to Mao Tse-tung's thought in motion pictures and eulogising Mao Tse-tung's thought in scripts. On the other hand, he went to great lengths to produce films on emperors, kings, generals, prime ministers, scholars and beauties as media for promoting the bourgeois and revisionist black line on literature and art.

"Revolutionary employees of Ch'angch'un Film Studio pledged to expose thoroughly and criticise Yüan's crimes and to pull him down and discredit him completely to ensure that Mao Tse-tung's thought can take deep root in the minds of all workers in the film industry."

Yüan Nai-ch'en (袁乃晨)

Playwright and film director.

Yüan Nai-ch'en was the co-writer and director of the film, "Folks of Two Families," produced by Ch'angch'un Film Studio. As such, he was taken to task by two soldiers in their letter to the editors of *Chieh-fang-chün Pao,* published on August 5, 1966.

Films, plays, books, and literary and art works branded as "poisonous weeds" or "poisoned arrows"

Early Spring in February (早春二月)

Produced by Peking Film Studio in 1963.

The film "Early Spring in February" was branded as a poisonous weed in the *Jen-min Jih-pao* of September 15, 1964 for seeking to whitewash class contradiction and propagate bourgeois individualism and humanism.

The film, based on the novel *February* written by Jou Shih (柔石) 30 years ago, posed the cardinal issue of right and wrong in the fields of art and literature — what characters should be praised and what ideas propagated by proletarian literature and art?

The Lin Family Shop (林家舖子)

Produced by Peking Film Studio, 1959.

The film "The Lin Family Shop" was roundly attacked in articles published in *Jen-min Jih-pao,* May 29, 1965, *Chung-kuo Ch'ing-nien Pao* of Peking, May 29, 1965, *Ta-kung Pao* of Peking, May 29, 1965, and *Kuang-ming Jih-pao* of Peking, May 29, 1965, for glorifying the bourgeoisie, vilifying the working class, covering up class exploitation, obliterating class contradiction, and preaching class co-operation.

The film was adapted by Hsia Yen (夏衍) in 1958 from a novel bearing the same title written by Shen Yen-ping (沈雁冰) under the pen name of Mao Tun in 1932.

When the film was first shown in 1959 and later in 1965, both Shen Yen-ping and Hsia Yen had been dismissed from their posts. Shen was sacked from his post of Minister of Culture in accordance with a decision of the 1st session of the 3rd NPC held at the end of 1964. Hsia Yen's dismissal from the post of Vice-Minister of Culture was approved by the State Council at its meeting on April 30, 1965.

194

Nightless City (不夜城)

Produced by Shanghai Film Studio.

The film "Nightless City" was denounced as a poisonous weed in the *Chung-kuo Ch'ing-nien Pao* of Peking, June 14, 1965, for glorifying the bourgeoisie, publicising the reactionary theory of bourgeois humanism and spreading the decadent bourgeois way of life.

The film was said to have taken the bourgeois stand in heaping praises on the capitalist. Therefore, "Nightless City," according to the paper, should be thoroughly exposed and criticised.

The film was also alleged, in the *Jen-min Jih-pao* of June 17, 1965, to have seriously distorted the peaceful transformation of the bourgeoisie by declaring that there was actually no class struggle in such "peaceful transformation."

Laying Siege to the City (兵臨城下)

A product of Ch'angch'un Film Studio; screenplay adapted by Pai Jen and Lin Nung.

This film was identified as a poisonous weed publicising revisionist ideas in the *Jen-min Jih-pao* of April 24, 1966. In was said that the film completely ran counter to Mao Tse-tung's thought on people's war and distorted the history of the War of Liberation. It did not model the image of the PLA heroes but spared no effort in portraying, eulogising and idealising the enemy. It did not depict the final battle between the revolutionary and counter-revolutionary forces but took the bourgeois stand and freely publicised the theory of class conciliation and the bourgeois theory of human nature.

The Press Gang (抓壯丁)

Produced by Pa I (August First) Film Studio of the People's Liberation Army.

This film was undesirable because it distorted history, vilified the working people, called for obliteration and reconciliation of the class struggle and openly defended and glossed over the guilt of the landlord class, according to an article in the *Jen-min Jih-pao* of May 12, 1966.

The film was said to have protected instead of hitting at the landlord class, glossed over instead of exposing the reactionary rule of the Kuomintang, vilified instead of praising the working people.

Sisters of the Stage (舞台姊妹)

> Produced by Hsia Yen and other persons advocating the motion picture tradition of the thirties.

The film was condemned as a big poisonous weed personally planted by Hsia Yen and other persons in an article in the *Jen-min Jih-pao* of May 16, 1966. The article called the film an anti-Party, anti-socialist black line contrary to Mao Tse-tung's thought — a reflection of the class struggle on the literary and art front.

The film eulogised the personal struggle of the bourgeoisie and opposed the socialist revolution for the promotion of proletarian and eradication of bourgeois ideology. It publicised and extolled bourgeois humanism, obliterated class contradictions and eliminated the class struggle.

In ideological content and form of presentation, the film was said to be a mixture of those vile and filthy things of the films of the thirties. It revived the bourgeois films of the thirties and was an example set by Hsia Yen and other persons for promoting the films of the thirties.

Red Sun (紅日)

> Based on the screenplay by Ch'ü Pai-yin, author of "Monologue on the Question of Creating New Films."

The film was labelled as a poisonous weed transposing light and darkness in an article published in *Jen-min Jih-pao* of May 29, 1966. It was said to have seriously tampered with history, vilified the People's Liberation Army and idealised the enemy.

In addition, the film had distorted the revolutionary war of the people and shamelessly heaped praises on the reactionary clique headed by Chiang Kai-shek.

The film was produced at the time when China was ravaged by natural calamities to serve the reactionary political needs of the class enemies, the article said.

Senior Li, Junior Li and Old Li (大李，小李，老李)

> Produced by Shanghai T'ienma Studio, directed by Hsieh Chin, and written by Yü Ling, Yeh Ming, Hsieh Chin and Liang Yen-ching.

Described as an "anti-Party, anti-socialist big poisonous weed," the film was called a serious challenge to the working class and a rabid attack against the proletarian regime in the *Jen-min Jih-pao* of June 15, 1966.

The film was said to have viciously attacked the socialist system, vilified the working class by every possible means and distorted Party guidelines for physical culture.

The film was alleged to have presented a gloomy picture of the socialist cause, giving the impression that production was run in a disorderly manner and that the masses of workers, denied democratic life, were opposed to the leadership everywhere.

Sailing a Thosuand Li against the Wind (逆風千里)

Produced by Chuchiang Film Studio and written by Chou Wan-ch'eng and Fang Huang in 1962.

The writer and the director of the film were accused in an article in the *Jen-min Jih-pao* of June 25, 1966 of idealising the reactionary troops of Chiang Kai-shek.

The article gave an account of interviews with the cadres and fighters of a certain People's Liberation Army unit participating in the shooting of the film on location.

The article charged that the standpoint, viewpoint, thoughts and feelings, and way of life of the writer and the director of the film were completely in accord with those of the Kuomintang reactionaries.

The Peach-Blossom Fan (桃花扇)

Produced by Sian Film Studio and written by Mei Ch'ien and Sun Ching.

Not an ordinary film about love affairs, the film was a political play praising the "Tunglin spirit" and advocating counter-revolutionary insurrection, according to the *Jen-min Jih-pao* of July 12, 1966.

The film was said to have been produced with the support and encouragement of the "black gang" headed by Chou Yang, former deputy director, CCP CC Propaganda Department.

The political designs and objectives of the writers of the film, according to the paper, were deeply engraved in the play.

The film was alleged to have vigorously publicised and extolled the counter-revolutionary "moral courage" of those who were loyal to the overthrown dynasty, and viciously vilified by insinuation the Communist Party and the dictatorship of the proletariat.

Football Fans (球迷)

Produced by Shanghai T'ienma Film Studio in 1962;
written and directed by Hsü Ch'ang-lin.

The film "Football Fans" was branded as "a big, anti-Party, anti-socialist poisonous weed linked with Chou Yang's black line for literature and art," in the *T'i-yü Pao* of Peking, August 17, 1966.

In the guise of a satirical comedy, this "counter-revolutionary" film was said to have frenziedly attacked the Party's general line for building socialism, the great leap forward and the people's commune.

The film also viciously cursed the leadership of the Communist Party and shamelessly disparaged the working class.

The film was made at a time when class enemies at home and abroad, taking advantage of China's economic difficulties brought about by three consecutive years of natural calamities, conducted a big anti-China chorus. The black gangsters in literary and art circles thought that their opportunity had come. Those at the higher and lower levels worked in collusion to form factions for selfish ends. They purposefully launched rabid attacks against the Party and socialism, and banged the gong to pave the way for the restoration of capitalism, the paper said.

The film was written and directed by a counter-revolutionary "fighter," with the assistance of Ch'ü Pai-yin, an advance guard of the black gang in film circles. Their back-stage "boss" was Chou Yang, ringleader of the black gang in literary and art circles, it added.

In an article in the *Jen-min Jih-pao* of August 17, 1966, the film "Football Fans" was called a "poisonous melon" grown on the anti-Party, anti-socialist vine of literature and art.

The film exhibited an abundance of bourgeois modes of life, such as bizarre costumes and other monstrosities, to spread the poisonous stuff of the bourgeoisie and modern revisionism. It made use of much ambiguous dialogue and obscure scenes to attack — by insinuation — the Communist Party, socialist society and proletarian dictatorship, the article alleged.

Folks of Two Families (二家人)

Produced by Ch'angch'un Film Studio, 1963; written
by Lin Mo-ch'en and directed by Yüan Nai-ch'en.

In the guise of depicting the struggle between the socialist and capitalist roads in the agricultural co-operation movement in the country-side, the film "Folks of Two Families"—called a big poisonous weed against the Party and socialism in a *Jen-min Jih-pao* article of August 5, 1966—viciously disparaged the poor peasants, agitated for independent operation of private plots and beat the drum for the restoration of capitalism.

The film was said to have taken the reactionary stand of the land-lord class and the bourgeoisie.

The same paper also denounced "Folks of Two Families" for distorting the class struggle in rural areas and attacking all the working people. It condemned the film for trying to incite the poor and lower-middle peasants to rise against the Communist Party with "a handful of anti-Party elements."

The August 5 *Chieh-fang-chün Pao* listed ten big crimes of the film "Folks of Two Families." The more serious ones were:

— The makers of the film spread poison and wanted to prepare for a capitalist restoration;
— The film viciously slandered the system of rural co-operatives;
— It attacked the Party's grain purchasing and selling policy, which was opposed to the interests of the people;
— Party leadership was completely ignored.

King of Ch'i Looks for a General (齊王求將)

Produced by Chuchiang Film Studio, 1962; directed by T'ao Chin and written by T'ao Chin and others.

The film "King of Ch'i Looks for a General" was branded as a big poisonous weed that agitated for a return to counter-revolution, according to the *Hung-wei Pao* of Canton, September 9, 1966.

Called an extremely reactionary, counter-revolutionary film, "King of Ch'i Looks for a General" was said to be a virulent attack on the leadership of the Communist Party, on socialism and the dictatorship of the proletariat. The film was also denounced for trying to incite the "overthrown class enemies" and dismissed officials to struggle for regaining their lost power.

Like "Hai Jui Dismissed from Office," "Hsieh Yao-huan" and "Li Hui-niang," the film "King of Ch'i Looks for a General" also satirised the present through incidents in the past and made oblique attacks.

Hai Jui Dismissed from Office (海瑞罷官)

A new historical play written by Wu Han, a former vice mayor of Peking.

The play "Hai Jui Dismissed from Office" was denounced for "making veiled criticism of contemporary people with ancient people," according to an article first published in *Wen-hui Pao* of Shanghai and reproduced in *Jen-min Jih-pao* of November 30, 1966.

The play idealised all "honest, incorrupt officials" as things which transcended class, implying that their existence was divorced from and independent of the dictatorship of the landlord class.   It advocated the idea that there was no need for the oppressed people to make revolution, to go through any serious struggle, and to smash the state machinery. Provided they bowed to "honest, incorrupt officials" and abided by the "law" of the feudal dynasty, they could wipe out the corrupt officials in one stroke and "lead a good life."

The play was said to have made it clear that "honest, incorrupt officials," not class struggle, provided the motive force for propelling history forward.

The article by Yao Wen-yüan, formerly chief editor of *Wen-hui Pao* of Shanghai and now a member of the group in charge of the cultural revolution under the CCP Central Committee, condemned the play as a poisonous weed.

Hsieh Yao-huan (謝瑤環)

A stage play written by T'ien Han in 1956.

T'ien Han's play "Hsieh Yao-huan" was identified as a poisonous weed and a counter-current in literature and art against socialism in an article carried in *Hsi-chü Pao,* No. 2, 1966.

The play was said to have glorified "speaking for the people" through the image of Hsien Yao-huan as the heroine of the play.

In denouncing the ideological content of "Hsieh Yao-huan" as reactionary, the article said that the play — in playing up and advocating "speaking for the people"—regarded the present relationship between the Communist Party and the people as identical to the antagonistic relationship between the feudal ruling group and the people.

The play was said to have compared the three difficult years brought about by natural calamities to the crisis of a feudal dynasty and vilified

200

the socialist society as one under the domination of bad characters, in this way making it impossible to implement correct guidelines and policies.

The article noted that the play "Hsieh Yao-huan" was "poisonous" in these aspects:

— It eulogised and promoted virtues that were above class...

— It depicted the hard and miserable life of the people, and their flight to other places...

— It traced the basic cause of the hard life of the people to the fact that they had lost their land...

Li Hui-niang (李慧娘)

A ghost play written by Meng Ch'ao in 1961.

The ghost play "Li Hui-niang" which appeared in 1961 when the class struggle was very acute was labelled a poisonous weed in an article carried in *Hsi-chü Pao,* No. 3, 1966.

Based on a certain historical theme, "Li Hui-niang" was said to have made veiled criticism of contemporary people with ancient characters.

In Act II of "Li Hui-niang," "P'ei Shun-ch'ing angrily denounces 'the misrule of the powerful, crafty ministers' on the one hand. On the other hand, after demanding Chia Szu-tao to explain 'why the people are robbed of their salt' and 'why private land is seized,' he points out that 'there are now people in distress all over the land under the rule of the Sung Dynasty.' "

As a ghost play, "Li Hui-niang" portrays the heroine as a malicious spirit with unlimited magic power and the incarnation of "righteousness."

Putting on the mantle of historical plays, "Li Hui-niang" was said to have tried to cover up its attack against realities. The play was described as a product of the appearance of the ideological counter-current which attempted to "overturn the socialist boat" during the three successive difficult years.

In "Li Hui-niang's" "In Place of a Postscript," the author declared that "the play was written to vent my emotional feelings and to make known what I had in mind."

Hai Jui's Memorial to the Emperor (海瑞上疏)

A stage play written by Chou Hsin-fang, prominent
Peking opera actor, T'ao Hsiung and Hsü Ssu-yen.

The play "Hai Jui's Memorial to the Emperor" was called a big poisonous weed in an article in the *Jen-min Jih-pao* of June 15, 1966.

The article noted that the play, just as "Hai Jui Scolds the Emperor" and "Hai Jui Dismissed from Office," was a poisonous spawn of the political line of Right opportunists. All these three plays sang the same tune, adopted the same counter-revolutionary approach and pursued the same counter-revolutionary objective.

The play which was first presented in 1959 and was again staged in Peking towards the end of 1961, was said to have echoed the big anti-China chorus conducted by American imperialists, modern revisionists and reactionaries of all countries.

On Our Ancient Scholars' Spirit and Method of Study
(談談我國古代學者的學習精神和學習方法)

A book written jointly by Wu T'ien-shih and Ma
Ying-po in 1961.

The book "On Our Ancient Scholars' Spirit and Method of Study" which appeared at a time when the "Three-Family Village" made its debut, was described in an article carried in *Chung-kuo Ch'ing-nien*, No. 13, 1966 as a big poisonous weed smearing the Party and the thought of Mao Tse-tung.

The book advocated that "after reading the teachings of ancient sages, one must not only understand them thoroughly but also abide by them strictly." This view was considered as an attempt to induce the younger generation to worship the ancients and an act to subvert proletarian dictatorship.

The book was said to have tried to defend the feudal educational system aimed at training students according to their aptitude and calibre —a system which was overtly opposed to the educational line laid down by the Communist Party.

In another article carried in the same periodical, the book "On Our Ancient Scholars' Spirit and Method of Study" was considered harmful to young people. Lauding the spirit of ancient scholars in pursuing their studies, the authors of the book tried to sell youths the method

202

Of study which was divorced from politics and fostered the bourgeois notion of seeking fame and personal gain.

The article noted that in the name of recommending the ancients' spirit and method of study to young people, the book was peddling feudal and capitalist merchandise, in an attempt to lure them away from revolutionary struggles and the teachings of Mao Tse-tung.

History of Development of Chinese Motion Pictures (中國電影發展史)

Published by Chinese Motion Picture Publishing House, 1963; edited by Ch'eng Hsi-hua.

The book "History of Development of Chinese Motion Pictures" was condemned as a "big anti-Party, anti-socialist poisonous weed" in an article published in *Jen-min Jih-pao* of April 19, 1966.

The book praised highly the work of Hsia Yen, T'ien Han and others, who the article said were trying to replace the Mao Tse-tung line for literature and art with a bourgeois line.

In another article carried in *Wen-i Pao,* No. 4, 1966, the book was called a "trump card" put down by the advocates of literature and art of the thirties.

The book was said to have distorted the history of the left-wing motion picture movement in the Kuomintang-occupied areas in the thirties, glossing over the weak points of the films produced at that time and evading the vital issues. It kept silent about the bourgeois theory of humanism, class conciliation and individualism which pervaded the left-wing films of that period.

Collecting Shells in the Sea of Art (藝海拾貝)

A book written by Ch'in Mu in popular language.

The book "Collecting Shells in the Sea of Art" was criticised in an article carried in *Wen-hsüeh P'ing-lun,* No. 2, 1966 because its views on the three questions of a fundamental character — orientation, class character and social function—deviated from the Marxist theories of literature and art.

The book left entirely untouched the point that literature and art must serve the workers, peasants and soldiers. It interpreted the policy of "letting a hundred flowers blossom" as a means of bringing about diversification in form, style and content to please the readers.

Talks on Basic Knowledge about the Party (關於黨的基本認識談話)

A book written and published by the Propaganda Department of the former CCP Peking Municipal Committee.

The book "Talks on Basic Knowledge about the Party" was condemned in an article carried in *Jen-min Jih-pao,* September 15, 1966 for attacking Mao Tse-tung's leadership in the Party and trying to propagate the "theory of class conciliation" of "modern revisionism."

The book, which runs to 65,000 words, was said to have entirely omitted to mention "the thought of Mao Tse-tung."

It was also said to have ignored class struggle and the dictatorship of the proletariat.

"Chairman Mao and the Party centre have always attached great importance to developing democracy within the Party as well as criticism and self-criticism..." according to the author of the article.

"However, we must also remember Chairman Mao's teaching that we must first of all distinguish friend from foe, and that our democracy is for the people and not for reactionaries...

"As for the hostile elements like them [the writers of "Talks on Basic Knowledge about the Party"]... they can only be told to behave themselves and cannot be allowed to speak and act as they please."

CHAPTER II

Policy Pronouncements on the Great Cultural Revolution

Official pronouncements in the form of Jen-min Jih-pao or Hung-ch'i editorials, reproduced in full or in part in this chapter, describe uninterrupted struggle on the ideological and cultural front in China for the past 16 years. This struggle is described as one between the forces attempting a political and economic restoration of capitalism and the forces opposing them.

This is a sharp and violent class struggle which is far from mere polemics on paper. Bourgeois intellectuals are charged with having tried to assert themselves and to shape public opinion for a come-back.

These policy documents draw attention to the revisionist intellectuals of the Petofi Circle who touched off the 1956 Hungarian Revolution and the fact that the Khrushchev revisionist group has usurped the leadership power of the Soviet Union.

The efforts of bourgeois revisionist groups to oppose the line of the great socialist cultural revolution, to resist the guiding principle on the question of class and class struggle, and finally to seize important cultural positions have the sole purpose, the articles say, of preparing public opinion for a counter-revolutionary coup and for turning proletarian dictatorship into bourgeois dictatorship. — Ed.

Everything reactionary is the same: if you don't hit it, it won't fall. This is also like sweeping the floor; as a rule, where the broom does not reach, the dust does not vanish of itself.

—Mao Tse-tung

(The Situation and Our Policy after the Victory in the War of Resistance against Japan—August 13, 1945).

A Vital Question That Touches People's Souls

The following editorials from the *Jen-min Jih-pao* sounded the call to carry forward the great cultural revolution of the proletariat. The revolution was to rage in the ideological and cultural fields against bourgeois representatives, notably a "horde of monsters" who had entrenched themselves. Once so established, they were charged with seeking to subvert socialism in an attempt to wipe out proletarian control.

Explaining that criticism, struggle and revolution can alone propel the socialist cause forward, these documents warn that the struggle against bourgeois representatives in literary and art circles is one of life and death.—Ed.

A Great Revolution That Touches People to Their Very Souls

China today is in a new era of great change after the seizure of political power by the proletariat and is in a new situation in which the socialist revolution becomes deeper every day. It finds itself in the strong current of a great socialist cultural revolution which touches people to their very souls.

The gradual deepening of the socialist revolution and of the socialist education movement inevitably brings the question of the proletarian cultural revolution to the fore. Whether or not you are genuinely in favour of the socialist revolution or whether you are even against the socialist revolution is bound to manifest itself in your attitude towards the proletarian cultural revolution. This is a question that touches people's souls, in other words, their world outlook, a question of whether the proletarian or the bourgeois world outlook dominates people's minds. It is a struggle between the two antagonistic world outlooks.

Like two armies facing each other in battle, the two antagonistic world outlooks, that is, the antagonistic world outlooks of the proletariat and the bourgeoisie, are locked in a struggle which invariably results in one vanquishing the other. Either you crush me, or I crush you. Either the East Wind prevails over the West Wind, or the West Wind prevails over the East Wind. There is no middle road.

The Party and Chairman Mao teach us to arm ourselves with the proletarian world outlook to change our subjective world while changing the objective world. But the representatives of the bourgeoisie and the bourgeois "scholars and authorities" insist on dragging us into the quagmire of the bourgeois world outlook and subverting socialism. Confronted by our sworn enemies, we must rally under the great banner of Mao Tse-tung's thought and wage resolute and relentless struggles against the anti-Party and anti-socialist bourgeois representatives and "scholars and authorities." Only by waging a resolute struggle against them and dissipating the evil bourgeois winds can people free themselves from the influence of bourgeois ideology, traditions and force of habit, pass the great test of socialist revolution and march forward in giant strides along the broad road of socialist revolution.

It is erroneous, contrary to Marxism-Leninism and at variance with dialectics to say that there are no contradictions in socialist society. How can there be no contradictions? There will still be contradictions after a thousand or ten thousand or even a hundred million years. Contradictions will exist in the universe even after the destruction of the earth and the extinction of the sun. All things are in a flux of contradiction, struggle and change. This is the Marxist-Leninist outlook. The essence of Marxism is critical and revolutionary. Its basic spirit is criticism, struggle and revolution. This alone can constantly propel our socialist cause forward.

Chairman Mao often quotes the saying, "the tree may prefer calm, but the wind will not subside," to tell us that class struggle is an objective fact and is independent of man's will. The bourgeoisie is daily trying to influence us and corrupt us. The current struggle has been provoked entirely by the representatives of the bourgeoisie. Moreover, they have been preparing and waging it for many years. We cannot avoid it even if we want to. Struggle is life. If you don't struggle against him, he will struggle against you. If you don't hit him, he will hit you. If you don't wipe him out, he will wipe you out. This is a life-and-death class struggle. It is dangerous to lose vigilance in such a struggle.

Chairman Mao says:

> ...while we recognise that in the general development of history the material determines the mental and social being determines social consciousness, we also—and indeed must—recognise the reaction of mental on material things, of social consciousness on social being and of the superstructure on the economic base.

Bourgeois ideology is still very powerful and exerts an immense influence in our country. The question of who will win out in the ideological sphere, the proletariat or the bourgeoisie, has not yet been settled.

We must have a firm grip on ideology and the superstructure, theoretical and academic work, literature and art, etc., so as to consolidate the ideological positions of the proletariat, strengthen the dictatorship of the proletariat and consolidate the economic base of socialism.

The representatives of the overthrown bourgeoisie are still trying to tighten their grip on ideology and the superstructure, theoretical and academic work, literature and art, etc. On the cultural front, they have worked hard to let emperors and kings, generals and prime ministers, scholars and beauties, foreign idols and dead men dominate the stage and have carried on anti-Party and anti-socialist propaganda with a view to moulding public opinion in preparation for the restoration of capitalism.

We must never regard our struggle against them as mere polemics on paper which do not affect the general situation. It was a number of revisionist literary men of the Petofi Club who acted as the shock brigade in the Hungarian events. The turbulent wind precedes the mountain storm. This is the prelude to the vain attempt of the revisionists at a counter-revolutionary restoration.

Therefore, the current sharp class struggle we are engaged in on the ideological and cultural front is a struggle to shatter all schemes for capitalist restoration ideologically and to dig out the ideological roots of revisionism, a struggle to strengthen the dictatorship of the proletariat and defend Mao Tse-tung's thought. This struggle must end in victory, and there is no doubt that it can and will end in victory.

We should attach great importance to the role of ideology, of proletarian and socialist ideology, of Marxism-Leninism and Mao Tse-tung's thought. For us communists, to attach no importance to the role of ideology would be philistine or mechanical materialism. We must arouse the enthusiasm of the people and broaden their horizon about the future by means of the great thought of Mao Tse-tung and our great just cause, so that they will unswervingly march ahead! The Chinese people must rid themselves of the influence of all the traditions and forces of habit of thousands of years left over by the exploiting classes and the influence of imperialism. Once freed from all these influences, they will generate a mighty force and play a powerful role. We must enhance our communist consciousness and consciously foster communist ideology. We must not be waverers, we must be thoroughgoing revolutionaries. We must always hold high the great red banner of Mao Tse-tung's thought, sweep away all monsters and carry the great proletarian cultural revolution through to the end.

(From a translation of an editorial carried in
Jen-min Jih-pao of June 2, 1966)

*   *   *

Sweep Away All Monsters

An upsurge is occurring in the Great Proletarian Cultural Revolution in socialist China whose population accounts for one-quarter of the world's total.

For the last few months, in response to the militant call of the Central Committee of the Chinese Communist Party and Chairman Mao hundreds of millions of workers, peasants and soldiers and vast numbers of revolutionary cadres and intellectuals, all armed with Mao Tse-tung's thought, have been sweeping away a horde of monsters that have entrenched themselves in ideological and cultural positions. With the tremendous and impetuous force of a raging storm, they have smashed the shackles imposed on their minds by the exploiting classes for so long in the past, routing the bourgeois "specialists," "scholars," "authorities" and "venerable masters" and sweeping every bit of their prestige into the dust.

Chairman Mao has taught us that class struggle does not cease in China after the socialist transformation of the system of ownership has in the main been completed. "The class struggle between the proletariat and the bourgeoisie, the class struggle between different political forces, and the class struggle in the ideological field between the proletariat and the bourgeoisie will continue to be long and tortuous and at times will even become very acute. The proletariat seeks to transform the world according to its own world outlook, and so does the bourgeoisie. In this respect, the question of which will win out, socialism or capitalism, is still not really settled."

The class struggle in the ideological field between the proletariat and the bourgeoisie has been very acute right through the 16 years since China's liberation. The current great socialist cultural revolution

210

is precisely a continuation and development of this struggle. The struggle is inevitable. The ideology of the proletariat and the ideology of all the exploiting classes are diametrically opposed to each other and cannot co-exist in peace. The proletarian revolution is a revolution to abolish all exploiting classes and all systems of exploitation; it is a most thoroughgoing revolution to bring about the gradual elimination of the differences between workers and peasants, between town and country, and between mental and manual labourers. This cannot but meet with the most stubborn resistance from the exploiting classes.

In every revolution the basic question is that of State power. In all branches of the superstructure — ideology, religion, art, law, State power — the central issue is State power. State power means everything. Without it, all will be lost. Therefore, no matter how many problems have to be tackled after the conquest of State power, the proletariat must never forget State power, never forget its orientation and never lose sight of the central issue. Forgetting about State power means forgetting about politics, forgetting about the basic theses of Marxism and switching to economism,[1] anarchism and utopianism and becoming muddle-headed. In the last analysis, the class struggle in the ideological field between the proletariat and the bourgeoisie is a struggle for leadership.

The exploiting classes have been disarmed and deprived of their authority by the people, but their reactionary ideas remain rooted in their minds. We have overthrown their rule and confiscated their property, but this does not mean that we have rid their minds of reactionary ideas as well. During the thousands of years of their rule over the working people, the exploiting classes monopolised the culture created by the working people and in turn used it to deceive, fool and benumb the working people in order to consolidate their reactionary State power. For thousands of years, theirs was the dominant ideology which inevitably exerted widespread influence in society. Not reconciled to the overthrow of their reactionary rule, they invariably try to make use of this influence of theirs surviving from the past to shape public opinion in preparation for the political and economic restoration of capitalism. The uninterrupted struggle on the ideological and cultural front in the 16 years from liberation up to the current exposure of the black anti-Party and anti-socialist line of the "Three-Family Village," big and small, has been a struggle between the forces attempting

211

restoration and the forces opposing restoration.

In order to seize State power, the bourgeoisie during the period of the bourgeois revolution likewise started with ideological preparations by launching the bourgeois cultural revolution. Even the bourgeois revolution, which replaced one exploiting class by another, had to undergo repeated reversals and witness many struggles — revolution, then restoration and then the overthrow of restoration. It took many European countries hundreds of years to complete their bourgeois revolutions from the start of the ideological preparations to the final conquest of State power.

Since the proletarian revolution is a revolution aimed at completely ending all systems of exploitation, it is still less permissible to imagine that the exploiting classes will meekly allow the proletariat to deprive them of all their privileges without seeking to restore their rule. The surviving members of these classes who are unreconciled will inevitably, as Lenin put it, throw themselves with a tenfold furious passion into the battle for the recovery of their lost paradise. The fact that the Khrushchev revisionist clique has usurped the leadership of the Party, army and State in the Soviet Union is an extremely serious lesson for the proletariat throughout the world. At present the representatives of the bourgeoisie, the bourgeois "scholars" and "authorities" in China are dreaming precisely of restoring capitalism. Though their political rule has been toppled, they are still desperately trying to maintain their academic "authority," remould public opinion for a come-back and win over the masses, the youth and the generations yet unborn from us.

The anti-feudal cultural revolution waged by the bourgeoisie ended as soon as it had seized power. The proletarian cultural revolution, however, is a cultural revolution against the ideology of all exploiting classes. This cultural revolution is entirely different in nature from the bourgeois cultural revolution. It is only after the creation of the political, economic and cultural prerequisites following the capture of State power by the proletariat that the broadest road is opened up for the proletarian cultural revolution.

The proletarian cultural revolution is aimed not only at demolishing all the old ideology and culture and all the old customs and habits, which, fostered by the exploiting classes, have poisoned the minds of the people for thousands of years, but also at creating and fostering among the masses an entirely new ideology and culture and entirely new customs and habits — those of the proletariat. This great task of transforming customs and habits is without any precedent in human history. As for all the heritage, customs and habits of the feudal and bourgeois classes, the proletarian world outlook must be used to subject them to thoroughgoing criticism. It takes time to clear away the evil habits of the old society from among the people. Nevertheless, our experience since liberation proves that the transformation of customs and habits can be accelerated if the masses are fully mobilised, the mass line is implemented and the transformation is made into a genuine mass movement.

As the bourgeois cultural revolution served only a small number of people, i.e., the new exploiting class, only a small number of people could participate in it. The proletarian cultural revolution, however, serves the broad masses of the working people and is in the interests of the working people who constitute the overwhelming majority of the population. It is therefore able to attract and unite the broad masses to take part in it. The bourgeois individuals who carried out the enlightenment invariably looked down upon the masses, treated them as a mob and considered themselves as the predestined masters of the people. In sharp contrast, proletarian ideological revolutionaries serve the people heart and soul with the object of awakening them, and work for the interests of the broadest masses.

The bourgeoisie, with its base selfishness, is unable to suppress its hatred for the masses. Marx said: "The peculiar nature of the material it (political economy) deals with, summons as foes into the field of battle the most violent, mean and malignant passions of the human breast, the furies of private interest." This also holds for the bourgeoisie when it has been overthrown.

The scale and momentum of the Great Proletarian Cultural Revolution now being carried on in China have no parallel in history, and the tremendous drive and momentum and boundless wisdom of the working people manifested in the movement far exceed the imagination of the lords of the bourgeoisie. Facts have eloquently proved that Mao Tse-tung's thought becomes a moral atom bomb of colossal power once it takes hold of the masses. The current great cultural revolution is immensely advancing the socialist cause of the Chinese people and undoubtedly exerting an incalculable, far-reaching influence upon the present and future of the world.

The stormy cultural revolution now under way in our country

213

has thrown the imperialists, the modern revisionists and the reactionaries of all countries into confusion and panic. At one moment, they indulge in wishful thinking saying that our great cultural revolution has shown that there are hopes of "a peaceful evolution" on the part of China's younger generation. A moment later, they become pessimistic, saying that all this has shown that communist rule remains very stable. Then again, they seem to be fearfully puzzled, saying that it will never be possible to find genuine "China hands" who can promptly pass accurate judgment on what is taking place in China. Dear Sirs, your wishful thinking invariably runs counter to the march of history. The triumphant progress of this great and unparalleled cultural revolution of the proletariat is already sounding the death knell not only of the remnant capitalist forces on Chinese soil, but of imperialism, modern revisionism and all reaction. Your days are numbered.

Illuminated by the great Mao Tse-tung's thought, let us carry the proletarian cultural revolution through to the end. Its victory will certainly further strengthen the dictatorship of the proletariat in our country, guarantee the completion of the socialist revolution on all fronts and ensure our successful transition from socialism to triumphant communism!

(From a translation of an editorial carried in
Jen-min Jih-pao of June 1, 1966)

NOTES

1. In communist parlance, this means the use of such material incentives as wage increases, back pay and bonuses to bribe the working people and corrupt them.

The Compass for the Great Cultural Revolution

In the editorials reproduced below in part, Lin Piao's success in the creative application of Mao Tse-tung's thought is hailed as an example for all China to follow. Giving prominence to Mao Tse-tung's thought, particularly on literature and art as expounded in "Talks at the Yenan Forum on Literature and Art," is described in these documents as the compass to follow in the great cultural revolution of the proletariat. The Great Proletarian Cultural Revolution is described as a struggle in defence of Mao's political thought concerning the cardinal issues of right and wrong, and as a sharp class struggle between the proletariat and the bourgeoisie which will affect the destiny of China and the Chinese Communist Party.—Ed.

Put Mao Tse-tung's Thought in the Forefront, Cadres Give the Lead at Every Level

The experience of China's revolutionary struggles in the past decades may be summarised in thousands of points, but in the final analysis, they boil down to one single point: Chairman Mao's works are the supreme guide for work in all fields; Mao Tse-tung's thought is the fundamental guarantee of victory for all work. When Mao Tse-tung's thought is placed in the forefront, our cause advances irresistibly and triumphantly. This was the case during the period of the new-democratic revolution; it is also the case during the period of the socialist revolution. This is true of the socialist revolution on the economic and political fronts; it is also true of the socialist revolution on the ideological and cultural fronts.

A great movement for the creative study and application of Chairman Mao's works has unfolded in the past few years among the masses of the workers, peasants, soldiers and revolutionary cadres. Mao Tse-tung's thought has penetrated deeper and deeper into the hearts and minds of the people and is being mastered by more and more people. For this reason, the socialist revolution has developed in greater scope and depth and socialist construction has advanced in ever bigger strides,

215

with one miracle after another being created in every field of work.

Comrade Lin Piao has issued the call: "Study Chairman Mao's works, follow his teachings, act in accordance with his instructions and be a good soldier of Chairman Mao," and he has initiated a movement in the People's Liberation Army for the creative study and application of Chairman Mao's works. This is a great, new development. Comrade Lin Piao's instruction — "Study Chairman Mao's works with certain problems in mind, study and apply them in a creative way, combine study with application, and study first what is needed most so as to gain prompt results" — has become the guide for the whole army in the study of Chairman Mao's works and it has yielded incalculable results. Nurtured by Mao Tse-tung's thought, large numbers of heroic people such as Lei Feng, Wang Chieh, Ouyang Hai, Mai Hsien-teh and Sun Lo-yi have appeared in the Liberation Army. They are examples for the whole people to emulate. The great success made by the Liberation Army in creatively studying and applying Chairman Mao's works has given a tremendous impetus to our revolutionary cause as a whole. Energetic emulation of the Liberation Army has become a universal call to action for all the people and all endeavours. In this emulation, the fundamental point is to learn from the Liberation Army how they persistently place Mao Tse-tung's thought in the forefront in all work and to learn from Comrade Lin Piao's extremely important instructions on the creative study and application of Chairman Mao's works.

The socialist education movement in China's vast countryside and in the cities, launched under the guidance of Mao Tse-tung's thought, is a struggle between the proletarian and bourgeois classes, between the two roads: socialism and capitalism; it is a great socialist revolutionary movement. The basic experience derived from it is also that Mao Tse-tung's thought must be placed in the forefront. Wherever Mao Tse-tung's writings are studied and applied well and penetrate into the hearts and minds of the people, there the movement is deep-rooted and thoroughgoing, the ideological outlook of the people undergoes revolutionary and radical change and a new situation appears in production.

Similarly in the Great Proletarian Cultural Revolution, we must ensure that Mao Tse-tung's thought is placed in the forefront. How are we to see through monsters? How are we to see through representatives of the bourgeoisie who have wormed their way into the Party? We must rely on Mao Tse-tung's thought and we must rely on it, too, to sweep away all monsters and thoroughly defeat those representatives

216

of the bourgeoisie who have wormed their way into the Party.

The watershed dividing Marxism-Leninism from revisionism and revolution from counter-revolution lies between the alternatives of whether one supports or opposes the placing of Mao Tse-tung's thought in the forefront, whether one supports putting Mao Tse-tung's thought in command, supports putting "politics in command," or one advocates money-making in command and the placing of professional work in command.

The creative study and application of Chairman Mao's works and the placing of Mao Tse-tung's thought in the forefront persistently in all work must rely on strong leadership by the Party committees at all levels, and the cadres giving the lead at all levels. This is a most important guarantee.

Some cadres busy themselves every day with meetings, giving instructions, telephoning and other daily tasks but do not study Chairman Mao's works well. We must know that we may do a thousand or ten thousand jobs, but if we forget to creatively study and apply Chairman Mao's works, then we forget politics, the class struggle and the dictatorship of the proletariat and become blockheads. This is very dangerous. If we depart from Mao Tse-tung's thought, we will not be able to do anything well and will lose our heads in the storm of the class struggle, not knowing which way to go. If we depart from Mao Tse-tung's thought, we will be corrupted by bourgeois ideology, become its captives and become revisionists. All Party cadres must thoroughly understand this and must regard creative study and application of Chairman Mao's works as a task of prime importance.

The masses of workers, peasants and soldiers have achieved very good results in creatively studying and applying Chairman Mao's works. The phenomenon in some places where cadres have not studied as well as the masses, and leading cadres have not studied as well as the ordinary cadres, must be speedily changed. Cadres must give the lead in studying and applying. In studying Chairman Mao's works, cadres must also learn from the workers, peasants and soldiers. Only by doing so can they talk about leading. Before they can become revolutionary leaders, cadres must first give the lead in the creative study and application of Chairman Mao's works.

Outstanding examples of cadres giving the lead in the study of Chairman Mao's works are to be found everywhere. Like the worker, peasant and soldier masses, they creatively study and apply Chairman

217

Mao's works and combine this study with application. They study in the process of class struggle, the struggle for production, and scientific experiment. They give the lead in study, work, physical labour and ideological remoulding. They join the masses in their work, physical labour, study and ideological revolutionisation. This is why they have a high proletarian class consciousness, do their work well and are really able to lead the masses well. They all place Mao Tse-tung's thought in the forefront in their work, place it in command of everything, and use it to push everything forward. The Party committees at all levels should take care to sum up and popularise their experience.

If cadres and the masses study Chairman Mao's works conscientiously, follow Chairman Mao's teachings, and act in accordance with Chairman Mao's instructions, their ideological outlook will be transformed, the relations between cadres and the masses will change, the way they work will change and the situation in production will change.

With the cadres giving the lead at all levels, the ranks of activists in studying Chairman Mao's works will grow steadily and their level will gradually rise. Thus a still broader and deeper mass movement will be formed for creatively studying and applying Chairman Mao's works, so that Mao Tse-tung's thought takes deep root in the minds of the masses and is really placed in the forefront in all work. This is the fundamental guarantee for carrying the socialist revolution through to the end, consolidating the dictatorship of the proletariat and adhering to the correct orientation for socialist construction.

It is the conclusion and the call of the Party to place Mao Tse-tung's thought in the forefront, and for cadres to give the lead at all levels.

(From a translation of an editorial carried in *Hung-ch'i*, No. 8, 1966)

*　　　*　　　*

The Compass for the Great Cultural Revolution

The sum of practice in struggle over the past 24 years has proved that the question of whether one supports or opposes Comrade Mao Tse-tung's line on literature and art establishes the line of demarcation between Marxism-Leninism and revisionism and between revolution and counter-revolution.

The talks of Comrade Mao Tse-tung at the Yenan Forum on

218

Literature and Art made a systematic criticism of the bourgeois line on literature and art of the 1930s represented by Comrade Chou Yang. Politically, the bourgeois line on literature and art of the 1930s represented by Chou Yang was the product of Wang Ming's Right capitulationism and Left opportunism; ideologically, it was the manifestation of the bourgeois and petty-bourgeois world outlook; and organisationally, it was sectarianism, working for the interests of the individual or of a small group.

For 24 years Chou Yang and company have consistently refused to carry out Comrade Mao Tse-tung's line on literature and art and stubbornly adhered to the bourgeois, revisionist black line on literature and art.

Since liberation, Chou Yang and company, bourgeois representatives within the Party, who usurped the leadership of literary and art circles, have stubbornly insisted on carrying through their bourgeois line on literature and art which is against the Party, against socialism and against Mao Tse-tung's thought. Under the control and influence of this black line came a spate of absurd theories and a profusion of poisonous weeds, creating a miasma in literary and art circles. They turned literature and art into tools to attack the dictatorship of the proletariat and into means to restore capitalism.

Comrade Mao Tse-tung pointed out in December 1963 that in all forms of art — drama, ballads, music, the fine arts, the dance, the cinema, poetry and literature, etc., — problems abounded; the people engaged in them were numerous; and in many departments very little had been achieved so far in socialist transformation. The "dead" still dominated in many departments. Wasn't it absurd that many communists showed enthusiasm in advancing feudal and capitalist art, but no zeal in promoting socialist art, Comrade Mao Tse-tung added.

In June 1964, Comrade Mao Tse-tung pointed out that in the past 15 years the literary and art circles for the most part (this did not apply to every individual) had not carried out the policies of the Party and had acted as high and mighty bureaucrats, had not gone to the workers, peasants and soldiers and had not reflected the socialist revolution and construction. In recent years, they had even slid to the verge of revisionism. If serious steps were not taken to remould them, they were bound at some future date to become groups like the Hungarian "Petofi Club."

These statements of Comrade Mao Tse-tung were directed precisely at Chou Yang and company.

In the course of the past few months the great cultural revolution, launched and led by the Party's Central Committee headed by Comrade Mao Tse-tung, has lifted the lid covering the dominance of the black line in literary and art circles during the 16 years since the founding of the Chinese People's Republic, has brought out into the open and exposed to the light of day one group of monsters after another, and has conducted a vast and powerful campaign of criticism and struggle against them. This great cultural revolution is a struggle in defence of Mao Tse-tung's thought concerning cardinal issues of right and wrong; it is an extremely intense, extremely sharp and extremely profound class struggle between the proletariat and the bourgeoisie. It is an issue of prime importance which affects the destiny and future of our Party and country.

It is most important at this moment to make a new study of these talks of Comrade Mao Tse-tung. This is of immense practical and far-reaching significance.

The talks are a compass which, in complex and acute class struggle, gives us guidance in finding our direction, and in distinguishing between fragrant flowers and poisonous weeds, between revolution and counter-revolution and between true revolution and sham revolution.

The talks are a "magic mirror" to detect demons, the sharpest weapon for thoroughly destroying all monsters. Facing it, all words and deeds which oppose the Party, oppose socialism and oppose Mao Tse-tung's thought will be shown up in their true form and will have no place to hide themselves.

The talks are the clarion that sounds the advance. They call on the broad masses of workers, peasants and soldiers to act as the main force, and on those who work in the field of literature and art to go among the workers, peasants and soldiers, to go into the heat of the struggle, to take an active part in this great cultural revolution, to repudiate thoroughly the reactionary culture of feudalism, capitalism and revisionism and to create an entirely new proletarian, socialist culture.

In this great cultural revolution, which touches the people to their very souls, when we master this sharpest of weapons, we shall be able to defeat all of the old ideology and culture and all of the old customs and habits and we shall be able to establish a thoroughly revolutionary proletarian world outlook.

(Extracts from a translation of a *Hung-ch'i* editorial note on reprinting "Talks at the Yenan Forum on Literature and Art")

Mao Tse-tung's Thought
Spurs the Cultural Revolution

The value of the Thought of Mao is further defined in the materials presented in this section. This thought is described as the guiding principle in different stages of China's socialist revolution. It is the most powerful ideological weapon, the target of which is imperialism, modern revisionism and all reactionaries.

The editorials trace the struggle against "anti-Party, revisionist" groups as far back as 1953. In the main, however, these editorials stress that Mao's theory of class, class contradiction and class struggle is completely and totally correct and that this theory represents a new development of Marxism-Leninism. It is exactly this creative theory of Mao, they say, that has spurred the great cultural revolution.—Ed.

Long Live Mao Tse-tung's Thought

Today (July 1, 1966) we commemorate the 45th anniversary of the founding of the Communist Party of China in the midst of the upsurge of China's Great Proletarian Cultural Revolution, in an excellent situation of magnificent revolutionary struggle of the people all over the world.

Our Party is a great, glorious and correct Party.

Our Party, founded and nurtured by Comrade Mao Tse-tung personally, is a Party armed with Marxism-Leninism, Mao Tse-tung's thought, a proletarian revolutionary Party that integrates theory with practice, maintains close ties with the masses of the people and has the spirit of conscientious self-criticism, a proletarian revolutionary Party which has gone through the most acute, the most arduous, the most protracted and the most complex struggles in revolutionary history.

Throughout the 45 years of our Party's history, Comrade Mao Tse-tung has closely integrated the universal truth of Marxism-Leninism with the concrete practice of the Chinese revolution and the world revolution. Our Party's great victories during those 45 years are the great victories of Mao Tse-tung's thought.

Mao Tse-tung's thought has been developed in the course of the practice of our people's democratic revolution, socialist revolution and socialist construction; it has been developed in the struggle of our Party and the Marxist-Leninists of various countries against imperialism and modern revisionism; it has been developed in the course of summing up the new experiences in the struggle of the oppressed people and oppressed nations against imperialism and the reactionaries of various countries; it has been developed in the course of summing up the new experiences in international proletarian revolution and proletarian dictatorship since the Great October Socialist Revolution; it has been developed in the course of drawing the grave, painful lesson from the fact that the Soviet Khrushchev clique has usurped Party, army and government leadership and has led the Soviet Union from the socialist system on to the road of restoration of capitalism.

A revolutionary leader like Comrade Mao Tse-tung who has undertaken such protracted, complex, acute and many-sided struggles is rare in history, just as Marx, Engels, Lenin and Stalin were. Precisely because Comrade Mao Tse-tung is on all occasions supremely skilled at applying Marxist-Leninist dialectical and historical materialism in summing up the new experiences in all kinds of revolutionary struggles, Mao Tse-tung's thought has been and is the sole correct guiding principle in the different stages of the Chinese revolution and a powerful ideological weapon of revolution in the hands of the oppressed people and oppressed nations against imperialism, modern revisionism and all reactionaries.

Mao Tse-tung's thought is Marxism-Leninism inherited and developed with genius, creatively and in an all-round way in the era in which imperialism is approaching complete collapse and socialism is advancing to victory all over the world; it is the acme of Marxism-Leninism in the present era; it is living Marxism-Leninism at its highest. Comrade Mao Tse-tung is the greatest Marxist-Leninist of the present era.

Lenin once said that Marxism "has had to fight for every step forward in the course of its life." Mao Tse-tung's thought has been developed in the struggle against all sorts of powerful enemies, in China and abroad, and it has also been developed in the struggle against various opportunist ideas within the Party.

There has been a red Marxist-Leninist line, with Mao Tse-tung's thought as its guiding principle, running right through the long history

222

of our Party ever since it was founded. Throughout the period of democratic revolution, the Party's correct line represented by Comrade Mao Tse-tung engaged in serious struggle with Right opportunist lines on two occasions and with "Left" opportunist lines on three occasions. Comrade Mao Tse-tung's position of leadership over the whole Party was established at the Tsunyi Meeting in January, 1935. As a result of the rectification campaign which went on throughout the Party from 1942 onwards, the Party's Seventh National Congress in 1945 established Mao Tse-tung's thought as the guiding ideology for our whole Party, the guiding principle for all the work of the Party.

At the Party's Seventh National Congress, Comrade Liu Shao-ch'i pointed out: Comrade Mao Tse-tung "is a creative Marxist of genius." The emergence and development of Mao Tse-tung's thought "is the greatest achievement and glory of our Party and the Chinese people in their long struggles and it will be a boon to our nation for generations and generations." And "it will make great and useful contributions to the struggle for the emancipation of the people of all countries in general, and of the nations in the East in particular."

The founding of the People's Republic of China marked the entry of our country into a new era, that of socialist revolution and the dictatorship of the proletariat. The socialist revolution is a revolution for the complete abolition of the exploiting classes and private ownership; it is incomparably more profound and incomparably broader than the democratic revolution. After the socialist transformation of the ownership of the means of production is completed in socialist society, classes and class contradictions still remain. Although the form of class struggle has changed, the class struggle does not end. During the period of the dictatorship of the proletariat, there is extremely complicated and sharp class struggle. The class enemy at home and abroad harbours bitter hatred towards our socialist cause. At home, the exploiting classes which have already been overthrown and are being gradually eliminated put up a desperate fight, desperate resistance. They still exist, and they are not reconciled to their defeat. They work in collusion with the new bourgeois elements that emerge, and constantly try to stage a counter-revolutionary come-back. Imperialism, modern revisionism and the reactionaries of all countries are constantly plotting in all sorts of ways to attack, to undermine, to disintegrate, and to subvert our socialist system. And this acute domestic and international class struggle is inevitably reflected within our Party.

223

In the 16 years since the founding of our People's Republic, the Marxist-Leninist leadership of the Central Committee of the Party headed by Comrade Mao Tse-tung has waged three big struggles against anti-Party revisionist cliques.

The first was against the anti-Party alliance of Kao Kang and Jao Shu-shih.

This struggle took place in 1953, at the crucial moment when China's socialist revolution began to develop on a large scale. The Party at that time put forward the general line for socialist industrialisation and the socialist transformation of agriculture, handicrafts and capitalist industry and commerce. In this situation, in which class relations in our country were undergoing violent change and the class struggle was extremely tense, these ambitious careerists and conspirators Kao Kang and Jao Shu-shih, agents of the bourgeoisie who had wormed their way into the Party, could no longer restrain themselves. Working energetically at their conspiratorial activities, they made a vain attempt to seize the highest Party and State power, in order to bring about a bourgeois counter-revolutionary come-back. The Central Committee of the Party headed by Comrade Mao Tse-tung fought these counter-revolutionary elements resolutely. And at the Fourth Plenary Session of the Seventh Central Committee of the Party in 1954, and at the Party conference in 1955, this anti-Party alliance was thoroughly exposed and smashed.

Thanks to the victory in this struggle, the whole Party rallied still more closely under the banner of Mao Tse-tung's thought and around the Party's Central Committee headed by Comrade Mao Tse-tung, thus ensuring the great victory in socialist transformation.

The second big struggle was against another small handful of people of a Right opportunist, or revisionist, anti-Party clique.

In 1958, the Central Committee of the Party headed by Comrade Mao Tse-tung put forward the general line of going all out, aiming high and achieving greater, faster, better and more economical results in building socialism. Inspired by it, the people of the whole country buoyantly went forward in a great new upsurge of socialist revolution and socialist construction. This was a new great leap forward. In the course of this great leap forward the people's communes emerged throughout the country's rural areas. Our Party's general line for building socialism, and our people's great leap forward and the people's communes which emerged under the guidance of this general line, threw the imperialists, the modern revisionists and the reactionaries at home and abroad into a great panic and aroused their greatest hatred, so that they launched a concerted and frenzied attack on us. At the Lushan meeting of the Party in 1959, a handful of ambitious bourgeois careerists and schemers who had wormed their way into our Party and who had the support of the Khrushchev revisionist clique launched a ferocious attack on the Party's Central Committee headed by Comrade Mao Tse-tung. They put forward a thoroughly revisionist programme intended to replace the Party's general line for building socialism, in the vain hope of dragging our country back on to the capitalist road.

Under the leadership of Comrade Mao Tse-tung and the Party's Central Committee, our Party rose in unison and dealt this anti-Party clique a resolute rebuff, thoroughly smashing its schemes and safeguarding the correct leadership of the Party's Central Committee headed by Comrade Mao Tse-tung, safeguarding the Party's unity and its general line for building socialism. This was followed by one victory of our people after another on all fronts. The seeds sown in the great leap forward in 1958 and 1959 have been proved to bear abundant fruits.

The victory in the struggle in 1959 against the anti-Party clique of Right opportunists was another great victory for Mao Tse-tung's thought. It was of great historic significance in our country's advance along the road of socialism.

The third big struggle is the one against the recently exposed counter-revolutionary clique which opposes the Party, opposes socialism and Mao Tse-tung's thought.

These anti-Party elements are representatives of the bourgeoisie who sneaked into the Party, government, army and cultural departments and usurped important posts. They are more insidious and cunning in their activities than the two previous anti-Party cliques which had been crushed. For a long period, they waved "red flags" to oppose the red flag and donned the cloak of Marxism-Leninism, of Mao Tse-tung's thought to oppose Marxism-Leninism, to oppose Mao Tse-tung's thought. They put up the deceptive signboard of supporting the Party and socialism, while carrying on counter-revolutionary intrigues against the Party and against socialism.

The question of the Great Proletarian Cultural Revolution came to the fore with the gradual deepening of our country's socialist revolution and the step-by-step development of the socialist education movement. Taking the reactionary stand of the bourgeoisie, this counter-revolutionary clique did their utmost to resist and oppose the line of the great socialist cultural revolution formulated by the Central Committee of the Party and Comrade Mao Tse-tung, to resist and oppose the guiding principle on the question of classes and class struggle in socialist society put forward by Comrade Mao Tse-tung at the Tenth Plenary Session of the Eighth Central Committee of the Party, and to oppose the carrying through to the end of the socialist revolution. From a number of important positions under their control in the fields of journalism, education, art and literature, in the academic field and in publishing and other branches of culture, they waged an all-out class struggle for the bourgeoisie against the proletariat, spread bourgeois, revisionist poison widely and launched frantic attacks against Mao Tse-tung's thought, against the Party's Central Committee headed by Comrade Mao Tse-tung, and against the socialist system. They tried in a hundred and one ways to shield the bourgeois Right, attack the proletarian revolutionaries, suppress the revolutionary movement of the worker, peasant and soldier masses, and resist and sabotage the Great Proletarian Cultural Revolution. They reached out to grab power in the Party, army and government. Their aim was to usurp the leadership of the Party, army and government and to restore capitalism. Once conditions ripened, they would have staged a counter-revolutionary coup d'état like the one staged by Khrushchev.

And their efforts to seize hold of the pen had the sole purpose of preparing public opinion for the restoration of capitalism and a counter-revolutionary coup.

The thorough exposure and smashing of this counter-revolutionary clique in the Great Proletarian Cultural Revolution is an immense new victory for Mao Tse-tung's thought. It is a great event, ensuring the continuous development of China's socialist revolution, consolidating the dictatorship of the proletariat, preventing a usurpation of leadership by revisionism and a come-back of capitalism, preventing a counter-revolutionary coup and counter-revolutionary subversion, a great event affecting the destiny of the whole Chinese people and, broadly speaking, also the destiny of the people of the world.

The three big struggles that have occurred inside our Party in the last 16 years have been struggles between Mao Tse-tung's thought and ideas which are against Mao Tse-tung's thought, struggles between the Marxist-Leninist line and the revisionist line, between the proletariat and the bourgeoisie, and between the road of socialism and the road of capitalism.

226

Chairman Mao Tse-tung has said: "Opposition and struggle between ideas of different kinds constantly occur within the Party; this is a reflection within the Party of contradictions between classes and between the new and the old in society. If there were no contradictions in the Party and no ideological struggles to resolve them, the Party's life would come to an end." He has also pointed out: "Class struggle is an objective matter which is independent of men's will. This means that it is inevitable and that it is impossible to avoid even if men want to. One can only guide it along its course of development and so wrest victory."

It is perfectly normal and in accord with objective laws that, after each big struggle, our Party has purged itself of the handful of the alien class elements who had wormed their way into it. Our Party has become ever more united and consolidated and its combat strength has increased following each of these struggles. Here there is no straw for imperialism, modern revisionism and the domestic and foreign reactionaries to clutch at, and it is futile for them to dream of it.

The three big struggles that have occurred inside our Party in the last 16 years show that the criminal activities of the anti-Party cliques were all directed towards staging counter-revolutionary coups and transforming the dictatorship of the proletariat into a dictatorship of the bourgeoisie. If their criminal schemes had not been exposed, they would undoubtedly have struck a vicious blow against the people.

If their schemes had succeeded, the proletarian State power, the State power of the people, gained after the sacrifice of so much blood over scores of years of fighting, would have been ruined overnight, and our people would again have been oppressed and exploited and made to live like beasts of burden. Imperialism would have made a comeback, Khrushchev revisionism would have ridden roughshod over us, and our country would once again have been reduced to a colony or semi-colony.

We communists, the revolutionary proletariat and all who support the socialist system and the dictatorship of the proletariat, must not take such matters lightly; we must deal with them very seriously.

We are entirely capable of seeing through and exposing these anti-Party cliques and thwarting their schemes, because our Party is one which has conducted revolution under the leadership of Comrade Mao Tse-tung for decades, because our Party is armed with Marxism-Leninism, Mao Tse-tung's thought, and is of the same flesh and blood as the masses and rich in revolutionary experience. There is nothing much to these anti-Party elements. Once their schemes are exposed, they are immediately besieged by the broad masses of the people and seen as the paper tigers that they really are.

The great thought of Mao Tse-tung is the biggest barrier to the schemes of all anti-Party cliques trying to stage a counter-revolutionary coup d'état. Consequently, they always direct their attacks against it. When there is any mention of Mao Tse-tung's thought, they get upset, start swearing and cursing, fly into a rage and even get quite hysterical, just like the imperialists and the Khrushchev revisionists. Whoever supports Mao Tse-tung's thought and advocates the study of it, is bound to meet with opposition and attacks from them; they spread rumours and slanders and are capable of anything, however foul. They especially fear the direct grasp of Mao Tse-tung's thought by the masses of workers, peasants and soldiers. They oppose the creative study and application of Chairman Mao's works by the masses of workers, peasants and soldiers, labelling it as "over-simplification," "philistinism" and "pragmatism." They issue prohibitions and bans to make Mao Tse-tung's thought inaccessible to the masses of workers, peasants and soldiers. However, the more they prohibit, ban and oppose, the more enthusiastically the masses of workers, peasants and soldiers show their love for Chairman Mao's works and study them with the greatest eagerness.

The historical experience of our Party during the past 45 years proves that Mao Tse-tung's thought is the soul and the source of life of our Party. The ambitious anti-Party careerists who plot to usurp Party, army and government power must debase, distort, attack and oppose Mao Tse-tung's thought. And to ensure that our Party never degenerates and our country never changes colour, we must always take Mao Tse-tung's thought as our Party's guiding ideology, as the common ideological foundation of unity and revolution for the entire Party. This is true today and will remain true a hundred or a thousand years from now, it will remain true for ever. One's attitude towards Mao Tse-tung's thought is the yardstick distinguishing the genuine revolutionary from the sham revolutionary and the counter-revolutionary, the Marxist-Leninist from the revisionist. Anyone who opposes Mao Tse-tung's thought, now or in the future, will be a mortal enemy of the revolution and the people and will be condemned by the whole Party and denounced by the whole nation.

As early as 21 years ago, Comrade Liu Shao-ch'i pointed out to the whole Party: "The important task now is to mobilise the entire Party to study and disseminate Mao Tse-tung's thought and to arm our membership and the revolutionary people with it, so that it becomes an irresistible force in practice."

Comrade Chou En-lai has said: "Arming our cadres and working people with Mao Tse-tung's thought is a vital prerequisite for carrying our socialist revolution forward to the end and for the smooth progress of our socialist construction. It is also the fundamental way to overcome bourgeois ideology, revisionism and dogmatism and prevent their emergence."

Comrade Lin Piao has pointed out: "China is a great socialist State of the dictatorship of the proletariat and has a population of 700 million. It needs unified thinking, revolutionary thinking, correct thinking. That is Mao Tse-tung's thinking." "It is essential to imbue the workers and peasants with Chairman Mao's thought through the creative study and application of his works. Only so can the mental outlook of the working people be changed and spiritual forces be transformed into tremendous material strength."

Comrade Teng Hsiao-p'ing has pointed out: "Our Party's greatest merit is that it has the guiding ideology represented by Mao Tse-tung's thought. Mao Tse-tung's thought has stood the test of history. The Chinese revolution was led to victory by no other set of ideas than Mao Tse-tung's thought. And since the victory of the revolution, it is under the guidance of Mao Tse-tung's thought that our socialist revolution and socialist construction have achieved such great successes and are continuously and triumphantly forging ahead."

The Chinese People's Liberation Army, personally founded by Comrade Mao Tse-tung, is an instrument of the dictatorship of the proletariat, loyal to the Party and loyal to the people. The People's Liberation Army launched the movement to creatively study and apply Chairman Mao's works, in response to the call issued by the Military Commission of the Central Committee of the Party and Comrade Lin Piao to "study Chairman Mao's works, follow his teachings, act in accordance with his instructions, and be good soldiers of Chairman Mao." This is a great initiative and has already had immeasurable effect.

The movement by hundreds of millions of the worker, peasant and soldier masses for the creative study and application of Chairman Mao's works is gaining momentum. It is a monumental ideological revolutionary movement unprecedented in human history. It is a

229

tremendous popularisation of Marxism-Leninism such as has never been known before. A vast country with a quarter of the world's population is becoming a vast school for the study of Marxism-Leninism, Mao Tse-tung's thought. When there are several hundred million people armed with Mao Tse-tung's thought, and millions of successors to the proletarian revolutionary cause armed with Mao Tse-tung's thought, then we shall be able to carry our socialist revolution through to the end, lead our country step by step through the transition from socialism to communism, and make still greater contributions to the world revolution.

The broad masses of the workers, peasants and soldiers, the revolutionary cadres and the revolutionary intellectuals must unite closely around the Party's Central Committee and Comrade Mao Tse-tung and resolutely adhere to the instructions of the Party's Central Committee: Remember, never forget, class struggle; remember, never forget, the dictatorship of the proletariat; remember, never forget, to give prominence to politics; remember, never forget, to hold high the great red banner of Mao Tse-tung's thought.

Long live the great Communist Party of China!

Long live the great leader, Chairman Mao!

Long live the great and invincible Mao Tse-tung's thought!

(From a translation of an editorial carried in Jen-min Jih-pao of July 1, 1966)

*   *   *

The Sunlight of the Party Illuminates the Road of the Great Cultural Revolution

Under the correct leadership of the Chinese Communist Party and Chairman Mao Tse-tung, the current great proletarian cultural revolution in our country, a revolution without parallel in history, is gaining victory step by step.

Chairman Mao has said: "The force at the very core that leads our cause is the Communist Party of China."

It is only under the leadership of the Chinese Communist Party that the Chinese people can be victorious in all their undertakings and struggles.

The victory of the democratic revolution which toppled the "three

230

great mountains"[1] was won under the leadership of the Chinese Communist Party.

All the great achievements in the socialist revolution and socialist construction have been brought about under the leadership of the Chinese Communist Party.

Likewise, it is only under the leadership of the Chinese Communist Party that the Great Proletarian Cultural Revolution is able to triumph.

In short, without the leadership of the Chinese Communist Party it is absolutely impossible for our country to become prosperous, rich and strong and establish the great socialist system free from exploitation of man by man. To think that these things could be achieved without such leadership would be a pure illusion.

Our Party has the great and invincible Mao Tse-tung's thought as the ideological basis for the unity of the whole Party and the revolution, and it has the firm and powerful leadership of its Central Committee at the core of which is Chairman Mao.

Our Party is built in accordance with Chairman Mao's ideas on Party building and his revolutionary style, and it is a proletarian revolutionary Party, one that integrates theory with practice, closely links itself with the masses and has the spirit of self-criticism.

Our Party has developed, grown and been consolidated in the course of struggle against powerful enemies both at home and abroad and against opportunism of all kinds within the Party, and has gone through the severe tests of protracted revolutionary struggles.

Our Party is one that, guided by Mao Tse-tung's thought, has experienced countless hardships with almost no equal in world history, skilfully steering past hidden shoals in fierce tempests and advancing from victory to victory.

Our Party enjoys the greatest prestige, unshakable prestige, among the people. Our Party represents the highest interests of the proletariat and the broad masses of the working people, and its relationship with the masses of the people is, as Chairman Mao says, like that between fish and water.

Therefore, our Party is worthy of being called a great Party, a glorious Party, a correct Party.

Under the leadership of the Party's Central Committee and Chairman Mao, the overwhelming majority of our Party organisations at all levels, and of our Party members and cadres are good and loyal to the proletariat, to the cause of communism, and to Marxism-Leninism,

Mao Tse-tung's thought. Although some Party members and Party organisations to one degree or another have manifested shortcomings and made mistakes, many of them will be able to rectify these through criticism and self-criticism with the help of the Party and the masses and under their education and supervision.

During the period of the socialist revolution and socialist construction, class struggle is still very acute, and the struggle between the socialist road and the capitalist road is extremely sharp and, furthermore, is protracted. The class struggle and the struggle between the two roads in society are inevitably reflected within our Party. To Marxists, this is nothing strange, but a normal phenomenon conforming to objective laws.

In our Party there is a small handful of anti-Party and anti-socialist representatives of the bourgeoisie. They are class enemies who have sneaked into our ranks or those degenerated elements who have been drawn away from our ranks. They usurped leadership in a number of units and departments. Such things have happened in the past, they have been found to exist now and they may occur again in the future. The fact that the Party can mobilise the masses to uncover them, dismiss such people from office, strip them of their power and resolutely remove them from our ranks testifies to the strong militancy, the unity and the consolidation of our Party.

The Great Proletarian Cultural Revolution is a revolution against the ideology of the bourgeoisie and all exploiting classes. As Chairman Mao has said, this is a great revolution that touches the people to their very souls. This great cultural revolution is not only a sharp class struggle in society, but, within the Party, it is bound to encounter resistance from those who have not joined the Party ideologically but cling stubbornly to bourgeois ideas.

The touchstone for every member of society, testing whether he supports the dictatorship of the proletariat and the socialist system or not, is his attitude towards the great cultural revolution.

Every Party organisation and every Party member will be tested in this great cultural revolution.

The leadership of the Chinese Communist Party armed with Mao Tse-tung's thought is the fundamental guarantee for victory in the Great Proletarian Cultural Revolution.

The great cultural revolution can take the correct direction, the revolutionary people can see and think clearly and the movement can develop in a healthy way only with the correct leadership of the Party.

Correct leadership by the Party means being good at following the mass line of "from the masses and to the masses," being good at consulting the masses, listening to their opinions, distinguishing right from wrong and dealing with different things in different ways.

Correct leadership by the Party means relying on the resolute proletarian revolutionaries, expanding the ranks of the Left, winning over the greatest majority, isolating and splitting up the minority and dealing blows with concentrated force against the diehard anti-Party and anti-socialist counter-revolutionary elements, who account for only a few per cent.

Correct leadership by the Party means constantly raising the proletarian political consciousness of the masses, adopting for the great majority the policy of unity-criticism-unity[2] and, through the movement, in the end uniting over 95 per cent of the people, including those Party members and non-Party people who have committed mistakes but are willing to correct them and admit the error of their ways.

All good Party members, good functionaries and good Party organisations should courageously take part in this revolution, arm themselves further with Mao Tse-tung's thought and lead the mass movement of this cultural revolution well. They should stand in the van of the movement and among the masses and not be afraid of them or dampen their enthusiasm.

As for some of the leading functionaries in our Party organisations at all levels, if they are not anti-Party and anti-socialist they should come to the battlefront without any mental burdens. They should be courageous in self-examination of their shortcomings and mistakes, and open-mindedly accept criticism from the masses. They should not become disgruntled and disheartened just because the masses have posted a few big-character posters and voiced some opinions.

Our Party and the masses of the people are proud of the guidance of the great Mao Tse-tung's thought and are proud of the leadership of the Central Committee of the Party armed with Mao Tse-tung's thought.

Chairman Mao Tse-tung's theory of classes, class contradictions and class struggle in the period of socialism is a new development of Marxism-Leninism. It is a proletarian revolutionary truth that has been tested and confirmed again and again. It is the irrefutable proletarian revolutionary science. This proletarian revolutionary science has been developed in the course of the practice of our socialist revolution and socialist construction. It has been developed in the struggle waged by our Party and the Marxist-Leninists of other countries against imperialism and modern revisionism. It has been developed through the serious and painful lesson that the Khrushchev clique of the Soviet Union usurped Party, army and government leadership in that country and led it away from the socialist system and on to the road to the restoration of capitalism.

The class struggle in China's Great Proletarian Cultural Revolution and the multitude of facts brought to light in this class struggle have added fresh proof of the correctness of Chairman Mao's theory of classes, class contradictions and class struggle during the period of socialism.

It is in accordance with this theory of Chairman Mao's which reflects the objective laws that we should conduct the struggle in this great cultural revolution and transform people's inner, subjective world and the objective world, so that we can carry out our socialist revolution and socialist construction better and make it possible for our country to achieve the future transition from socialism to communism.

The road of our Great Proletarian Cultural Revolution is illuminated by the sunlight of Mao Tse-tung's thought and the leadership of the Central Committee of the Party.

We shall be invincible provided we resolutely work in accordance with Mao Tse-tung's thought and the instructions of the Central Committee of the Party and Chairman Mao, strengthen the Party's correct leadership of the movement and link leadership by the Party closely with the masses.

In the end, no monsters can escape exposure under the sunlight of Mao Tse-tung's thought and of the Party. Under this sunlight, under the watchful eyes of millions of awakened masses, no monsters can possibly succeed in their attempts to gain something by trickery, to reverse right and wrong, to fish in troubled waters, and to create confusion in people's minds. Still more impossible is it for them to slip through and hope to escape their destined failure.

NOTES

1. Imperialism, feudalism and bureaucratic capitalism.
2. This means to start off with a desire for unity and resolve contradictions through criticism or struggle so as to achieve a new unity on a new basis.

(From a translation of an editorial carried in
Jen-min Jih-pao of June 24, 1966)

*   *   *

Forward along the High Road of Mao Tse-tung's Thought

We celebrate our great National Day this year at a time when the Great Proletarian Cultural Revolution is in high tide and when our country's socialist revolution has developed to a new, deeper and more extensive stage. This is a most unusual festival, a festival that brims with high revolutionary spirit as never before and a festival that gives the greatest cause for rejoicing.

The 17 years since the founding of the People's Republic of China have been 17 years in which the people of the whole country have forged triumphantly ahead by holding aloft the great red banner of Mao Tse-tung's thought. Extremely brilliant achievements have been registered in these 17 years in the fields of politics, economics, military affairs and culture. Our achievements have won enthusiastic praise from revolutionary people all over the world and have made the imperialists, modern revisionists and reactionaries of all countries tremble with fear. New socialist China stands high and firm in the East, bringing about tremendous changes in the revolutionary struggles of the whole world.

How were our great successes over the 17 years achieved? Our basic experiences may be summed up in one, that is, as Chairman Mao has said, to keep a firm hold on the key link — the struggle between the two classes, the proletariat and the bourgeoisie, and the struggle between the two roads, the road of socialism and the road of capitalism. Our victories are victories of the proletariat in its struggle against the bourgeoisie, victories of the socialist road in its struggle against the capitalist road.

In his report to the Second Plenary Session of the Seventh Central Committee of the Chinese Communist Party, held in March 1949, Chairman Mao pointed out that after the countrywide victory of the Chinese revolution and the solution of the land problem, the basic contradiction in the country would be the contradiction between the working class and the bourgeoisie. This means that the contradiction between the working class and the bourgeoisie runs right through the entire historical course of socialism and right through all sectors of socialist society.

The historical experience of the 17 years proves that once the key link — the struggle between the two classes and the two roads — is grasped, our proletarian revolutionary cause develops, forges ahead and flourishes with great liveliness. If any place or department relinquishes this key link, an ill wind will blow up there, and that place or department will lose its bearings and suffer setbacks.

At the National Working Conference called by the Political Bureau of the Central Committee of the Chinese Communist Party in January 1965, Comrade Mao Tse-tung told us:

Throughout the period of transition there exist class contradictions, the class struggle between the proletariat and the bourgeoisie, the struggle between the two roads of socialism and capitalism. If we forget this fundamental theory and fundamental practice of our Party of the past ten years and more, we will go astray.

The proletarian cultural revolution marks a new stage in the struggle between the two classes and between the two roads.

The present great cultural revolution has a very wide scope. We are out to sweep away all ghosts and monsters and, in the realm of ideology and on a grand scale, to eradicate the "four olds" [old ideas, old culture, old customs and old habits] of the exploiting classes and foster the "four news" [new ideas, new culture, new customs and new habits] of the proletariat. Inevitably, this touches the political and economic life of society. This great cultural revolution is directed at striking down a handful of bourgeois rightists, striking down those within the Party who are in authority and who are taking the capitalist road.

The struggle between the masses of workers, peasants and soldiers, revolutionary cadres and revolutionary intellectuals on the one hand and a handful of people within the Party who are in authority and who are taking the capitalist road on the other is a concentrated expression of the present stage of the struggle between the proletariat and the bourgeoisie and between socialism and capitalism.

How is it possible that a handful of people who are in power and who are taking the capitalist road could emerge within the Party? This is decided by the law of class struggle. Under the dictatorship of the proletariat, the overthrown exploiting classes invariably try in every possible way to corrupt cadres of the Communist Party and find agents within our Party. At the Second Plenary Session of the Seventh Central Committee of the Party, Chairman Mao counselled us that we must guard against the "sugar-coated bullet attacks" of the bourgeoisie. This was a warning to all members of the Communist Party. The great majority of them have stood the test. But, there are a handful of people who have been hit by the bourgeoisie's sugar-coated bullets. They are no longer the representatives of the proletariat but of the bourgeoisie.

The people within the Party who are in authority and who are taking the capitalist road are a handful of counter-revolutionary revisionists. They have been waving "red flags" to oppose the red flag. They are men of the Khrushchev type. Whenever they have an opportunity, they will plot to usurp the leadership of the Party the army and the government. They are our most dangerous and our main enemy. The overthrown exploiting classes place their hopes of a come-back chiefly on them. The exploiting classes carry out activities for a comeback mainly through them or under their protection. Therefore, only by striking down those people within the Party who are in authority and who are taking the capitalist road can we smash the plots of the exploiting classes for a come-back, further consolidate the dictatorship of the proletariat and promote the development of the socialist cause.

The Decision of the Central Committee of the Chinese Communist Party Concerning the Great Proletarian Cultural Revolution, or the 16 Points, drawn up under the personal guidance of Chairman Mao, is a product of the struggle between two lines, a product of the victory of the proletarian revolutionary line, represented by Chairman Mao, over the bourgeois reactionary line. The promulgation of the 16-point decision has won the enthusiastic support of the broad masses of revolutionary people and advanced the Great Proletarian Cultural Revolution to a new high. The entire revolutionary situation is very fine and it is getting still finer every day.

But the struggle between the two lines has not yet come to an end. In some places and units, the struggle is still very acute and complicated. There are a very small number of people who adopt new forms to deceive the masses and act against the 16-point decision, they stubbornly persist in the bourgeois reactionary line and, to attain their own ends, do their utmost to use the form of inciting the masses to struggle against each other.

The bourgeois reactionary line must be thoroughly criticised and repudiated. Only by thoroughly criticising and repudiating it and sweeping away all its influence can the 16-point decision of the proletariat be carried through and implemented; only then can the struggles [against those persons in authority who are taking the capitalist road], criticisms and repudiations [of the reactionary bourgeois academic "authorities" and the ideology of the bourgeoisie and all other exploiting classes] and transformations [of education, literature and art and all other parts of the superstructure that do not correspond to the socialist economic base] be carried out in society, schools and colleges and other cultural departments; only then can there be a clear-cut idea of what to struggle against, what to criticise and what to transform; only then can there be a clear-cut idea of whom to rely on in waging the struggles, carrying out the criticisms and the transformations; only then can the task of struggle, of criticism and repudiation and of transformation be successfully fulfilled. If the erroneous line of the past is continued, or the error of suppressing the masses is repeated, or the inciting of students to struggle against each other goes on, or the revolutionary masses who were dealt blows in the past are not liberated, and so on — all this constitutes acting against and undermining the 16-point decision. In those circumstances, how could the struggles, the criticisms and repudiations and the transformations be carried out correctly?

To criticise and repudiate or not to criticise and repudiate the bourgeois reactionary line — this is the pivot on which hinges the question whether or not the 16-point decision on the cultural revolution can be carried through and implemented, whether or not the struggles, criticisms and repudiations, and transformations can be carried out correctly and extensively. Here to resort to eclecticism will not do.

The struggle between the two lines in the Great Proletarian Cultural Revolution is a reflection of the class struggle inside the Party. We must approach this question from the viewpoint of materialist dialectics, not from the viewpoint of metaphysics or that of a philistine.

Chairman Mao has said: "Opposition and struggle between ideas of different kinds constantly occur within the Party; this is a reflection within the Party of contradictions between classes and between the new and the old in society. If there were no contradictions in the Party and no ideological struggles to resolve them, the Party's life would come to an end."

Chairman Mao has also said: In the circumstances in which a non-antagonistic contradiction between correct and incorrect ideas occurs in the Communist Party, "if the people who have committed errors persist in them and aggravate them, there is the possibility that this contradiction will develop into antagonism."

The Party's Central Committee holds that comrades who have committed errors on matters of orientation or errors of line in the Great Proletarian Cultural Revolution, should face up to their errors, rectify them and return to the correct stand and correct line, instead of going so far as to act against the Party.

Those who persist in the erroneous line are only a handful. They are divorced from the people, opposed to the people and to Mao Tse-tung's thought. So they are bound to fail. Those masses who are for a time hoodwinked and deceived by them will certainly wake up and draw a line of demarcation between them and themselves and oppose them.

Holding high the great red banner of Mao Tse-tung's thought, Comrade Lin Piao, close comrade-in-arms of Chairman Mao, has called for the development of a mass movement for the creative study and application of Chairman Mao's works. This movement, spreading from the People's Liberation Army to the masses of the people throughout the country, has achieved great results. The movement is putting Mao Tse-tung's thought deeper into the hearts of the people. When hundreds of millions of people are armed with Mao Tse-tung's thought, they constitute the most reliable guarantee for the victory of the Great Proletarian Cultural Revolution. The forward leap in the mental outlook of the masses of the people will inevitably be transformed into a tremendous material force.

Over the past 17 years, Comrade Mao Tse-tung has always firmly grasped the development of the basic contradiction within socialist society, posing the problems and solving them. Now that socialist society in China has developed to its present stage, Comrade Mao Tse-tung has advanced the theory and line for the Great Proletarian Cultural Revolution; this is a great development of Marxism-Leninism and a great creation in the history of the communist movement.

The historical experience of the international proletariat, and particularly the historical lesson of the emergence of revisionist rule in the Soviet Union, teaches us that only by waging a great proletarian cultural revolution, by thoroughly criticising and repudiating the ideology of all exploiting classes, by criticising and repudiating the reactionary bourgeois academic "authorities," by transforming education, art and literature, and everything in the superstructure that does not correspond to the socialist economic base, by uprooting the bourgeois agents hidden in the Party and by destroying bourgeois ideology and fostering proletarian ideology on a grand scale — only by so doing can we consolidate the dictatorship of the proletariat, prevent the emergence of revisionist rule, prevent the restoration of capitalism and ensure the victorious advance of our cause in the direction of socialism and communism.

Day in and day out, the revisionist leading group of the Soviet Communist Party and other traitors and scabs are madly cursing our Great Proletarian Cultural Revolution. Why these curses of theirs? It is because they realise that the influence of China's Great Proletarian Cultural Revolution cannot be held in check. It will inevitably awaken proletarian revolutionaries in their countries and arouse the masses of revolutionary people to rise up in opposition to them. Their throne is tottering.

The law of history is unalterable. All reactionaries at home and abroad can never evade the punishment that will be meted out to them by history. They will all be buried by their grave diggers, the revolutionary masses.

No matter how the enemy curses or how he attacks, the great Chinese people, with big strides and heads erect, will always march along their own road, the road of triumph, the road of Mao Tse-tung's thought; they will carry the Great Proletarian Cultural Revolution through to the end and will carry forward every undertaking in socialist revolution and socialist construction from victory to victory.

(From a translation of an editorial carried in
Hung-ch'i, No, 13, 1966)

A Great School of Mao Tse-tung's Thought

The editorials reproduced in this section lay emphasis on turning China into a great school of Mao Tse-tung's thought. In this school, the millions of China will become critics of the old and builders of a new world. The People's Liberation Army, called an instrument of proletarian dictatorship, is held up as an example for the entire country to follow. In line with Mao's thinking on "army building," the PLA itself is to be a great school for the study, implementation, dissemination and safeguarding of the thought of Mao Tse-tung. The *Hung-ch'i* editorial reveals that military professionalism, as opposed to absolute concentration on ideological matters, has at times got out of hand in the PLA. Such professionalism is labelled bourgeois and is condemned.
—Ed.

The Whole Country Should Become A Great School of Mao Tse-tung's Thought

Full 39 years have elapsed since the founding of the Chinese People's Liberation Army.

This great people's army founded by Comrade Mao Tse-tung himself and directly led by him has always maintained and carried forward the glorious tradition of being "at the same time a fighting force, a working force and a production force" throughout the past decades — both in the protracted and arduous fighting against the class enemy at home and abroad during the years of revolutionary wars, and, since the nationwide victory, in the course of shouldering the task of defending and building up the socialist motherland and safeguarding peace in the Far East and the whole world. In recent years, in accordance with the instructions of the Central Committee of the Chinese Communist Party, the Military Commission of the Party's Central Committee and Comrade Lin Piao, the Liberation Army has held aloft the great red banner of Mao Tse-tung's thought, undertaken the creative study and application of Chairman Mao's works, vigorously given prominence to proletarian politics, developed the "three-eight" working style,[1] participated in the socialist education movement and the Great Proletarian Cultural

Revolution, taken part and helped in socialist construction, and made another big stride forward along the road to becoming an even more highly proletarianised, revolutionised and militant army.

The masses of people in our country have always seen the Liberation Army as an example from which to learn. Since 1964, in response to the great call of Comrade Mao Tse-tung, the people throughout the country have set going an enthusiastic movement for learning in a big way from the Liberation Army. This has played a tremendous role in advancing our country's socialist revolution and socialist construction.

Comrade Mao Tse-tung recently pointed out: The People's Liberation Army should be a great school. In this great school, our armymen should learn politics, military affairs and culture. They can also engage in agricultural production and side occupations, run some medium-sized or small factories and manufacture a number of products to meet their own needs or for exchange with the State at equal values. They can also do mass work and take part in the socialist education movement in the factories and villages. After the socialist education movement is over, they can always find mass work to do, so that the army will forever be at one with the masses. They should also participate in the struggles of the cultural revolution to criticise the bourgeoisie whenever they occur. In this way, the army can concurrently study, engage in agriculture, run factories and do mass work. Of course, these tasks should be properly co-ordinated, and a distinction should be made between the primary and secondary tasks. Each army unit should engage in one or two of the three fields of activity — agriculture, industry and mass work, but not in all three at the same time. In this way, our army of several million will be able to play a very great role indeed.

It has been Comrade Mao Tse-tung's consistent idea that the people's army should be run as a great school of revolution. We did so in the past. Now, in the light of the new conditions, Comrade Mao Tse-tung has .put higher demands on the Liberation Army.

Comrade Mao Tse-tung has called on the people of the whole country to turn China's factories, rural people's communes, schools, trading undertakings, service trades and Party and government organisations into great schools for revolutionisation like the Liberation Army.

Comrade Mao Tse-tung has pointed out:

While the main activity of the workers is in industry, they should at the same time also study military affairs, politics and culture. They,

242

too, should take part in the socialist education movement and in criticising the bourgeoisie. Where conditions permit, they should also engage in agricultural production and side occupations, as is done at the Taching Oilfield.

While the main activity of the peasants in the communes is in agriculture (including forestry, animal husbandry, side occupations and fisheries), they, too, should at the same time study military affairs, politics and culture. Where conditions permit, they should also collectively run some small factories. They should also criticise the bourgeoisie.

This holds good for students too. While their main task is to study, they should in addition to their studies, learn other things, that is, industrial work, farming and military affairs. They should also criticise the bourgeoisie. The period of schooling should be shortened, education should be revolutionised, and the domination of our schools by bourgeois intellectuals should by no means be allowed to continue.

Where conditions permit, those working in commerce, in the service trades and in Party and government organisations should also do the same.

This brilliant idea of Comrade Mao Tse-tung is of great historic significance.

Comrade Mao Tse-tung has summed up all of China's experience in socialist revolution and socialist construction, studied all the experience of the international proletarian revolution and the dictatorship of the proletariat since the October Revolution, in particular drawing serious lessons from the carrying out of the restoration of capitalism by the Khrushchev revisionist clique in the Soviet Union, and has creatively provided the scientific answers to the questions of how to prevent a restoration of capitalism, consolidate the dictatorship of the proletariat and guarantee the gradual transition to communism.

The idea set forth by Comrade Mao Tse-tung that every field of work should be made into a great school for revolutionisation, where people take part both in industry and agriculture, in military as well as civilian affairs — such is our programme.

By acting in accordance with what Comrade Mao Tse-tung has said, it will be possible to elevate the proletarian ideology of our people very considerably, push forward the revolutionisation of people's thinking, and help them to break away from all the old ideology, culture, customs and habits surviving from the old society. Hence it will be possible to build socialism with still greater, faster, better and more economical results, and more quickly root out the social and ideological bases for capitalism and revisionism.

By acting in accordance with what Comrade Mao Tse-tung has said, it will be possible to promote the step-by-step narrowing of the gap between workers and peasants, town and countryside and mental and manual labour; to prevent abnormal urban and industrial development; to enable intellectuals to become at the same time manual workers and manual workers at the same time intellectuals; and to train hundreds of millions of new communist people who have a high degree of political consciousness and are developed in an all-round way.

By acting in accordance with what Comrade Mao Tse-tung has said, it will be possible to turn all the people into soldiers and greatly strengthen our combat preparedness. Should imperialism dare to invade us, it will be drowned in the great ocean of people's war.

By acting in accordance with what Comrade Mao Tse-tung has said, the 700 million people of our country will all become critics of the old world as well as builders and defenders of the new world. With hammer in hand they will be able to do factory work, with hoe, plough or harrow they will be able to do farming, with the gun they will be able to fight the enemy, and with the pen they will be able to express themselves in writing.

In this way, the whole country will be a great school of Mao Tse-tung's thought, a great school of communism.

It is in accordance with this idea of Comrade Mao Tse-tung that the Chinese People's Liberation Army has worked in the last few decades and is still continuously developing and improving itself. The Liberation Army is the best great school for studying Mao Tse-tung's thought. All factories, rural people's communes, schools, shops, service trades, and Party and government organisations in the country must follow the example set by the Liberation Army and turn themselves into great schools of Mao Tse-tung's thought.

The broad masses of the workers, peasants and soldiers, the revolutionary cadres and revolutionary intellectuals, and all members of the Communist Party should draw inexhaustible strength, wisdom and courage from this brilliant instruction of Comrade Mao Tse-tung, and struggle to fulfil the great historic task put forward by the Party and Comrade Mao Tse-tung.

(From a translation of an editorial carried in
Jen-min Jih-pao of August 1, 1966)

*   *   *

Make Our Army A Great School of Mao Tse-tung's Thought

Our great leader Chairman Mao Tse-tung recently gave us an extremely important directive on army building.

Chairman Mao said: The People's Liberation Army should be a great school. In this great school, our armymen should learn politics, military affairs and culture. They can also engage in agricultural production and side occupations, run some medium-sized or small factories and manufacture a number of products to meet their own needs or for exchange with the State at equal values. They can also do mass work and take part in the socialist education movement in the factories and villages. After the socialist education movement is over, they can always find mass work to do, so that the army will forever be at one with the masses. They should also participate in the struggles of the cultural revolution to criticise the bourgeoisie whenever they occur. In this way, the army can concurrently study, engage in agriculture, run factories and do mass work. Of course, these tasks should be properly co-ordinated, and a distinction should be made between the primary and secondary tasks. Each army unit should engage in one or two of the three fields of activity — agriculture, industry and mass work, but not in all three at the same time.

Chairman Mao said: In this way, our army of several million will be able to play a very great role indeed.

This directive of Chairman Mao is a great call to our army made under the circumstances that the Great Proletarian Cultural Revolution is developing vigorously in China and the class struggle is becoming more acute and complicated both at home and abroad, and it is a great call issued under the circumstances that our army is carrying out the instructions of the Military Commission of the Central Committee of the Chinese Communist Party and Comrade Lin Piao and is creatively studying and applying Chairman Mao's works, energetically giving prominence to politics and making great progress in all fields of work. It is a great call which demands that our army should go forward to a still higher stage along the road to becoming an extremely proletarianised and extremely militant army.

Chairman Mao wants us to run our army as a great school. Working mainly as a fighting force, it concurrently studies, engages in agriculture, runs factories and does mass work; it carries on and further develops the fine traditions of our Party and our army, and trains and tempers millions of successors to the proletarian revolutionary cause, so that our people's army of several million can play a still greater role in the cause of socialist revolution and socialist construction. It is a great school for the study, implementation, dissemination and safeguarding of Mao Tse-tung's thought.

It is now 39 years since Chairman Mao himself created this army of ours. It is a worker and peasant army under the absolute leadership of the Chinese Communist Party and built in accordance with the principles of Marxism-Leninism, a people's army of a totally new type, completely different from the feudal warlord or bourgeois armies.

At an early stage in the creation of our army, Chairman Mao clearly pointed out that it should certainly not confine itself to fighting, but should be an armed body for carrying out the political tasks of the revolution. In the famous resolution at the Kutien Congress, Chairman Mao wrote: "The Red Army fights not merely for the sake of fighting but in order to conduct propaganda among the masses, organise them, arm them, and help them to establish revolutionary political power. Without these objectives, fighting loses its meaning and the Red Army loses the reason for its existence."

Chairman Mao set our army three great tasks, namely, fighting, mass work and production. He pointed out that our army was always a fighting force, and at the same time it was a working force and a production force.

On the eve of nationwide victory, Chairman Mao said: "The army is a school." And "we must look upon the field armies with their 2,100,000 men as a gigantic school for cadres."

In the past decades, our army has done precisely what Chairman Mao has taught us to.

The directive recently given by Chairman Mao constitutes the most recent summing up of our army's experience in previous decades and represents a development of Chairman Mao's consistent thinking on army building in the new historical conditions. This directive is of great historic and strategic significance for enabling our army to preserve forever its distinctive character as a people's army, for consolidating the dictatorship of the proletariat, for pushing forward China's socialist revolution and socialist construction, strengthening national defence, bringing the mighty force of people's war into full play and countering possible attacks by US imperialism and its accomplices.

Chairman Mao's thinking on army building constitutes the most

246

thorough, correct and comprehensive body of proletarian ideas on army building.

Chairman Mao's thinking on army building is diametrically opposed to the purely military viewpoint in which consideration is given solely to military affairs in complete disregard of politics, reducing the army's task merely to fighting; it is diametrically opposed to all bourgeois military ideas.

Throughout the 39 years' history of our army, the struggle between Chairman Mao's thinking and line on army building and bourgeois military ideas of various kinds has never ceased. This was true of the entire period of the democratic revolution, and is equally true of the period of the socialist revolution.

In the 16 years since the founding of the People's Republic of China, we have waged three big struggles against representatives of the bourgeois military line who wormed their way into the Party and the army.

The first big struggle started after the conclusion of the war to resist US aggression and aid Korea. Under the pretext of "regularisation" and "modernisation," a handful of representatives of the bourgeois military line, making a complete carbon copy of foreign practice, vainly attempted to negate our army's historical experience and fine traditions and to lead our army on to the road followed by bourgeois armies. The bourgeois military dogmatism which they tried to push through was strongly resisted and opposed by the broad masses of cadres and fighters in our army. Responding to Chairman Mao's call of "Down with the slave mentality! Bury dogmatism!", the 1958 Enlarged Session of the Military Commission of the Central Committee of the Chinese Communist Party smashed their frantic attack and defended Chairman Mao's thinking and line on army building.

The second big struggle took place at the same time as our Party's struggle against the Right opportunist anti-Party clique in 1959. Taking advantage of the important posts they had usurped in the army, the principal members of the anti-Party clique — who were exposed at the Party's Lushan Conference — made a great effort to do away with the Party's absolute leadership over the army, to abrogate political work, to reject the army's tasks of participating in socialist construction and doing mass work, and to abolish the local armed forces and the militia; in this way, they tried to completely negate Chairman Mao's thinking on the people's army and people's war. They vainly hoped to refashion our army according to the bourgeois, revisionist military line so that it would become an instrument for their usurping leadership of the Party and the Government, and for realising their personal ambitions. The Enlarged Session of the Military Commission held after the Party's Lushan Conference thoroughly settled accounts with them in regard to their crimes and dismissed them from office. This was a great victory for Mao Tse-tung's thought!

Since he took charge of the work of the Military Commission of the Party's Central Committee, Comrade Lin Piao has most resolutely and thoroughly implemented Chairman Mao's thinking and line concerning army building. In 1960, with the attention and guidance of the Party's Central Committee and Chairman Mao, the Enlarged Session of the Military Commission presided over by Comrade Lin Piao went further in eradicating the influence of the bourgeois military line, corrected the orientation in political work, adopted the "Resolution Concerning the Strengthening of Political and Ideological Work in the Armed Forces," and carried on and developed the spirit of the Kutien Congress, and thus established a new milestone in our army's road of advance. In the last few years, under the leadership of the Military Commission of the Party's Central Committee and Comrade Lin Piao, the whole army has held high the great red banner of Mao Tse-tung's thought and creatively studied and applied Chairman Mao's works, given prominence to politics, upheld the "four firsts,"[2] vigorously fostered the "three-eight" working style, given full scope to democracy in the three main fields of work,[3] launched the "four-good" companies campaign,[4] and taken part in the socialist education movement and the Great Proletarian Cultural Revolution, took part in and supported socialist construction, so that an excellent, flourishing situation has emerged in the revolutionisation of our army and in all other fields of work.

The third big struggle took place not long ago. Exposed in this struggle were representatives of the bourgeoisie who had usurped important posts in the army and were important members of the counter-revolutionary anti-Party, anti-socialist clique recently uncovered by our Party. They had opposed the Party's Central Committee and Mao Tse-tung's thought, had overtly agreed to but covertly opposed Comrade Lin Piao's directives on giving prominence to politics, had talked about putting politics in command but in practice had put military affairs first, technique first and work first. They had waved "red flags" to oppose the red flag and vigorously spread eclecticism, i.e., opportunism, in the vain attempt to substitute a bourgeois military line for Chairman

Mao Tse-tung's proletarian military line. Our Party's thorough exposure and repudiation of the handful of anti-Party careerists is a great new victory for Mao Tse-tung's thought!

The representatives of the bourgeoisie, who were exposed in these big struggles of our army since the founding of the People's Republic of China, opposed Chairman Mao's principle of building our army into a powerful, revolutionary army of the proletariat, opposed absolute leadership by the Party over the army, opposed political work and opposed the mass line. What they wanted was bourgeois regularisation and not proletarian revolutionisation. They discarded our army's glorious traditions, reduced its three great tasks to the single task of training in combat skill in peace-time and fighting in times of war. In short, everything they did was the diametrical opposite of Chairman Mao's thinking on army building and on turning our army into a great school. Their criminal aim was to turn our army into a bourgeois army serving a few careerists, an army divorced from Mao Tse-tung's thought, from proletarian politics, from the masses of the people and from productive labour.

The struggle between the two sets of ideas, the two different lines, on army building is a reflection within the army of the struggle between the proletariat and the bourgeoisie, between the road of socialism and the road of capitalism. So long as classes and class struggle still exist, this struggle will never end. At home and abroad, the class enemy who is hoping, in vain, to cause our country to change colour, will first of all try to make our army change colour. The tiny handful of representatives of the bourgeoisie who worm their way into our army will always step forward and try to stir up trouble whenever the class struggle becomes very intense. However, under the brilliant light of the great thought of Mao Tse-tung, the broad masses of cadres and fighters in our army, including some who have been temporarily misled, will invariably be able to detect their ugly features, expose them to the light of day and frustrate their conspiracies.

The history of our army over the decades has proved to the hilt that Chairman Mao's thinking and line on army building represent irrefutable truth and are our army's lifeline. At no time and in no circumstances is it permissible for us to depart in the slightest from the orbit of Chairman Mao's thinking and line on army building.

We must respond with enthusiasm to the great call of Chairman Mao Tse-tung, take over and develop the fine traditions of our army and run it as a great school.

We shall resolutely learn politics, military affairs and culture in accordance with Chairman Mao's directive. We shall play an active part in the socialist education movement and the great proletarian cultural revolution. Everyone should take up the sharpest weapon, Mao Tse-tung's thought, to criticise the bourgeoisie. We should at all times hold ourselves ready to crush any possible attack by US imperialism and its accomplices.

We shall resolutely adhere to Chairman Mao's directive that the army should concurrently study, engage in agriculture, run factories and do mass work. Everyone should take part in productive labour and forever maintain the distinctive character of working people. Everyone should do mass work, abide by the three main rules of discipline and the eight points for attention,[5] so that the army will always be at one with the masses. Militia work should be done well and the idea of people's war[6] should be implanted among the masses of the people. We must enthusiastically take part and help in socialist construction, actively help with local work, learn modestly from the local districts and strengthen the unity between the army and the local districts.

To run this great army school well, the most important and fundamental thing is to study and apply Chairman Mao Tse-tung's works creatively. It is necessary to study and to apply in the course of struggle. This great school must forever hold high the great red banner of Mao Tse-tung's thought and always give prominence to proletarian politics, use Mao Tse-tung's thought as the guide for all work and arm everyone with Mao Tse-tung's thought.

This great school of ours is a great school of Mao Tse-tung's thought!

We must run this great school of Mao Tse-tung's thought well!

Let us march forward valiantly under the great banner of Mao Tse-tung's thought!

(From a translation of an editorial carried in *Hung-ch'i* of August 1, 1966.)

NOTES

1. The "three-eight" working style (which in Chinese is written in three phrases and eight additional characters) means firm, correct political orientation; a plain, hard-working style; flexibility in strategy and tactics; and unity, alertness, earnestness and liveliness.

2. The "four firsts" are: First place must be given to man in handling the relationship between man and weapons; to political work in handling the relationship between political and other work; to ideological work in relation to other aspects of political work; and, in ideological work, to the ideas currently in a person's mind as distinguished

250

from ideas in books.

3. "Democracy in the three main fields of work" means democracy in the political, the economic and the military fields.

4. The "four-good" title of honour is given to companies which are good in political and ideological work, in the "three-eight" working style, in military training and in arranging their daily life.

5. The three main rules of discipline are a) Obey orders in all your actions; b) Don't take a single needle or piece of thread from the masses; c) Turn in everything captured. The eight points for attention are: a) Speak politely; b) Pay fairly for what you buy; c) Return everything you borrow; d) Pay for anything you damage; e) Don't hit or swear at people; f) Don't damage crops; g) Don't take liberties with women; h) Don't ill-treat captives.

6. This refers to Mao Tse-tung's military strategy of using the countryside to surround the cities in the case of fighting a major war.

Revisionist Roots of
Counter-revolutionary Group

Editorials reproduced below in full reveal
that certain leading members of the former
CCP Peking Municipal Committee are revisionists donning the cloak of Marxism-Leninism
for the purpose of exercising bourgeois dictatorship over the proletariat in the field of education
in particular. The former president of Peking
University—called a base from which bourgeois
revisionists woo the younger generation away
from the proletariat—and a handful of "bourgeois royalists" are singled out for attack for
pursuing the revisionist line advocated by the
former Peking Municipal Party Committee.—Ed.

New Victory for Mao Tse-tung's Thought

This paper publishes two important items of news today (June 4,
1966). One is about the decision of the Central Committee of the
Communist Party of China on the reorganisation of the Peking Municipal
Committee of the Party, with the appointment of Comrade Li Hsüeh-feng,
First Secretary of the North China Bureau of the Party's Central Committee, as concurrently First Secretary of the new Peking Municipal Committee of the Party, and Comrade Wu Te as Second Secretary. The other
item announces that the newly reorganised Peking Municipal Committee
of the Chinese Communist Party has decided that Lu P'ing and P'eng
P'ei-yun be dismissed from all their posts and that the Peking University
Party Committee be reorganised. The newly reorganised Peking
Municipal Party Committee also decided to send a work team to the
university to lead the great socialist cultural revolution and to act as
the Peking University Party Committee.

These two items of news, after being broadcast over the radio at
four o'clock yesterday afternoon, immediately received the warm support
of the worker and peasant masses as well as of government organisations,

colleges and schools, people's organisations and the People's Liberation Army units in Peking. The people are elated; and their universally expressed opinion is that these decisions of the Central Committee and the newly reorganised Peking Municipal Committee of the Party are very wise and absolutely correct. This is a new victory for Mao Tse-tung's thought.

A black anti-Party and anti-socialist line ran through the leadership given by the former Peking Municipal Committee of the Party.

A number of the principal leading members of the former Peking Municipal Party Committee are not Marxists but revisionists.

The anti-Party and anti-socialist counter-revolutionary clique of "Three-Family Village" was uncovered during the great socialist cultural revolution. The roots of this counter-revolutionary clique lay in the former Peking Municipal Committee of the Party.

For a considerable period of time, *Ch'ien Hsien,* the *Pei-ching Jih-pao* and the *Pei-ching Wan-pao* became instruments of this counter-revolutionary clique for spreading revisionist poison, in a futile attempt to restore capitalism. The former Peking Municipal Committee of the Party was at the very root of this.

For a considerable period of time, many departments of the Peking Party and government organisations carried out not the line of Marxism-Leninism and Mao Tse-tung's thought mapped out by the Central Committee of the Chinese Communist Party, but a revisionist line. They were instruments not of the proletariat for exercising dictatorship over the bourgeoisie but of the bourgeoisie for exercising dictatorship over the proletariat. The former Peking Municipal Committee of the Party was at the very root of this.

The former Peking Municipal Committee of the Party also carried out an anti-Party and anti-socialist line in education. Peking University was a most stubborn bulwark under its control. As many students of Peking University have revealed, its educational policy was not the training of successors for the proletarian revolutionary cause but the training of successors for the bourgeoisie.

The workers, peasants and soldiers in Peking and the many revolutionary cadres and revolutionary intellectuals have for a long time been resisting and fighting against the black anti-Party and anti-socialist line of the former Peking Municipal Party Committee. They have kept firmly to the instructions of the Central Committee of the Party and Chairman Mao Tse-tung, have done a great deal of work and made

253

their contribution to the socialist revolution and socialist construction. More than 95 per cent of the people and more than 95 per cent of the cadres in the Peking area support Chairman Mao and the Central Committee of the Party. Now that they know the real facts of the matter, those who were temporarily misled are immediately rallying and going into action against the black anti-Party and anti-socialist line of the former Peking Municipal Party Committee.

There is today a vigorous revolutionary situation in Peking University. The poster put up by seven comrades, including Nieh Yüan-tzu, written in big characters, was the opening shot. Everyone in the university was inspired and there was widespread joy as soon as the contents of this poster were broadcast on the radio and published in the newspapers. The proletarian revolutionaries are elated and the ranks of the Left have rapidly expanded. Tens of thousands of big-character posters have descended on the heads of the anti-Party and anti-socialist elements like a rain of shells. The active support given by all universities and colleges in Peking has greatly enhanced the revolutionary power and prestige of the proletariat. The "royalists" have panicked, they have become completely isolated. Under the leadership of the work team sent in by the new Municipal Party Committee, the students, faculty members and workers are firmly settling things and combating the anti-Party and anti-socialist crimes of Lu P'ing and the others.

In appearance, these counter-revolutionary anti-Party and anti-socialist cliques looked very tough. Their control and blockade were iron-clad and impenetrable. But once Chairman Mao Tse-tung and the Central Committee of the Party issued the clarion call to carry out the Great Proletarian Cultural Revolution, once the masses stood up, the counter-revolutionary features of these cliques were quickly exposed. Like all reactionaries, they were simply paper tigers.

The situation in our country is excellent. The people of the whole country have boundless love for Chairman Mao and the Central Committee of the Chinese Communist Party, Mao Tse-tung's thought has penetrated people's minds, the political consciousness of the masses is higher than it has ever been and tremendous successes have been registered in the socialist revolution and construction. No one who opposes Chairman Mao, Mao Tse-tung's thought, the Party's Central Committee, the dictatorship of the proletariat or the socialist system can escape the censure and condemnation by the whole Party and the whole nation, whoever he may be, whatever high position he may hold and however much of a veteran he may be. The only possible result is his total ruination.

We are firmly convinced that under the leadership of the newly reorganised Peking Municipal Committee of the Chinese Communist Party, the erroneous line of the former Municipal Party Committee and the effects of this line will be thoroughly eradicated. Tremendous successes in the Great Proletarian Cultural Revolution in Peking are certain. Now, all work in Peking is bound to be well done.

(From a translation of an editorial in Jen-min Jih-pao of June 4, 1966)

*   *   *

To Be Proletarian Revolutionaries or Bourgeois Royalists?

Responding to the great call of Chairman Mao Tse-tung and the Central Committee of the Chinese Communist Party, Peking University has set the Great Proletarian Cultural Revolution in dynamic motion. The proletarian revolutionaries in the university who were formerly repressed have risen to their feet. They have overthrown the rule of the bourgeois royalists headed by Lu P'ing. A struggle to smash the intrigues for the restoration of capitalism is developing successfully and the bourgeois royalists have found themselves heavily encircled by the masses.

With its long history, Peking University holds one of the most important positions in the field of education in our country. Some anti-Party, anti-socialist leading members of the former Peking Municipal Committee of the Party who adhered to a revisionist line always took Peking University as a base from which to win away the younger generation from the proletariat.

Stubbornly implementing the revisionist line of the former Peking Municipal Committee of the Party, that handful of royalists, Lu P'ing and company, exercised the dictatorship of the bourgeoisie in Peking University. Under their rule certain departments in the university, while nominally retaining the banner of the dictatorship of the proletariat, actually engaged in criminal activities against it. They carried out a bourgeois and revisionist line in education and went to great lengths to lead the students astray on to the road of revisionism and train them as successors for the bourgeoisie.

Lu P'ing and a handful of other royalists lauded to the skies the bourgeoisie's so-called academic authorities and allowed them to spread their poisonous ideas freely among the students and to systematically propagate bourgeois and revisionist ideology. They tried to oust the revolutionary teachers and relentlessly attacked them.

Lu P'ing and a handful of other royalists painstakingly cultivated students who accepted their revisionist policy in education, provided them with all kinds of facilities and gave them special care and attention. They tried to breed revisionist seedlings and spread them around.

Lu P'ing and a handful of other royalists intensely hated the students of worker and peasant origins and those students who rejected their whole set of revisionist policies in education. These royalists devised many ways of restricting, squeezing out, obstructing, and discriminating against these good students all the way from the entrance examination to the lectures, and from the final examination to the assignment of jobs on graduation. They went so far as to engage in ruthless struggles against these students.

Lu P'ing and a handful of other royalists desperately resisted and sabotaged the socialist education movement. During this movement, the revolutionary teachers and students of Peking University brought to light a great number of the anti-Party and anti-socialist statements and actions of Lu P'ing and other royalists and presented a vast amount of material showing their implementation of revisionist policy in education. But they put up a stubborn resistance. Under the direct guidance of the former Peking Municipal Committee of the Party, they launched a frantic counter-offensive in which they hit back and took revenge. They trumped up charges against the revolutionaries, attacked them and labelled them, organised things so as to hedge them in and made one round of attacks after another against them. The cruel struggle against a number of activists lasted as long as seven months. This was one extremely serious counter-revolutionary event that occurred in 1965.

Lu P'ing and a handful of other royalists did not scruple to hound those who would not obey their orders, accusing them of undermining organisational discipline and opposing the leadership. Indeed they showed a very strong Party spirit, but it was the Party spirit of the bourgeois royalists, the counter-revolutionary Party spirit of revisionism.

Indeed they had organisational discipline and leadership, but it was the organisational discipline of the bourgeois royalists and the counter-revolutionary leadership of revisionism. We must tell this bunch of lords that it was precisely the proletarian Party spirit which opposed your Party spirit. It was the conscious observance of the organisational discipline of the proletarian revolution and proletarian dictatorship which destroyed your organisational discipline. It was the conscious support and defence of the leadership of the Central Committee of the Chinese Communist Party headed by Chairman Mao Tse-tung which opposed your leadership. The people who did this are fine comrades, proletarian revolutionaries, the vanguards of Peking University's proletarian revolution. The Central Committee of the Chinese Communist Party headed by Chairman Mao certainly supports the proletarian revolutionaries in overthrowing your leadership and bringing down your bunch of royalists.

The struggle at Peking University is one between proletarian revolutionaries and bourgeois royalists, between Marxism-Leninism, Mao Tse-tung's thought on the one hand and revisionism on the other, between the proletarian line and the bourgeois line in education, between revolution and counter-revolution, and it is an extremely sharp class struggle.

The struggle by the bourgeoisie to win the younger generation away from the proletariat is an important part of the class struggle in socialist society. In the last analysis, the struggle between the two lines and the two roads of socialism and capitalism in the field of education is a question of whether the younger generation will be brought up to become successors to the proletariat or successors to the bourgeoisie. This great issue is one of crucial importance which concerns the destiny and future of our Party and State.

In its illusions about "peaceful evolution" in socialist New China, imperialism is pinning its hopes on the younger generation. Its futile dream is that our younger generation will take not the road of Marxism-Leninism and Mao Tse-tung's thought, but the road of revisionism. Lu P'ing and company who, in the sphere of education, obstinately pursued the revisionist line of the former Peking Municipal Party Committee exactly fitted the needs of imperialism.

Mao Tse-tung's thought is taking deeper and deeper root in the hearts and minds of the people of China. It is impossible for anyone to block access by the masses to Mao Tse-tung's thought. Even in that stubborn stronghold in which Lu P'ing and company was entrenched for so many years, the overwhelming majority of the students, the faculty and other staff members support Chairman Mao and Mao Tse-tung's thought, support our Party and its Central Committee. A great many of the students, faculty and other staff members there have all along held high the great red banner of Mao Tse-tung's thought and waged resolute struggles against Lu P'ing and company.

The struggle at Peking University is a typical instance of the struggle between the bourgeoisie who wants to restore capitalism and the proletariat who opposes a restoration. Every revolutionary comrade will derive very valuable experience from it and learn the lessons.

The unfolding of the Great Proletarian Cultural Revolution confronts educational workers, youth and students, confronts all cultural workers and everyone else with this sharp question — which side are you on in the life-and-death class struggle between the proletariat and the bourgeoisie, between the socialist and the capitalist road; to be a proletarian revolutionary or a bourgeois royalist? Everyone must choose for himself.

We are confident that the overwhelming majority, that is, over 95 per cent of the population, will surely repudiate the bourgeois royalists and stand on the side of the proletarian revolutionaries, will firmly rally around Chairman Mao Tse-tung and the Party's Central Committee and carry the cause of socialist revolution and the Great Proletarian Cultural Revolution in China through to the end!

(From a translation of an editorial in Jen-min Jih-pao of June 5, 1966)

*　　　*　　　*

Thoroughly Criticise and Repudiate the Revisionist Line of the Former CCP Peking Municipal Committee

The Great Proletarian Cultural Revolution is advancing with great rapidity and intensity. One group of monsters and demons after another has been exposed, and one reactionary bastion after another has been shattered. The broad masses of workers, peasants and soldiers, of Party cadres and revolutionary intellectuals in Peking, with the direct support of Chairman Mao Tse-tung and the Central Committee of

258

the Party, have exposed and overthrown the former Peking Municipal Party Committee, that insidious anti-Party and anti-socialist clique. The counter-revolutionary revisionist true colours of some of the principal leading members of the former Peking Municipal Party Committee have been fully brought out into the open.

This is an excellent, important event in the history of the dictatorship of the proletariat in our country and a new victory for Mao Tse-tung's thought.

A black line opposed to the Party, to socialism and to Mao Tse-tung's thought ran through the leadership exercised by some of the principal leading members of the former Peking Municipal Party Committee. The main point of this black line was opposition to the proletarian revolution, to the dictatorship of the proletariat, and to the correct line of the Central Committee of the Party and Comrade Mao Tse-tung, and the carrying out of a counter-revolutionary, revisionist line. This was manifested in the following respects:

First, Resistance to the Great Proletarian Cultural Revolution. Some of the principal leading members of the former Peking Municipal Party Committee deeply feared the Great Proletarian Cultural Revolution, and they stubbornly opposed and sabotaged that great cultural revolution. Their counter-revolutionary, revisionist line was exposed precisely in the course of the current great cultural revolution. Under the direct leadership of Chairman Mao and the Party's Central Committee, the Shanghai Municipal Committee of the Chinese Communist Party started the criticism of Wu Han's "Hai Jui Dismissed From Office," and sounded the clarion call for the Great Proletarian Cultural Revolution. The Shanghai *Wenhui Pao* printed Comrade Yao Wen-yüan's article "On the New Historical Drama Hai Jui Dismissed From Office" and this angered the gang of revisionist lords in the former Peking Municipal Party Committee. They made unscrupulous attacks on the Shanghai Municipal Party Committee, and flagrantly acted against Comrade Mao Tse-tung's instructions. They regarded Comrade Yao Wen-yüan's article as dangerous floods and wild beasts, and used the propaganda organs in their hands to try in every way possible to resist and block the article. They resorted to all sorts of vile and vicious tricks to suppress and deal blows at all proletarian revolutionaries who persist in Comrade Mao Tse-tung's correct line, and to shield the sinister anti-Party and anti-socialist counter-revolutionary gangsters. Even after Comrade Mao Tse-tung criticised the former Peking Municipal Party Committee,

259

they continued to carry out organised and planned resistance in an attempt "to save the queen by sacrificing the knights." The editorial note of *Ch'ien Hsien* (Frontline) and *Pei-ching Jih-pao* (Peking Daily) on April 16 was a concentrated expression of the counter-revolutionary double-dealing tricks they played. Further, they carried out a series of clandestine, underground and illegal activities, clung desperately to their positions and collected information about proletarian revolutionaries in preparation for a counter-offensive. This series of anti-Party activities paved the way for their own complete downfall. Thus, the counter-revolutionary features of the gang of representatives of the bourgeoisie who had long hidden themselves in the Party were brought to light.

Second, Opposition to the Socialist Education Movement in the Urban and Rural Areas. The opposition of the former Peking Municipal Party Committee to the Great Proletarian Cultural Revolution was the continuation and development of their consistent opposition over the past few years to the socialist education movement in the urban and rural areas and to the socialist revolution. They opposed and resisted the policy of the urban and rural socialist education movement formulated by Chairman Mao and the Party's Central Committee; they opposed the full mobilisation of the masses to lift the lid† on the class struggle; they protected the Party members who were in power at the basic level in the urban and rural areas and were taking the road of capitalism; and they protected the landlords, rich peasants, counter-revolutionaries, bad elements and rightists. As the urban and rural socialist education movement developed in depth, they lost no time in "applying the brake," and worked vigorously to reverse decisions on closed cases; they backed up the landlords, rich peasants, counter-revolutionaries, bad elements and rightists; they attacked the poor peasants, lower-middle peasants and revolutionary activists and carried out organised and planned counter-attacks in revenge. This line of the former Peking Municipal Party Committee was precisely a line of opposing socialist revolution and of restoring capitalism.

Third, Abandonment of the Viewpoint of Classes and Class Struggle in an Attempt to Bring About a "Peaceful Evolution." The former Peking Municipal Party Committee stubbornly opposed and resisted Comrade Mao Tse-tung's guiding principles regarding classes and class struggle in socialist society. They were opposed to taking class struggle as the key link in all fields of work: in culture, education, industry, agriculture, finance and trade, etc. They were opposed to giving

260

prominence to proletarian politics and, instead, they gave prominence to bourgeois politics. Because they have abandoned the viewpoint of classes and class struggle of Marxism-Leninism, of Mao Tse-tung's thought, they could not but sink into the quagmire of Khrushchev revisionism. What they carried into effect was, in reality, such revisionist rubbish as Khrushchev's "Party of the entire people" and "State of the whole people." Their bourgeois nature was clearly revealed. On various fronts, they ruthlessly suppressed and dealt blows at the proletarian revolutionary Left and revolutionary masses, and did all they could to let loose monsters of all kinds. This small handful of counter-revolutionary revisionists carried out "peaceful evolution" in some units and departments of the Peking Municipal Party and government organisations, and, as a result, the leadership of these was usurped by representatives of the bourgeoisie.

Fourth, Transformation of the Dictatorship of the Proletariat Into a Dictatorship of the Bourgeoisie. The small handful of counter-revolutionary revisionists in the former Peking Municipal Party Committee waved the flag of the dictatorship of the proletariat, but, in reality, they did their utmost to carry out bourgeois dictatorial rule. Arrogantly, arbitrarily and without any sense of democracy, they suppressed and attacked the broad masses of workers, peasants and soldiers, of Party cadres and revolutionary intellectuals. Their "democracy" was the democracy of a handful of representatives of the bourgeoisie who opposed the Party, opposed socialism and opposed Mao Tse-tung's thought, the democracy of a handful of reactionary bourgeois "academic authorities," the democracy of a handful of landlords, rich peasants, counter-revolutionaries, bad elements and rightists. They were a bunch of despots, a bunch of Lords of Hell.

Fifth, Preparation of Public Opinion for the Restoration of Capitalism and Subversion of Proletarian Political Power. The small handful of counter-revolutionary revisionists of the former Peking Municipal Party Committee laid special stress on preparing public opinion for the restoration of capitalism and the subversion of the proletarian political power. They used *Ch'ien Hsien* (Frontline), *Pei-ching Jih-pao* (Peking Daily) and *Pei-ching Wan-pao* (Peking Evening News) as their tools to oppose the Party, socialism and Mao Tse-tung's thought and to spread revisionist poison. Making use of the newspapers, journals, radio broadcasts, books, lectures, literary works, films, plays, operas, etc., which they were able to control, they poured out a great deal of poison to corrode and corrupt the people of the whole country. All this was done with a view to preparing conditions for the restoration of capitalism.

Sixth, Opposition to the Educational Policy Put Forward by Chairman Mao and the Party's Central Committee, and Application of a Bourgeois and Revisionist Educational Policy. Some schools under the control of some of the principal leading members of the former Peking Municipal Party Committee, instead of serving proletarian politics, worked in the interests of a bourgeois restoration. Instead of cultivating successors to the proletarian revolutionary cause, they groomed new bourgeois intellectuals. While showing great care and consideration for bourgeois elements, they discriminated against and persecuted the broad masses of revolutionary teachers and students. Peking University under their control was a typical stubborn stronghold of reaction.

Seventh, Opposition to the Creative Study and Application of Chairman Mao's Works. The small handful of members of the former Peking Municipal Party Committee did their utmost to oppose the creative study and application of Chairman Mao's works by the broad masses of workers, peasants and soldiers and cadres. Harbouring intense hatred for Mao Tse-tung's thought, they reacted against any mention of it and swore and flew into a rage. They attacked and suppressed the masses of workers, peasants and soldiers and revolutionary cadres who followed Chairman Mao's teachings and acted in accordance with his instructions. This handful of counter-revolutionary revisionists did all kinds of evil. What they dreaded most was to be shown up in their true colours under the sunlight of Mao Tse-tung's thought. Above all they dreaded mastery by the broad masses of the infinitely powerful weapon of Mao Tse-tung's thought to overthrow their reactionary rule.

Eighth, Recruitment of Deserters and Acceptance of Mutineers and Formation of Cliques for Their Own Selfish Interests. In order to push through their revisionist political line, these principal leading members of the. former Peking Municipal Party Committee pursued a "feudal guild" organisational line of forming cliques for their own selfish interests. Using such base means as handing out official posts, lavishing promises, and recruiting deserters and accepting mutineers, they bought over and gained the allegiance of a group of people as a band of loyal confederates who acted as their faithful lackeys.

Ninth, Erection of a Tight Barricade Against the Party's Central Committee. The small handful of anti-Party elements in the former Peking Municipal Party Committee regarded the Peking municipality

262

as an "independent kingdom," watertight and impenetrable, and nobody was allowed to intervene or criticise it — it was like a tiger whose backside no one dared to kick. On the other hand, they themselves reached out everywhere with their grasping hands. They were a gang of conspirators and careerists.

Tenth, Waving "Red Flags" to Oppose the Red Flag. The main reason why these anti-Party, anti-socialist, revisionist elements were able to conceal themselves for a considerable period of time was that they waved "red flags" to oppose the red flag, carried the signboard of Marxism-Leninism to oppose Marxism-Leninism, carried the signboard of Mao Tse-tung's thought to oppose Mao Tse-tung's thought, carried the signboard of the dictatorship of the proletariat to oppose the dictatorship of the proletariat, and carried the communist signboard to engage in anti-communist intrigues. These manoeuvres by the principal leading members of the former Peking Municipal Party Committee were almost identical with those of Khrushchev. They are persons of the Khrushchev type.

Step by step the Central Committee of the Party perceived the revisionist line of the principal leading members of the former Peking Municipal Party Committee. But the full exposure of their revisionist nature required a certain course of time and certain "soil and weather" conditions. Even a poisonous snake comes out of its hole only in certain weather conditions, and the moment these poisonous snakes came out of their holes, they were captured by Chairman Mao and the Party's Central Committee and immediately crushed by the broad masses of Party cadres and the people.

The exposure of this sinister gang of some of the principal leading members of the former Peking Municipal Party Committee who were against the Party, against socialism and against Mao Tse-tung's thought is an excellent thing, a normal phenomenon in Party life. Comrade Mao Tse-tung told us long ago that if there were no contradictions and no struggles in the Party, the Party's life would come to an end. Under certain conditions, the contradictions within the Party can change from being non-antagonistic to being antagonistic ones. The fact that our Party was able in good time to detect and destroy the reactionary bastion of the former Peking Municipal Party Committee, which was completely controlled by a handful of revisionists, is a fine demonstration of the power and strength of our Party and the exceptional wisdom and greatness of the leadership given by Chairman Mao and the Party's Central

Committee.

Some of the principal leading members of the former Peking Municipal Party Committee are very good teachers by negative example. What we learn from all this is that in order to push ahead the Great Proletarian Cultural Revolution and wrest back the leadership usurped by the bourgeoisie in the field of culture, we must first of all expose, criticise and struggle against the representatives of the bourgeoisie who have wormed their way into the Party, government, army and various circles in the field of culture. The struggle against these revisionists who are against the Party, against socialism and against Mao Tse-tung's thought is a struggle between attempts at staging a capitalist restoration and efforts to thwart such attempts and a struggle to prevent the dictatorship of the proletariat from changing into a dictatorship of the bourgeoisie.

High in spirit, the broad masses of workers, peasants and soldiers and of the Party cadres and revolutionary intellectuals in Peking are arming themselves with Mao Tse-tung's thought and using it as their weapon for combat and criticism in the Great Proletarian Cultural Revolution. Under the leadership of the new Peking Municipal Party Committee, they are sweeping away all monsters with the tremendous force of a thunderbolt.

For a long time, the broad masses of workers, peasants and soldiers, of the Communist Party and the Communist Youth League members, and of the revolutionary intellectuals in Peking resisted and fought against the black anti-Party, anti-socialist line of the former Peking Municipal Party Committee. They cherish boundless love for Chairman Mao and support the Party's Central Committee without reservation. Keeping to the instructions of the Party's Central Committee and Chairman Mao, they have done a great deal of work and made their own contributions to the cause of socialist revolution and socialist construction. Upwards of 95 per cent of the people, and more than 95 per cent of the cadres in Peking, will certainly unite on the basis of Mao Tse-tung's thought, take what Chairman Mao says as the supreme instruction for all kinds of work and, under the leadership of the new Peking Municipal Party Committee, thoroughly eradicate the influence of the counter-revolutionary revisionist line of the former Peking Municipal Party Committee and score new victories on all fronts.

(From a full translation of an editorial in *Hung-ch'i,* No. 9, 1966)

A Great Ideological Revolution

A call is made in the editorials reproduced below to criticise the old bourgeois ideology and culture and the influence they exert. These documents declare that the deepening of a great socialist cultural revolution is always preceded by a gigantic struggle in the ideological field and heralded by a great ideological revolution. The bourgeoisie is charged with using the reactionary slogan of "Liberty, equality and fraternity" to deceive the working people and oppose proletarian dictatorship in the vain hope of regaining their lost "paradise."—Ed.

We Are Critics of the Old World

The rapid and vigorous development of China's Great Proletarian Cultural Revolution is shaking the world.

Some people say, "The 700 million Chinese are all critics."

Irrespective of who says this, and whether it makes them happy or unhappy, this saying reflects the fact that China's broad masses of workers, peasants and soldiers and revolutionary cadres and revolutionary intellectuals, using as their weapon the thought of Mao Tse-tung, have started to criticise the old world, old things and old thinking on an unprecedented scale.

We criticise the system of exploitation, the exploiting classes, imperialism, modern revisionism, all reactionaries, landlords, rich peasants, counter-revolutionaries, bad elements and rightists.

We criticise the representatives of the bourgeoisie and bourgeois "scholars and authorities."

We criticise the bourgeois conception of history, bourgeois academic theories, pedagogy, journalism, and theories of art and literature, and all bad plays, films and works of literature and art.

In sum, we criticise the old world, the old ideology and culture, and old customs and habits which imperialism and all exploiting classes use to poison the minds of the working people, we criticise all non-proletarian ideology, all reactionary ideology which is antagonistic to Marxism-Leninism, to Mao Tse-tung's thought.

Why should we criticise all this?

We do this because it is absolutely necessary for the consolidation of the dictatorship of the proletariat and the building of socialism and communism, and it corresponds to the laws of historical development. Lenin held that after the overthrow of the bourgeoisie, for a long period its strength surpasses that of the proletariat, and that, particularly in the field of ideology, for a long time it still remains predominant and very stubborn. And it uses this in every way to make ideological preparations and get public opinion ready for the restoration of capitalism. This is fully illustrated by the sharp and protracted struggles on the ideological and cultural front between the two classes and two roads in the 17 years since the liberation of China, and especially by the struggle between the bourgeoisie plotting a restoration and the proletariat opposing a restoration, a struggle which of late has come to the fore.

Chairman Mao told us long ago that everything reactionary is the same: if you don't hit it, it won't fall. This is also like sweeping the floor; as a rule, where the broom does not reach, the dust does not vanish of itself. This applies to everything in the world. We want to build the new world so we must destroy the old; we want to create the new ideology and culture of socialism and communism so we must subject the old bourgeois ideology and culture, and the influence they exert, to thoroughgoing criticism and clear them out.

The essence of Marxism-Leninism is critical and revolutionary. Its essentials are to criticise, to wage struggle and make revolution. What we practise is the militant philosophy of dialectical materialism. Struggle is life. As we go forward along the correct path of struggle, our fighting power will grow and we will be better able to advance our great cause.

Chairman Mao has often emphasised that "there is no construction without destruction, no flowing without damming and no moving forward without a holding back." Destruction here means criticism, means revolution. Destruction necessarily calls for reasoning, and reasoning is construction; destruction comes first, and in the course of it there is construction. The formation and development of Marxism-Leninism and Mao Tse-tung's thought have taken place in the incessant struggle to destroy the ideological system of the bourgeoisie.

266

Chairman Mao says:

> What is correct always develops to the course of struggle with what is wrong. The true, the good and the beautiful always exist in comparison with the false, the evil and the ugly, and grow in struggle with the latter.

Who is to be counted on in making criticism? We must count on the broadest masses of the people, on the workers, peasants and soldiers, the revolutionary cadres and the revolutionary intellectuals. During the revolutionary war, the masses of people used arms to criticise the old world and seize power; since victory, they have been using criticism as their weapon against all the evils left over by imperialism and the landlord and bourgeois classes. Only when all the 700 million people take up Mao Tse-tung's thought, the sharpest of all weapons, to make criticism can there be a clean-up on the broadest scale of the dust left hidden by the bourgeoisie in every corner and a thorough uprooting to the greatest depth of the ideology of the exploiting classes which have been in a monopolistic and dominant position for the past thousands of years. Only when the broadest masses master the proletarian world outlook and criticise the bourgeois world outlook, master Marxism-Leninism, Mao Tse-tung's thought, and criticise revisionist ideas, will there be the guarantee of China's socialist revolution being carried through to the end and of its step-by-step transition from socialism to communism.

The fact that "700 million people are critics" is stupendous, it is an epoch-making event. This in itself shows that the thinking of our 700 million people has been emancipated, that they have risen to full height and that they are no longer slaves of the old culture and old ideas of imperialism and the exploiting classes. It is not at all accidental that our 700 million people have become critics. It is something new that has arisen in the conditions of the dictatorship of the proletariat. It is something new, born of the brilliance of Mao Tse-tung's thought. It is a new phenomenon, an inevitable product of the integration of Mao Tse-tung's thought with the broad masses of workers, peasants and soldiers. It represents the great awakening of the Chinese people.

The birth and deepening of any great revolutionary movement is inevitably preceded by a gigantic struggle in the ideological field and heralded by a great ideological revolution. In the history of the proletarian revolution, every major polemics has been the prelude to and signal for a revolutionary leap forward. In China, each of the many major polemics in the ideological field in the 17 years since liberation has blazed the trail for the locomotive of revolution. The great cultural revolution now under way, on a scale never known before, necessarily foreshadows a development of the socialist revolution by leaps and bounds and a new big leap forward in China's socialist construction.

Once the people have risen, the enemy falls. In China, the broad masses of workers, peasants and soldiers, the revolutionary cadres and revolutionary intellectuals have risen, and the representatives of the bourgeoisie and the bourgeois "scholars and authorities" will fall. In the movement of criticism that is developing on an unprecedentedly wide scale in the tremendous cultural revolution, a great new era is now emerging on the horizon, an era in which the whole of the 700 million Chinese people are people of wisdom.

Let us welcome this great new era with open arms.

(From a translation of an editorial in *Jen-min Jih-pao* of June 8, 1966)

*   *   *

Tear Aside the Bourgeois Mask of 'Liberty, Equality and Fraternity'

There is an upsurge in the Great Proletarian Cultural Revolution in China today. This surging tide is forcefully pounding away at all the decadent ideological and cultural positions held by the bourgeoisie and the feudal survivals. Holding high the great red banner of Mao Tse-tung's thought, the workers, peasants and soldiers, the revolutionary cadres and revolutionary intellectuals have launched a fierce counteroffensive against the black anti-Party and anti-socialist line of the bourgeoisie. This is a serious, acute and complex political struggle, a struggle between the proletariat and the bourgeoisie, between socialism and capitalism, between revolution and counter-revolution, between Marxism-Leninism and revisionism; it is a life-and-death class struggle. In no way is this struggle a trivial matter; it is a matter of prime importance that affects the destiny and future of our Party and State; it is a matter of prime importance that affects what our Party and State will look like in the future, and also affects the world revolution.

Basing himself on the fundamental theses of Marxism-Leninism and the historical experience of the dictatorship of the proletariat, Chairman Mao Tse-tung has comprehensively and systematically analysed classes and class struggle in socialist society and creatively developed Marxist-Leninist theory on the dictatorship of the proletariat. Chairman Mao teaches us that class contradiction still exists and class struggle does not die out in socialist society after the completion of the socialist transformation of the ownership of the means of production. There is struggle between the proletariat and bourgeoisie, between the socialist and capitalist roads throughout the stage of socialism. The socialist revolution must be carried through to the end on the political, economic, and ideological and cultural fronts in order to ensure the successful building of socialism and prevent the restoration of capitalism. It is precisely Chairman Mao's theory on classes and class struggle in socialist society, on the proletarian revolution and the dictatorship of the proletariat, on the need to carry out the socialist revolution not only in the matter of ownership but also in the field of ideology, that provides the correct line and guiding principles which we must follow in this great socialist cultural revolution.

With ulterior motives, a handful of representatives of the bourgeoisie, who had wormed their way into our Party, covered up the true class nature of the struggle and twisted this serious political struggle into a "purely academic problem" and a "discussion of different opinions." They hoisted aloft the black bourgeois banner of "liberty, equality and fraternity" in opposition to the line of the proletarian cultural revolution advanced by the Party's Central Committee headed by Chairman Mao Tse-tung. They ranted along these lines: "full expression should be given to different opinions (including those opposed to Marxism-Leninism)," "everyone is equal before the truth," "one should not be arbitrary like a scholar-tyrant or overwhelm others by the use of one's position or power," and cried that "care" and "prudence" must be exercised in the struggle against the anti-Party and anti-socialist monsters and that they should not be "held in such a tight grip" and so on. Their vicious motive was: to deceive the masses of the people, muddy the waters, mix up the proletarian and the bourgeois class fronts and shift the target of the struggle; to encourage the bourgeois Right and frustrate the proletarian Left, protect the bourgeois Right and attack the proletarian Left. Their motive was to bring about bourgeois liberalisation and revisionism and reduce proletarian rule to chaos so that they could capture power from the proletariat and restore capitalism when the opportunity arose.

Messrs. bourgeois "authorities!" You are experts at making mistakes. Your appraisal of the situation was entirely wrong. Your estimation of the consciousness and strength of the workers, peasants and soldiers was entirely wrong. Your estimation of the power of the Party's leadership and the dictatorship of the proletariat was again entirely wrong. You cannot possibly succeed in using the tattered banner of "liberty, equality and fraternity" to cover up your attack on the Party and socialism. Equally, you cannot possibly succeed in using that banner as a "protective umbrella" to cover your retreat. All the more is it impossible for you to realise your vain hope of making us relinquish the dictatorship of the proletariat and deal with you monsters on the footing of liberty, equality and fraternity, and allow you to impose your dictatorship over us. You are demons in human shape. Don't imagine that you wolves, once in sheep's clothing, can deceive people. The worker, peasant and soldier masses, the revolutionary cadres and revolutionary intellectuals, armed with Mao Tse-tung's thought, are firm and clear-sighted and their banner is bright and distinctive. We have torn aside your sordid camouflage of counter-revolution and caught you red-handed. We shall strip you of your disguises and expose you in all your ugliness.

You Messrs. bourgeois "authorities" talked glibly about "liberty" and put great stress on the "opening wide" policy in an underhand attempt to distort this policy of the Party and wipe out its class content. Your "opening wide" was to meet the needs of your own class and bring about bourgeois liberalisation. It was opposed to the Party's leadership, the dictatorship of the proletariat and the thought of Mao Tse-tung.

"Isn't it the Party's policy to 'open wide'?" This was the pretext put forward by Messrs. bourgeois "authorities." Yes, we are firmly in favour of the policy of opening wide. Chairman Mao said: "We choose the policy of opening wide, because it is the policy which will help to consolidate our country and develop our culture." He also said: "To 'open wide' means to let all people express their opinions freely, so that they dare to speak, dare to criticise and dare to debate." In discussing this question, Chairman Mao specially pointed out that "we still have to wage a protracted struggle against bourgeois and petty-bourgeois ideology. It is wrong not to understand this and to give up ideological struggle. All erroneous ideas, all poisonous weeds, all ghosts and monsters, must be subjected to criticism; in no circumstance should they be allowed to spread unchecked." Our policy of "opening wide" is a firm proletarian class policy and is distinguished by proletarian political criteria. But your so-called "opening wide" encourages

270

the bourgeoisie alone and not the proletariat. It permits only such bourgeois "authorities," "specialists" and "scholars" as yourselves to spread their poison without allowing the worker, peasant and soldier masses and the revolutionary cadres and revolutionary intellectuals to hit back. In a word, under the pretext of "opening wide," you are actually opposing the Party and socialism.

Weren't these the facts? For years, Messrs. bourgeois "authorities," you turned loose a horde of monsters to spread their load of poison, without let-up for a single day, in co-ordination internationally with the big anti-China chorus of the imperialists, the modern revisionists and all reactionaries. Your poisonous products filled our newspapers, radio, magazines, books, textbooks, lectures, literary works, films, plays, operas and ballads, fine arts, music, dancing, etc. You never advocated the need to accept proletarian leadership, and never asked anyone for approval of what you did. Yet when we launched a counter-attack on the ideological and cultural front, what attitude did you take towards the worker, peasant and soldier masses and towards the proletarian Left? You shelved everything critical of the poisonous weeds, holding some things back for as long as several years. You set up one taboo after another, put on airs and deliberately turned simple matters into mysteries to scare off the workers, peasants and soldiers. You lavished praise on the so-called academic "authorities" of the bourgeoisie and showed hostility to and suppressed the militant, new emerging forces representing the proletariat. You would not allow the workers, peasants and soldiers to rise up and overthrow the bourgeois "authorities," you would not allow them to make revolution.

Obviously, the "liberty" you wanted was nothing but liberty to set up the "Three-Family Village" gangster inn, liberty to spread the villainous "Evening Chats at Yenshan," liberty to stage widely such unsavoury plays and films as "Hsieh Yao-huan," "Li Hui-niang," "Hai Jui Dismissed from Office," and "Laying Siege to the City," liberty to complain that the Right opportunists had been wronged and to encourage them to stage a come-back, liberty to pour cold water on the enthusiasm of the worker, peasant and soldier masses for creatively studying and applying Mao Tse-tung's works and to use the big stick on them, liberty to spread widely the decadent and degenerate landlord, bourgeois and revisionist ideology to pave the way for the restoration of capitalism. The "liberty" you wanted was liberty to attack the Party and socialism, to attack the dictatorship of the proletariat, and to attack Mao Tse-tung's

271

thought. In short, you wanted the liberty of counter-revolution. Chairman Mao has said:

> Freedom and democracy do not exist in the abstract, only in the concrete. In a society rent by class struggle, if there is freedom for the exploiting classes to exploit the working people, there is no freedom for the working people not to be exploited, and if there is democracy for the bourgeoisie, there is no democracy for the proletariat and other working people.

Our socialist system certainly will not allow freedom of speech to counter-revolutionaries; this freedom is permitted only among the people. You want to oppose the leadership of the Party and socialism but we will never give you this freedom. If you were allowed freedom to oppose the Party and socialism, the revolution would suffer defeat, the people would suffer disaster and this would lead the country to destruction.

Messrs. bourgeois "authorities!" You harped on "equality," alleging that "everybody is equal before the truth." This is an out-and-out bourgeois slogan, an extremely reactionary slogan which protects the bourgeoisie and opposes the proletariat, Marxism-Leninism and Mao Tse-tung's thought.

Did you really practise equality? No, not in the least. How wildly and tyrannically you attacked the proletariat! You revered as sacred, as priceless, all the things that came from the bourgeois "specialists" and "scholars," and, giving them your whole attention, you published them, advertised them, performed them and lauded them. As for the products of the workers, peasants and soldiers, even their good articles on the creative study and application of Chairman Mao's works, you dismissed contemptuously. You dared to denigrate them as typically "philistine," "oversimplified," and "pragmatic" and forthwith consigned them to the back shelf. Is that equality? You spread a lot of poison, yet the moment we counter-attacked you yelled "everyone is equal before the truth." Indeed, you clamped the label "scholar-tyrants" on the proletarian Left and maligned our counter-attack as "arbitrary," as "overwhelming others by the use of position or power." Let us ask, what is a "scholar-tyrant," and who is a "scholar-tyrant?" Does not the proletariat need dictatorship, does it not need to prevail over the bourgeoisie? Is it not necessary for proletarian learning to prevail over and eliminate bourgeois learning? By your actions you have been in fact making a last-ditch fight, rejecting criticism, attacking the

272

proletarian Left and giving support to real bourgeois scholar-tyrants. Is that, too, equality?

Were you really talking of the truth? No. You embarked on a conspiracy under the smokescreen of "truth." You used undermining tactics, utterly stripping truth of its class nature. Don't you know that there is only class truth in class society and no such thing as abstract truth above classes? Each particular plant yields its own particular fruit; each class speaks in its own terms. Different classes always hold different views on what is truth and what is falsehood, what constitute fragrant flowers and what poisonous weeds. The "fragrant flowers" you glorify are, to us, simply poisonous weeds which we shall uproot. The "truth" you uphold is exactly the bourgeois falsehood we oppose. Truth is objective. There can be only one truth and who after all arrives at the truth depends not on subjective boasting but on objective practice. The only criterion of truth is the revolutionary practice of the millions of people. Only the proletariat, which is the most advanced and most revolutionary class, can understand the objective laws of social development and grasp the truth. Mao Tse-tung's thought is the acme of Marxism-Leninism in the present era, living Marxism-Leninism at its highest, the powerful ideological weapon in the hands of the proletariat and the revolutionary people all over the world, the great truth in this great era of ours. Mao Tse-tung's thought is the truth that conforms to the laws of development of socialist society, the laws of development of nature, and the needs of proletarian revolution. In making Mao Tse-tung's thought our supreme guide and leadership we show that we indeed love the truth, uphold the truth and adhere to the truth. You made a hullabaloo about "everybody is equal before the truth." Putting it plainly, what you meant was opposition to Mao Tse-tung's thought, substituting for the great thought of Mao Tse-tung the reactionary ideology of the bourgeoisie and the revisionists. This was the great conspiracy you conceived!

Chairman Mao teaches us that the struggle between the proletariat and the bourgeoisie, between the truth of Marxism and the fallacies of the bourgeoisie and all exploiting classes, is a matter of the East wind prevailing over the West wind or vice versa; in this connection there can never be any such thing as equality. What equality can be permitted in such fundamental matters as the proletarian struggle against the bourgeoisie, the dictatorship of the proletariat over the bourgeoisie, the dictatorship of the proletariat in the realm of the superstructure including the various fields of culture, and the continuous work that the proletariat has to do in clearing out the bourgeois representatives who have wormed their way into the Communist Party and waved "red flags" to oppose the red flag, etc.? For decades the old social democratic parties, and in the last ten years or so, the modern revisionists, have never allowed the proletariat any equality with the bourgeoisie. They entirely deny that the history of mankind for several thousand years has been one of class struggle, they entirely deny proletarian class struggle against the bourgeoisie, proletarian revolution against the bourgeoisie and the dictatorship of the proletariat over the bourgeoisie. On the contrary, they are faithful lackeys of the bourgeoisie and imperialism, and, hand in hand with them cling to the ideology of bourgeois oppression and exploitation of the proletariat and to the social system of capitalism while opposing the ideology of Marxism-Leninism and the socialist system of society. They are anti-communist and anti-popular counter-revolutionaries. Their struggle against us is one of life and death in which there is no such thing as equality. Hence, our struggle against them is inevitably one of life and death; our relationship with them can never be that of equality but that in which one class suppresses the other, *i.e.,* a relationship in which the proletariat exercises absolute rule or dictatorship over the bourgeoisie; nor can it be anything else, such as, for example, a so-called relationship of equality, a relationship of peaceful co-existence between the exploited and exploiting classes, or a relationship of benevolence, justice and so on.

Messrs. bourgeois "authorities!" On the black banner you monsters displayed, you inscribed the word "fraternity." What do you mean by "fraternity?" You ardently love the bourgeoisie and intensely hate the proletariat. That is your conception, the bourgeois conception, of "fraternity."

Let us now see what they really love, these philanthropists who are filled with the spirit of "fraternity." When the anti-Party and anti-socialist gang feverishly attacked the Party in order to give it a heavy "blow on the head" and "pour dog's blood on its head," in the hope of overthrowing the Party leadership, you bosses behind the scenes gave them the green light, beat the drum for them, summoned the wind and the waves, forgot yourselves in your excitement and acclaimed them in the belief that good days were in store for you just around the corner. But your sweet dream was short-lived and your dirty anti-Party and anti-socialist camouflage was soon torn down. Then, when you threw away your shield and armour and fled in panic you hastily hoisted the tattered flag of "fraternity" and assumed a hypocritic air of impartiality and justice, while proclaiming that "those with reactionary academic viewpoints" must be allowed to "reserve their views" and not be "prevented from making revolution" and not "be held in a tight grip," and so on. This was really an example of birds of a feather flocking together. What care and consideration you showed for that anti-Party and anti-socialist gang of yours! As for the staunch proletarian Left, they were a thorn in your flesh and you wanted to "rectify" their "working style" and "purge" them. You longed to devour them. How firm was your bourgeois stand! What a clear distinction you maintained then between love and hate!

Chairman Mao teaches us: "There is absolutely no such thing in the world as love or hatred without reason or cause." He also teaches us:

> We definitely do not apply a policy of benevolence to the reactionaries and towards the reactionary activities of the reactionary classes. Our policy of benevolence is applied only within the ranks of the people, not beyond them to the reactionaries or to the reactionary activities of reactionary classes.

Messrs. bourgeois "authorities!" You are birds of a feather with imperialism, modern revisionism and the reactionaries abroad, and with the landlords, rich peasants, counter-revolutionaries, bad elements and rightists at home. There is no compatibility between you and us, and the struggle between you and us is irreconcilable. You have never had "fraternal love" for us, nor shall we ever have any for you. Your hatred for our great Party of the proletariat and the people was so bitter that you employed the meanest of tricks and would not feel content till you utterly destroyed them. How then can we talk about "fraternal love" for you? We must never be tender-hearted to the enemies of the revolution. To be tender-hearted to you would mean cruelty to the proletariat and to the millions of working people. We must never mistake the wolf for the lamb or arsenic for sugar. We shall never be deceived by you "tigers with smiling faces." We must reply in kind. We must deal you destructive blows, make your names reek to high heaven and defeat and overthrow you completely. We must thoroughly sweep away all "pests" that harm the people!

"Liberty, equality and fraternity" is the decadent and reactionary world outlook of the bourgeoisie. Two centuries have passed since this slogan was first raised by the French bourgeoisie in the 18th

275

century. Although when they led the French revolution, this slogan had an anti-feudal progressive aspect, it is a hypocritical one used by the bourgeoisie to defend their private class interests. The bourgeoisie made use of this slogan during the democratic revolution to deceive the working people, seize State power from the feudal landlord class and establish a bourgeois dictatorship. After their seizure of power, the bourgeoisie continued to use the slogan to lull the working people, cover up their sanguinary rule and consolidate the dictatorship of the bourgeoisie. The liberty proclaimed by the bourgeoisie amounts to nothing more than liberty for them to exploit wage labour and plunder colonies, and on the other hand, liberty for the labouring people to be exploited and the people in the colonies to be plundered. The equality proclaimed by the bourgeoisie means nothing more than equality for them to exploit wage labour and equality for the working people to be exploited. The fraternity proclaimed by the bourgeoisie means nothing more than an attempt to exploit and enslave more and more people, and a demand that the exploited and oppressed people should be grateful for the bourgeois exploitation. Marx and Engels once said that the vampire would not lose its hold so long as there was a muscle, a nerve, a drop of blood to be exploited. This is the reactionary essence of the bourgeois slogan of "liberty, equality and fraternity."

The bourgeoisie never reconcile themselves to their defeat once their State power is overthrown by the proletarian revolution. Invariably they resort to every kind of conspiracy and disruption, and, through their agents who have infiltrated the revolutionary ranks, they employ the reactionary slogan of "liberty, equality and fraternity" to deceive and lull the working people and oppose the dictatorship of the proletariat in the vain hope of restoring their lost "paradise." In opposing the proletarian revolution and proletarian dictatorship, the old social-democrats adopted the black banner of "liberty, equality and fraternity." In order to backtrack from socialism to capitalism, and to oppose and undermine people's revolution throughout the world, the Khrushchev modern revisionists have also taken up this reactionary banner and even incorporated it into the notorious programme of the CPSU. In 1956, the Hungarian "Petofi Club" also used this black banner to incite the masses to stage a counter-revolutionary rebellion. The bourgeois rightists in our country in 1957 hoisted the same banner in their frenzied attack on the Party and socialism. At the Lushan meeting the Right opportunists who were dismissed from office also vigorously spread

276

this reactionary slogan in their opposition to the Party's Central Committee, to the Party's correct line and to Mao Tse-tung's thought. Now, Messrs. bourgeois "authorities," you have also plucked this rubbish from history's dustbin, tried to pretty it up and made it your anti-Party, anti-socialist standard, your programme of action against Mao Tse-tung's thought and your magic weapon to obstruct and undermine the great socialist cultural revolution. You have stepped into the shoes of the bourgeoisie and revisionists past and present, at home and abroad, set up cliques for your selfish interests, and tried every trick to mislead the public and match strength with the proletariat, in the hope of undermining the dictatorship of the proletariat and restoring capitalism. You are racking your brains in vain! You are daydreaming! Your fate cannot be better than that of your fore-runners and brothers-in-crime!

Our socialist society still rests on class antagonism. Although the landlord and the bourgeois classes have been overthrown, they are not yet completely eliminated. We have confiscated the property of the exploiting classes, but we cannot confiscate their reactionary ideas. Persons of these classes are still living and they are not reconciled. They inevitably try to stage a come-back. They form a minuscule minority of the whole population, but their power of resistance is proportionately much greater. The spontaneous forces of the urban and rural petty-bourgeoisie ceaselessly engender new bourgeois elements. Some unwholesome elements come into the workers' ranks as these expand. There are also some people in the Party and government organs who degenerate. Further, imperialism, modern revisionism and the reactionaries of all countries are always making efforts, in one way or another, to have a go at us. All this exposes our country to the danger of a restoration of capitalism. We absolutely must not ignore this danger. Just as we must raise our vigilance a hundred-fold against the external enemy; so, too, we must not lower our guard against the enemy at home. While paying serious attention to the enemy with guns, we must not lose sight of the enemy without guns. A wolf in sheep's clothing is more dangerous than an ordinary wolf, and even more dangerous than a pack of wolves. The enemy holding a red flag is more dangerous than the enemy with a white one. Sugar-coated bullets kill people. Smiling tigers eat people. We must never engross ourselves in work and forget politics just because we have a host of problems to deal with. To forget politics, to forget class struggle, would be to forget the fundamental theses of Marxism-Leninism and Mao Tse-tung's thought. This would be blind carelessness and sheer idiocy. We must follow the instructions of the Party's Central Committee and never for a single instant forget class struggle, the dictatorship of the proletariat and the primary place of politics, and never for a single instant forget to hold high the great red banner of Mao Tse-tung's thought.

Marxism-Leninism is critical and revolutionary in nature. Its basic point is criticism, struggle and revolution. Towards everything bourgeois and revisionist, we must adopt not reformist but thoroughgoing revolutionary methods. In dealing with the enemy of revolution, we cannot rely on persuasion but on struggle. If you don't struggle against him, he will struggle against you. If you don't hit him, he will hit you. Without destruction, there will be no construction. Destruction means criticism and revolution. Destruction comes first and construction comes in the course of destruction. Messrs. bourgeois "authorities," you say we are "dynamiters" and "clubs." You are right. We want to be proletarian "dynamiters" so as to blow to bits all the anti-Party, anti-socialist gangster villages and inns. We want to be "golden clubs" of the proletariat so as to rout all monsters. We shall smash anyone who tries to oppose the Party and socialism, the dictatorship of the proletariat and Mao Tse-tung's thought. No matter what his "authority," no matter how high his post, the whole nation and the whole Party will rise to denounce him.

At the present time, we are facing an excellent situation. The whole world situation is excellent, and so is China's. Ours is a Party that has been making revolution for dozens of years under the leadership of Chairman Mao Tse-tung, a Party that is armed with Marxism-Leninism and Mao Tse-tung's thought, a Party closely linked with the masses, possessing rich revolutionary experience and a glorious revolutionary tradition, a Party that has withstood storm and stress in protracted revolutionary struggles; ours is a glorious, great and correct Party. Any monsters, schemers or careerists who plan to capture our bastion from within and stage in China the ugly drama of Khrushchev's usurpation of Party, army and State power will knock their heads against a brick wall, lose all standing and reputation and end in utter failure. We must use the great Mao Tse-tung's thought and the great, just cause of communism to inspire the revolutionary enthusiasm of the working people of our country, broaden their vistas of the future and press forward unswervingly. The masses of the workers, peasants and soldiers, the revolutionary cadres and revolutionary intellectuals of our country must rally closely around the Party's Central Committee and Chairman Mao Tse-tung, raise aloft the great red banner of Mao Tse-tung's thought, smash the rabid attack of the bourgeois gangsters, resolutely tear down the black banner of bourgeois "liberty, equality and fraternity," sweep away all monsters and carry the great socialist cultural revolution through to the end.

(From a translation of an editorial in *Jen-min Jih-pao* of June 4, 1966)

The Struggle between Two Lines

Editorials reproduced below explain that once the broad masses, meaning those organised and oriented groups, understand the "general orientation of struggle" set by Mao Tse-tung, they will know whom they should denounce and overthrow in what is called Lu Hsün's harsh and merciless spirit of "beating a mad dog in the water," his spirit of daring to make revolution and to struggle.

Without identifying the "small handful of persons in power in the Party," the articles admit that manifestations of bourgeois ideology are so widespread and resistance to the supremacy of the Maoist line so strong as to hamper the progress of the Great Proletarian Cultural Revolution.

The articles reveal that the struggle between proletarian and bourgeois lines has never ceased for a moment since 1949 when the Chinese Communist Party won political power. This struggle in the ideological and cultural spheres has become so complex and acute that on numerous occasions in the past bourgeois representatives had fought back in every possible way to oppose the Maoist line, shaping public opinion for the restoration of capitalism and challenging the dictatorship of the proletariat over the bourgeoisie in the broad fields of ideology and culture.—Ed.

Victory for the Proletarian Revolutionary Line Represented by Chairman Mao

At present, the situation of the Great Proletarian Cultural Revolution is very fine. Characteristic of this very fine situation is the fact that the broad masses have really been mobilised. Just as Chairman Mao has said, "This is a movement of a momentous scale. It has indeed mobilised the masses. It is of very great significance to the revolutionisation of the thinking of the people throughout the country."

The broad revolutionary masses have acquired a better understanding of the proletarian revolutionary line represented by Chairman Mao. The orientation of their struggle has become still clearer and their fighting spirit has soared still higher. They study and apply Chairman

280

Mao's works creatively in the struggle, pushing the mass movement of studying Chairman Mao's works to a new high. The movement of the Great Proletarian Cultural Revolution is developing in a more penetrating, more extensive and healthier manner.

Of late, in response to Chairman Mao's call to "pay attention to State affairs," the broad masses, conscientiously turning their minds to the struggle between the two lines in the great proletarian revolution, have unfolded a mass criticism and repudiation of the bourgeois reactionary line. This mass criticism and repudiation has spread to all provinces, municipalities, departments, colleges and schools throughout the country. All errors in contravention of Chairman Mao's line and all sorts of manifestations of the bourgeois reactionary line have been exposed, criticised and repudiated by the broad masses.

The broad revolutionary masses have risen to criticise and repudiate the bourgeois reactionary line. This is an important indication that the broad masses have indeed been mobilised and that the current situation is very fine. It shows that the proletarian revolutionary line represented by Chairman Mao is penetrating ever deeper into people's hearts and the bourgeois reactionary line has gone bankrupt.

It is a very fine thing that the masses have themselves directly grasped Chairman Mao's correct line and have undertaken an extensive and profound mass criticism and repudiation of the erroneous line; it is a very fine thing that the masses in their hundreds of millions are paying such attention to State affairs. It is acting as a great spur to comrades who have a very poor understanding of the work of leadership in this Great Proletarian Cultural Revolution and whose leadership has been far from conscientious or effective. It is a great help to those comrades who follow the bourgeois line, for them to correct their mistakes. It is a most important guarantee that the erroneous line will be rectified further and its bad influence eradicated, and that the proletarian revolutionary line and the 16-point decision concerning the great cultural revolution will be correctly applied and carried out.

The struggle between the two lines has all along centred on the question of one's stand and attitude towards the masses. The proletarian revolutionary line represented by Chairman Mao is this: to trust the masses, rely on them, respect their initiative, and have them educate and liberate themselves; to boldly arouse the masses to struggle against the handful of persons in authority within the Party who are taking the capitalist road, to give free rein to the masses to struggle against all

281

ghosts and monsters in society and to carry out the struggles [against those persons in authority who are taking the capitalist road], criticisms and repudiations [of the reactionary bourgeois academic "authorities" and the ideology of the bourgeoisie and all other exploiting classes] and transformations [of education, literature and art and all other parts of the superstructure that do not correspond to the socialist economic base].

The bourgeois reactionary line, however, runs counter to this. Certain representative personages who have put forward this line are against the masses educating and liberating themselves. In dealing with the masses, they resorted to the "tutelage" practised by the Kuomintang; they treat the masses as if they were ignorant and incapable and look upon themselves as men of wisdom and resourcefulness; they suppress the masses and stifle their initiative; they shift the targets for attack and direct their spearhead against the revolutionary masses, branding them as "counter-revolutionaries," "anti-Party elements," "rightists," "pseudo-leftists but genuine rightists," and so forth.

These two lines are sharply opposed to each other. One is the mass line of Chairman Mao, the other is the line of the bourgeoisie which opposes and suppresses the masses; one is the revolutionary line of the proletariat which is carrying the Great Proletarian Cultural Revolution through to the end, the other is the bourgeois line of opposing revolution which wants to lead the Great Proletarian Cultural Revolution in the opposite direction and wants to strangle it in its cradle.

Without destruction there can be no construction. Without opposing the reactionary line of the bourgeoisie and eradicating the influence of this erroneous line, it is impossible to correctly and thoroughly implement the revolutionary line of the proletariat.

A great amount of work is needed before the evil influence of the bourgeois reactionary line can be eradicated. The bourgeois reactionary line has its social basis which is mainly in the bourgeoisie. The erroneous line has a certain audience inside the Party, because there exist the handful of persons inside the Party who are in power and are taking the capitalist road, and who regard this erroneous line as their protective talisman; and because there are still a considerable number of muddle-headed people inside the Party whose world outlook has not been remoulded or has not been effectively remoulded. A process is required for these comrades to return from the erroneous line to the correct line.

Distinctions should be made among those who have committed errors of line. Those (there are only one, two or several persons) who have put forward the erroneous line should be distinguished from those who have put it into effect; those (these are a minority) who have consciously implemented the erroneous line should be distinguished from those (there is a large number of these) who have done it unconsciously; we should differentiate between those who have put it into practice to a serious extent and those to a not so serious extent; differentiate between those who cling to their mistakes and those who are willing to correct them and are already in the process of doing so.

Generally speaking, the contradictions between those comrades who committed errors of line on the one hand and the Party and the masses on the other are still contradictions among the people. Provided that they can correct their errors, return to the correct stand and carry out the Party's correct line, it is not only possible for them to become cadres of the second category [comparatively good] or of the third category [those who have made serious mistakes but have not become anti-Party, anti-socialist rightists], it is also possible for them to develop into cadres of the first category [good]. Nevertheless, these comrades must be sharply told that no matter who they are, and no matter how great their past achievements, if they cling to the erroneous line, the nature of the contradictions between them and the Party and the masses will change; the non-antagonistic contradictions then may become antagonistic contradictions and they will slide down the anti-Party and anti-socialist road.

The mark distinguishing rectification of errors from stubborn adherence to them is the attitude towards the masses and whether they have publicly admitted before the masses that they have carried out the erroneous line; whether they have made serious efforts to reverse the decisions passed on those of the revolutionary masses who have been branded as "counter-revolutionaries," "anti-Party elements," "rightists," "pseudo-leftists but genuine rightists;" and whether they have publicly rehabilitated them and support the revolutionary actions of the revolutionary masses.

A Communist who has committed an error of line should be courageous enough to admit his errors, critically examine those errors and join the masses to criticise and repudiate his own errors. Chairman Mao has taught us: "Countless revolutionary martyrs have laid down their lives in the interests of the people, and our hearts are filled with pain as we the living think of them — can there be any personal interest, then, that we would not sacrifice or any error that we would not discard?"

In the course of criticising and repudiating the erroneous line, the policy of "learning from past mistakes to avoid future ones" and "curing the sickness to save the patient" — a policy which Chairman Mao has consistently advocated — should be adopted towards those comrades who have committed errors of line, "in order to achieve the two-fold objective of clarity in ideology and unity among comrades." The revolutionary masses and revolutionary youth who have stood up energetically to criticise and repudiate the erroneous line should all pay attention to this teaching of Chairman Mao's. As to some of the masses who have been hoodwinked for a time by the erroneous line, they should not be blamed, nor should such labels as "Royalists" be stuck on them; instead, patient efforts should be made to help them and to unite with them.

Those comrades who have committed errors of line should modestly, sincerely and wholeheartedly listen to the criticisms of the masses, and, as Chairman Mao has repeatedly taught us, "shedding the ugly mantle of pretentiousness and becoming a willing pupil." They should stand together with the revolutionary masses and with them eradicate the evil influences caused by the bourgeois reactionary line. No feelings of antagonism should result because of some excesses in words and actions by the masses in the course of criticism and repudiation. Instead one should see that the masses' main orientation is correct, understand how they feel, have faith in the majority of the masses and have faith that the masses are reasonable.

Those comrades who have committed errors must get rid of the many "fears" in their minds. In the final analysis, these "fears" are being afraid of the masses and afraid of revolution. They should act according to Chairman Mao's instructions and replace "fear" with "daring," "self" with "public" and "having faith in oneself" with "having faith in the masses." Only by doing so can errors be corrected, can they take the initiative instead of being passive, and give leadership in the Great Proletarian Cultural Revolution in accordance with Chairman Mao's line.

All comrades who want to make revolution, let us unite and push forward the Great Proletarian Cultural Revolution under the great banner of Mao Tse-tung's thought and on the basis of the revolutionary proletarian line represented by Chairman Mao.

(From a full translation of an editorial in *Hung-ch'i,* No. 14, 1966)

*   *   *

Commemorating Lu Hsün—Our Forerunner in the Cultural Revolution

The Great Proletarian Cultural Revolution surges to a new high in its advance along the revolutionary line represented by Chairman Mao Tse-tung. The broad revolutionary masses are thoroughly criticising and repudiating the bourgeois reactionary line. It is in this excellent situation, and in a spirit of militant pride that we commemorate Lu Hsün — our forerunner in the cultural revolution.

Chairman Mao has given the most comprehensive, the most penetrating appraisal of Lu Hsün. He said: Lu Hsün was "the greatest and the most courageous standard-bearer of this new cultural force." He was "the chief commander of China's cultural revolution;" "representing the great majority of the nation, Lu Hsün breached and stormed the enemy citadel; on the cultural front he was the bravest and most correct, the firmest, the most loyal and the most ardent national hero, a hero without parallel in our history."

The life of Lu Hsün was a life of struggle. He always stood at the forefront of the times, waging an unswerving struggle to overthrow imperialism and its lackeys, sweep away the old culture of the exploiting classes, and spread and promote the new culture of the masses.

The old semi-feudal, semi-colonial system and culture of the China of the past was a prison that kept the masses incarcerated and rigidly shackled their minds. Lu Hsün had an implacable hatred for all man-eating systems and cultures. He sounded "the call to charge forward" to "clear out" and "sweep away" all the old forces, old ideas, old cultures, old customs and habits and trample them down, whether they were ancient canons, rare texts, sacred oracles, precious idols, traditional recipes or secret nostrums. With the fighting spirit of a man "breaking through all snares and traps," he attacked the old world courageously. He put daring above all else and boldly declared war on all the enemies, using his pen as a javelin to throw at the enemy's heart. He was fearless in face of threats, of isolation, of detraction and slander, of overt or covert persecution, of death itself. "Fierce-browed, I coolly defy a thousand pointing fingers" — Lu Hsün always despised the "flunkeyism" of being "servile and submissive" to the enemy. He broke completely with old traditions and old forces. He was a genuine revolutionary, free from the slightest trace of philistinism; he had not a moment's regret for the death of the old world. He repudiated the old world in the most merciless way. The force of his pen was such that the enemy was vanquished wherever it pointed.

Destruction comes first, and construction comes in the course of destruction. A new world can only be discovered in the course of repudiating the old world. This was precisely the course followed by Lu Hsün. He once said that at first, he had no idea what the new was like. It was in the course of struggling against the old system and old culture, and especially in the struggle against such reactionary bourgeois ideas as "the theory of human nature," "humanitarianism" and "vulgar evolutionism" and in the struggle against the Trotskyite gang that he found Marxism and learnt the Marxist theory of class struggle. With this weapon he observed society, attacked the enemy and at the same time constantly "dissected himself" to transform his world outlook and consciously temper himself into a revolutionary. It was through such sharp class struggles that Lu Hsün was transformed from a radical democrat into a great communist fighter. He firmly believed that "the future belongs to the newly rising proletariat alone" and placed the hopes of the Chinese revolution in the Chinese Communist Party led by Chairman Mao.

Today, as we commemorate Lu Hsün, we must follow Chairman Mao's teachings and learn from Lu Hsün's utterly fearless fighting spirit and spirit of thoroughgoing revolution.

The phrase "beating a mad dog in the water" is an outstanding expression of Lu Hsün's thoroughgoing revolutionary spirit. Lu Hsün resolutely opposed any talk of "forgiving" or "showing mercy" to the enemy. He sharply rebutted the drivel which vilifies the spirit of "beating a mad dog in the water" as "going to extremes" or "being too harsh in hating evil." He clearly pointed out that "the nature of the dog" would not change and that if it were allowed "to crawl back on to the bank" and catch its breath, it would some day "bite to death" many revolutionaries. We say: Listen, you who are always charging us with "going to extremes!" Can we talk about "forgiving" in regard to our class enemies at home or abroad, the counter-revolutionary revisionists or the handful of persons who are in authority and are taking the capitalist road? Can we allow them to rise up again some day to "bite to death" revolutionaries? No! We must learn from Lu Hsün's thoroughgoing revolutionary spirit of "beating a mad dog in the water," and beat them to the earth so that they never get up again.

Lu Hsün bitterly hated those seemingly "fair" and "just"

"peace-makers," the "fence-sitters" who pretend to be "unbiased" between two armies locked in battle. "Conciliation" or "eclecticism" means "obliterating the difference between good and bad" and "serving as the enemy's jackal." To practise eclecticism in a life-and-death class struggle means in fact to stand on the side of the enemy. At every crucial moment in the class struggle, the eclectics invariably raise a hue and cry or mumble complaints. But history has booked these characters for a tragic role. There is no middle road in the present struggle between Marxism-Leninism and modern revisionism with the CPSU leadership at its centre. Those who advocate a middle road will inevitably slip down into the quagmire of revisionism.

In the Great Proletarian Cultural Revolution, there is also no middle road in the struggle between the proletarian revolutionary line represented by Chairman Mao and the bourgeois reactionary line. To practise conciliation and eclecticism in this struggle between the two lines is, in fact, to defend the bourgeois reactionary line and oppose the proletarian revolutionary line. Every revolutionary should do as Lu Hsün did: "enthusiastically uphold what is right" and "spiritedly attack what is wrong," be clear-cut in what he loves and hates and persist in a principled stand.

From start to finish, in the revolutionary struggle, Lu Hsün fought on stubbornly and unyieldingly, no matter how long and tortuous the road or how many the difficulties, dangers and obstacles on the way. He opposed those who regarded the revolution as something simple, easy, and all plain sailing, and who would be thrown into a state of "despair and despondency" whenever things got difficult. This was the "tenacious" fighting spirit that Lu Hsün firmly upheld, this was that revolutionary staunchness characterised by down-to-earth effort, dauntlessness and defiance of all difficulties and refusal to give up before the aim is achieved. Enemy encirclement and persecution made him all the more resolute. The enemy encirclement and persecution brought out and tempered Lu Hsün's fighting spirit. Lu Hsün did not feel alone when dark clouds obscured the sky and he was isolated. This was because he breathed the same air as the masses and threw in his lot with them, because he stood with Chairman Mao, the great leader of the Chinese people. At the time, although on the surface he was isolated, truth was on his side; he represented the interests of the proletariat and the broad masses of working people of China and the path of historical advance.

287

Reactionary encirclement and attack brings out and tempers the revolutionary Left. Such are the dialectics of history. In the Great Proletarian Cultural Revolution, all comrades of the Left should understand this truth, and be fearless in the face of twists and turns, encirclement and isolation, consciously tempering themselves in the class struggle and making themselves into staunch and steeled fighters.

"Head-bowed, like a willing ox I serve the children" — Lu Hsün had confidence in the people and a great love for them. Because of this, Lu Hsün was adept at discovering the new-born forces in society and resolutely supported them. Throughout his life, Lu Hsün carried the banner for the emerging new things in society, cheered for their growth and sounded the clarion to clear the way for them. He spared no effort to "bring forth a large number of new fighters." With great enthusiasm he concerned himself with the growth of the young generation and encouraged them to go into battle. He saw China's hopes and future in the proletariat, in the masses of the people and in the revolutionary youth, and this strengthened his revolutionary confidence and militant courage. One's attitude towards new things emerging in society, of supporting or not supporting or opposing them, is an important criterion of whether one is a revolutionary, or not a revolutionary or opposes the revolution. Proletarian revolutionaries can see the infinite vitality and the great future development of a new thing as soon as it emerges on the horizon and they will enthusiastically greet it and resolutely support it. As for the political philistines, they are blind, they cannot see the new things, or else dare not support them for fear of getting their fingers burnt. Representatives of the decaying forces heap scorn and abuse on, and ruthlessly seek to overthrow and destroy new emerging things. In the Great Proletarian Cultural Revolution, new, revolutionary things are constantly emerging and the newly emerging forces are continuously growing stronger. Before them, one must swiftly show one's attitude and make a choice.

What most of all deserves emulating in Lu Hsün was his boundless esteem and love for the great leader Chairman Mao. In his early years he had "wandered," but once he had found Marxism, especially after he had found the Communist Party of China represented by Chairman Mao and had found the revolutionary line represented by Chairman Mao, he became resolute, obeyed orders and willingly became "a foot soldier" and "an ordinary soldier" in the proletarian revolution. Ignoring the white terror of the Kuomintang reactionaries, the lies and slanders of the Trotskyite gang and the deceit and attacks of the Chou Yangs, Lu Hsün resolutely followed Chairman Mao from start to finish and courageously defended the correct line represented by Chairman Mao.

"The heart of the hero in his old age is as stout as ever." The older Lu Hsün grew the stronger his revolutionary will and the more pronounced became his militant youthful vigour. What force inspired him? It was the Communist Party of China represented by Chairman Mao; it was our great teacher Chairman Mao. Genuine revolutionaries must all be like Lu Hsün, resolutely follow Chairman Mao, follow him for ever, and march forward along the way pointed out by Chairman Mao. Today, we are much luckier than Lu Hsün in that we can hear Chairman Mao's instructions in person. We must make revolution throughout our lives, read Chairman Mao's writings throughout our lives, study Mao Tse-tung's thought throughout our lives, and be for ever loyal to Chairman Mao, loyal to the people and loyal to the cause of communism.

Thirty years have elapsed since our forerunner in the cultural revolution, Lu Hsün, left us, but his revolutionary spirit lives on in the heart of every revolutionary comrade.

In the tempestuous waves of the Great Proletarian Cultural Revolution we need people of unyielding proletarian integrity armed with Mao Tse-tung's thought; we need all-round revolutionary pathbreakers with penetrating insight, and wisdom and courage. The revolutionary spirit of Lu Hsün and his experience in struggle are a precious heritage. We must act according to Chairman Mao's teachings, emulate Lu Hsün's example, use Mao Tse-tung's thought as our guide, and take over the carry forward Lu Hsün's spirit of daring to make revolution and being good at making revolution, of daring to struggle and being good at struggling. We must hold still higher the great red banner of Mao Tse-tung's thought, thoroughly criticise and repudiate the bourgeois reactionary line, resolutely implement the proletarian revolutionary line represented by Chairman Mao, and carry the Great Proletarian Cultural Revolution through to the end.

(From a full translation of an editorial in
Hung-ch'i, No. 14, 1966)

*   *   *

Long Live the Great Proletarian Cultural Revolution

Under the direct leadership of Chairman Mao Tse-tung and the Central Committee of the Chinese Communist Party, a great mass proletarian cultural revolution without parallel in history is swiftly and vigorously unfolding with the irresistible force of an avalanche.

Holding high the great red banner of Mao Tse-tung's thought, the masses of workers, peasants and soldiers and the masses of revolutionary cadres and revolutionary intellectuals are sweeping away the representatives of the bourgeoisie who have wormed their way into the Party, the monsters of all kinds and all forms of decadent bourgeois and feudal ideology. An unprecedentedly favourable situation has arisen on the political, ideological and cultural fronts.

This is an extremely acute and complex class struggle to foster what is proletarian and eradicate what is bourgeois in the superstructure, in the realm of ideology — a life-and-death struggle between the bourgeoisie attempting to restore capitalism and the proletariat determined to prevent it. This struggle affects the issue of whether the dictatorship of the proletariat and the economic base of socialism in our country can be consolidated and developed or not, and whether or not our Party and country will change colour. It affects the destiny and future of our Party and our country as well as the destiny and future of world revolution. It is most important that this struggle should not be taken lightly.

Why is it imperative that the proletarian cultural revolution be launched? Why is this revolution so important?

Comrade Mao Tse-tung has scientifically summed up the international historical experience of the dictatorship of the proletariat and put forth the theory of contradiction, classes and class struggle in socialist society. He constantly reminds us never to forget the class struggle, never to forget to put politics first and never to forget to consolidate the dictatorship of the proletariat, and that we must take various measures to prevent a revisionist usurpation of leadership, to prevent a capitalist restoration. He points out that the overthrow of political power is necessarily preceded by efforts to seize hold of the superstructure and ideology in order to prepare public opinion, and that this is true both of the revolutionary and the counter-revolutionary classes. Proceeding from this fundamental point of departure, Comrade Mao Tse-tung has called on us to launch the class struggle in the ideological

290

field to foster what is proletarian and eradicate what is bourgeois.

Here is a great truth, a great development of Marxism-Leninism.

History shows that the bourgeoisie first took hold of ideology and prepared public opinion before it seized political power from the feudal landlord class. Starting from the period of the "Renaissance," the European bourgeoisie persistently criticised feudal ideology and propagated bourgeois ideology. It was in the 17th and 18th centuries, after several hundred years of preparation of public opinion, that the bourgeoisie seized political power and established its dictatorship in one European country after another.

Marx and Engels began propagating the theories of communism more than a century ago. They did so to prepare public opinion for the seizure of political power by the proletariat. The Russian proletarian revolution culminated in the seizure of political power only after decades of preparation of public opinion. Our own experience is even fresher in our minds. When the Chinese proletariat began to appear on the political scene, it was weak and unarmed. How was the revolution to start? It started with the propagation of Marxism-Leninism and the exposure of imperialism and its lackeys in China. The struggle of the Chinese proletariat for the seizure of political power began precisely with the May 4th cultural revolution.

In the final analysis, the history of the seizure of political power by the Chinese proletariat is a history of Mao Tse-tung's thought gripping the masses of workers, peasants and soldiers. As the masses have aptly put it: "Without Mao Tse-tung's thought, there would have been no New China." By integrating Marxism-Leninism with the practice of the Chinese revolution, Comrade Mao Tse-tung, the great revolutionary standard-bearer, changed the whole face of the Chinese revolution. Historical experience shows that Mao Tse-tung's thought enabled us to gain the increasing support of the masses, to have armed forces and guns, to set up one revolutionary base area after another, to seize political power bit by bit and finally to take over political power throughout the country.

Having seized political power, the proletariat has become the ruling class and the landlord and capitalist classes have become the ruled. The landlord class and the reactionary bourgeoisie will never be reconciled to being ruled or to their extinction. They are constantly dreaming of a restoration through subversion of the dictatorship of the proletariat, so that they can once again ride on the backs of the working people.

They still have great strength. They have money, extensive social contacts and international links, and experience in counter-revolution. In particular, the ideology of the exploiting classes still has a very big market. Some unsteady elements in the revolutionary ranks are prone to be corrupted by this ideology and consequently become counter-revolutionaries. Moreover, the spontaneous influence of the petty-bourgeoisie ceaselessly engenders capitalism. Having seized political power the proletariat still faces the danger of losing it. After being established the socialist system still faces the danger of a capitalist restoration. Failure to give this serious attention and take the necessary steps will end in our Party and our country changing colour and will cause tens of millions of our people to lose their lives.

Bourgeois and feudal ideologies are one of the most important strongholds of the overthrown landlord and capitalist classes after the socialist transformation of the ownership of the means of production has been effected. Their efforts at restoration are first of all directed at getting their hold over ideology and using their decadent ideas in every possible way to deceive the masses. The seizure of ideology and the moulding of public opinion are the bourgeoisie's preparation for the subversion of the dictatorship of the proletariat. And when the opportunity is ripe, they will stage a coup to seize political power in one way or another.

After the establishment of socialist relations of production, the Soviet Union failed to carry out a proletarian cultural revolution in earnest. Bourgeois ideology ran rife, corrupting the minds of the people and almost imperceptibly undermining the socialist relations of production. After the death of Stalin, there was a more blatant counter-revolutionary moulding of public opinion by the Khrushchev revisionist group. And this group soon afterwards staged its "palace" coup to subvert the dictatorship of the proletariat and usurped Party, military and government power.

In the 1956 Hungarian counter-revolutionary incident, the counter-revolutionaries also prepared public opinion before they took to the streets to create disturbances and stage riots. This counter-revolutionary incident was engineered by imperialism and started by a group of anti-communist intellectuals of the Petofi Club. Imre Nagy, who at that time still wore the badge of a communist, was "fitted out with a king's robe" and became the chieftain of the counter-revolutionaries.

International historical experience of the dictatorship of the proletariat shows that this dictatorship cannot be consolidated, nor can the socialist system be consolidated, unless a proletarian cultural revolution is carried out and persistent efforts are made to eradicate bourgeois ideology. Bourgeois ideas spreading unchecked inevitably leads to the subversion of the dictatorship of the proletariat and the emergence of such representatives of the bourgeoisie as Khrushchev, who will seize political power through a "palace" coup or a military coup, or a combination of both. If the dictatorship of the proletariat is to be consolidated, if a country under the dictatorship of the proletariat is to advance in a socialist and communist direction, a proletarian cultural revolution is imperative; proletarian ideology must be fostered and bourgeois ideology eradicated and the ideological roots of revisionism must be pulled out completely and the roots of Marxism-Leninism, of Mao Tse-tung's thought, must be firmly implanted.

Socialist revolution and socialist construction demand energetic efforts in many fields of work. Running through this work there must be a red line, which is nothing other than the class struggle between the proletariat and the bourgeoisie, the struggle between the socialist and the capitalist roads, and the class struggle between the proletariat and the bourgeoisie in the field of ideology.

Comrade Mao Tse-tung teaches us:

> The class struggle between the proletariat and the bourgeoisie, the class struggle between the different political forces, and the class struggle in the ideological field between the proletariat and the bourgeoisie will continue to be long and tortuous and at times will even become very acute. The proletariat seeks to transform the world according to its own world outlook, and so does the bourgeoisie. In this respect, the question of which will win out, socialism or capitalism, is still not really settled.[1]

The purpose of the proletarian cultural revolution is to settle the question of "who will win" in the ideological field between the proletariat and the bourgeoisie. It is a protracted and difficult historical task that runs through every field of work.

Some comrades regard the debates in the press between the proletariat and the reactionary bourgeoisie as "trivial, paper polemics" of literary men. Immersed in their work, some comrades are not concerned with the struggle on the ideological and cultural fronts and pay no heed to the class struggle in the field of ideology. This is absolutely wrong and most dangerous. If bourgeois ideology is allowed to run wild, the dictatorship of the proletariat will become the dictatorship of the bourgeoisie, and the socialist system will become a capitalist system, or a semi-colonial, semi-feudal system. We must shout to these people: Comrades! The enemy is sharpening his sword, he wants to cut off our heads, he wants to overturn our State power. How is it that you see it and hear it and take no notice?

Both the seizure and consolidation of political power depend on the pen as well as the gun. If we are to safeguard and carry forward the revolutionary cause, we must not only hold on firmly to the gun but must take up the proletarian pen to blast and sweep away the pen of the bourgeoisie. Only by sweeping away all bourgeois ideology can we consolidate proletarian political power and keep an ever firmer hold on the proletarian gun.

A good look at the class struggle on the ideological and cultural fronts makes one stirred to the soul.

The struggle on the ideological and cultural fronts between the proletariat and the bourgeoisie, between Marxism and anti-Marxism, has never ceased for a moment since the founding of the Chinese People's Republic. After the establishment of socialist relations of production this class struggle in the ideological field has become ever deeper, ever more complex and acute.

In 1957 the bourgeois rightists launched a frenzied attack against the Party and socialism. Before the alliance of the reactionary politicians headed by Chang Po-chün and Lo Lung-chi came out into the open in this offensive, bourgeois rightist intellectuals had already scattered a good many poisonous weeds around; one after another, there emerged a number of counter-revolutionary notions, political programmes and films and novels. These were obviously efforts to prepare public opinion for the bourgeois rightists to seize political power.

Under the wise leadership of the Party's Central Committee and Chairman Mao, the Chinese people repulsed this wild offensive of the bourgeois rightists and won an important victory on the political and ideological fronts.

Then in 1958, under the great red banner of the general line for socialist construction, the Chinese people embarked with boundless enthusiasm and energy on the great leap forward in every field of work and set up the people's communes in a big way. At the same time, the masses of workers, peasants and soldiers zealously took to studying Chairman Mao's works and applying his thought in a creative way. A revolution also began on the ideological and cultural fronts.

From 1959 to 1962, China suffered temporary economic difficulties as a result of sabotage by the Soviet revisionists and three successive years of serious natural calamities. But difficulties could not intimidate the revolutionary Chinese people. They worked hard and courageously forged ahead under the wise leadership of the Party's Central Committee and Chairman Mao. Within a few years they had overcome the difficulties and brought about an excellent situation. However, in these few years of economic difficulties, monsters had come out of their hiding places one after another. The offensive of the reactionary bourgeoisie against the Party and socialism reached a degree of utmost fury.

In the field of philosophical studies, Yang Hsien-chen[1] blatantly spread the fallacy denying the identity of idea and being in an attempt to hold back the masses of workers, peasants and soldiers from bringing their subjective initiative into play and to oppose the great leap forward. Subsequently, he came out with the theory of "two combined into one," thus providing philosophical "grounds" for the extremely reactionary political line which advocated the liquidation of struggle in our relations with imperialism, the reactionaries and modern revisionism, and reduction of assistance and support to the revolutionary struggle of other peoples, as well as the extension of plots for private use and of free markets, the increase of small enterprises with sole responsibility for their own profits or losses, and the fixing of output quotas based on the household. The so-called "authorities" representing the bourgeoisie who had wormed their way into the Party wildly brandished the three cudgels of "philistinism," "over-simplification" and "pragmatism" to oppose the workers, peasants and soldiers from studying Chairman Mao's works and applying his thought in a creative way. Moreover, exploiting their positions and powers, they forbade the press to publish philosophical articles written by workers, peasants and soldiers. At the same time, under the guise of studying the history of philosophy, certain bourgeois "specialists" widely propagated the ideas of "liberty, equality and fraternity" and lavished praise on Confucius, making use of this mummy to publicise their whole set of bourgeois ideas.

In the field of economic studies, Sun Yeh-fang and company put forward a whole set of revisionist fallacies. They wanted to put profit and money in command to oppose putting Mao Tse-tung's thought and politics in command. They vainly attempted to change the socialist relations of production and turn socialist enterprises into capitalist ones.

In the field of historical studies, a pack of bourgeois "authorities" launched unscrupulous attacks on the revolution in historical studies which began in 1958. They opposed putting Marxism-Leninism, Mao Tse-tung's thought, in command in historical research and spread the notion that historical data are everything. They used what they called "historicism" to counter the Marxist-Leninist theory of class struggle. They bitterly hated those revolutionary research workers in history who made critical appraisals of emperors, kings, generals and prime ministers and gave prominence to the peasants and the peasant wars. They extolled the emperors, kings, generals and prime ministers to the skies while energetically vilifying the peasants and peasant wars. They were the bourgeois "royalists" in the field of historical studies. Among them, some were inveterate anti-Communists. These include Wu Han and Chien Po-tsan.

In the field of literature and art, the representatives of the bourgeoisie spared no effort to propagate the whole revisionist line in literature and art to oppose Chairman Mao's line, and vigorously propagated what they called the traditions of the 1930s. Typical were their theories on "truthful writing," on "the broad path of realism," on "the deepening of realism," on opposition to "subject-matter as the decisive factor," on "middle characters," on opposition to "the smell of gunpowder," on "the merging of various trends as the spirit of the age," and on "discarding the classics and rebelling against orthodoxy." Under the "guidance" of these theories, there appeared a wave of bad, anti-Party, anti-socialist operas and plays, films and novels, and histories of the cinema and of literature.

In the field of education, the representatives of the bourgeoisie did their utmost to oppose the educational policy advanced by Chairman Mao, which is aimed at enabling the educated to develop morally, intellectually and physically and become socialist-minded, cultured working people. They spared no effort in opposing the part-work, part-study educational system and propagating the educational "theories" and systems of Soviet revisionism. They made desperate efforts to win the younger generation away from us in the vain hope of training them into heirs of the bourgeoisie.

In the field of journalism, the representatives of the bourgeoisie exerted themselves to oppose the guiding role of journalism, and advocated the bourgeois conception of "imparting knowledge." They vainly attempted to strangle the leadership of Marxism-Leninism, of Mao Tse-tung's thought, in journalistic work, hoping to give free currency to bourgeois contraband and wrest from us our journalistic base.

The most reactionary and fanatical element in this adverse current was the anti-Party "Three-Family Village" gang. They had many bases — newspapers, magazines, forums and publishing organisations. Their long arms reached out to all corners of the cultural field and they usurped some positions of leadership. Their nose for anything reactionary was extremely sharp and their writings showed extremely close and prompt co-ordination with anything reactionary in the political atmosphere. Under direction, organised, acting according to plan and with set purposes, they prepared public opinion for the restoration of capitalism and the overthrow of the dictatorship of the proletariat.

Playing the main role in this adverse current were the representatives of the bourgeoisie who had sneaked into the Party. They waved "red flags" to oppose the red flag and donned the cloak of Marxism-Leninism, of Mao Tse-tung's thought, to oppose Marxism-Leninism and Mao Tse-tung's thought. Dressing themselves up as "authorities" on Marxism, as "authorities" clarifying the Party's policies, they wantonly spread poison and deceived the masses. They took advantage of their positions and powers, on the one hand to let loose all kinds of monsters, and on the other hand to suppress the counter-attacks of the proletarian Left. They are a bunch of schemers who put up the signboard of communism behind which they actually peddled anti-Party and anti-socialist poison. They are a most dangerous bunch.

We have constantly fought back against the attacks launched by the bourgeoisie from 1959 onwards. Especially since last November, when Comrade Yao Wen-yüan published his article "On the New Historical Drama 'Hai Jui Dismissed from Office'" and sounded the clarion of the Great Proletarian Cultural Revolution, a mass counter-offensive against the bourgeoisie's attacks has opened up.

In this counter-attack the political consciousness of the broad masses of workers, peasants, soldiers, revolutionary cadres and revolutionary intellectuals has risen to an unprecedented level and their fighting power has enormously increased. The battles fought by the masses have shattered and uprooted the "Three-Family Village" anti-Party clique. And its roots lay nowhere else than in the former Peking Municipal Party Committee. A black anti-Party and anti-socialist line ran through the leadership of the former Peking Municipal Committee of the Communist Party. Some of its leading members are not Marxist-Leninists, but revisionists. They controlled many bases and media and exercised a dictatorship over the proletariat. They are a clique of careerists and conspirators. Their plots were exposed and they were defeated. The Central Committee of our Party reorganised the Peking Municipal Party Committee and established a new one. This decision was very wise and absolutely correct. It was a new victory for Mao Tse-tung's thought.

From the moment we launched this large-scale counter-attack last year, the representatives of the bourgeoisie who wormed their way into the Party and waved "red flags" to oppose the red flag, were thrown into utter confusion. They hurriedly invoked five "talismans" to support and shelter the bourgeois rightists and suppress and attack the proletarian Left.

One of these "talismans" was raised in the name of "opening wide."

The representatives of the bourgeoisie, who wormed their way into the Party and waved "red flags" to oppose the red flag, tried their best to distort the Party's "opening wide" policy by removing its class content and twisting it into bourgeois liberalisation. They allowed only the bourgeois rightists to "speak out" and did not allow the proletarian Left to enter the contest. They allowed only the bourgeois rightists to attack and did not allow the proletarian Left to counter-attack. They let the rightists "open" as wide as they could while they either shelved the counter-attacking manuscripts sent in by those of the Left or compelled the authors to rewrite them in the light of their ideas. They said that "Hai Jui Dismissed from Office" should not be criticised from a political angle, otherwise this would affect the "opening wide" and people would not dare to speak up. We would like to ask these lords: Did you just "open" very slightly? Haven't you attacked the Party politically in the manner of a warrior brandishing his sword or drawing his bow? Why did you prohibit the proletariat from "opening wide" to counter-attack the bourgeois rightists politically? In fact, your "opening wide" gave the green light to all the bourgeoisie and the red light to hold back the proletariat.

Another "talisman" went by the name of "construction before destruction."

Pretending to be "dialecticians," the representatives of the bourgeoisie, who wormed their way into the Party and waved "red flags" to oppose the red flag, set up a clamour about "construction before destruction" when the proletariat countered the bourgeois attack. And on the pretext of "construction before destruction," they would not allow the proletariat to destroy bourgeois ideology, to attack the reactionary political citadel of the bourgeoisie. "Construction before destruction" is opposed to dialectics and Mao Tse-tung's thought. Comrade Mao Tse-tung constantly teaches us that there is no construction without destruction. It is precisely destruction that we want to come first. Destruction means revolution, it means criticism. Destruction necessarily calls for reasoning, and reasoning is construction. Marxism-Leninism, Mao Tse-tung's thought, has all developed in the struggle to destroy bourgeois ideology, Right and "Left" opportunism. Historical dialectics is nothing other than destruction before construction and construction in the course of destruction. Is not Marxism-Leninism, Mao Tse-tung's thought — the greatest truth ever known since time immemorial — construction? We would like to ask those bourgeois lords, what is it you want to construct? Obviously, only bourgeois, reactionary ideology and not proletarian, revolutionary ideology. When the proletariat, employing Marxism-Leninism, Mao Tse-tung's thought, irresistibly countered the bourgeois attack and set to work to destroy bourgeois ideology, the clamour you set up about "construction before destruction" was precisely for the purpose of protecting the rightists and preventing the Left from counter-attacking. It was opposition to the proletarian cultural revolution.

A third "talisman" came under the head of opposing and holding back the growth of "Left scholar-tyrants."

Whenever the proletarian Left countered bourgeois attacks, the representatives of the bourgeoisie, who wormed their way into the Party and waved "red flags" to oppose the red flag, on the pretext of wanting to be "meticulous" and "profound," condemned the Left as being "crude" and acting like a "cudgel." During the present great counter-offensive against bourgeois attacks, they again invoked the "talisman" of opposing and holding back the growth of "Left scholar-tyrants" in a vain attempt to hold the proletarian Left down and suppress it. This would never do. We say that the tag of "scholar-tyrant" fits you bourgeois representatives and "academic authorities" perfectly. You lords who wormed your way into the Party and shielded and backed the bourgeois scholar-tyrants are the big Party-tyrants and scholar-tyrants — tyrants who do not read the newspapers and books, who are divorced from the masses and devoid of knowledge, and who try to overwhelm others by the use of your power. The proletarian Left always insists on the truth of Marxism-Leninism, the truth of Mao

Tse-tung's thought, and relies on scientific contention and evidence in criticising bourgeois ideology. The proletarian Left has nothing in common with "scholar-tyrants." We shall enter the lists against the bourgeois "scholar-tyrants" with colours flying and denounce you, the small handful of big Party-tyrants and scholar-tyrants. We tell you lords, who malign the Left as a "cudgel," that the Left is the steel cudgel, the golden cudgel, of the proletariat. And we shall use this cudgel to smash the old world to smithereens, defeat your handful of big Party-tyrants and scholar-tyrants and destroy your underworld kingdom. This is what is called the dictatorship of the proletariat.

Another "talisman" went by the name of "purely academic discussion."

In order to cover up the bourgeois rightists attacks on the Party and socialism and, at the same time, to suppress the counter-attacks of the proletarian Left, the representatives of the bourgeoisie, who wormed their way into the Party and waved "red flags" to oppose the red flag, described the class struggle in the realm of ideology as a "purely academic discussion." We would ask these lords: Is there really anything academic about Wu Han's "Hai Jui Scolds the Emperor" and "Hai Jui Dismissed from Office" and the anti-Party and anti-socialist double-talk of Teng T'o, Liao Mo-sha and company? The so-called "purely academic discussion" is a fraud the bourgeoisie often plays. There is nothing "purely academic" in class society; everything academic is based on the world outlook of a given class, is subordinate to politics and serves the politics and economy of a given class in one way or another. In the course of our present full-scale counter-offensive, the representatives of the bourgeoisie held up the "talisman" of so-called "purely academic discussion" and opposed putting politics first in order to cover up the vital political issue concerning the anti-Party "Three-Family Village" or "Four-Family Village" gangster inns, to put bourgeois politics first and oppose putting proletarian politics first, and to drag this great struggle to the Right and divert it on to a revisionist course.

Still another important "talisman" of theirs was what they called: "Everybody is equal before the truth," "everyone has his share of erroneous statements" and "it is all a muddle."

In the course of the proletarian counter-offensive against the bourgeoisie, the representatives of the bourgeoisie, who wormed their way into the Party and waved "red flags" to oppose the red flag, invoked this "talisman," on the one hand to get their own men to hang on to

300

their positions and not retreat an inch, and on the other hand to create confusion so that they could fish in troubled waters and await an opportunity to counter-attack.

The out-and-out bourgeois slogan of "everybody is equal before the truth" is thoroughly hypocritical. There can be no equality at all between opposing classes. Truth has its class nature. In the present era, the proletariat alone is able to master objective truth because its class interests are in complete conformity with the objective laws. The reactionary and decadent bourgeoisie has long been completely divorced from the truth. Its so-called "truth" can be nothing more than a fallacy that runs counter to the tide of the times and the objective laws. There can be no equality whatsoever between the proletariat and the bourgeoisie, between proletarian ideology and bourgeois ideology, between proletarian truth and bourgeois fallacy. The only question involved is whether the East wind prevails over the West wind or vice versa. Can any equality be permitted on such basic questions as the struggle of the proletariat against the bourgeoisie, the dictatorship of the proletariat over the bourgeoisie, the dictatorship of the proletariat in the sphere of the superstructure including the various fields of culture, and the continual cleansing of the proletarian ranks of representatives of the bourgeoisie who have wormed their way into the Party and wave "red flags" to oppose the red flag? The old social democrats in the decades gone by and the modern revisionists in the past decade and more have never permitted the proletariat to enjoy equality with the bourgeoisie. In bringing up the slogan "everybody is equal before the truth," the representatives of the bourgeoisie who wormed their way into the Party wanted to bolster up the anti-Party and anti-socialist elements while suppressing the counter-attacks of the Left. We would like to ask these lords: Weren't you prating about equality with your tongue in your cheek? Why did you withhold from publication articles by the Left, while you permitted the rightists alone to publish their numerous poisonous weeds? What equality was this? We have to tell you bluntly, we absolutely will not permit you any equality with the proletariat. Our struggle against you is one of life and death. With regard to your kind of anti-Party and anti-socialist gangs, dictatorship is the only thing.

The argument that "everyone has his share of erroneous statements" and "it is all a muddle" was a great conspiracy. We consider that first of all a line of demarcation must be drawn between classes,

301

between revolution and counter-revolution. In the course of under-standing objective events, the revolutionary Left may commit one error or another, but these cannot be mentioned in the same breath as the anti-Party, anti-socialist and counter-revolutionary speeches and actions of the bourgeois rightists; the two things are radically different. In the present great cultural revolution the principal contradiction is the antagonistic one between, on the one hand, the broad masses of the work-ers, peasants, soldiers, revolutionary cadres and revolutionary intellec-tuals, and, on the other hand, you the handful of anti-Party and anti-socialist representatives of the bourgeoisie. This is a contradiction between revolution and counter-revolution, an irreconcilable contradic-tion between the enemy and ourselves. As for your counter-revolu-tionary speeches and actions, we must subject them all to merciless criti-cism and sound the call for attack. Bourgeois academic ideas in general must, of course, come under criticism, but that is different from the treatment befitting anti-Party and anti-socialist elements such as you are. In dealing with ordinary bourgeois scholars, we shall go on pro-viding them with suitable conditions of work and let them remould their world outlook in the course of their work, provided they do not oppose the Communist Party and the people. When we hit back at the attacks by the bourgeoisie, the bourgeois representatives who sneaked into our Party set up the clamour about "everyone has his share of erroneous statements" and "it is all a muddle" with no other aim than holding the Left in a tight grip, of revenging themselves by creating a great muddle. This was just a waste of effort. We go by Chairman Mao's guidance and make a distinction between the Left, the middle and the Right; we rely on the Left, combat the Right and win over, unite with and educate the majority so as to carry the Great Proletarian Cultural Revolution through to the end.

All these "talismans" of the bourgeois representatives who sneaked into the Party and waved "red flags" to oppose the red flag, were all directed at one goal — the subjection of the proletariat to their dictator-ship. They already usurped some leading positions and applied dictator-ship over us in various fields of culture. We have to recapture all these positions and overthrow these bourgeois representatives.

A striking feature of the bourgeois representatives who sneaked into the Party is their opposition to the red flag while waving "red flags."

How can we recognise them? The only way is "to read Chair-man Mao's works, follow his teachings and act on his instructions."

Mao Tse-tung's thought is the acme of Marxism-Leninism in the present era, it is living Marxism-Leninism at its highest. The theory and practice of Comrade Mao Tse-tung may be likened to the ceaseless movement of the sun and moon in the skies and the endless flow of the rivers and streams on earth. Comrade Mao Tse-tung's works are the highest directives for all our work. The watershed between Marxism-Leninism and revisionism, between revolution and counter-revolution, lies in whether one supports Mao Tse-tung's thought and acts in accordance with it or whether one rejects it and refuses to act in accordance with it.

We endorse and support all that is in keeping with Mao Tse-tung's thought. We shall fearlessly struggle against and overthrow anybody who opposes Mao Tse-tung's thought, no matter how high the position he holds and how great the "fame" and "authority" he enjoys.

The representatives of the bourgeoisie who wormed their way into the Party look like a "colossus." Yet in fact, like all reactionaries, they are only paper tigers.

Mao Tse-tung's thought is the steering gear, and the workers, peasants and soldiers are the main force in the proletarian cultural revolution. This being so, we can certainly defeat every kind of monsters and win victory after victory in the proletarian cultural revolution.

Maliciously and gleefully, the landlords, rich peasants, counter-revolutionaries, bad elements and rightists at home and the imperialists and revisionists abroad think that they can gain some advantage while we are unmasking and criticising the anti-Party "Three-Family Village" gang. We have to tell the reactionaries at home and abroad that they are as stupid as a donkey. The exact purpose of unmasking the anti-Party "Three-Family Village" gang, subjecting them to criticism and sweeping away all the monsters is to eliminate your agents within our Party and our country and remove the "time-bomb" on which you place your hopes. As the Great Proletarian Cultural Revolution develops in depth, we shall implant Mao Tse-tung's thought still more firmly among the people all over the country and completely dig out the roots of re-visionism and of the restoration of capitalism. History will ruthlessly deride you silly donkeys.

The reactionaries at home and abroad have spread the lie that we are attacking all intellectuals. This is nonsense. China's Great Prole-tarian Cultural Revolution is directed against a handful of evil men who put up the signboard of communism behind which they peddled their anti-communist wares; it is directed against a handful of anti-Party, anti-socialist and counter-revolutionary bourgeois intellectuals. With regard to the great number of intellectuals who came over from the old society, our policy is to unite with them, educate and remould them. And the ranks of the proletarian intellectuals are steadily growing in the course of the great cultural revolution.

Revolutionary people, let us all unite still more closely on the basis of Mao Tse-tung's thought!

Holding high the great red banner of Mao Tse-tung's thought, and the great red banner of the proletarian cultural revolution, let us go forward in triumph!

Long live the Great Proletarian Cultural Revolution!

(From a full translation of an editorial in *Hung-ch'i,* No. 8, 1966)

NOTES

1. Mao Tse-tung, "On the Correct Handling of Contradictions among the People."

*　　　*　　　*

China in the Midst of Hight-Tide of the Great Proletarian Cultural Revolution

A high-tide of the Great Proletarian Cultural Revolution has been unfolding vigorously throughout China for several months, in response to the great call of the Central Committee of the Chinese Communist Party and Chairman Mao Tse-tung. This is a great revolutionary movement aimed at consolidating the dictatorship of the proletariat and advancing the cause of socialism.

Hundreds of millions of workers, peasants and soldiers, revolutionary cadres and revolutionary intellectuals, armed with Mao Tse-tung's thought, have been writing articles, holding discussions and putting up posters written in big characters to sweep away the monsters of all kinds entrenched in ideological and cultural positions, and to foster proletarian ideology and liquidate bourgeois ideology with great vigour. Those who echo the imperialists and the reactionary bourgeois "specialists," "scholars" and "authorities" have been routed, one group after another, with every bit of their prestige swept into the dust. The reactionary strongholds controlled by members of the sinister anti-Party and anti-socialist gangs have been breached, one after another. The magnitude, impact, intensity and strength of this Great Proletarian Cultural Revolution are without precedent in history. The whole of China is a vast scene of seething revolution.

Chairman Mao Tse-tung has all along taught the Chinese people that the socialist revolution on the economic and political fronts alone is not enough. It is necessary to carry out thoroughgoing socialist revolution on the ideological and cultural fronts as well. Chairman Mao has pointed out that, with the deepening of China's socialist revolution, the issue of the proletarian cultural revolution would inevitably come to the forefront. The proletarian revolution demands the complete destruction of the old decadent culture of the capitalist and feudal classes and the creation of a brand-new socialist culture which serves proletarian politics and the workers, peasants and soldiers. The overthrown capitalist class and other exploiting classes, however, are stubbornly entrenched in ideological and cultural positions and spread the cultural viruses of capitalism and feudalism so as to serve bourgeois politics, pave the way for the restoration of capitalism and prepare public opinion for subversion of the proletarian State power. As a result, class struggle in the ideological and cultural fields between the proletariat and the bourgeoisie has become inevitable, and at times is even very sharp.

Shortly after the socialist transformation of the ownership of the means of production was basically completed in 1956, the bourgeois rightists mounted attacks in 1957, and a sharp class struggle took place. These attacks were repulsed by the Chinese people under the leadership of the Communist Party.

Between 1959 and 1962, anti-China waves were stirred up by the imperialists and modern revisionists who took advantage of the temporary difficulties resulting from sabotage by the Khrushchev revisionists and serious natural calamities in China. In co-ordination with the imperialists and modern revisionists, the reactionary bourgeois forces within the country availed themselves of this opportunity to unleash another series of frantic attacks against the proletariat. The representatives of the bourgeoisie entrenched in academic, educational, journalistic, literary and art, publishing and other cultural fields unleashed frenzied attacks on the dictatorship of the proletariat, the socialist system, and leadership by the Communist Party and Chairman Mao Tse-tung.

305

These anti-Party and anti-socialist criminal activities of the bourgeoisie aroused strong indignation among the masses of workers, peasants and soldiers, revolutionary cadres and revolutionary intellectuals. The revolutionary masses have waged uninterrupted struggle against them. The signal for the counter-offensive in full force by the proletariat against the reactionary bourgeoisie was given by Yao Wen-yüan's article "On the New Historical Play 'Hai Jui Dismissed from Office' " carried by the Shanghai *Wen-hui Pao* on November 10 last year, which raised the curtain on the current upsurge of the great cultural revolution.

Between publication of Yao Wen-yüan's article last November and April of this year, the revolution revolved mainly around criticism and exposure of Wu Han's anti-Party and anti-socialist crimes. Wu Han served US imperialism as a cultural servant. He was personally groomed by the reactionary politician Hu Shih and consistently worshipped the US and was pro-Chiang Kai-shek and anti-Communist. He wormed his way into the revolutionary ranks on the eve of the country's liberation and later became Vice-Mayor of Peking. Posing as a revolutionary cadre while engaged in counter-revolutionary dealings, Wu Han is in fact a lackey of US imperialism.

Starting in 1959, Wu Han wrote a series of reactionary articles and drama to attack the Communist Party, the socialist system and the dictatorship of the proletariat. In his drama and his articles on Hai Jui, he used the story of the dismissal from office 400 years ago in the Ming dynasty of this Chinese feudal bureaucrat to distort history, satirise the present and complain about the "injustice" done to the anti-Party and anti-socialist Right opportunists who were "dismissed" from office by the Chinese people in 1959, and to encourage them to stage a come-back.

Yao Wen-yüan's article of last November and "The Reactionary Nature of 'Hai Jui Scolds the Emperor' and 'Hai Jui Dismissed from Office' " written by Chi Pen-yu and " 'Hai Jui Scolds the Emperor' and 'Hai Jui Dismissed from Office' Are Two Big Poisonous Weeds Against the Party and Socialism" by Kuan Feng and Lin Chieh, both published early in April this year, exposed Wu Han's reactionary political character, thus bringing the struggle in criticising Wu Han to the key issue of the class struggle between the proletariat and the bourgeoisie and between the road of socialism and the road of capitalism. Numerous articles were also published by most newspapers and periodicals in the country, unfolding further criticism of Wu Han. The history of Wu Han's anti-Communist and anti-popular true colours as a servant of US imperialism has thus been more clearly revealed.

The secrets of the Three-Family Village were unmasked more fully from the beginning to the end of May this year. The Three-Family Village represents an anti-Party and anti-socialist clique which includes Teng T'o, Wu Han and Liao Mo-sha. Teng T'o is a renegade who insinuated himself into the Party once again and is a rightist who was not caught but slipped through in 1957. Over the last few years, he usurped the post of member of the Secretariat of the Peking Municipal Committee of the Chinese Communist Party. Liao Mo-sha is a bourgeois representative who wormed his way into the Party and usurped the post of Director of the United Front Department of the Peking Municipal Party Committee over the last few years. Using as their instruments the fortnightly *Ch'ien Hsien,* the *Pei-ching Jih-pao* and the *Pei-ching Wan-pao,* sponsored by the Peking Municipal Party Committee, Teng T'o, Wu Han and Liao Mo-sha wrote large numbers of miscellaneous articles starting in 1959, releasing a whole series of anti-Party and anti-socialist poisonous arrows to prepare public opinion for the restoration of capitalism.

On May 8 this year, the *Chieh-fang-chün Pao* published "Open Fire at the Black Anti-Party and Anti-Socialist Line!" by Kao Chu and the *Kuang-ming Jih-pao* brought out "Heighten Our Vigilance and Distinguish the True from the False" by Ho Ming, exposing the plot of *Ch'ien Hsien* and the *Pei-ching Jih-pao* to make a bogus criticism of Teng T'o's anti-Party and anti-socialist crimes while in fact covering them up and to wage a bogus struggle against him while in fact shielding him. At the same time, the two papers mentioned above published material under the title "Teng T'o's 'Evening Chats at Yenshan' Is Anti-Party and Anti-Socialist Double-Talk."

The *Chieh-fang Jih-pao* and the *Wen-hui Pao* in Shanghai on May 10 published "On 'Three-Family Village'" by Yao Wen-yüan which made a systematic and comprehensive exposure and criticism of the sinister Three-Family Village gang, dealing it vital blows. The article pointed out: "The course of events from the criticism of 'Hai Jui Dismissed from Office' to that of Three-Family Village has been one of stirring class struggle. It is a great revolution in the political, ideological and cultural fields. Faced with so arduous and militant a task, we must dare to make revolution." It said: "All those who oppose Mao Tse-tung's thought, obstruct the advance of the socialist revolution,

307

or are hostile to the interests of the revolutionary people of China and the world should be exposed, criticised and knocked down, whether they are 'masters' or 'authorities,' a Three-Family or a Four-Family Village, and no matter how famous they are, what influential positions they hold, by whom they are directed or supported, or how numerous their flatterers are."

On May 11, the magazine *Hung-ch'i* printed the article "On the Bourgeois Stand of *Ch'ien Hsien* and the *Pei-ching Jih-pao*" by Chi Pen-yu, which revealed that these two publications and the *Pei-ching Wan-pao* themselves for a long time had been instruments of Teng T'o, Wu Han and Liao Mo-sha in their frantic attacks on the Party and socialism.

Jen-min Jih-pao on May 14 printed "Expose Teng T'o's Anti-Party and Anti-Socialist Features" by Lin Chieh. It pointed out that Teng T'o and company had followed a black anti-Party and anti-socialist line and actively worked for the restoration of capitalism.

When the Three-Family Village gangster inn was exposed, the masses of workers, peasants and soldiers, revolutionary cadres and revolutionary intellectuals began holding discussions and writing articles indignantly condemning the criminal activities of the handful of anti-Party and anti-socialist elements.

Since early June this year, it has been further revealed that the sinister Three-Family Village gang had its roots in the former Peking Municipal Committee of the Chinese Communist Party.

Starting on June 1, the *Jen-min Jih-pao* published a series of editorials entitled "Sweep Away All Monsters," "A Great Revolution That Touches the People to Their Very Souls," "Capture the Positions in the Field of Historical Studies Seized by the Bourgeoisie," "Tear Aside the Bourgeois Mask of 'Liberty, Equality and Fraternity,'" "To Be Proletarian Revolutionaries or Bourgeois Royalists?" and others. These editorials analysed the current situation in the great cultural revolution, refuted the absurd views of the reactionary bourgeoisie to resist the proletarian cultural revolution and put forward the fighting tasks of developing the great cultural revolution even more profoundly.

The editorial entitled "Sweep Away All Monsters" pointed out that this Great Proletarian Cultural Revolution is aimed at exposing thoroughly the black anti-Party and anti-socialist line that runs through all Three-Family Villages, big and small, and at "demolishing all the old ideology and culture and all the old customs and habits, which, fostered by the exploiting classes, have poisoned the minds of the people for thousands of years, and creating and fostering among the masses an entirely new ideology and culture and entirely new customs and habits — those of the proletariat."

A poster in big characters written by Nieh Yüan-tzu and six others at Peking University was broadcast on June 1, exposing the plot of members of the sinister Three-Family Village gang who tried to put up a last-ditch fight through their control at the university.

In a commentator's article entitled "Hail the Big-Character Poster at Peking University," the *Jen-min Jih-pao* on June 2 called on the proletarian revolutionaries to rise up in a thoroughgoing revolution and crush all the sinister anti-Party and anti-socialist gangs and organisations and their discipline completely.

Waving the black flag of "liberty, equality and fraternity," members of the sinister anti-Party and anti-socialist gangs are countering the line for the proletarian cultural revolution of the Central Committee of the Party headed by Chairman Mao Tse-tung. In the editorial entitled "Tear Aside the Bourgeois Mask of 'Liberty, Equality and Fraternity,'" the *Jen-min Jih-pao* made a systematic criticism of the deceptive, hypocritical and reactionary nature of this bourgeois slogan and revealed the real purpose of these elements of the sinister gangs which is to oppose the dictatorship of the proletariat and to carry out the dictatorship of the bourgeoisie.

Two items of news were released on June 3: The Central Committee of the Chinese Communist Party decided to reorganise the Peking Municipal Committee of the Party and appointed new secretaries; and the new Peking Municipal Committee decided to reorganise the Party Committee of Peking University. In its editorial the following day entitled "New Victory for Mao Tse-tung's Thought," the *Jen-min Jih-pao* pointed out that the roots of the counter-revolutionary Three-Family Village clique were in the former Peking Municipal Committee of the Party. Shot through with a black anti-Party and anti-socialist line, it was not an instrument of the proletariat to exercise dictatorship over the bourgeoisie but an instrument of the bourgeoisie to exercise dictatorship over the proletariat. The decision of the Central Committee of the Party to reorganise the Peking Municipal Committee was a historic victory in China's Great Proletarian Cultural Revolution, a new victory for the great thought of Mao Tse-tung.

The masses of workers, peasants and soldiers, revolutionary cadres and revolutionary intellectuals in Peking and all other parts of the country, full of revolutionary enthusiasm, joy and inspiration, have warmly supported the decision of the Central Committee of the Party to reorganise the Peking Municipal Committee and warmly hailed this new victory.

At present, this Great Proletarian Cultural Revolution is, with the power of a thunderbolt, becoming ever more profound, and it is developing with the momentum of an avalanche, pounding with great power to smash all the decadent ideological and cultural positions still in the hands of the bourgeoisie and the feudal remnant forces and sweeping away the reactionary ideological and decadent cultural influences of imperialism.

This Great Proletarian Cultural Revolution is taking place under the direct leadership of the Central Committee of the Party and Chairman Mao Tse-tung. Four brilliant works of Chairman Mao—"On New Democracy," "Talks at the Yenan Forum on Literature and Art," "On the Correct Handling of Contradictions among the People" and "Speech at the Chinese Communist Party's National Conference on Propaganda Work"—are an important part of the great Mao Tse-tung's thought, which represents the summit of the contemporary Marxist-Leninist world outlook and theories of literature and art and is the supreme guide for China's great cultural revolution.

The masses of workers, peasants and soldiers and revolutionary cadres, who are armed with Mao Tse-tung's thought, have become the main force in storming and shattering the old bourgeois culture. Large numbers of excellent articles written by workers, peasants, students and cadres have appeared in the press in all parts of the country. In this struggle, the masses of workers, peasants and soldiers have displayed to the full their talent and wisdom and a younger generation of Marxist-Leninists is growing up. Gone for ever is the historical period in which culture was monopolised by bourgeois "scholars," "specialists" and "authorities."

Revolutionary proletarian culture is growing rapidly in the struggle to overthrow bourgeois culture. China's ancient Peking opera, the most stubborn of strongholds, was taken by storm in the past few years with the emergence of Peking operas on contemporary revolutionary themes like "The Red Lantern," "Shachiapang," "Taking the Bandits' Stronghold" and "Raid on White Tiger Regiment." Foreign classical art forms like the ballet, symphonic music and sculpture have undergone

310

a revolutionary transformation with the emergence of the ballet "The Red Detachment of Women," the symphony "Shachiapang" and the sculptures "Compound Where Rent Was Collected," etc. These fine works of art have been approved by the masses of workers, peasants and soldiers, and enthusiastically acclaimed by Chinese and foreign audiences. With the development in depth of the Great Proletarian Cultural Revolution, all departments in the cultural field of our country will inevitably appear in an entirely new light, bringing forth an increasing number of works that are excellent both in ideological content and artistic form, and an increasing number of highly scientific and revolutionary theses.

The Great Proletarian Cultural Revolution is in essence aimed at safeguarding the dictatorship of the proletariat. Imperialism and modern revisionism seek to subvert the political power of the proletariat both by force of arms and by cultural infiltration and ideological poisoning. Every counter-revolutionary restoration starts in the realm of ideology so as to mould public opinion. This is what happened in the usurpation of the leadership of the Soviet Party and State by the Khrushchev revisionist group and in the 1956 Hungarian counter-revolutionary riots. The great victory of our great cultural revolution is also a great victory in chopping off the claws of imperialism, digging out the roots of revisionism and preventing a capitalist restoration.

All the revolutionary peoples of the world are watching with great attention and warmly acclaiming the great victory of our great cultural revolution. However, a small handful of terror-stricken imperialists, modern revisionists and reactionaries of various countries are babbling about it.

Some reactionaries gloatingly take a malicious delight in this, as if the rule of the proletariat in China had hit some snag and they could profit by it. The illusions of these "lord-masters" are soon smashed to smithereens by facts. By sweeping away monsters of all kinds, we are digging out the social foundation of imperialism and modern revisionism within our country. The political power of the proletariat is now firmer than ever.

Some reactionaries slanderously allege that we are "destroying culture." Well, we want not only to destroy but to eradicate the decadent culture of imperialism and modern revisionism. Only by destroying and eradicating such things is it possible really to draw benefit from the fine culture created in the course of history and to develop the new culture of the proletariat to the full.

311

Some reactionaries vilify us by saying that the spearhead of our struggle is "directed against all intellectuals." This is sheer nonsense. The spearhead of our Great Proletarian Cultural Revolution is directed against a small handful of anti-Communist villains who have donned the cloak of communism and a small handful of anti-Party, anti-socialist and counter-revolutionary bourgeois intellectuals. The policy of the Communist Party towards the mass of intellectuals coming from the old society is one of uniting with, educating and remoulding them. The ranks of the proletarian intellectuals are growing with each passing day in the great cultural revolution.

An excellent situation prevails throughout China, with an all-round rise in the national economy and a steady, healthy development of the upsurge in economic construction. Through the great cultural revolution, Mao Tse-tung's thought has taken deeper root in people's minds, the revolutionary spirit of the masses of the people has been brought into full play and the leadership of the Party and the dictatorship of the proletariat have been consolidated and strengthened. This great cultural revolution will ensure the triumphant advance of the Chinese people along the road of socialism and communism.

The unprecedented great revolutionary change now taking place in China, which accounts for a quarter of the world's population, will inevitably have an immeasurably profound world-wide bearing on the history of mankind.

(Reproduced in full from Chinese Literature,
No. 8, 1966)

CHAPTER III

The Army's Role in the Cultural Revolution

The People's Liberation Army, as directed by Defence Minister Lin Piao, has taken an ever increasing role in the Great Proletarian Cultural Revolution. In every way, the army is held up for emulation for all of China.

The PLA began playing the part of the vanguard shortly after the current "revolution" got under way. Its policies and ideological decisions were propagated in the Liberation Army Daily, the army newspaper under the editorial control of the General Political Department of the PLA. Reproduced in this section are the important statements of policy from this newspaper.

The editorials stress the importance of implementing Mao Tse-tung's theory of class and class struggle, of toppling the small handful of persons in power within the Chinese Communist Party who have taken the capitalist road and issue demands to sweep away the "monsters and demons" with the objective of consolidating the dictatorship of the proletariat.

In a series of speeches at mass Peking rallies, Lin Piao further expounded the Army view. Placing himself in the position of speaking for Mao Tse-tung, Lin constantly called for the use of Mao's political thoughts on the struggle of class against class. He called for unity in the thinking of the people of the entire country, interpreting the Mao Tse-tung line as the line of the Great Proletarian Cultural Revolution and defining this as a new development in the current revolution.

Lin Piao also called on the People's Liberation Army to carry forward the mass movement for study of Mao Tse-tung's works. The more important of this series of statements are reproduced in this section.—Ed.

"We will strike down those in power who take the road of capitalism, strike down the reactionary bourgeois authorities, strike down all bourgeois royalists, oppose all actions to suppress the revolution, and strike down all monsters and demons!

"We will vigorously destroy all the old ideas, old culture, old customs and old habits of the exploiting classes... We will sweep away all vermin and remove all obstacles!"

—Lin Piao

(Speech at the first mass Peking rally held on August 18, 1966)

The Army Organ Takes Over

In the following editorials in *Chieh-fang-chün Pao*, official organ of the CCP Central Committee's Military Commission which controls the General Political Department of the People's Liberation Army, the whole country is urged to carry the Great Proletarian Cultural Revolution through to the end.

Not until June 1966 did the army paper take over from both *Jen-min Jih-pao*, official organ of the CCP Central Committee, and *Hung-ch'i,* theoretical journal of the Party centre, the job of waging "a sharp class struggle" to eliminate the "black anti-Party line" and foster proletarian ideology in academic work, education, journalism, literature, stage art and other spheres of culture.

The documents of the army newspaper warn that a "scholars' rebellion," formed along the line of the Petofi Circle of Hungary, may erupt into a counter-revolution to usurp proletarian leadership. The articles call upon one and all in China to be vigilant against "enemies without guns" and against "sugar-coated bullets" on ideological and political fronts.—Ed.

Never Forget the Class Struggle

The publication of our editorial "Hold High the Great Red Banner of Mao Tse-tung's Thought and Actively Participate in the Great Socialist Cultural Revolution" has evoked a great response both inside and outside our army. The broad masses of workers, peasants and soldiers and revolutionary cadres, showing a high degree of revolutionary enthusiasm, have sent in articles and letters; they are actively participating in the struggle and voicing their deep indignation at the black anti-Party and anti-socialist line in the cultural field. They understand that the current great polemic on the cultural front is definitely not a question concerning only a few articles, plays and films, nor is it merely an academic debate. It is an extremely sharp class struggle. It is a struggle to defend Mao Tse-tung's thought, a struggle on a cardinal issue of right and wrong. It is an acute, protracted struggle on the question of which will win out in the realm of ideology, the proletariat or the bourgeoisie.

We must energetically foster proletarian ideology and liquidate bourgeois ideology in academic work, education, journalism, literature and art and other spheres of culture. This is a crucial question affecting the deepening of our country's socialist revolution at the present stage, a question concerning the overall situation, and an issue of prime importance affecting the destiny and future of our Party and State as well as the world revolution. We revolutionary fighters should none of us stand aloof or be indifferent to this struggle. We must respond to the call of the Party, hold high the great red banner of Mao Tse-tung's thought, take an active part in this class struggle and resolutely carry the great socialist cultural revolution through to the end.

Chairman Mao Tse-tung teaches us that classes and class struggle continue to exist in socialist society and that the struggle between the road of socialism and the road of capitalism still goes on. The socialist revolution on the economic front (in the ownership of the means of production) is insufficient and cannot be consolidated by itself. There must also be a thoroughgoing socialist revolution on the political and ideological fronts. A very long period of time is needed to decide which will win out in the struggle between socialism and capitalism in the political and ideological fields. Several decades will not suffice; anywhere from one to several centuries will be required for success.

In fact, as Chairman Mao has pointed out, there has never been a year, a month or even a day in the 16 years since liberation when the class struggle on the cultural front has halted. We have had, for instance, the criticism of the film "The Life of Wu Hsün" in 1951, the criticism of the book *"Studies in the 'Dream of the Red Chamber'"* and then of the reactionary ideas of Hu Shih in 1954, the criticism of Hu Feng and the struggle against his counter-revolutionary clique in 1955, the counter-attack against the fanatical onslaught of the bourgeois rightists on the cultural front in 1957, the emergence of numerous bourgeois and revisionist poisonous weeds in the form of films, dramas and literary works since 1959 and our struggle against them, the criticism of Yang Hsien-chen's theory of "two combining into one" in 1964, and the current great polemic which, begun with the criticism of Wu Han's "Hai Jui Dismissed from Office," is now being carried to a greater depth.

316

One struggle has followed another, each increasingly profound. After we are rid of this black line, others may appear and the struggle must go on. This shows that class struggle is independant of man's will and is inevitable. The anti-Party and anti-socialist elements will stubbornly show their bourgeois nature by every possible means. You cannot expect them to do otherwise. These people give verbal support to socialism, but in reality they are infatuated by capitalism and cling to the corpse of the bourgeoisie. They are hostile to the dictatorship of the proletariat and have a deep-seated resentment against and hatred of the Party and socialism. Whenever there is a suitable climate, they will give vent to these feelings, and whenever some wind stirs the grass, they will raise their ugly heads. After being repeatedly exposed, criticised and dealt blows by the broad masses, they will resort to more covert, crafty, round-about and zigzag tactics to continue their attacks on the Party and socialism.

The noteworthy thing is that in the present new situation of class struggle, the attacks launched against us by this handful of anti-Party and anti-socialist elements have new features. They are waving "red flags" to oppose the Red Flag and donning the cloak of Marxism-Leninism and Mao Tse-tung's thought to oppose Marxism-Leninism and Mao Tse-tung's thought. Taking advantage of the functions and powers given them by the Party and Government, they have put some departments and units under their control, resisted the leadership of the Party and committed anti-Party and anti-socialist crimes through the instruments in their hands. These people are mostly so-called authorities, and they are rather "well known" in society. They are still worshipped by some people who do not know the facts. They think that they still possess enough capital to have a trial of strength with the proletariat and they desperately defend the stronghold of bourgeois ideology. Their anti-Party and anti-socialist activities are not isolated or accidental but are in tune with the international anti-China chorus raised by the imperialists, the modern revisionists and the reactionaries, in line with the activities of the overthrown reactionary classes within our country to attempt a come-back and in co-ordination with the anti-Party activities of the Right opportunists within our Party. Their anti-Party and anti-socialist activities are to a certain extent deceptive and are extremely harmful. Our struggle with them is a life-and-death one. We must be fully aware of this and maintain sharp vigilance. As for those who have turned out a number of bad works but are at one with the Party and socialism, their shortcomings and errors can be rectified in the course of practice. A strict distinction should be made between these comrades and the handful of anti-Party and anti-socialist elements.

Before our nation-wide victory, Chairman Mao Tse-tung warned us:

> After the enemies with guns have been wiped out, there will still be enemies without guns, they are bound to struggle desperately against us; we must never regard these enemies lightly. If we do not now raise and understand the problem in this way, we shall commit very grave mistakes.

Restoration of capitalism invariably takes the form either of violence or of "peaceful evolution," or of a combination of both. US imperialism and the other class enemies at home and abroad attempt not only to overthrow us by violence but also to conquer us by "peaceful evolution," by the use of "sugar-coated bullets." In a hundred and one ways, they are spreading reactionary political and ideological viruses and the bourgeois way of life in an attempt to corrupt and corrode the Communists, the proletariat and the other revolutionary people, hoping to bring about the degeneration of some weak-minded persons in our ranks into bourgeois elements and to make socialism gradually retrogress to capitalism. It is indeed a profound lesson that the Soviet Union, the first great socialist State founded by Lenin and born amid the salvoes of the October Revolution, has been going down the road of capitalist restoration through a process of "peaceful evolution" under the control and manipulation of a handful of revisionists who have usurped the leadership of the Party and State.

Chairman Mao Tse-tung teaches us:

> Class struggle, the struggle for production and scientific experiment are the three great revolutionary movements for building a mighty socialist country. These movements are a sure guarantee that Communists will be free from bureaucracy and immune against revisionism and dogmatism, and will for ever remain invincible. They are a reliable guarantee that the proletariat will be able to unite with the broad working masses and realise a democratic dictatorship. If, in the absence of these movements, the landlords, rich peasants, counter-revolutionaries, bad elements and ogres of all kinds were allowed to crawl out, while our cadres were to shut their eyes to all this and in many cases fail even to differentiate between the enemy and ourselves but were to collaborate with the enemy and become corrupted and demoralised, if our cadres were thus dragged into the enemy camp or the enemy were able to sneak into our ranks, and if many of our workers, peasants, and intellectuals were left defenceless against both the soft and the hard tactics of the enemy, then it would not take long, perhaps only serveral

318

years or a decade, or several decades at most, before a counter-revolutionary restoration on a national scale inevitably occurred, the Marxist-Leninist Party would undoubtedly become a revisionist party or a fascist party, and the whole of China would change its colour.

We must keep this teaching of Chairman Mao Tse-tung's firmly in our minds and never forget the class struggle in the period of socialism; we must never ignore the battle against the enemies without guns.

Chairman Mao also teaches us that "any given culture (as an ideological form) is a reflection of the politics and economics of a given society, and the former in turn has a tremendous influence and effect upon the latter" and that "a cultural revolution is the ideological reflection of the political and economic revolution and is in their service." He further says:

> ... while we recognise that in the general development of history the material determines the mental and social being determines social consciousness, we also — and indeed must — recognise the reaction of mental on material things, of social consciousness on social being and of the superstructure on the economic base.

In the 16 years since liberation, the economic base of socialism and the political power of the dictatorship of the proletariat have been established in China and are daily growing stronger. The socialist revolution on the economic and political fronts has won great victories. However, the political viewpoints and the ideology of the overthrown bourgeoisie and other exploiting classes still have strong influence. They not only impede the development of the economic base of socialism but are actively employing bourgeois and revisionist culture to pave the way for the restoration of capitalism. The question of which will win out in the ideological sphere is far from settled. We must pay great attention to the reaction of the superstructure on the economic base and to the class struggle in the ideological sphere. The victory of the socialist revolution on the economic and political fronts cannot be consolidated without the victory of the socialist revolution in the ideological sphere.

We must never think that the wild attack launched against us by this handful of revisionist and bourgeois elements is merely a "scholars' rebellion" which will amount to nothing much. We must never regard our struggle against them as only paper polemics that have no effect on the overall situation. In fact, every counter-revolutionary restoration starts in the realm of the mind—including ideology, the superstructure,

319

theoretical and academic work, literature and art — so as to mould public opinion. This was what happened when the Khrushchev revisionists usurped the leadership of the Soviet Communist Party. Likewise, in Hungary in 1956, it was a number of revisionist and bourgeois writers, artists and intellectuals who organised the "Petofi Club" and acted as the shock brigade in the counter-revolutionary riots. The present furious attacks against our Party and against socialism by a handful of revisionist and bourgeois elements in our country represent their attempt to realise their fond dream of restoring capitalism. If we are not vigilant against these enemies without guns, do not counterattack them resolutely, but give bourgeois ideas free rein and allow their plots to be carried out, there is the danger that the foundations of our socialism will be undermined and that our country will change its colour.

The Chinese People's Liberation Army is an army of workers and peasants founded and led by the Party and Chairman Mao; it is the mainstay of the dictatorship of the proletariat and the defender of the cause of socialism. We must keep close watch on the enemies with guns and be ready at all times to defeat armed attacks by US imperialism and its lackeys; at the same time, we must be highly vigilant against the enemies without guns and firmly crush the bourgeoisie's criminal plots against the Party and against socialism. The cadres and men of our army should not only be brave soldiers charging through enemy fire on the battlefield but also staunch proletarian fighters against "sugar-coated bullets" on the political and ideological fronts. We must follow Chairman Mao's teachings, fully recognise the protracted, tortuous and complex nature of the class struggle in the period of socialism and never forget the existence of class struggle. We must arm our minds with Mao Tse-tung's thought and observe, analyse and deal with everything from the viewpoint of class struggle and with the method of class analysis. We must criticise erroneous things, uproot poisonous weeds and strike down ogres of all kinds whenever we see them; we must never allow them to run wild and incite and create trouble.

It is on the basis of Chairman Mao's theory on the existence of classes and class struggle in socialist society that Comrade Lin Piao issued his directive on giving prominence to politics. Politics is the struggle of class against class. To give prominence to politics means that we must give prominence to proletarian politics, take Mao

Tse-tung's thought as the guide and class struggle as the key link, and wage the struggle to foster proletarian ideology and liquidate bourgeois ideology.

Our armed forces do not live in a vacuum. Through various channels, class struggles in society will inevitably be reflected in our armed forces and in the mind of every one of us. We must never underestimate the influence on us of the class struggle in the ideological sphere.

Good works of literature and art and good articles can help raise our political consciousness and heighten our fighting will. But bad films, plays, novels and articles, if we do not examine them, criticise them and boycott them, will poison our minds, gradually transform us and lead us on to the wrong track. Historical experience proves that no enemy, however ferocious and whatever his tricks, is to be feared. What is to be feared is that we ourselves should relax vigilance and let ourselves be disarmed mentally. The present great socialist cultural revolution is a most vivid, most practical education in class struggle and is also a test for every cadre and man in our army politically and ideologically. Every comrade must closely follow and give great attention to the development of the present great cultural revolution with a high sense of political responsibility and great revolutionary fervour, and actively join this great struggle to get himself tempered, educated and remoulded and raise his political consciousness in the process.

The era of Mao Tse-tung is the era in which the workers, peasants and soldiers master revolutionary theory. They are demonstrating their role as the main force in this great socialist cultural revolution. Although the "scholars," "specialists" and "professors" who oppose the Party and socialism don all sorts of cloaks, strike grand poses and deliberately turn simple things into mysteries, they can neither daunt nor mislead us. We have the all-conquering weapon of Mao Tse-tung's thought and ardent hearts loyal to the Party, to socialism and to Mao Tse-tung's thought. Truth is with us. The cadres and men of our army have a firm and clear-cut political stand, keen political awareness and discerning eyes. They can distinguish between the enemy and ourselves and between right and wrong.

Provided we make efforts to study and apply Chairman Mao's works creatively, arm ourselves with his thought, dare to despise the "authority" of the revisionist and bourgeois elements and dispel blind faith in them, we will certainly be able to see through the true features of these ogres and monsters and expose them to the light of day. Let us hold ever higher the great red banner of Mao Tse-tung's thought, resolutely destroy the black anti-Party and anti-socialist line of the bourgeoisie and the revisionists, and carry the great socialist cultural revolution through to the end!

(From a full translation of an editorial in
Chieh-fang-chün Pao of May 4, 1966)

*   *   *

Hold High the Great Red Banner of Mao Tse-tung's Thought and Actively Participate in the Great Socialist Cultural Revolution

Chairman Mao Tse-tung has taught us that classes and class struggle continue to exist in socialist society. He has said that in China "the class struggle between the proletariat and the bourgeoisie, the class struggle between the different political forces, and the class struggle in the ideological field between the proletariat and the bourgeoisie will continue to be long and tortuous and at times will even become very acute."

The struggle to foster what is proletarian and liquidate what is bourgeois on the cultural front is an important aspect of the class struggle between the proletariat and the bourgeoisie, between the socialist road and the capitalist road and between proletarian ideology and bourgeois ideology. The proletariat seeks to change the world according to its own world outlook, and so does the bourgeoisie. Socialist culture should serve the workers, peasants and soldiers, should serve proletarian politics, and should serve the consolidation and development of the socialist system and its gradual transition to communism. Bourgeois and revisionist culture serves the bourgeoisie, serves the landlords, rich peasants, counter-revolutionaries, bad elements and rightists, and paves the way for the restoration of capitalism. If the proletariat does not seize hold of the cultural positions, the bourgeoisie is bound to do so. This is a sharp class struggle.

Since the remnant forces of the bourgeoisie in our country are still fairly large, since there are still a fairly large number of bourgeois intellectuals, since the influence of bourgeois ideology is still fairly strong and since their methods of fighting us have become increasingly sly and insidious, we shall find it difficult to see the struggle that is taking place and may fall victim to the sugar-coated bullets of the bourgeoisie or we may even lose our positions, if we slacken our vigilance or relax in the least. In this respect, the issue of which will win, socialism or capitalism, is not yet settled. The struggle is inevitable. Failure to handle it properly will give rise to revisionism.

Our People's Liberation Army, the people's armed forces created and led by the Chinese Communist Party and Chairman Mao, is the most loyal tool of the Party and the people, and the mainstay of the dictatorship of the proletariat. It has always played an important role in the revolutionary cause of the proletariat, and it will do so in this great socialist cultural revolution as well. We must acquire a deeper understanding of the situation with respect to the class struggle in the ideological field, hold high the great red banner of Mao Tse-tung's thought and unswervingly carry the socialist cultural revolution through to the end together with all the people of our country and make the literary and art work of our armed forces play a powerful part in giving prominence to politics and promoting the revolutionisation of the people.

The past 16 years have witnessed sharp class struggles on the cultural front.

In both stages of our revolution, the new democratic stage and the socialist stage, there has existed a struggle between two classes and two lines on the cultural front, i.e., the struggle between the proletariat and the bourgeoisie for leadership on this front. In the history of our Party, the struggles against both "Left" and Right opportunism also included struggles between the two lines on the cultural front.

Wang Ming's line was a bourgeois trend which was once rampant within our Party. In the rectification movement which started in 1942, Chairman Mao gave a thorough theoretical refutation first of Wang Ming's political, military and organisational lines and then, immediately afterwards, of the cultural line represented by him. Chairman Mao's "On New Democracy" and "Talks at the Yenan Forum on Literature and Art" are the most complete, the most comprehensive and the most systematic historical summaries of this struggle between the two lines on the cultural front. They have carried on and developed the Marxist-Leninist world outlook and theory on literature and art.

323

After our revolution entered the socialist stage, a whole series of important struggles on the cultural front were waged under the direct leadership of the Central Committee of the Party and Chairman Mao, such as the criticism of the film "The Life of Wu Hsün,"[1] the criticism of the book "Studies in the Dream of the Red Chamber,"[2] the struggle against the Hu Feng counter-revolutionary clique,[3] the struggle against the rightists, and the great socialist cultural revolution of the last three years. Chairman Mao's two works, "On the Correct Handling of Contradictions Among the People" and "Speech at the Chinese Communist Party's National Conference on Propaganda Work," are the most recent summaries of the historical experience of the movements for revolutionary ideology and literature and art in China and other countries. They represent a new development of the Marxist-Leninist world outlook and theory on literature and art.

These four brilliant works form an important part of the great thought of Mao Tse-tung. They represent the peak of the contemporary Marxist-Leninist world outlook and theory on literature and art. They are the supreme guide for our work in literature and art and suffice for the needs of our proletariat for a long time.

In the decade and more since the founding of our People's Republic, a black anti-Party and anti-socialist line running counter to Mao Tse-tung's thought has existed in our literary and art circles. This black line is a combination of bourgeois ideas on literature and art, modern revisionist ideas on literature and art and what is called the literature and art of the 1930s (in the Kuomintang areas of China). Its typical expressions are such theories as those of "truthful writing,"[4] "the broad path of realism,"[5] "the deepening of realism,"[6] opposition to "subject matter as the decisive factor,"[7] "middle characters,"[8] opposition to "the smell of gunpowder,"[9] and "the merging of various trends as the spirit of the age."[10] Most of these theories were refuted long ago by Chairman Mao in his "Talks at the Yenan Forum on Literature and Art".

In film circles there are people who advocate "discarding the classics and rebelling against orthodoxy," in other words, discarding the classics of Marxism-Leninism and Mao Tse-tung's thought and rebelling against the orthodoxy of people's revolutionary war. As a result of the influence or domination of this bourgeois and modern revisionist counter-current in literature and art, there are only a small number of good or basically sound works among post-liberation works about people's wars, the people's armed forces and other military subjects which truly praise revolutionary heroes and serve the workers, peasants and soldiers and socialism; some are anti-Party and anti-socialist poisonous weeds, while many works are somewhere in between. Some works distort the historical facts, concentrating on the portrayal of erroneous lines instead of the correct line; some describe heroic characters who, however, always violate discipline, or create heroes only to make them die in an artificially tragic ending. Some works do not present heroic characters but only "middle" characters who are actually backward people, caricatures of workers, peasants or soldiers; in depicting the enemy, they fail to expose his class nature as an exploiter and oppressor of the people, and even go so far as to prettify him. Then there are other works concerned only with love and romance, pandering to philistine tastes and claiming that love and death are eternal themes. All such bourgeois, revisionist trash must be resolutely opposed.

The struggle between the two roads on the front of literature and art in society is bound to be reflected in the armed forces, which do not exist in a vacuum and cannot possibly be an exception to the rule. Our armed forces are the chief instrument of the dictatorship of the proletariat. Without the people's armed forces led by the Party there would have been neither the victory of our revolution nor the dictatorship of the proletariat and socialism, and the people would have nothing. Inevitably, therefore, the enemy will try by every means to undermine our armed forces from all sides; and they will inevitably use literature and art as a weapon to corrupt our armed forces. We must be very much on our guard against this.

However, not everybody shares this view. Some claim that the problem of the orientation of literature and art in our armed forces is already solved, that what remains is mainly the problem of raising our artistic level. This fallacy is most pernicious and is not based on concrete analysis. In point of fact, some works of literature and art of our armed forces are taking the right direction and have reached a comparatively high artistic level; some are taking the right direction but their artistic level is low; some have serious defects or mistakes in both political orientation and artistic form; and some are anti-Party and anti-socialist poisonous weeds. During the great upheavals in the class struggles on the literary and art front since liberation, some literary and art workers in the army have failed to pass the test, committing major or minor mistakes. This shows that literary and art work in

325

the armed forces has also been influenced to a greater or lesser degree by the black anti-Party and anti-socialist line.

In accordance with the instructions of the Central Committee of the Party and Chairman Mao, we must actively participate in the great socialist revolution on the cultural front, completely eliminate this black line and liquidate its influence on the armed forces. After we are rid of this black line, still others may appear and the struggle must go on. This is an arduous, complex, long-term struggle which will take dozens of years, perhaps hundreds. It is vital for the revolutionising of our armed forces, for the future of the Chinese revolution and for the future of the world revolution that we should unswervingly carry the great socialist cultural revolution through to the end.

Since the 10th Plenary Session of the 8th Central Committee of the Party in September 1962, when Chairman Mao called upon the whole Party and the entire Chinese people never to forget classes and class struggle, the struggle to foster what is proletarian and liquidate what is bourgeois on the cultural front has developed further.

The last three years have seen a new situation in the great socialist cultural revolution. The most outstanding example is the emergence of Peking operas on contemporary revolutionary themes. Those working to reform Peking opera, led by the Central Committee of the Party and Chairman Mao and armed with Marxism-Leninism and Mao Tsetung's thought, have launched a heroic and tenacious offensive against the literature and art of the feudal class, the bourgeoisie and the modern revisionists.

Peking opera, formerly the most stubborn of strongholds, has thus been radically revolutionised, both in ideological content and in artistic form, and this has started a revolutionary change in literary and art circles. Peking operas with contemporary revolutionary themes like "The Red Lantern," "Shachiapang," "Taking the Bandits' Stronghold" and "Raid on the White Tiger Regiment," the ballet "Red Detachment Women," the symphony "Shachiapang" and the sculptures "The Rent Collection Courtyard" have been approved by the broad masses of workers, peasants and soldiers, and enthusiastically acclaimed by Chinese and foreign audiences. They are pioneer efforts which will have a profound and far-reaching impact on the socialist cultural revolution. They effectively prove that even that most stubborn stronghold Peking opera can be taken by storm and revolutionised and that foreign classical art forms like the ballet, symphonic music and sculpture can also be remoulded to serve our purpose. This should give us still greater confidence in revolutionising other forms of art. At the same time, these successes deal a powerful blow at conservatives of various descriptions and at such views as the "box-office value" theory, the "foreign currency value" theory and the theory that "revolutionary works cannot travel abroad."

Another outstanding feature of the great socialist cultural revolution in the past three years is the widespread mass activity of workers, peasants and soldiers on the ideological and literary and art fronts. Workers, peasants and soldiers are now writing many fine philosophical articles which express Mao Tse-tung's thought in a practical way. They are also producing many fine works of literature and art to praise the triumph of our socialist revolution, the big leap forward on all the fronts of socialist construction, our new heroes, and the brilliant leadership of our great Party and our great leader Chairman Mao. The numerous poems by workers, peasants and soldiers which appear on wall newspapers and blackboards are especially noteworthy, since both in content and form they represent an entirely new age.

During these few years an excellent situation in the cultural work of our armed forces has also emerged. Since Comrade Lin Piao took charge of the affairs of the Military Commission of the Central Committee of the Party, he has taken a firm grip on literary and art work and given us many important instructions. The Resolution on Strengthening Political and Ideological Work in the Armed Forces passed at the enlarged meeting of the Military Commission in 1960 clearly specifies that literary and art work in the armed forces "must, in close conjunction with the tasks of the armed forces and in the context of their ideological situation, serve the cause of fostering proletarian ideology and liquidating bourgeois ideology and consolidating and improving fighting capacity." Most of our literary and art workers in the armed forces have given prominence to politics, creatively studied and applied the works of Chairman Mao, lived with the companies or in the villages and factories, taken an active part in the socialist education movement, linked themselves with workers, peasants and soldiers, further tempered themselves and remoulded their ideology, and raised their level of proletarian consciousness. As a result, they have produced excellent plays like "On Guard Beneath the Neon Lights," excellent novels like "The Song of Ouyang Hai," and some fairly good reportage, soldiers' poems, music, dances and fine art. A number of promising

327

writers and artists have emerged.

Of course, these are merely the first fruits of our socialist cultural revolution, the first step in a long march of ten thousand *li*. In order to safeguard and extend this achievement, to carry the socialist cultural revolution through to the end, we must work hard for a long time. The literary and art workers of our armed forces must strive to make a worthy contribution.

To create a new socialist literature and art, we must foster good models, and leading comrades must see to this themselves. Only when we have good models and successful experience in producing them will our arguments prove convincing, and will we be able to consolidate the positions we hold.

We should have the courage to blaze new trails, to create new and original socialist and proletarian works. The basic task of socialist literature and art is to strive to create heroic workers, peasants and soldiers armed with Mao Tse-tung's thought. Chairman Mao has pointed out:

> If you are a bourgeois writer or artist, you will eulogise not the proletariat but the bourgeoisie, and if you are a proletarian writer or artist, you will eulogise not the bourgeoisie but the proletariat and working people: it must be one or the other.

So the class struggle between the proletariat and the bourgeoisie on the literary and art front centres on which class to eulogise, which class to portray heroes from, and which class to choose men from to occupy the dominant position in works of literature and art. Here lies the line of demarcation in the literature and art of different classes.

The fine qualities of the heroes who have appeared from among the workers, peasants and soldiers nurtured by Mao Tse-tung's thought are the epitome of the proletarian class character. We should enthusiastically create heroic images of workers, peasants and soldiers. We should create typical characters and not confine ourselves to actual persons and events. Chairman Mao has said that "life as reflected in works of literature and art can and ought to be on a higher plane, more intense, more concentrated, more typical, nearer the ideal, and therefore more universal than actual everyday life." This means that our writers must sum up the material from real life accumulated over a long period to create typical characters of various kinds.

To create heroic characters successfully, we must adopt the method of combining revolutionary realism with revolutionary romanticism, and must not adopt the bourgeois method of critical realism or romanticism.

Writers in the armed forces should make it their glorious task to depict revolutionary wars, propagate Chairman Mao's theory of people's war, and create heroic characters in revolutionary wars. When we write about revolutionary wars, we must first be clear about their nature—ours is the side of justice, the enemy's is the side of injustice. Our works must show our arduous and heroic struggles and sacrifices, but must also display revolutionary heroism and revolutionary optimism. While depicting the cruelty of war, we should not dwell excessively on its horrors. While depicting the arduousness of the revolutionary struggle, we should not dwell excessively on the sufferings. The cruelty of a revolutionary war and revolutionary heroism, the arduousness of the revolutionary struggle and revolutionary optimism are the unity of opposites, but we must be clear which is the principal aspect of the contradiction; otherwise, if we put the emphasis wrongly, a bourgeois pacifist trend will emerge. While depicting the people's revolutionary war, whether in the stage in which guerrilla warfare was primary and mobile warfare supplementary, or in the stage in which mobile warfare was primary, we must correctly show the relationship between the regular forces, the guerrillas and the people's militia and between the armed masses and the unarmed masses under the leadership of the Party.

It is no easy matter to produce good models of proletarian literature and art. Strategically we must make light of this task, but tactically we must take it seriously. To create a fine work is an arduous process, and the comrades in charge of literary and art work must never adopt a bureaucratic or casual attitude towards it but must work hard, sharing the writers' joys and hardships. As far as possible, they must get their material first hand. They should not be afraid of failures or mistakes. They should allow for failures and mistakes and let people correct their mistakes. They must rely on the masses, get the opinions of the masses and refer back to the masses, so that by repeatedly undergoing the test of practice over a long period a work may become better and better and achieve the unity of revolutionary political content and the highest possible perfection of artistic form. In the course of practice they must sum up their experience in good time, gradually grasping the laws of various forms of art. Otherwise, no good models can be produced.

There are many important revolutionary historical and contemporary themes which urgently need portrayal in a planned and systematic way. A powerful nucleus of truly proletarian writers and artists will be trained in the process.

The socialist cultural revolution must overthrow certain things and establish others. If certain things are not thoroughly overthrown, others cannot be truly established. To carry out the socialist cultural revolution and create a new socialist literature and art, we must emancipate our minds and overcome superstition.

We must overcome our superstitious reverence for what is called the literature and art of the 1930s (in the Kuomintang areas of China). At that time the Left-wing literary and art movement followed Wang Ming's "Left" opportunist line politically; organisationally it practised closed-doorism and sectarianism; and its theory of literature and art was virtually that of such Russian bourgeois literary critics as Belinsky,[11] Chernyshevsky[12] and Dobrolyubov,[13] bourgeois democrats of tsarist Russia who had bourgeois ideas, not Marxist ones. The bourgeois-democratic revolution is a revolution in which one exploiting class opposes another. It is only the socialist revolution of the proletariat that finally destroys all exploiting classes. Therefore, we must not take the ideas of any bourgeois revolutionary as the guiding principle in our proletarian ideological or literary and art movements. There were of course good things in the 1930s too, namely, the militant Left-wing literary and art movement led by Lu Hsün. Towards the end of the 1930s, some Left-wing leaders influenced by Wang Ming's Right capitulationist line abandoned the Marxist-Leninist class standpoint and put forward the slogan of "a literature of national defence." That was a bourgeois slogan. It was Lu Hsün who put forward the proletarian slogan, "Literature of the masses for the national revolutionary war." Some Left-wing writers and artists, notably Lu Hsün, also raised the slogans that literature and art should serve the workers and peasants and that the workers and peasants should create their own literature and art. However, no systematic solution was found for the basic problem of how to integrate writers and artists with the workers, peasants and soldiers. The great majority of these men were followers of bourgeois nationalism and democracy, a number of whom failed to pass the test of the democratic revolution, while others have not given a good account of themselves under the test of socialism.

We must overcome blind reverence for Chinese and foreign

classical literature. The classical literature and art of China and those of Europe (including Russia) have exercised a considerable influence on our literary and art circles, and some people have looked on them as models and accepted them in their entirety. But Chairman Mao has taught us that "uncritical transplantation or copying from the ancients and the foreigners is the most sterile and harmful dogmatism in literature and art." Ancient and foreign works should be studied too, and refusal to study them would be wrong; but we must do so critically, making the past serve the present and foreign things serve China.

As for the relatively good revolutionary literary and art works of the Soviet Union, which appeared after the October Revolution, they too must be analysed and not blindly worshipped or, still less, blindly imitated. Blind imitation can never become art. Literature and art can only spring from life which is their sole source. This is borne out by the whole history of ancient and modern literature and art, both Chinese and foreign.

All leading personnel in literary and art work as well as writers and artists must practise democratic centralism, support the practice of "letting all people have their say" and oppose the practice of "what I say goes." We must follow the mass line and see to it that politics are given prominence. In the past, writers sometimes produced a piece of work and, turning a deaf ear to the opinions of the masses, forced the leadership to nod in approval. This way of doing things is very bad. The cadres in charge of literature and art should always bear in mind two points in dealing with creative work in literature and art: first, they must be good at listening to the opinions of the masses; second, they must be good at analysing these opinions, accepting those which are right and rejecting those which are wrong. There are no perfect works of literature and art, but if a work is basically good, we should point out its shortcomings and errors so that it can be improved upon. Bad works should not be hidden away but brought out for appraisal by the masses. We must not be afraid of the masses but should have firm faith in them, for they can give us much valuable advice. And through such appraisal those whose ideas are confused will improve their powers of discrimination.

We must encourage revolutionary, militant, mass criticism of literature and art, break the monopoly of literary and art criticism by a few "critics" (those going in a wrong direction or lacking in militancy).

We must place the weapon of criticism of literature and art in the hands of the masses of workers, peasants and soldiers and integrate professional critics with critics from among the masses. We must make this criticism more militant and oppose unprincipled vulgar praise. We must reform our style of writing, encourage the writing of short, popular articles, transform our literary and art criticism into daggers and hand-grenades and learn to handle them effectively in close combat.

Of course, we must at the same time write some longer, systematic articles of greater theoretical depth. We must present the facts and reason things out, not use jargon to frighten people. This is the only way to disarm the self-styled critics of literature and art. Critics must give warm support to works which are good or fundamentally sound, while pointing out their shortcomings in a helpful manner. And principled criticism must be made of bad works. In the theoretical field, typical fallacies on literature and art must be thoroughly and systematically criticised. We must not mind being blamed for "brandishing the stick." When some people accuse us of over-simplification and crudity, we must make our own analysis. Some criticisms we make are basically correct but are not sufficiently convincing because the analysis and the evidence adduced are inadequate. These should be improved. Some people who start by accusing us of over-simplification and crudity drop the charge when they gain a better understanding. But when the enemy condemns our correct criticisms as over-simplified and crude, we must stand firm. We must have regular criticism of literature and art; it is an important method of waging the struggle in the field of literature and art as well as of Party guidance of the work in this field. Without correct literary and art criticism we cannot maintain a correct orientation in literature and art or enable creative work to flourish.

To carry out a thoroughgoing socialist cultural revolution we must re-educate the cadres in charge of literature and art and reorganise the ranks of writers and artists. As far back as the struggle on the Chingkang Mountains, the Workers' and Peasants' Red Army set up a red contingent of writers and artists under the direct leadership of Chairman Mao and the brilliant guidance of the resolution of the Kutien meeting. During the War of Resistance Against Japan, with the growing political and military strength of our Party and army, our contingent of writers and artists made great headway. In the base areas and in the armed forces, we trained a considerable number of revolutionary literary and art workers. Especially after the publication of the "Talks at the Yenan Forum on Literature and Art," they maintained the correct orientation, persisted in the path of integrating themselves with the workers, peasants and soldiers, and played a positive role in the revolution. The question now is that, after the liberation of the whole mainland, some people were unable to resist the corrupting influence of bourgeois ideas when we entered the large cities, with the result that they have fallen out in the course of our advance. And the newcomers among the literary and art workers in the armed forces have brought with them the influence of various bourgeois views on literature and art. There are also a small number of people who have not been remoulded at all, but cling stubbornly to the bourgeois stand.

Our literature and art is a proletarian literature and art, a Party literature and art. What distinguishes us above all from other classes is the principle of the proletarian Party spirit. We must realise that the spokesmen of other classes also have their principle of party spirit, and a very strong one too. We must firmly abide by the principle of the proletarian Party spirit and combat corruption by bourgeois ideology in the following three fields, i.e., the ideas guiding creation in literature and art, the organisational line and working style. We must draw a clear line between our ideology and bourgeois ideology; we must never peacefully co-exist with it.

The literary and art workers in our armed forces have various problems, but for the majority of them, the question is to acquire a correct understanding, to receive more education and to attain a higher level. We must regard Chairman Mao's writings as our supreme guide, seriously study and grasp his teachings on literature and art, and pay special attention to putting them into practice and creatively applying what we learn to our thinking and actions, so that we really master Mao Tse-tung's thought. We must carry out his instructions and "for a long period of time unreservedly and whole-heartedly go among the masses of workers, peasants and soldiers, go into the heat of the struggle, go to the only source, the broadest and richest source," to integrate ourselves with the workers, peasants and soldiers, remould our thinking, raise the level of our political consciousness and whole-heartedly serve all the people of China and of the world, with no thought of fame or profit and without fear of hardship or death. We must make it our life-time endeavour to study Chairman Mao's works, devote ourselves to the revolution and remould our thinking. Only thus can we carry out Comrade Lin Piao's instructions and be ready to pass any stiff test with flying colours in our thinking, our life and our professional skills. Only thus can our literary and art work better serve the workers, peasants and soldiers, serve socialism and help to consolidate and raise the fighting capacity of our armed forces.

An upsurge of the great socialist cultural revolution has taken shape and is now assuming the form of a mass movement. This great revolutionary tide will wash away the mire of all the old bourgeois ideas on literature and art and usher in a new epoch of socialist proletarian literature and art. Confronted with this excellent revolutionary situation, we should be proud to be thoroughgoing revolutionaries. Our socialist revolution is a revolution to eliminate the exploiting classes and all systems of exploitation once and for all and to root out all exploiting class ideas which are injurious to the people. We must have the confidence and courage to do things never previously attempted. We must raise still higher the great red banner of Mao Tse-tung's thought and, under the leadership of the Central Committee of the Party, Chairman Mao and the Military Commission, actively participate in the great socialist cultural revolution, unswervingly carry it through to the end and strive to create a new socialist literature and art worthy of our great country, our great Party, our great people and our great army.

NOTES

1. "The Life of Wu Hsün" was a pernicious film slandering the revolutionary tradition of the Chinese people and advocating bourgeois reformism and capitulationism. Wu Hsün was a landlord's toady in the Ch'ing dynasty, but the film presented him as a great man who was willing to sacrifice himself to provide the sons of poor peasants with a chance to study. A *Jen-min Jih-pao* editorial of May 20, 1951 sternly pointed out the reactionary nature of this film and called on the whole country to criticise it. This was the first large-scale criticism of reactionary bourgeois ideas after the establishment of New China.

2. Yu P'ing-po, the author of "Studies in the 'Dream of the Red Chamber'," evaluated the novel from an idealist viewpoint, using bourgeois methods of textual research. In September 1954 a nation-wide movement was launched to criticise it. This was a struggle between proletarian and bourgeois ideology and against bourgeois idealism.

3. The Hu Feng counter-revolutionary clique: Hu Feng was a renegade who sneaked into the ranks of the revolution. After liberation he organised a secret clique among literary and art circles to carry out counter-revolutionary activities. In 1954 he presented a 300,000-character "suggestion" to the Central Committee of the Party, viciously attacking the Party's policy and Mao Tse-tung's teachings on literature and art. In May and June, 1955 *Jen-min Jih-pao* published three collections of material on Hu Feng's counter-revolutionary clique, thoroughly exposing and smashing its counter-revolutionary plot.

4. The theory of "truthful writing" was advocated by the revisionists. The counter-revolutionary Hu Feng was an exponent of it, and so was Feng Hsüeh-feng. They had ulterior motives and under the cover of "truthful writing" tried to oppose the class character and tendency of socialist literature and art, as well as the use of the socialist spirit in literature and art to educate the people. They advocated "truthful

writing" in order to seek out the "seamy side" of life in socialist society and the rotten things left over from history, so as to paint our splendid socialist society in dark colours.

5. The theory of "the broad path of realism" was advocated by some anti-Party and anti-socialist writers and artists who, opposing Chairman Mao's "Talks at the Yenan Forum on Literature and Art," argued that it was out of date and urged that a different and broader path should be found. This was the nature of "the broad path of realism" advocated by Chin Chao-yang and others. In their view, the correct, broad path of serving the workers, peasants and soldiers was too narrow, was "hard-boiled dogmatism" and "confined writers to an unalterable, narrow path." They argued that each author should write whatever he pleased according to his "different personal experience of life, education and temperament and artistic individuality." They wanted writers to abandon the worker-peasant-soldier orientation and explore "new fields which would give unlimited scope to their creativeness."

6. Shao Ch'üan-lin, formerly Vice-Chairman of the Chinese Writers' Union, advanced the theory of "the deepening of realism" while advocating "writing about middle characters." According to this theory, writers should depict "the old traits" in the people, summarise "the spiritual burdens of individual peasants through the centuries" and create complex "middle characters." They should write about "every-day" events to "reveal the greatness in trivial things" and attempt to show "the rich diversity of the world in a crumb of rice." To Shao Ch'üan-lin, the only realist writing was that depicting "middle characters" riddled with inner contradictions, summarising "the spiritual burdens of individual peasants through the centuries" and presenting the "painful stages" of the peasants' transition from an individual to a collective economy. This, he contended, was the only way to "deepen realism," whereas praising the revolutionary heroism of the people and describing the heroes among them was neither true nor realistic. This theory of "the deepening of realism," which was taken directly from bourgeois critical realism, is thoroughly reactionary.

7. The theory of opposition to "subject matter as the decisive factor," which was opposed to the socialist view of literature and art, found keen support from T'ien Han, Hsia Yen and others. Proletarian writers must consider what subject matter is of value to the people before they start writing and a specific subject should be selected and written up in order to foster proletarian ideology and liquidate bourgeois ideology and encourage the masses to be firm in taking the socialist road. But to advocates of this theory, these correct views were restrictions and fetters which "must be thoroughly eliminated." Under the pretext of enlarging the scope of subject matter, they proposed discarding the classics of revolution and rebelling against the orthodoxy of war. They argued that too many of our films dealt with the revolution and armed struggle and that unless a break was made, no really new films could be produced. Other advocates of this theory were in favour of writing works with "human interest," "love of mankind," "insignificant people" and "minor events." The aim of these proposals was actually to lead literature and art astray from the path of serving proletarian politics.

8. The chief exponent of the theory of "middle characters" was Shao Ch'üan-lin. He put forward this proposal time and again between the winter of 1960 and the summer of 1962. He slandered the vast majority of our poor and lower-middle peas-ants as people in an "intermediate state" vacillating between socialism and capitalism. He hoped that more writing about middle characters would undermine readers' faith in socialism and serve to curb or oppose the creation of heroes of the socialist age in works of literature and art.

9. Opposition to "the smell of gunpowder": Modern revisionist literature plays up the horrors of war and propagates the philosophy of survival and capitulationism to sap the people's fighting will and serve the needs of the imperialists. In recent years there were also some people in China who repeatedly clamoured that our writing reeked of gunpower and our stage bristled with guns, and that this was inartistic. They wanted writers to discard the classics of revolution and rebel against the orthodoxy of war. This theory was in essence a reflection of the revisionist trend in our literary and art circles.

10. "The merging of various trends as the spirit of the age" was an anti-Marxist-Leninist fallacy put forward by Chou Ku-ch'eng, who denied that the spirit of the age is the spirit which propels the age fowrard and that the representative of this spirit is the advanced class which propels the age forward. He argued that the spirit of the age was a "merging" of the "different ideologies of different classes," and that it included "pseudo-revolutionary, non-revolutionary and even counter-revolutionary ideas." This was a thoroughly reactionary theory aimed at class conciliation.

11. V.G. Belinsky (1811-1848) was a Russian democrat, literary critic, thinker and writer on aesthetics who opposed the serf system and the despotic rule of the tsar in his literary criticism.

12. N. G. Chernyshevsky (1828-1889) was a Russian democrat, critic and writer who upheld revolutionary democratic ideas and opposed the tsar and serfdom.

13. N. A. Dobrolyubov (1836-1861) was a Russian democrat and critic of literature and art who engaged in activities against the rule of the tsar and the serf system.

(From a full translation of an editorial, together with notes, carried in *Chieh-fang-chün Pao* of April 18, 1966)

Mao Tse-tung's Line for Revolution

The *Chieh-fang-chün Pao* editorials reproduced below give a detailed account of the struggle between the proletariat and the bourgeoisie in the spheres of ideology and culture since the Great Proletarian Cultural Revolution was launched.

In no uncertain terms, the documents of the army organ give warning that the 1956 "counter-revolutionary riots" in Hungary were started by revisionist intellectuals of the Petofi Circle and that a Khrushchev-type coup may also occur in China. The editorials call upon all "revolutionary" officers and men of the People's Liberation Army to conduct the Great Proletarian Cultural Revolution to a victorious conclusion by eliminating the "black, anti-Party and anti-socialist line" dominating ideological and cultural spheres.

The "proletarian revolutionary line" personally laid down by Mao Tse-tung is described in the editorials as a "powerful ideological weapon" for wiping out all "monsters and demons" who attack the Chinese Communist Party and socialism in what is called a "life-and-death class struggle."—Ed.

Essential Points for Propaganda and Education

In response to the militant call of the Central Committee of the Chinese Communist Party and Chairman Mao Tse-tung, the high tide of the Great Proletarian Cultural Revolution has been sweeping through the whole of China in the last few months with tempestuous force. Armed with Mao Tse-tung's thought, the several hundred million workers, peasants and soldiers and the masses of revolutionary cadres and revolutionary intellectuals are clearing out the many monsters entrenched in the ideological and cultural positions. The so-called "Three-Family Villages" or "Four-Family Inns," the bourgeois "experts," "scholars," "authorities" and "respected masters" and their like have been routed and their arrogance has been completely shattered. This great cultural revolution has no parallel in scale, in sweep, in strength or in momentum. It is already spurring the socialist cause in China

337

forward with great vigour and undoubtedly is having and will continue to have an immeasurably profound and far-reaching impact on the world revolution. All commanders and fighters in our army should actively plunge right into this great revolution, open fire at the black anti-Party and anti-socialist line and temper themselves and raise their level in the revolution.

Chairman Mao has always put great emphasis on the class struggle on the ideological and cultural fronts. During China's "New Democracy" period, Chairman Mao gave a thorough theoretical refutation of the bourgeois cultural line. Chairman Mao's "On New Democracy" and "Talks at the Yenan Forum on Literature and Art" are the most complete, the most comprehensive and the most systematic historical summing-up of this struggle between the two lines on the cultural front. They have carried on and developed the Marxist-Leninist world outlook and Marxist-Leninist theory on literature and art.

After China entered the stage of socialist revolution and socialist construction, the two works of Chairman Mao, "On the Correct Handling of Contradictions Among the People" and "Speech at the Chinese Communist Party's National Conference on Propaganda Work," were published. They are the most recent summing-up of the historical experience of the movements for the revolutionary ideology and literature and art in China and other countries. They represent a new development of the Marxist-Leninist world outlook and Marxist-Leninist theory on literature and art.

These works of Chairman Mao's have given a systematic exposition of the revolutionary new culture of the proletariat, formulated the line and the concrete principles and policies of the proletarian cultural revolution, and affirmed that literature and art should serve proletarian politics, serve the workers, peasants and soldiers, serve the consolidation and development of the dictatorship of the proletariat and the socialist system. Chairman Mao's great thinking on the new culture of the proletariat is our powerful weapon in waging the cultural revolution and the sole criterion for distinguishing fragrant flowers from poisonous weeds and revolution from counter-revolution; it is our Party's supreme guide in leading the cultural revolution.

Over a long period, however, a handful of representatives of the bourgeoisie within and without the Party countered Chairman Mao's brilliant ideas with a black anti-Party and anti-socialist line of their own. In the academic, educational, journalistic, literary, artistic, publishing and other cultural spheres they used all sorts of insidious and devious methods to oppose Chairman Mao's line on the proletarian cultural revolution and contend with the proletariat tooth and nail for leadership. They spread bourgeois and revisionist ideology in a thousand and one ways in such ideological fields as the press, radio broadcasting, periodicals, books and text-books, lectures, literary and art works, the cinema, the theatre, ballads, the fine arts, music and dancing, making frenzied attacks on our socialist system, the dictatorship of the proletariat, our great Party, our great leader Chairman Mao and the great thought of Mao Tse-tung.

They usurped the leadership in some departments, newspapers, and periodicals, turned monsters of all kinds loose and refused to carry out Party policy. The reality in these departments was that the bourgeoisie was exercising dictatorship over the proletariat and not the proletariat exercising dictatorship over the bourgeoisie. Bourgeois representatives of this sort include Yang Hsien-chen, the former President of the Higher Party School of the Central Committee of the Chinese Communist Party, Hsia Yen, the former Vice-Minister of Culture, T'ien Han, the former Chairman of the Union of Chinese Stage Artists, Yang Han-sheng, the former Secretary-General of the All-China Federation of Literary and Art Circles, and Chien Po-tsan, Vice-President of Peking University, who had been exposed earlier; and Teng T'o, former member of the Secretariat of the Peking Municipal Committee of the Chinese Communist Party, Wu Han, Vice-Mayor of Peking, Liao Mo-sha, the former Director of the Department of United Front Work of the Peking Municipal Committee of the Chinese Communist Party, and Lu P'ing, the former President of Peking University, who have now been exposed, and those who backed and shielded them.

Over a long period they made use of their positions and power to spread their poison and level wild attacks on our Party, thus stirring up a bourgeois and revisionist adverse current. Among the big anti-Party and anti-socialist poisonous weeds that emerged under the domination and influence of this adverse current were "Evening Chats at Yenshan," "Notes from Three-Family Village," "Hai Jui Scolds the Emperor," "Hai Jui Dismissed from Office," "Hsieh Yao-huan," "Li Hui-niang," "The Pressgang," "Laying Siege to the City," "Red Sun," "Threshold of Spring," "Sisters of the Stage," and "The Lin Family Shop."

Soon after China's liberation, the film world produced that big

339

poisonous weed, "The Life of Wu Hsün." Wu Hsün was a lackey of the feudal forces. When the Chinese people were struggling against imperialism and the feudal rulers in the latter years of the Ch'ing Dynasty, he never lifted a finger against the reactionary ruling class; on the contrary, he carried on frantic propaganda for feudal culture and abjectly did everything possible to curry favour with the feudal ruling class. Yet the film "The Life of Wu Hsün" portrayed him as a "great personality" who made self-sacrifice to provide opportunities for the children of poor peasants to get an education. The film smeared the revolutionary tradition of the Chinese people and spread bourgeois reformism and capitulationism. Acting on the instructions of the Party's Central Committee and Chairman Mao, the *Jen-min Jih-pao* on May 20, 1951, published an editorial seriously pointing out the reactionary nature of "The Life of Wu Hsün" and calling for a nation-wide criticism of the film. This was the first large-scale criticism of reactionary bourgeois ideas after the founding of New China.

From September 1954 onward, the criticism of the book "Studies in the 'Dream of the Red Chamber'" and of the reactionary ideas of Hu Shih was conducted. To distort and erase the positive, anti-feudal significance of the "Dream of the Red Chamber," the author of the book, Yü P'ing-po (a professor at Peking University), using the approach of bourgeois idealism, formalism and scholastic textual research, declared that it was the autobiography of Ts'ao Hsüeh-ch'in. Yü P'ing-po's methods were a complete carry-over of the line of the reactionary comprador-bourgeois scholar Hu Shih. An inveterate enemy of communism and the people, Hu Shih had twice been Kuomintang ambassador to the United States; in 1919, he published the reactionary article, "Study Problems More and Talk Less About 'isms'," opposing Marxism-Leninism as the guide for the Chinese revolution in the hope of leading the Chinese youth down the devious road of evading reality and class struggle. A serious nation-wide criticism of these bourgeois idealist ideas was undertaken, thoroughly repudiating and discrediting the various kinds of disciples of Hu Shih.

In May 1955, the whole nation hit back effectively at the Hu Feng counter-revolutionary clique. Hu Feng was a renegade who had wormed his way back into the ranks of the revolution. After liberation, he organised a sinister gang in literary and art circles to carry out counter-revolutionary activities. In a 300,000-character "suggestion" which he presented to the Central Committee of the Party in 1954, he venomously attacked the Party's literary and art policy and Mao Tse-tung's thought on literature and art. During May and June of 1955, the *Jen-min Jin-pao* published three collections of material on Hu Feng's counter-revolutionary clique, thoroughly smashing its counter-revolutionary plot and exposing a number of major and minor Hu Feng elements.

In 1957, taking advantage of the rectification movement launched by our Party, the bourgeois rightists launched a wild onslaught on the Party. Their dream was to create a Hungarian-type incident in China and stir up chaos, so that they could come forward "to clear up the mess," replace the Party and bring about a capitalist come-back in China. The Party and Chairman Mao led the whole people in waging a vigorous struggle against the rightists and thus repulsed this frenzied attack by the bourgeoisie.

In 1959, the Right opportunists in the Party attacked the Party's Central Committee at the Lushan meeting. Co-ordinating with them both before and after this event, the "Three-Family Village" sinister gang attacked the Party without let-up for several years, bringing out "Hai Jui Scolds the Emperor" and "Hai Jui Dismissed from Office" and then publishing their "Evening Chats at Yenshan" and "Notes from Three-Family Village" in the fortnightly *Ch'ien Hsien,* the *Pei-ching Jih-pao* and the *Pei-ching Wan-pao.*

Monsters and demons came out of their lairs in other cultural fields, too, and we waged tit-for-tat struggles against them. The current great cultural revolution is the continuation and deepening of these struggles.

This series of struggles has been carried out under the direct leadership of the Party's Central Committee and Chairman Mao. In September 1962, at the 10th Plenary Session of the 8th Central Committee of the Party, Chairman Mao issued his great call: "Never Forget the Class Struggle." Then on a number of occasions in 1963, 1964 and 1965 he gave extremely important instructions on the question of the cultural revolution.

Chairman Mao pointed out in December 1963 that in all forms of art — drama, ballads, music, the fine arts, the dance, the cinema, poetry and literature, etc., — problems abounded; the people engaged in them were numerous; and in many departments very little had been achieved so far in socialist transformation. The "dead" still dominated in many departments. Wasn't it absurd that many Communists

341

showed enthusiasm in advancing feudal and capitalist art, but no zeal in promoting socialist art, Chairman Mao added.

In June 1964, during the rectification movement within the All-China Federation of Literary and Art Circles and its affiliated associations, Chairman Mao pointed out that in the past 15 years these associations and most of their publications (a few said to be good) for the most part (this did not apply to every individual) had not carried out the policies of the Party and had acted as high and mighty bureaucrats, had not gone to the workers, peasants and soldiers and had not reflected the socialist revolution and construction. In recent years, they had even slid to the verge of revisionism. If serious steps were not taken to remould them, they were bound at some future date to become groups like the Hungarian "Petofi Club."

On many other occasions, too, Chairman Mao has given important verbal instructions on the question of the cultural revolution.

These instructions of Chairman Mao's have given a great impetus to the struggle to foster what is proletarian and eradicate what is bourgeois in the cultural fields. A new situation has emerged in China's cultural revolution in the last three years, under the personal care of Chairman Mao, and guided by his line on the proletarian cultural revolution. The most outstanding examples of revolutionary art have been the Peking operas on contemporary revolutionary themes such as "Red Lantern," "Shachiapang," "Taking the Bandits' Stronghold" and "Raid on the White Tiger Regiment," the ballets "Red Detachment of Women" and "The White-Haired Girl," the symphonic music "Shachiapang," the sculptures "Rent Collection Courtyard" and the recent revolutionary music festival "Shanghai Spring."

Another example of this revolutionary situation is the extensive, mass activity of the workers, peasants and soldiers on the ideological, literary and art fronts. They have done many fine essays in philosophy, showing skill in expressing Mao Tse-tung's thought in a practical way and created many outstanding works of literature and art in praise of China's socialist revolution and construction, of the new heroes of our era and our great Party and great leader.

In the last few years, too, many literary and art workers in the army have given prominence to politics, creatively studied and applied Chairman Mao's works, gone to the basic units and integrated themselves with the workers, peasants and soldiers. The result has been the creation of such fine works as "On Guard Beneath the Neon

342

Lights," "A Great Wall Along the South Coast" and "Song of Ouyang Hai," and the emergence of such fine units as the seaborne cultural team of the Canton army units and the Haifang cultural troupe of the Nanking army units. At the same time, countless small but effective amateur teams of performers and groups of singers that give prominence to politics have emerged in the army units.

At a meeting of the central leadership of the Chinese Communist Party in September 1965, Chairman Mao pointed to the need to subject reactionary bourgeois ideology to criticism. In November *Wen-hui Pao*, under the leadership of the Communist Party organisation in Shanghai, took the lead in publishing Comrade Yao Wen-yuan's article "On the New Historical Drama *'Hai Jui Dismissed from Office'*," it was the opening shot in the criticism of Wu Han and his ilk. Then the *Chieh-fang-chün Pao* reprinted the article and pointed out that "Hai Jui Dismissed from Office" was a big poisonous weed.

Since the end of February 1966 *Hung-ch'i* has carried articles by Yin Ta, Kuan Feng, Chi Pen-yu and other comrades. The *Chieh-fang-chün Pao* published two editorials, entitled "Hold High the Great Red Banner of Mao Tse-tung's Thought and Actively Participate in the Great Socialist Cultural Revolution" and "Never Forget the Class Struggle", on April 18 and May 4 respectively. Since May 8 *Hung-ch'i*, the *Chieh-fang-chün Pao, Kuang-ming Jih-pao* and Shanghai's *Chieh-fang Jih-pao* and *Wen-hui Pao* have carried a series of articles which exposed the bourgeois, anti-Party stand of *Ch'ien Hsien*, the *Pei-ching Jih-pao* and the *Pei-ching Wan-pao* and launched a counter-attack against Teng T'o and a handful of other anti-Party elements and their supporters. Immediately, masses of workers, peasants and soldiers throughout the country plunged into the struggle to smash the "Three-Family Village." Rapidly and with irresistible power, the great cultural revolution swept forward and attained a high-tide of unprecedented magnitude. In recent years, besides, the revolutionary masses have exposed and criticised a number of reactionary views on philosophy and history and a number of bad plays and films.

Beginning June 1 this year, the *Jen-min Jih-pao* has published a series of important editorials, including "Sweep Away All Monsters," "A Great Revolution That Touches People to Their Very Souls," "Capture the Positions in the Field of Historical Studies Seized by the Bourgeoisie," "New Victory for Mao Tse-tung's Thought," "Tear Aside the Bourgeois Mask of 'Liberty, Equality and Fraternity'," and

343

"To Be Proletarian Revolutionaries or Bourgeois Royalists?" which give a profound explanation of the tremendous significance of the great cultural revolution and provide powerful guidance for the present struggle. On June 2, the press published the big-character poster put up by Nieh Yüan-tzu and six other comrades of Peking University which exposed the criminal anti-Party, anti-socialist acts committed by Lu P'ing and company. On the afternoon of June 3 the Central Committee of the Chinese Communist Party announced the decision to reorganise the Peking Municipal Committee of the Chinese Communist Party and, at the same time, declared that Comrade Li Hsüeh-feng, First Secretary of the North China Bureau of the Central Committee of the Chinese Communist Party, had been appointed concurrent First Secretary of the Peking Municipal Committee of the Chinese Communist Party, and Comrade Wu Teh its Second Secretary. The new, reorganised Peking Municipal Committee made the decision to relieve Lu P'ing, President of Peking University and concurrent Secretary of the University Party Committee, and P'eng Pei-yün, Deputy Secretary, of all their posts. The work team sent by the new Municipal Committee is providing leadership for the great socialist cultural revolution at Peking University and it is exercising the functions of the University Party Committee. The decisions of the Central Committee and the new Peking Municipal Committee of the Chinese Communist Party won immediate, enthusiastic support of the people in the capital and throughout the country and carried the tide of the nation-wide great cultural revolution to a new high. Now with its great momentum the high-tide of the great cultural revolution is pounding at all the corrupt ideological and cultural positions still held by the bourgeoisie and the survivals of feudalism.

Over the past 16 years, there has been one struggle after another on the ideological and cultural fronts, each more profound than the one before. Far from being isolated and accidental phenomena, these struggles are manifestations of the deepening class struggle in China and abroad. A handful of representatives of the bourgeoisie, constantly and stubbornly trying to assert themselves, have been desperately holding on to their bourgeois ideological stronghold and engaging in frantic anti-Party and anti-socialist activities. Make trouble, fail, make trouble again, fail again, till their doom — that is the logic of all reactionaries. This handful of bourgeois representatives is certainly no exception to the rule.

344

We know from the historical experience of the proletarian revolution that the basic question in every revolution is that of State power. We conquered the enemy in the country and seized State power by the gun. They can all be overthrown, be it imperialism, feudalism or the bureaucrat capitalist class; millionaires, billionaires and trillionaires can be toppled, whoever they may be. And their property can be confiscated. However, confiscation of their property does not amount to confiscation of the reactionary ideas in their minds. Daily and hourly they are always dreaming of a come-back, dreaming of restoring their lost "paradise." Although they are only a tiny percentage of the population, their political potential is quite considerable and their power of resistance is out of all proportion to their numbers.

Socialist society emerges out of the womb of the old society. It is not at all easy to eradicate the idea of private ownership formed in thousands of years of class society and the forces of habit and the ideological and cultural influence of the exploiting classes associated with private ownership. The spontaneous forces of the petty bourgeoisie in town and country constantly give rise to new bourgeois elements. As the ranks of the workers grow in number and extent, they take in some elements of the complex background. Then, too. a number of people in the ranks of the Party and State organisations degenerate following the conquest of State power and living in peaceful surroundings. At the same time, on the international plane the imperialists headed by the United States and the reactionaries of various countries are trying hard to eliminate us by using the counter-revolutionary dual tactics of threats of war and "peaceful evolution." And the modern revisionist group with the leadership of the Soviet Communist Party as the centre is also trying by hook or by crook to topple us. If we were to forget about class struggle and drop our guard in these circumstances, we would be in danger of losing State power and allowing capitalism to make a come-back.

Our struggle against the bourgeoisie is a protracted one. As Chairman Mao teaches us:

> In China, although in the main socialist transformation has been completed with respect to the system of ownership, and although the large-scale and turbulent class struggles of the masses characteristic of the previous revolutionary periods have in the main come to an end, there are still remnants of the overthrown landlord and comprador classes, there is still a bourgeoisie, and the remoulding of the petty bourgeoisie has only just started. The class struggle is by no means over. The class struggle between the proletariat and the bourgeoisie, the class

345

struggle between the different political forces, and the class struggle in the ideological field between the proletariat and the bourgeoisie will continue to be long and tortuous and at times will even become very acute. The proletariat seeks to transform the world according to its own world outlook, and so does the bourgeoisie. In this respect, the question of which will win out, socialism or capitalism, is still not really settled.

Our struggle against the representatives of the bourgeoisie on the ideological and cultural fronts is not just "paper polemics" that are of no great consequence, but a class struggle between the bourgeoisie and the proletariat, between the road of capitalism and the road of socialism. It is a struggle to determine which will win out, capitalism or socialism, a struggle between Marxism-Leninism, Mao Tse-tung's thought on the one hand and capitalist and revisionist ideology on the other, a struggle between the bourgeoisie scheming to restore capitalism and the proletariat determined to prevent it. There must be no minimising of this point, nor the slightest lack of vigilance in this regard.

The anti-Party and anti-socialist activities of the bourgeoisie's representatives on the ideological and cultural fronts are intended to open up a road to the restoration of capitalism.

We know from the historical experience of the proletariat that the bourgeoisie invariably uses two tactics in working for a counter-revolutionary come-back. One is armed suppression of the proletarian revolution. The world's first dictatorship of the proletariat, established in 1871 by the French proletariat in Paris, eventually failed as a result of counter-revolutionary armed suppression. After the victory of the October Revolution, Russia was subjected to the combined attack of 14 capitalist-imperialist countries and counter-offensives by the land-lord and capitalist White Guards attempting a come-back, and it was only after three full years of war that the new-born revolutionary regime was made secure. The armed counter-attacks of the bourgeoisie, whether alone or in collusion with the forces of international reaction, are an obvious, military form of staging a come-back. It is easier to see and to notice, and people are more alert to it. The other form of staging a come-back is "peaceful evolution." It starts operating in the sphere of ideology in order to prepare public opinion for a come-back, for subversion and a counter-revolutionary coup d'état. Once the conditions are ripe, they will seize State power and restore the dictatorship of the bourgeoisie. People often fail to see this, fail to take note of this and are not vigilant against it.

346

The role of advance guard in the 1956 counter-revolutionary riots in Hungary was played precisely by a group of revisionist men of letters of the "Petofi Club." The Tito clique of Yugoslavia had long before defected through "peaceful evolution." The Khrushchev revisionist group used the same method to bring about a capitalist restoration in the Soviet Union. We must never, never forget these historical lessons paid for in blood.

Such were the methods adopted by the handful of representatives of the overthrown bourgeoisie in China who have now been brought to light. They tightened their grip on ideology and the superstructure, theoretical and academic work, literature and art, etc. On the cultural front they made efforts to see that emperors and kings, generals and prime ministers, scholars and beauties, foreign idols and dead men dominate the stage and conducted anti-Party and anti-socialist propaganda. Using the tactics of nibbling away, they tried to devour our positions in ideology mouthful by mouthful. By their infiltration tactics, they wanted to infect our minds with bourgeois ideas, bit by bit. They used extremely underhand and cunning tricks. For a long time they controlled a number of Party propaganda media and waved "red flags" to oppose the red flag. They launched wanton attacks on the Party under the guise of telling stories, imparting knowledge and carrying out academic research. They corrupted young people with the bourgeois idea of "making one's own way" and of achieving personal fame and career, in order to win the masses and the younger generation away from our Party. Usurping the name of the Party, they drew all the monsters and demons of society into their gangsters' inns and staged frantic counter-revolutionary activities.

What they were doing was to prepare the political, ideological and organisational ground for the restoration of capitalism. The means they used, while differing in minor points, were the same in essentials as those of the "Petofi Club" in Hungary and those used by Khrushchev. It would be very dangerous if we failed to see this point!

Therefore, with regard to the anti-Party and anti-socialist articles and booklets and the poisonous anti-Party and anti-socialist operas, plays and films written by the bourgeois "scholars," "specialists" and "writers," who were supported and shielded by back-stage manipulators, we must not adopt such an attitude as: "when scholars staged a rebellion, they could not succeed if they tried for three years," or "a few eels cannot stir up big waves and overturn boats." Nor can we take the view that after having seized State power all is well and propitious and we can sleep soundly. If we pay attention only to construction, to production and to culture and education, if we think only of dealing with the Chiang Kai-shek gang and US imperialism but neglect the possibility that the bourgeoisie can still work for a come-back and subvert us from within, and if we are not clear-headed and allow the bourgeois careerists to carry out their plots, then history will judge us as criminals.

Precisely for this reason, the present struggle has great and far-reaching significance:

First, we are conducting the Great Proletarian Cultural Revolution to defend the dictatorship of the proletariat.

If we do not carry out this revolution but allow the representatives of the bourgeoisie to carry out their schemes of restoring capitalism, some incident of the Hungarian type or some counter-revolutionary coup d'état of the Khrushchev type is bound to occur. At such a moment, the possibility would arise that the Chiang Kai-shek gang would return to the mainland and that great numbers of landlords and despots and their armed bands would hit back and take retaliation, our Party and our country would fall into rack and ruin, we ourselves would be killed and history be drastically pushed back. Gone would be the fruits of the revolutionary struggles waged by the Chinese people during the past hundred years and more, years in which fresh forces continually came forward to take the place of those who fell shedding their blood and sacrificing their lives. The Chinese people would once more become the beasts of burden of imperialism, the bourgeoisie and the feudal class.

As Chairman Mao has pointed out:

> If the landlords, rich peasants, counter-revolutionaries, bad elements and ogres of all kinds were allowed to crawl out, while our cadres were to shut their eyes to all this and in many cases fail even to differentiate between the enemy and ourselves but were to collaborate with the enemy and become corrupted and demoralised, if our cadres were thus dragged into the enemy camp or the enemy were able to sneak into our ranks, and if many of our workers, peasants, and intellectuals were left defenceless against both the soft and the hard tactics of the enemy, then it would not take long, perhaps only a few years or a decade, or several decades at most, before a counter-revolutionary restoration on a national scale inevitably occurred, the Marxist-Leninist Party would undoubtedly become a revisionist party or a fascist party, and the whole of China would change its colour.

Second, the Great Proletarian Cultural Revolution is having and

348

will have an incalculably profound and far-reaching effect on the world of our time and of the future.

The first socialist country, the Soviet Union, was dragged by Khrushchev revisionism on to the road of capitalist restoration. Now all the oppressed people and oppressed nations of the whole world place their hopes on the revolutionary New China. Under the leadership of the Party's Central Committee, holding high the great red banner of Marxism-Leninism, of Mao Tse-tung's thought, persisting in their firm stand against imperialism, modern revisionism and reactionaries of various countries, and greatly deflating the enemy's arrogance and boosting the morale of the people, the Chinese people have set a brilliant example for the people of the whole world. Our country has become the base of the world revolution. Our Party has become the standard bearer of the world revolution. Mao Tse-tung's thought is the beacon of the world revolution. If these anti-Party and anti-socialist elements made China change its colour, who can say how many more of the oppressed people in all countries would die, how much more suffering they would have to endure and by how many years the victory of the world revolution would be delayed.

By their anti-Party and anti-socialist activities, the handful of representatives of the bourgeoisie interacted internationally with imperialism, modern revisionism and all reactionaries. And their exposure is a serious blow to the class enemy abroad; it removed a hidden time-bomb inside our Party. With the deepening of China's great cultural revolution, the propaganda machinery of the imperialists, modern revisionists and all reactionaries has gone into top gear and they are bombarding us with their anathemas. By negative example, this proves the great significance of this struggle of ours.

Third, the Great Proletarian Cultural Revolution is a training in actual class struggle for every one of our comrades.

This struggle makes us clear all the dust from our eyes once more and gives us a deeper insight into the fact that socialist society is a society with classes and class struggle. It is not enough and not secure to have only a socialist revolution on the economic front and socialist transformation of the ownership of means of production; there must also be a thoroughgoing socialist revolution on the political and ideological front. And a long, long time — decades or even centuries — will be required to decide the issue of which will win in the struggle in the political and ideological field, socialism or capitalism. When one black line is eliminated, yet another will appear. Some representatives of the bourgeoisie have been found out, while others who are as yet undiscovered still nestle in our midst. Since the enemy uses the most underhand and cunning means in its efforts to restore capitalism, our exposure of them develops our ability to conduct class struggle and makes us understand its complexity.

Our Party, government, armed forces and workers in all fields of culture do not live in a vacuum. Naturally, the sharp class struggle finds its reflection within them. There is nothing strange in the fact that a handful of representatives of the bourgeoisie wormed their way into our Party, government and armed forces and various cultural fields. It is an inevitable law of the class struggle. Our class enemies know that a citadel is most easily taken if attacked from within. And so, they always use every possible trick to "pull somebody out or put someone in" in order to sneak into our ranks or find their agents within our Party. We cannot prevent this, much as we might wish to do so. As Chairman Mao has pointed out: "There is nothing that does not contain contradiction; without contradiction nothing would exist," and "Opposition and struggle between ideas of different kinds constantly occur within the Party; this is a reflection within the Party of contradictions between classes and between the new and the old in society. If there were no contradictions in the Party and no ideological struggles to resolve them, the Party's life would come to an end."

Our Party and armed forces have developed and grown from strength to strength precisely in the tit-for-tat struggles over the last few decades against the various erroneous lines and against the class enemies of various kinds who wormed their way into the Party and the armed forces.

In the course of our Party's history, didn't we see the divisive criminal activities of renegades such as Ch'en Tu-hsiu and Chang Kuo-t'ao? Didn't we see the anti-Party conspiracy of Kao Kang and Jao Shu-shih since the founding of New China? Didn't we see the attacks on the Party by the Hu Feng counter-revolutionary clique and the bourgeois rightists? Were there not also attacks on the Party by Right opportunist elements during the Lushan meeting? Didn't they befoul the atmosphere for a short time? But what was the outcome? One by one they failed ignominiously. They became completely isolated as soon as they were exposed. They were unable to halt or obstruct the development of our revolution and construction. The earth revolved as usual and the wheel of history continued to roll forward. And today, too, a handful of representatives of the bourgeoisie have concealed themselves very carefully, climbed to high positions and operated very cunningly, but to what avail? One by one they are being exposed and their real character shown up as paper tigers!

All this fully demonstrates the great power of Mao Tse-tung's thought. It shows that our Party is politically, ideologically and organisationally consolidated and united as never before, a Party that has been tested in storm and stress, a Party that is closely linked with the masses, has a wealth of experience of struggle and a fine revolutionary tradition; it is a great, glorious and correct Party. The handful of anti-Party and anti-socialist elements are just so much ugliness that cannot stand the light of day, a swarm of buzzing blowflies. Our present era is one in which the worker, peasant and soldier masses are grasping hold of Mao Tse-tung's thought. Provided we equip our minds with Mao Tse-tung's thought and wipe the dust from our eyes, these elements will not be able to stand up to a single blow. We need not in the least fear their anti-Party and anti-socialist activities; what we should fear is relaxation of vigilance on our part which would land us in their traps.

The exposure by us in this struggle of the group of anti-Party and anti-socialist elements who sneaked into our Party, government and armed forces and all fields of culture, is another important victory for our socialist revolution and a great victory for Mao Tse-tung's thought.

The historical experience of the proletariat teaches us that it is far more difficult to maintain and consolidate State power than to seize it. A bourgeois revolution is considered complete with the capture of State power. But the purpose of our proletarian revolution is to wipe out all exploiting classes and systems; it is the most thoroughgoing revolution destined step by step to eliminate the gap between the workers and the peasants, between town and countryside and between mental and manual labour. Therefore, the seizure of the State power is only the first step in a long march of ten thousand *li*. The dictatorship of the proletariat is our very life. We must rely on it to smash all the schemes for a come-back by the enemy at home and abroad. As Chairman Mao has pointed out:

> Like food and clothing, this power is something a victorious people cannot do without even for a moment. It is an excellent thing,

351

a protective talisman, an heirloom, which should under no circumstances be discarded before the thorough and total abolition of imperialism abroad and of classes within the country.

Our army is the mainstay of the dictatorship of the proletariat. All counter-revolutionaries are mortally afraid of our army and hate it with an inveterate hatred. Didn't the bourgeois rightist "alliance of Chang Po-chün and Lo Lung-chi" openly proclaim in 1957 that the Liberation Army was the greatest obstacle to their ascent to power? They invariably try to exert influence of one kind or another on the army and, through the various propaganda media under their control, to spread poison and corrupt our men behind the guns in an attempt to get our guns to serve them. Naturally, their schemes will not succeed. This is because ours is an army created by Chairman Mao Tse-tung himself, a people's army tempered in tens of years of revolutionary wars, one that has withstood great storm and stress and is highly proletarianised and revolutionised. Nevertheless, if we relax our vigilance, they will seize the chance to get in.

This has been proved by events in the last few years.

Didn't some cultural and art establishments of our army put on such bad plays and make such bad films like "The Pressgang?" Didn't some people write a number of bad works? Weren't there some people who propagated Yang Hsien-chen's fallacy of "two combining into one?" Didn't some people praise such anti-Party, anti-socialist big poisonous weeds as "Evening Chats at Yenshan?" Didn't some people, corrupted by them, fail in fighting will, show reluctance to remain in military service, and even defend the "Three-Family Village" gang? These people constituted only a pitiful handful. Yet all this took place in our people's army. Can we take them lightly? How can we permit such things to go on developing and allow their influence to spread?

Precisely for these reasons, we must be deeply concerned over the class struggle in the ideological field. We must never regard it as a trifling matter, one that has nothing to do with us, or something that concerns only literary men. We must never allow individuals of the Khrushchev type to nestle in our midst, never must we relax political and ideological vigilance and allow such rascals to stuff our minds with poisonous weeds! Guns are mindless. If the minds of the men behind the guns change, the guns will serve a different object. Whoever forgets this has forgotten the basic theses of Marxism-Leninism; he is a simpleton.

We must respond to the great call of Chairman Mao and pay close attention to the struggle in the ideological field, raise our proletarian political consciousness to a very high level, keep our eyes wide open and our sense of smell very sharp. Through every storm and whatever stress, we must see things clearly, take up a firm position, stand all tests and adhere to our proletarian stand. We must never allow the anti-Party, anti-socialist elements and their supporters to capture any position in our army. We must join actively and energetically in this great struggle, thoroughly criticise the anti-Party, anti-socialist poisonous weeds and eradicate their influence.

Chairman Mao teaches us:

> It has been proved that the enemy cannot conquer us by force of arms. However, the flattery of the bourgeoisie may conquer the weak-willed in our ranks. There may be some Communists, who were not conquered by enemies with guns and were worthy of the name of heroes for standing up to these enemies, but who cannot withstand sugar-coated bullets; they will be defeated by sugar-coated bullets. We must guard against such a situation.

Many facts brought to light in the current great cultural revolution show that at all times our enemies attempt to overthrow us with sugar-coated bullets. Have not some among us been poisoned or misled by the enemy because their bourgeois-individualist world outlook has not yet been remoulded? This tells us that bourgeois individualism is the root of all evil. There is a struggle between Communist and individualist ideas in the minds of our comrades in general and it goes on every day. The existence of this struggle is an objective fact and there can be no escaping from it. Proletarian ideology can overcome bourgeois-individualist ideology only if one carries on the struggle consciously, in the same way as washing one's own face every day. If we relax in this battle, individualism will grow and from small beginnings will develop into huge proportions. Therefore, every comrade must still more consciously undertake the revolutionising of his mind, overcome bourgeois individualism of all kinds, learn from Lei Feng, Wang Chieh, Mai Hsien-teh, Chiao Yu-lu, the Good Eighth Company on Nanking Road and other heroes and advanced units, wholeheartedly serve the people, and allow no monsters to find any foothold amongst us.

The proletarian cultural revolution is a great revolution that reaches into the very souls of people. Its purpose is not only to demolish all the old ideology and culture and old customs and habits which have been fostered by the exploiting classes and poisoned the minds of the people for thousands of years, but also to create and cultivate among the masses an entirely new, proletarian ideology and culture and entirely new proletarian customs and habits. This great undertaking to transform established traditions and practices is without precedent in human history. We must use the proletarian world outlook to thoroughly criticise all the feudal and bourgeois heritage, all the customs and habits of the feudal and capitalist classes. In this struggle we must foster proletarian ideology and destroy bourgeois ideology in a big way. We must oppose evil works which spread bourgeois ideas and tastes, oppose all perverse trends and vulgar practices, and launch many-sided cultural activities which are rich in revolutionary educational significance, read revolutionary books, sing revolutionary songs, perform revolutionary plays, see revolutionary films, tell revolutionary stories, listen to revolutionary broadcasts and ceaselessly consolidate and raise the fighting capacity of our army.

The most fundamental task of the Great Proletarian Cultural Revolution of our country is to study and apply Mao Tse-tung's thought in a creative way and popularise it in the course of the stormy class struggle, so that it becomes integrated with the masses of workers, peasants and soldiers. Every comrade should earnestly undertake the study of Chairman Mao's works and the application of his thought in a creative way, and in the course of struggle take a step forward in grasping Mao Tse-tung's thought.

We should take up the various questions arising in the present great cultural revolution and turn to and earnestly study the relevant writings or extracts from Chairman Mao's works. These include, for instance, his expositions on classes and class struggle in socialist society, on the consolidation of the dictatorship of the proletariat, on the line for the cultural revolution, on the protracted and complex nature of the class struggle in the ideological field, on how to distinguish fragrant flowers from poisonous weeds, on ideological remoulding, and so on.

In accordance with the basic principles of Marxism-Leninism, Chairman Mao has summed up the practical experience of the Chinese and world revolutions and the tragic lesson of the Soviet Party and State being usurped by the modern revisionist clique; he has formulated systematic theories and policies for the period of socialism concerning the need to keep a vigorous grip on the class struggle, persist in the dictatorship of the proletariat, prevent and oppose modern revisionism

354

and prevent the restoration of capitalism; he has thus greatly enriched and developed Marxist-Leninist theory on the dictatorship of the proletariat. In this great cultural revolution, we must advance our study and comprehension of these instructions of Chairman Mao and take them as the supreme guide to all our work and our sole criterion for distinguishing right from wrong, truth from falsehood.

In a complex struggle, we must distinguish genuine Marxism-Leninism from sham Marxism-Leninism and fragrant flowers from poisonous weeds. We should resolutely support and steadfastly carry out all that conforms to Mao Tse-tung's thought. As for anyone who contravenes or opposes Mao Tse-tung's thought, we will expose him to the light of day, repudiate and discredit him thoroughly no matter what high position he holds or whatever "authority" he is.

Mao Tse-tung's thought is the acme of Marxism-Leninism in our epoch. It is living Marxism-Leninism at its highest and the sharpest weapon to combat imperialism, modern revisionism and all reactionaries. In the magic mirror of Mao Tse-tung's thought, all monsters will be revealed for what they are. Once again the Great Proletarian Cultural Revolution is providing a vivid demonstration of the fact that once Mao Tse-tung's thought is grasped by the masses of workers, peasants and soldiers, it becomes a mighty material force. People armed with Mao Tse-tung's thought are the greatest fighting force; they have the greatest courage, wisdom and unanimity of will. When they grasp Mao Tse-tung's thought, which is both a political telescope and a political microscope, the worker, peasant and soldier masses have the highest criterion to distinguish right from wrong, they have the vantage ground from which to see far ahead, and they can discern the essence through the appearance. People who possess Mao Tse-tung's thought have the keenest nose and the sharpest eyes, and no anti-Party, anti-socialist element can escape their notice no matter what tricks he plays.

This is exactly why the enemy fears Mao Tse-tung's thought most of all and has the greatest hatred for it. But the more the enemy opposes it, the more ardently we love it. We must persist in studying Chairman Mao's works and applying his thought creatively. The revolution requires it, the situation requires it, the struggle against the enemy requires it, good preparatory work for smashing the US imperialist war of aggression requires it, and the prevention of and opposition to revisionism and the thwarting of capitalist restoration require it. Mao Tse-tung's thought is our very life. Anyone who opposes it will be condemned by the whole Party and denounced by the whole nation.

The Chinese People's Liberation Army is a people's army personally created by Chairman Mao. Every one of our comrades has grown up nourished by Mao Tse-tung's thought. The Central Committee of the Party, Chairman Mao, the Military Commission of the Central Committee and Comrade Lin Piao have all called on us to join in criticising reactionary bourgeois ideas and to play a major role in the great cultural revolution. We are determined not to fall short of their expectations.

We shall conscientiously study the instructions of the Party's Central Committee and Chairman Mao on the great cultural revolution and be thoroughgoing revolutionaries. Alongside the people of the whole country, we shall completely destroy the black anti-Party, anti-socialist line, safeguard our dictatorship of the proletariat, safeguard the Central Committee of the Party, Chairman Mao and Mao Tse-tung's thought.

In taking part in the great cultural revolution, we must go further in giving prominence to politics, in putting the "four good"† on a solid footing and in strengthening our combat-readiness. While struggling against the enemy without guns, we should give close attention to the enemy with guns. Should US imperialism dare to impose war on the Chinese people, we shall definitely annihilate it resolutely, thoroughly, wholly and completely.

We must determinedly adhere to the directives of the Party's Central Committee, the Military Commission and Comrade Lin Piao to study Chairman Mao's works, follow his teachings, act in accordance with his instructions, and be good soldiers of Chairman Mao. We must never forget the class struggle, never forget the dictatorship of the proletariat, never forget to give promenence to politics and never forget to hold high the great red banner of Mao Tse-tung's thought—so that we shall carry our cause of socialist revolution and socialist construction forward from one great new victory to another!

(From a full translation of "Raise High the Great Red Banner of Mao Tse-tung's Thought and Carry the Great Proletarian Cultural Revolution Throught to the End" in *Chieh-fang-chün Pao* of June 6, 1966)

*   *   *

356

Mao Tse-tung's Thought Is the Telescope and Microscope of Our Revolutionary Cause

The current great socialist cultural revolution is a great revolution to sweep away all monsters and a great revolution that remoulds the ideology of people and touches their souls. What weapon should be used to sweep away all monsters? What ideology should be applied to arm people's minds and remould their souls? The most powerful ideological weapon, the only one, is the great Mao Tse-tung's thought.

Mao Tse-tung's thought is our political orientation, the highest instruction for our actions; it is our ideological and political telescope and microscope for observing and analysing all things. In this unprecedented great cultural revolution, we should use Mao Tse-tung's thought to observe, analyse and transform everything, and, in a word, put it in command of everything. We should use Mao Tse-tung's thought to storm the enemy's positions and seize victory.

Chairman Mao teaches us:

> After the enemies with guns have been wiped out, there will still be enemies without guns: they are bound to struggle desperately against us; we must never regard these enemies lightly.

Our struggle against the black anti-Party, anti-socialist line and gangsters is a mighty, life-and-death class struggle. The enemies without guns are more hidden, cunning, sinister and vicious than the enemies with guns. The representatives of the bourgeoisie and all monsters, including the modern revisionists, often oppose the red flag by hoisting a red flag and oppose Marxism-Leninism and Mao Tse-tung's thought under the cloak of Marxism-Leninism and Mao Tse-tung's thought when they attack the Party and socialism, because Marxism-Leninism and Mao Tse-tung's thought are becoming more popular day by day, our Party and Chairman Mao enjoy an incomparably high prestige and the dictatorship of the proletariat in our country is becoming more consolidated. These are the tactics that the revisionists always use in opposing Marxism-Leninism. This is a new characteristic of the class struggle under the conditions of the dictatorship of the proletariat.

The many facts exposed during the great cultural revolution show us more clearly that the anti-Party and anti-socialist elements are all careerists, schemers and hypocrites of the exploiting classes. They indulge in double-dealing. They feign compliance while acting in opposition. They appear to be men but are demons at heart. They speak human language to your face, but talk devil's language behind your back. They are wolves in sheep's clothing and man-eating tigers with smiling faces. They often use the phrases of Marxism-Leninism and Mao Tse-tung's thought as a cover while greatly publicising diametrically opposed views behind the word "but" and smuggling in bourgeois and revisionist stuff. Enemies holding a false red banner are ten times more vicious than enemies holding a white banner. Wolves in sheep's clothing are ten times more sinister than ordinary wolves. Tigers with smiling faces are ten times more ferocious than tigers with their fangs bared and their claws sticking out. Sugar-coated bullets are ten times more destructive than real bullets. A fortress is most vulnerable when attacked from within. Enemies who have wormed their way into our ranks are far more dangerous than enemies operating in the open. We must give this serious attention and be highly vigilant.

In such a very complicated and acute class struggle, how are we to draw a clear-cut line between the enemy and ourselves and maintain a firm stand? How are we to distinguish between revolutionaries and counter-revolutionaries, genuine revolutionaries and sham revolutionaries, and Marxism-Leninism and revisionism? We must master Mao Tse-tung's thought, the powerful ideological weapon, and use it as a telescope and a microscope to observe all matters. With the invincible Mao Tse-tung's thought, with the scientific world outlook and methodology of dialectical materialism and historical materialism which have been developed by Chairman Mao, and with the sharp weapon of Chairman Mao's theory of classes and class struggle, we have the highest criterion for judging right and wrong. We are able to penetrate deeply into all things and to recognise the whole through observation of the part. We can see the essence behind outward appearance, and clear away the miasma to achieve profound insight into things and thus monsters of all sorts will be unable to hide themselves. We can stand on an eminence, become far-sighted and view the whole situation, the future and the great significance and far-reaching influence of the great socialist cultural revolution. We can advance without the slightest fear and stand in the forefront of the great socialist cultural revolution.

Chairman Mao teaches us, "The proletariat seeks to transform the world according to its own world outlook, so does the bourgeoisie."

In the sharp clash between the two world outlooks, either you crush me, or I crush you. It will not do to sit on the fence; there is no middle road. The overthrown bourgeoisie, in their plots for restoration and subversion, always give first place to ideology, take hold of ideology and the superstructure. The representatives of the bourgeoisie, by using their position and power, usurped and controlled the leadership of a number of departments, did all they could to spread bourgeois and revisionist poison through the media of literature, the theatre, films, music, the arts, the press, periodicals, the radio, publications and academic research and schools, etc., in an attempt to corrupt people's minds and perpetrate "peaceful evolution" as ideological preparation and preparation of public opinion for capitalist restoration. If our proletarian ideology does not take over the position, then the bourgeois ideology will have free rein; it will gradually nibble away and chew you up bit by bit. Once proletarian ideology gives way, so will the superstructure and the economic base and this means the restoration of capitalism. Therefore, we must arm our minds with Mao Tse-tung's thought and establish a firm proletarian world outlook. We must use the great Mao Tse-tung's thought to fight and completely destroy the bourgeois ideological and cultural positions.

Mao Tse-tung's thought is the acme of Marxism-Leninism in the present era. It is living Marxism-Leninism at its highest. It is the powerful, invincible weapon of the Chinese people, and it is also a powerful, invincible weapon of the revolutionary people the world over. Mao Tse-tung's thought has proved to be the invincible truth through the practice of China's democratic revolution, socialist revolution and socialist construction, and through the struggle in the international sphere against US imperialism and its lackeys and against Khrushchev revisionism. Chairman Mao has, with the gifts of genius, creatively and comprehensively developed Marxism-Leninism. Basing himself on the fundamental theses of Marxism-Leninism, Chairman Mao has summed up the experience of the practice of the Chinese revolution and the world revolution, and the painful lesson of the usurpation of the leadership of the Party and the State of the Soviet Union by the modern revisionist clique, systematically put forward the theory concerning classes, class contradictions and class struggle that exist in socialist society, greatly enriched and developed the Marxist-Leninist theory on the dictatorship of the proletariat, and put forward a series of wise policies aimed at opposing and preventing revisionism and the restoration of capitalism. All this ensures that our country will always maintain its revolutionary spirit and never change its colour, and it is of extremely great theoretical and practical significance to the revolutionary cause of the international proletariat. Every sentence by Chairman Mao is the truth, and carries more weight than ten thousand ordinary sentences. As the Chinese people master Mao Tse-tung's thought, China will be prosperous and ever-victorious. Once the world's people master Mao Tse-tung's thought which is living Marxism-Leninism, they are sure to win their emancipation, bury imperialism, modern revisionism and all reactionaries lock, stock and barrel, and realise communism throughout the world step by step.

The most fundamental task in the great socialist cultural revolution in our country is to eliminate thoroughly the old ideology and culture, the old customs and habits which were fostered by all the exploiting classes for thousands of years to poison the minds of the people, and to create and form an entirely new, proletarian ideology and culture, new customs and habits among the masses of the people. This is to creatively study and apply Mao Tse-tung's thought in tempestuous class struggle, popularise it and let it become closely integrated with the masses of workers, peasants and soldiers. Once the masses grasp it, Mao Tse-tung's thought will be transformed into a mighty material force. Facts show that those armed with Mao Tse-tung's thought are the bravest, wisest, most united, most steadfast in class stand and have the sharpest sight. In this great, stormy cultural revolution, the masses of workers, peasants and soldiers are playing the role of the main force — this is the result of their efforts in creatively studying and applying Mao Tse-tung's thought and arming their ideology with it. This is another eloquent proof of the fact that when the masses of workers, peasants and soldiers master the political telescope and microscope of Mao Tse-tung's thought, they are invincible and ever-triumphant. None of the monsters can escape their sharp sight, no matter what the tricks used or what the clever camouflage employed, "36 stratagems" or "72 metamorphoses." Not a single bourgeois stronghold can escape thorough destruction.

The attitude towards Mao Tse-tung's thought, whether to accept it or resist it, to support it or oppose it, to love it warmly or be hostile to it, this is the touchstone to test and the watershed between true revolution and sham revolution, between revolution and counterrevolution, between Marxism-Leninism and revisionism. He who wants to make revolution must accept Mao Tse-tung's thought and act in accordance with it. A counter-revolutionary will inevitably disparage, distort, resist, attack and oppose Mao Tse-tung's thought. The "authorities" of the bourgeoisie and all monsters, including the modern revisionists, use every means to slander Mao Tse-tung's thought, and they are extremely hostile to the creative study and application of Mao Tse-tung's works by the masses of workers, peasants and soldiers. They wildly attack the creative study and application of Mao Tse-tung's works by workers, peasants and soldiers as "philistinism," "oversimplification" and "pragmatism." The only explanation is that this flows from their exploiting class instinct. They fear Mao Tse-tung's thought, the revolutionary truth of the proletariat, and particularly the integration of Mao Tse-tung's thought with the worker, peasant and soldier masses. Once the workers, peasants and soldiers master the sharp weapon of Mao Tse-tung's thought, all monsters have no ground left to stand on. All their intrigues and plots will be thoroughly exposed, their ugly features will be brought into the broad light of day and their dream to restore capitalism will be utterly shattered.

The class enemy won't fall down if you don't hit him. He still tries to rise to his feet after he has fallen. When one black line is eliminated, another appears. When one gang of representatives of the bourgeoisie has been laid low, a new one takes the stage. We must follow the instructions of the Central Committee of the Communist Party of China and never forget the class struggle, never forget the dictatorship of the proletariat, never forget to give prominence to politics, never forget to hold aloft the great red banner of Mao Tse-tung's thought. We must firmly give prominence to politics. We must creatively study and apply still better Chairman Mao Tse-tung's works, putting stress on the importance of application. We must consider Chairman Mao's works the supreme directive for all our work. We must master Mao Tse-tung's thought and pass it on from generation to generation. This is dictated by the needs of the revolution, the situation, the struggle against the enemy, the preparations to smash aggressive war by US imperialism, of opposing and preventing revisionism, preventing the restoration of capitalism, of building socialism with greater, faster, better and more economical results and of ensuring the gradual transition from socialism to communism in China. Chairman Mao is the radiant sun lighting our minds. Mao Tse-tung's thought is our lifeline. Those who oppose Mao Tse-tung's thought, no matter when they do so and what kind of "authorities" they are, will be denounced by the entire Party and the whole nation.

(From a full translation of an editorial in *Chieh-fang-chün Pao* of June 6, 1966)

Lin Piao's Call to the Army

In the articles reproduced below in full,
Defence Minister Lin Piao calls upon the People's Liberation Army to push forward the mass
movement for study of Mao Tse-tung's works
in an attempt to destroy bourgeois ideas and
establish the supremacy of Mao's thought.

Lin's directions to the Army are said to be
applicable to the whole country because they
will help unify the thinking of the people of the
whole country on the basis of Mao's thought.
This is the practice in the current Great
Proletarian Cultural Revolution.—Ed.

Carry the Mass Movement for the Creative Study and Application of Chairman Mao's Works to a New Stage

Comrade Lin Piao has recently given extremely important directions on the study of Chairman Mao's works in the Chinese People's
Liberation Army, calling on the entire army to carry forward to
a new stage the mass drive for the creative study and application of
Chairman Mao's works. Comrade Lin Piao's directions were communicated to a recent meeting of cadres of the Air Force by Comrade Hsiao
Hua, Director of the General Political Department of the People's Liberation Army.

Comrade Lin Piao said: Mao Tse-tung's thought is the science
of revolution, it is proletarian truth which has stood the test of prolonged
revolutionary struggles, it is Marxism-Leninism conforming closest
to reality, it is the unified programme of action for the whole Party,
the whole army and the people of the whole country. The whole Party,
the whole army and the people of the whole country must be thoroughly
imbued with Mao Tse-tung's thought and our thinking must be unified
with it.

Comrade Lin Piao said: The Great Proletarian Cultural Revolution
is now being carried out throughout the country, and a new situation

and a new order of things have appeared in the study of Chairman Mao's works by the whole Party and the whole nation. The army must adapt itself to this situation and carry the mass movement for creatively studying and applying Chairman Mao's works to a new stage. The army must truly become a great school of Mao Tse-tung's thought. The great red banner of Mao Tse-tung's thought must be raised higher than ever. We must get a still firmer grip on the study of Chairman Mao's works and put it on a still more solid footing, we must bring about a new order of things and raise our study to a new level. Every comrade must do his utmost truly to grasp Mao Tse-tung's thought, truly to master it.

At the meeting of the Air Force cadres, Comrade Hsiao Hua urged all comrades in the army to respond resolutely and energetically to Comrade Lin Piao's call. He said that Comrade Lin Piao's extremely important and timely directions placed still greater demands on the army, and gave a new and powerful impetus to the mass drive for the study of Chairman Mao's works which was developing in depth, and they would have profound and far-reaching influence on the building of the PLA into a still more revolutionised army.

Comrade Hsiao Hua said: Why has our army work developed so rapidly and scored such great achievements in the few years since Comrade Lin Piao took charge of the work of the Military Commission of the Central Committee of the Chinese Communist Party? There may be thousands of reasons but they can be summed up in this single point — the holding aloft of the great red banner of Mao Tse-tung's thought, the study and application of Chairman Mao's works in a creative way, the placing of politics in the forefront. Practice has proved that tremendous changes will take place in the ideology and work of a unit when it holds aloft the great red banner of Mao Tse-tung's thought, studies and applies Chairman Mao's works in a creative way, puts politics in the forefront, persists in the "four firsts" and makes a great effort to revolutionise people's thinking.

In fighting a war, our armed forces have always relied on the men's political consciousness, on their courage, on the political factor, on the "four firsts." The fighting strength of a unit is dependent on political work, on political education, on the education in Mao Tse-tung's thought. People armed with Mao Tse-tung's thought are the most courageous, the most intelligent and the most revolutionary. An army that is equipped with Mao Tse-tung's thought has the greatest fighting power and is an army that will be ever-victorious and invincible in the world. We must equip and educate the armed forces with Mao Tse-tung's thought. When the work of education in Mao Tse-tung's thought is done successfully and the men's proletarian consciousness is raised, the result is courage, creativeness, a sense of organisation and discipline, a capacity to stand up to hardship and a revolutionary spirit. And like mushrooms after rain, there will emerge heroes of the type of Lei Feng, Ou-yang Hai, Wang Chieh, Mai Hsien-teh and Liu Ying-chün.

Comrade Lin Piao has pointed out that although, as far as the work of the whole army is concerned, it is very complicated and circumstances differ, yet in this particular respect the situation is at once both complicated and yet not so complicated, there are differences and yet there are no differences. That is to say, everything must be unified through Mao Tse-tung's thought. Since the work of the army as a whole is so complicated, what is it that must be taken hold of? The most fundamental thing is to take hold of education in Mao Tse-tung's thought, the placing of politics in the forefront. When this is done well, all kinds of work will receive an impetus and can be done well. If you don't take hold of this, you will never get results and inevitably you will lose your bearings however hard you strive and sweat on other matters. Out of all the thousands of things they must do, the Party Committees, the political organs and the leading cadres at all levels must have a firm grasp of the study of Chairman Mao's works, put politics in the forefront, stress the revolutionisation of people's thinking and turn the army into a great school of Mao Tse-tung's thought. Here lies the fundamental thing, the core and soul, in our army building.

Comrade Hsiao Hua said: The aim of the Great Proletarian Cultural Revolution is utterly to destroy bourgeois ideology and vigorously establish the supremacy of Mao Tse-tung's thought. The whole country is now engaged in vigorous study of the works of Chairman Mao. Our army must do better than before in studying Chairman Mao's works and bring about a new order of things, reach a new level and achieve new results. We must study better and better every year. We must not stand still but must continue to forge ahead. We must not become complacent but must raise our level, must develop, must make creative contributions and sum up our new experiences. Otherwise we may lag behind, lag behind the situation and behind the people throughout the country.

The great masses of cadres and fighters of our army are infinitely loyal to Chairman Mao and have unbounded love for him. They are infinitely loyal to Mao Tse-tung's thought and have unbounded love for it. When the news reached the army of Chairman Mao's swim in the Yangtse River, and of the several occasions when he received the revolutionary teachers and students, the knowledge that Chairman Mao was very fit and well was a matter of the greatest happiness and inspiration to the commanders and fighters throughout the army. They all said that Chairman Mao's good health was the greatest happiness for the whole Party, the whole army and the whole nation. There were resounding acclamations of long life to Chairman Mao throughout barracks and camps. The masses of cadres and fighters have extremely profound class feeling for our great leader Chairman Mao. Only with deep and rich proletarian feeling can we study Chairman Mao's works well.

The method of study should still follow Comrade Lin Piao's instructions, that is: they should be studied with problems in mind, they should be studied and applied in a creative way, study should be combined with practice, one should study first what is urgently needed so as to get quicker results and one should try hard to apply what one studies. Practice has proved that this is the best method of studying Chairman Mao's works and solving problems. Comrade Lin Piao has said: The question now is not whether we do or do not study but whether we can truly grasp and apply what we study. To grasp and apply truly, we must combine study with reality. Only by linking it with reality can we understand it, fix it in our minds and apply it. Without linking it with reality, we cannot understand it, fix it in our minds and apply it. We must link up with reality and carry out repeated education, dissemination, study and practice. We should not regard the army as still the same old one, as if nothing has changed. Actually things are changing every day. Don't be afraid of repetition. Link up with reality, link up with ideology and link up with work, and we will no longer be repetitive.

Comrade Hsiao Hua said: Comrade Lin Piao has instructed us that the army must implement the thought of Mao Tse-tung in order to resist revisionist ideology and all sorts of exploiting class ideology, to strengthen revolutionisation, to elevate our class consciousness, to raise our understanding of policy and improve our way of thinking. Comrade Lin Piao has stressed that not only the fighters but also the cadres must study the "three much-read articles."† It is very easy to read these articles. But to apply them truly is not so easy. We must study these three articles as maxims. These must be studied at all levels. We must apply what we study so as to revolutionise our thinking. These instructions of Comrade Lin Piao must be implemented with great earnestness.

Comrade Hsiao Hua said: Comrade Lin Piao has always implemented Mao Tse-tung's thought and carried out his correct line most faithfully, firmly and thoroughly. At every crucial turn in the history of the Chinese revolution, Comrade Lin Piao has resolutely taken his stand on the side of Chairman Mao and carried out uncompromising struggle against every kind of "Left" and Right erroneous line and has courageously safeguarded Mao Tse-tung's thought. Since he took charge of the work of the Military Commission of the Central Committee of the Chinese Communist Party, Comrade Lin Piao has held the great red banner of Mao Tse-tung's thought on high, creatively applied Mao Tse-tung's thought and put forward a series of important measures for the strengthening of the revolutionisation of the army. He has called on the whole army to launch a mass movement for the study of the works of Chairman Mao and has also pushed forward throughout the country a vigorous mass drive among workers, peasants and soldiers for the creative study and application of Chairman Mao's works. Comrade Lin Piao is Chairman Mao's closest comrade-in-arms, his best student and the best example in creatively studying and applying Chairman Mao's works. The comrades of our whole army should learn from Comrade Lin Piao and follow his example in holding high the great red banner of Mao Tse-tung's thought, creatively studying and applying Chairman Mao's works, and consistently and unswervingly disseminating and safeguarding Mao Tse-tung's thought.

Comrade Hsiao Hua spoke about the tremendous significance of the great proletarian cultural revolution in our country and its great successes. He also gave important directions concerning the work in the Air Force.

(Reproduced in full from an article in *Peking Review*, No. 42, 1966)

*   *   *

Mao Tse-tung's Thought Must Be Studied
Conscientiously and Diligently

Comrade Lin Piao recently called on the People's Liberation Army to carry forward the mass movement for the creative study and application of Chairman Mao's works to a new stage. These directions are fully applicable both to the whole army and to the whole Party and the entire people. They are extremely important and timely for all.

Over many years, the People's Liberation Army has held aloft the great red banner of Mao Tse-tung's thought, given prominence to proletarian politics, creatively studied and applied Chairman Mao's works, and made great achievements in revolutionising thinking, work and other matters. It has set a brilliant example for the people throughout the country.

In 1964, Comrade Mao Tse-tung issued a great call to the people throughout the country, urging them to go all out in learning from the Liberation Army. Following the example of the Liberation Army, the people of the whole country have strengthened political and ideological work and developed a vigorous mass movement for the creative study and application of Chairman Mao's works. Large numbers of advanced units and outstanding people have come forth on all fronts in the creative study and application of Chairman Mao's works in the short space of a few years. The unprecedented Great Proletarian Cultural Revolution, which is eliminating bourgeois ideology and promoting Mao Tse-tung's thought in a thoroughgoing way, has created a new situation in the whole Party and the entire country in the mass movement for the creative study and application of Chairman Mao's works.

We are now in a new era of world revolution and at a new stage in our country's socialist revolution. The situation of class struggle at home and abroad is changing greatly. Only by studying Chairman Mao's works still more consciously and conscientiously and mastering Mao Tse-tung's thought, the powerful ideological weapon of the proletariat, can we cope with the new situation and new changes in the class struggle and push the wheel of revolution forward.

Comrade Lin Piao has pointed out: Mao Tse-tung's thought is the science of the proletarian revolution, it is proletarian truth which has stood the test of prolonged revolutionary struggles, it is Marxism-Leninism conforming closest to reality, it is the unified programme of action for the whole Party, the whole army and the people of the whole

368

country.

However complex the work and however varied the conditions on the various fronts in our country, there is one point in common, i.e., to unify our thinking with Mao Tse-tung's thought. When the creative study and application of Chairman Mao's works is successfully grasped, politics is placed in the forefront and men's ideology is revolutionised, every kind of work receives an impetus and can be done well.

In the past few years, the Liberation Army has accumulated rich experience in the creative study and application of Chairman Mao's works.

(1) Study for revolution. Chairman Mao has said: "Our comrades must understand that we study Marxism-Leninism not for display, nor because there is any mystery about it, but solely because it is the science which leads the revolutionary cause of the proletariat to victory." We likewise study Chairman Mao's works for the sake of the Chinese revolution and the world revolution. We must be imbued with the firm determination to engage in revolution our whole lifetime, study Chairman Mao's works our whole lifetime and remould our ideology our whole lifetime, making the study of Chairman Mao's works the first need in our lives. On this ideological basis, everyone will have a high degree of consciousness in study, have drive and tenacity and find time to study, and no obstacle can stop him and no difficulty can subdue him.

(2) Study with deep and rich proletarian feeling. Comrade Lin Piao has said: "Mao Tse-tung's thought reflects the objective laws of the domestic and international class struggle; it reflects the fundamental interests of the proletariat, of the working people." Only when one holds fast to the proletarian standpoint, is imbued with deep and rich proletarian feeling and has boundless love for, loyalty to and faith in Chairman Mao and Mao Tse-tung's thought, can he understand Chairman Mao's works deeply, apply them well and really "do things in the way Chairman Mao says."

(3) Make great effort to apply what one studies. Comrade Lin Piao has said: "Chairman Mao's works should be studied with problems in mind, they should be studied and applied in a creative way, study should be combined with practice, one should study first what is urgently needed so as to get quick results and should make great effort to apply what one studies." This method of study is a method of combining theory with practice; it is the most effective Marxist method of study

369

and has been tested in practice. We must link our study of Chairman Mao's works closely with the current class struggle inside and outside the country and with the policies of the Party, link it closely with our own thinking and work, using the "arrow" of Mao Tse-tung's thought to shoot at the "target" of ideological and practical problems. It is necessary to pay special attention to making great effort to remould one's bourgeois world outlook, eliminate selfishness and build up devotion to the public interest, energetically eradicate bourgeois ideas and vigorously foster proletarian ideas.

(4) Study and apply in the course of struggle. Comrade Mao Tse-tung has said: "In order to have a real grasp of Marxism, one must learn it not only from books, but mainly through class struggle, through practical work and close contact with the masses of workers and peasants." When a person studies and applies Chairman Mao's works creatively and truly grasps Mao Tse-tung's thought in the course of sharp and complicated class struggle, he is able to see clearly, stand firmly and withstand any pressure so that "typhoons cannot shake him and thunderbolts cannot shatter him." At the same time, he receives an education from both the positive and negative side, draws experience and lessons, and tempers and improves himself in the teeth of great storms and waves.

(5) Study the particularly important articles constantly and the basic points of view repeatedly. Comrade Lin Piao has urged the armed forces to regard Chairman Mao's works as required study. "Both cadres and fighters should select a number of articles which are most closely related to the current practical struggle as their required lessons for intensive study, understand their essence and use them to solve practical problems current in the armed forces." He has also advocated the study of quotations from Chairman Mao by linking them up with reality and the memorising of a number of revolutionary maxims. Thus, through repeated study and application, many of Chairman Mao's basic points of view will gradually go deep into people's minds and take root.

(6) Cadres should take the lead in study. Study Chairman Mao's writings, follow his teachings and act according to his instructions and be his good fighters — these four phrases are not addressed to fighters alone, but first of all to cadres, particularly senior cadres. Whether a cadre raises the red banner of Mao Tse-tung's thought high or not, whether he studies Chairman Mao's works well or not, this is the criterion of first importance in judging whether he is a good cadre or a bad one. There are now large numbers of young people who have done very well

in the study of Chairman Mao's works. If the comrades who are cadres do not study conscientiously, they will inevitably fall behind.

The Great Proletarian Cultural Revolution which is now developing is a great school for the creative study and application of Chairman Mao's works. This revolution, which is extremely sharp, complex and profound, is storming every corner of social life and touches everyone to the very soul. To the revolutionary masses and cadres, the mighty waves of the Great Proletarian Cultural Revolution that have been surging forward during the past few months under the banner of Mao Tse-tung's thought provide a lesson not in the form of a lesson given in a school, a test not in the form of a test taken in a classroom; it is ten thousand times more profound than a lesson in school, it is ten thousand times more exacting than a test in a classroom.

The Great Proletarian Cultural Revolution is a great revolution to unify the thinking of the people throughout the country with Mao Tse-tung's thought; it is a great undertaking that will have its bearing on many later generations, an undertaking to dig out the roots of revisionism, prevent capitalist restoration and ensure China's transition from socialism to communism, step by step.

In the storms of struggle, large numbers of new, courageous fighters armed with Mao Tse-tung's thought are maturing quickly. Mao Tse-tung's thought is changing the outlook of the whole society and the mental outlook of people still further. Bathed in the sunlight of Mao Tse-tung's thought, our great motherland shines with brilliance.

Let our whole Party, our whole army and all our people study Chairman Mao's works conscientiously and diligently and in a thoroughgoing way, truly master Mao Tse-tung's thought and truly and quickly turn the whole country into a great school of Mao Tse-tung's thought!

(Reproduced from an article in *Peking Review*, No. 42, 1966)

* * *

The Army and People throughout the Country Are Determined To Master Mao Tse-tung's Thought

Comrade Lin Piao has recently given instructions, calling on the Chinese People's Liberation Army to carry forward to a new stage the mass movement for the creative study and application of Chairman

371

Mao's works. This call received resolute and warm support and response from the commanders and fighters of the whole Liberation Army and the broad masses of revolutionary people throughout the country.

Comrade Lin Piao points out in his instructions: Mao Tse-tung's thought is the science of revolution, it is proletarian truth which has stood the test of prolonged revolutionary struggles, it is Marxism-Leninism conforming closest to reality, it is the unified programme of action for the whole Party, the whole army and the people of the whole country. The whole Party, the whole army and the people of the whole country must be thoroughly imbued with Mao Tse-tung's thought and our thinking must be unified with it. The Great Proletarian Cultural Revolution is now being carried out throughout the country, and a new situation and a new order of things have appeared in the study of Chairman Mao's works by the whole Party and the whole nation. The army must adapt itself to this situation and carry the mass movement for creatively studying and applying Chairman Mao's works to a new stage. The army must truly become a great school of Mao Tse-tung's thought. The great red banner of Mao Tse-tung's thought must be raised higher than ever. We must get a still firmer grip on the study of Chairman Mao's works and put it on a still more solid footing. We must bring about a new order of things and raise our study to a new level. Every comrade must do his utmost truly to grasp Mao Tse-tung's thought, truly to master it.

Upon learning of these instructions, the army and the people of the whole country unanimously held that they are extremely important and timely, that they reflect their aspirations and are a tremendous new motivating force in the nation's deepening mass movement for the study of Chairman Mao's works.

Many leading cadres of PLA units headed work teams which have gone to companies, warships, airfields, warehouses, hospitals and border defence outposts to propagate Comrade Lin Piao's call and explain its great significance to cadres and fighters at the basic level. Many units have organised propaganda teams, put up wall-newspapers or blackboard bulletins and posted, both inside and outside their barracks, leaflets and slogans carrying important sections from the instructions so that everyone can see, hear and remember them, and translate them into action.

Discussions of Comrade Lin Piao's call were organised throughout the army immediately after the cadres and fighters had heard about it.

Unanimously they pointed out: Comrade Lin Piao has made higher demands on the whole army in the creative study and application of Chairman Mao's works at a time when the Great Proletarian Cultural Revolution has come to a high tide and a new situation and a new order of things have appeared in the study of Chairman Mao's works by the whole Party and the whole nation. This shows his great concern for the political development of all cadres and fighters. This is a beacon light guiding the whole army in studying Mao Tse-tung's thought well and in its advance along the road to thorough proletarianisation and militancy.

A political instructor of an armed unit stationed on the Tibetan plateau said: "Comrade Lin Piao has repeatedly taught us that Mao Tse-tung's thought is the science of revolution, it is proletarian truth which has stood the test of prolonged revolutionary struggles, it is Marxism-Leninism conforming closest to reality, it is the unified programme of action for the whole Party, the whole army and the people of the whole country. We have one hundred per cent belief in this correct thesis. We respond to Comrade Lin Piao's call without any reservation. We pledge to be infinitely loyal to Chairman Mao, to love him with a boundless love, to have boundless faith in and boundless veneration for Mao Tse-tung's thought and be his good fighters."

Fighters of the 9th Company of an army railroad unit said that, determined to follow the way pointed out by Comrade Lin Piao, they will imprint Mao Tse-tung's invincible thought in their minds, infuse it into their blood and express it in their actions.

Many units of the navy and the armed forces under the Wuhan, Foochow and Sinkiang Commands have summed up their experience in study in the light of Comrade Lin Piao's new directions. In accordance with them, they are determined to get a still firmer grip on the study of Chairman Mao's works and put it on a still more solid footing, to widen the scope of study, always take as their guiding principles the "three much-read articles"—"Serve the People," "In Memory of Norman Bethune" and "The Foolish Old Man Who Removed the Mountains," make great efforts to remould their world outlook, and quickly carry forward to a new stage the mass movement for the creative study and application of Chairman Mao's works.

Filled with their boundless love for Chairman Mao, the commanders and fighters of the army units spare on efforts to pass on Comrade Lin Piao's instructions to the masses of the people near where they are stationed.

One army unit under the Peking Command has organised 36 propaganda and cinema teams which have made lantern slides of Comrade Lin Piao's instructions to carry out propaganda in the area of Hsingtai, Hopei Province. Many army units under the Wuhan Command have sent out a large number of instructors to make Comrade Lin Piao's instructions known among the masses of the people. The commanders and fighters of the army units seize this chance of conducting propaganda among the masses to learn from the local activists in studying Chairman Mao's works, acquainting themselves with their outstanding deeds and experience so that they can do a still better job in organising study in their own units.

Workers, peasants, revolutionary teachers and students, young Red Guard fighters and revolutionary cadres have held many discussions. They have unanimously expressed their determination to follow closely the Liberation Army, learn from it still better, raise the great red banner of Mao Tse-tung's thought still higher, take a firmer hold of the study of Chairman Mao's works, put it on a still more solid footing and make Mao Tse-tung's thought a programme of their own actions.

At one meeting, Wang Yi-tai, a young worker of the Peking Thermal Power Plant, said: It is all right if we miss a meal but it will not do for us not to study Chairman Mao's writings. We must study and apply what we have studied for the revolution; we must make study and application our lifetime work and devote our whole life to making revolution.

Wang Yu-fa, a member of the heroic No. 32111 Drilling Team who, disregarding all danger, threw himself into the battle to put out a raging fire and save a gas well after an accidental conflagration in June this year (see *Peking Review*, No. 40, 1966) and who came to our capital to participate in the National Day festivities, said in Peking: Comrade Lin Piao's call is not only a mobilisation order for the whole army but also a clarion call to the entire people. If the 700 million people have truly grasped Mao Tse-tung's thought, then imperialism, revisionism and all reactionaries are not worth a straw and we shall be able to thoroughly smash the entire old world to pieces and create a bright red new world.

Over 600 representatives of minority nationalities from various parts of our motherland who also came to the capital to participate in the National Day festivities, in their native tongues said excitedly at discussion meetings: Comrade Lin Piao's instructions are very timely and are very important. We, people of all nationalities, must resolutely implement them and initiate a new high tide in the creative study and application of Chairman Mao's writings and turn every field of work into a great school of Mao Tse-tung's thought. Khaichhung, an emancipated Tibetan serf and now deputy-head of a township, said: I am resolved, at all times and in any task I tackle, to follow Comrade Lin Piao's instructions to give priority to the creative study and application of Chairman Mao's writings. Kalzang-Wang Drub, an emancipated serf, said: "Chairman Mao is the reddest and brightest sun in the hearts of us emancipated serfs. I will always be Chairman Mao's good student."

Some cadres and group leaders of the Poor Peasant Association of the Youth Brigade of the Ying-menkou People's Commune on the outskirts of Chengtu, an outstanding farm unit of Tachai type in Szechwan Province, held discussions during the work breaks. Brigade leader Chu Hai-ching said: We should immediately organise all commune members to study Comrade Lin Piao's call, put the study of Chairman Mao's works on a still more solid footing and bring about a new order of things.

Red Guard fighters hailing from various parts of the country who are the shock force in the Great Proletarian Cultural Revolution unanimously pledged to act also as the shock brigade in the mass drive for the creative study and application of Chairman Mao's works. Red Guard fighters in Tsinan, Kunming, Kweiyang and Sining warmly responded to Comrade Lin Piao's call in different ways — some made suggestions on how to study, others worked out their study plans, still others held meetings and discussions on the instructions. They unanimously pledged themselves to thoroughly carry out Comrade Lin Piao's instructions and pay particular attention at present to bringing the problems existing in their minds, which have arisen in the great cultural revolution, into their creative study and application of Chairman Mao's works. They are determined to resolutely defend the revolutionary line of the proletariat and thoroughly repudiate the reactionary line of the bourgeoisie and strive to fulfil the tasks of struggling against and crushing those persons in authority who are taking the capitalist road, criticising and repudiating the reactionary bourgeois academic "authorities" and the ideology of the bourgeoisie and all other exploiting classes and transforming education, literature and art and all other parts of the superstructure that do not correspond to the socialist economic base.

Lin Piao Speaks at Mass Peking Rallies

Speaking at five mass Peking rallies on behalf of Mao Tse-tung, Lin Piao explained that the object of the Great Proletarian Cultural Revolution was to crush all "counter-revolutionary" revisionists, bourgeois rightists and reactionary persons in power who followed the capitalist path, and to strike down all "monsters and demons" who tried to suppress the cultural revolution.

He declared that the "revolutionary torrents" of the masses would wash away all the "sludge and filthy water" left over from the old society, removing all obstacles in the course of the Great Proletarian Cultural Revolution. — Ed.

Speaking at the first mass rally of revolutionary students and teachers held in Peking's Tienanmen Square, Lin Piao said:

"Mao Tse-tung's thought marks a completely new stage in the development of Marxism-Leninism. It is the highest level of Marxism-Leninism in the present era. It is Marxism-Leninism of the present era for remoulding the very souls of the people. It is the most powerful ideological weapon of the proletariat.

"The masses are the makers of history. Once they master Mao Tse-tung's thought, they will become the wisest and the most courageous people, capable of displaying inexhaustible strength!

"With the wise leadership of Chairman Mao and having mastered Mao Tse-tung's thought which is the sharpest weapon, we will be invincible and all-conquering and will achieve complete victory in the Great Proletarian Cultural Revolution!

"We firmly support your proletarian revolutionary spirit of daring to break through, to act, to make revolution and to rise up.

"Our Chairman Mao is the supreme commander of this Great Proletarian Cultural Revolution. Chairman Mao is the commander-in-chief. Under the guidance of the great commander-in-chief and faithfully following the instructions of our commander-in-chief — Chairman Mao, we will certainly make the great cultural revolution

376

advance triumphantly and win great victory!

"The Great Proletarian Cultural Revolution initiated by Chairman Mao is a great creation in the communist movement and a great creation for the socialist revolution!

"The Great Proletarian Cultural Revolution is aimed precisely at eliminating bourgeois ideology, establishing proletarian ideology, remoulding people's souls, revolutionising their ideology, digging out the roots of revisionism, and consolidating and developing the socialist system.

"We will strike down those in power who take the road of capitalism, strike down the reactionary bourgeois authorities, strike down all bourgeois royalists, oppose all actions to suppress the revolution, and strike down all monsters and demons!

"We will vigorously destroy all the old ideas, old culture, old customs and old habits of the exploiting classes, and transform all those parts of the superstructure that do not correspond to the socialist economic base. We will sweep away all vermin and remove all obstacles!

"We will make vigorous efforts to establish proletarian authorities and the new ideas, new culture, new customs and new habits of the proletariat. In a word, we will work with great energy so that Mao Tse-tung's thought achieves complete ascendancy. We will enable hundreds of millions of people to grasp Mao Tse-tung's thought, ensure that it seizes all ideological positions, apply it in transforming the mental outlook of the entire society, and transform Mao Tse-tung's thought, this great spiritual force, into a great material force.

"The current great cultural revolution is a tremendous event affecting the fate and the future of our Party and our country!

"On what do we rely to make this great cultural revolution successful? We rely on the great thought of Mao Tse-tung as well as on the wisdom and strength of the masses of the people.

"Chairman Mao is the most outstanding leader of the proletariat and the greatest genius of the present era. Chairman Mao has the strongest faith in the masses of the people. He pays the greatest attention to them. He gives the strongest support to the revolutionary movement of the masses of the people. His heart is one with the hearts of the revolutionary masses!

"The great cultural revolution is a long-term task. It will last a very long time. So long as bourgeois ideology exists, we will fight on.

"This is a great campaign, a general attack on the ideas of the bourgeoisie and all other exploiting classes. Under the leadership of Chairman Mao, we must launch fierce attacks on bourgeois ideology, old customs and old forces of habit! We must thoroughly topple, smash and discredit the counter-revolutionary revisionists, bourgeois rightists and bourgeois reactionary authorities, and they must never be allowed to rise again!"

(Reproduced from NCNA English Service
dated August 18, 1966)

*   *   *

*In his speech at the second mass Peking rally
on August 31, Lin Piao said:*

"On behalf of our great teacher, great leader, great supreme commander and great helmsman Chairman Mao, I extend greetings to the students coming from all parts of the country and to you all! On behalf of the Central Committee of the Party, I greet you all!

"Students, you have come to Peking and are exchanging experience in the great cultural revolution with revolutionary teachers and students of Peking. You have travelled a long way and worked hard! We believe that after your return, you will work even better in accordance with Chairman Mao's instructions and the 16-point decision issued by the Central Committee of the Party, to break all resistance, overcome all difficulties and develop the Great Proletarian Cultural Revolution with even greater vigour and vitality!

"The present situation in the Great Proletarian Cultural Revolution is very fine!

"The great cultural revolution has already touched on politics and on economics. The struggle (against and crushing of those persons in authority who are taking the capitalist road), the criticism and repudiation (of the reactionary bourgeois academic "authorities" and the ideology of the bourgeoisie and all other exploiting classes) and the transformation (of education, literature and art and all other parts of the superstructure that do not correspond to the socialist economic base) in the schools have extended to the whole of society. The revolutionary torrents of the masses are washing away all the sludge and filthy water left over from the old society, and are transforming the entire social outlook of our country.

378

"Young revolutionary fighters, Chairman Mao and the Party's Central Committee warmly acclaim your proletarian revolutionary spirit of daring to think, to speak, to act, to break through and to make revolution. You have done many good things. You have put forward many good proposals. We are greatly elated, and we warmly support you! Firmly oppose any attempt to suppress you! Your revolutionary actions are very fine! We hail you, and salute you!

"We must act in accordance with Chairman Mao's teachings, dare to struggle and dare to make revolution and be good at waging struggles and at making revolution. We must take Mao Tse-tung's thought as our compass in the Great Proletarian Cultural Revolution and carry out the 16-point decision seriously, thoroughly, fully and in an over-all way.

"We must, in accordance with Chairman Mao's teachings, distinguish who are our enemies and who are our friends. Attention should be paid to uniting with the great majority, and concentrating all forces to striking at the handful of bourgeois rightists. The main target of the attack is those persons in power who have wormed their way into the Party and are taking the capitalist road. It is essential to hold fast to this main orientation in the struggles.

"We must act in accordance with the teachings of Chairman Mao Tse-tung, and carry out the struggles by reasoning and not by coercion or force. Don't hit people. This applies too in struggling against those persons in power who are taking the capitalist road and against the landlords, rich peasants, counter-revolutionaries, bad elements and rightists. Struggling against them by coercion or force can only touch their skins. Only by reasoning is it possible to touch their souls. Only by reasoning, exposing them fully and criticising them profoundly is it possible to thoroughly show their counter-revolutionary features, isolate them to the maximum, discredit them, pull them down and smash them.

"Provided we earnestly read Chairman Mao's works, follow his teachings and act in accordance with his instructions, the Great Proletarian Cultural Revolution can certainly achieve great victories! Let imperialism, modern revisionism and all reactionaries tremble before our victories!"

(Reproduced from NCNA English service
dated August 31, 1966)

*   *   *

Addressing the third mass Peking rally, Lin Piao declared:

"Chairman Mao and the Party Central Committee firmly support you! The broad masses of the workers, peasants and soldiers also firmly support you! Your revolutionary actions have shaken the whole of society and administered a shock to the dross and remnant evils left over from the old world. In your vigorous fight to destroy the 'four olds' (old ideas, old culture, old customs and old habits) and foster the 'four news' (new ideas, new culture, new customs and new habits), you have scored brilliant results. You have created utter consternation among those in power who are taking the capitalist road, the reactionary bourgeois 'authorities,' and the bloodsuckers and parasites. You have acted correctly and done well!

"Chairman Mao teaches us that the fundamental contradiction which the Great Proletarian Cultural Revolution should solve is the contradiction between the two classes, the proletariat and the bourgeoisie, and between the two roads, the socialist and the capitalist. The present movement's main target of attack is those within the Party who are in power and taking the capitalist road. Bombard the headquarters and you bombard the handful of people in power who are taking the capitalist road. Our country is a socialist country under the dictatorship of the proletariat. The leadership of our country is in the hands of the proletariat. It is precisely for the purpose of consolidating and strengthening our dictatorship of the proletariat that we must pull down the small handful of people in power who are taking the capitalist road. It is very clear that unlike us, the small handful of reactionary bourgeois elements, the elements belonging to the five categories of former landlords, former rich peasants, counter-revolutionaries, bad elements and rightists who have not changed, oppose the dictatorship exercised over them by the broad masses of revolutionary people headed by the proletariat. They are trying to bombard our headquarters of the proletarian revolution. Can we tolerate such actions of theirs? No, we must smash the tricky schemes of these monsters and demons, we must see them through, we must not let their schemes come true. They are only a small handful, but they can deceive some good people at times. We must keep firmly to the general orientation of our struggle. Any deviation from this general orientation will lead us astray.

"Like the workers, peasants and soldiers, be forever loyal to Chairman Mao, to Mao Tse-tung's thought, to the Party and to the people, and temper yourselves in the great storm of the revolutionary struggle to become successors to the proletarian revolutionary cause.

"Under the leadership of Chairman Mao, our great leader, great teacher, great supreme commander and great helmsman, and under the banner of Mao Tse-tung's thought, let the worker, peasant and soldier masses and the revolutionary students unite, let all revolutionary comrades unite, and carry the Great Proletarian Cultural Revolution through to the end."

(Reproduced from NCNA English service
dated September 15, 1966)

*   *   *

Speaking at the fourth mass Peking rally on October I,
Lin Piao Said:

"Today is the great festival of the 17th anniversary of the founding of the People's Republic of China. On behalf of our great leader Chairman Mao, the Central Committee of the Party and the Government of the People's Republic of China, I most warmly salute the workers, peasants and soldiers, the revolutionary teachers and students, the revolutionary Red Guards and other militant youth organisations, the revolutionary people of all nationalities and the revolutionary cadres throughout the country, and extend hearty welcome to our friends from different countries of the world!

"The 17 years that have elapsed since the founding of the People's Republic of China have been no ordinary years. They are years which have witnessed earth-shaking changes in China. They are years which have witnessed earth-shaking changes in the world as well.

"Comrade Mao Tse-tung led the Chinese people in carrying out the revolution, and they traversed a tortuous path beset with all kinds of hardships. Our domestic and foreign enemies were strong, but in the end they were overthrown and driven out by the Chinese people. The imperialists headed by the United States, all the reactionaries and the modern revisionists — all these paper tigers have been punctured by the Chinese people and all the revolutionary people of the world.

"In the short space of 17 years, the Chinese people have completely changed the face of old China. This is a highly meritorious deed performed by the masses of the Chinese people under the leadership of

381

Comrade Mao Tse-tung. We are convinced that all the oppressed peoples and oppressed nations of the world will take their own paths in the light of their own countries' conditions and seize final victory as the Chinese people did.

"Today, we are celebrating this great festival amidst the upsurge of the Great Proletarian Cultural Revolution. This revolution is a great revolution, an entirely new and creative revolution, carried out after the seizure of political power by the proletariat. It is to overthrow through struggle the small handful of persons within the Party who have been in authority and have taken the capitalist road, to sweep away all ghosts and monsters in our society, and to break the old ideas, culture, customs and habits of the exploiting classes and foster the new ideas, culture, customs and habits of the proletariat, with a view to further consolidating the dictatorship of the proletariat and developing the socialist system.

"The historical experience of the dictatorship of the proletariat in the world teaches us that if we fail to do so, the rule of revisionism will come about and the restoration of capitalism will take place. Should this come to pass in our country, China would go back to its former colonial and semi-colonial, feudal and semi-feudal road, and the imperialists and reactionaries would again ride roughshod over the people. The importance of our great cultural revolution is therefore perfectly clear.

"At present, hundreds of millions of people have been aroused. The revolutionary people feel proud and elated, while the reactionary bourgeoisie has been completely discredited. We are forging ahead. We have already laid the corner-stone of great victory.

"The Great Proletarian Cultural Revolution is promoting the revolutionisation of people's minds and has thus become a powerful motive force for the development of socialist production in our country. This year is the first year of our Third Five-Year Plan. The plan for this year's industrial production is expected to be overfulfilled, and as for agriculture another good harvest is to be reaped. New heights are being scaled in China's science and technology. Our great motherland has never been so prosperous and so full of vigour. Our national defence has never been so strong.

"Chairman Mao long ago pointed out that the class struggle between the proletariat and the bourgeoisie and the struggle between the roads of socialism and capitalism exist throughout the historical period of

382

socialism. The Great Proletarian Cultural Revolution constitutes a new stage in the struggle between the two classes and between the two roads. In the course of this revolution, the struggle is still going on between the revolutionary proletarian line represented by Chairman Mao and the bourgeois line of opposing revolution. Those who cling to the erroneous line are only a small handful of persons, who divorce themselves from the people, oppose the people and oppose Mao Tse-tung's thought, and this spells their certain failure.

"Comrades and friends! At present, an excellent situation prevails in the world. The great upheavals of the past few years in the world show that the days of imperialism headed by the United States, modern revisionism and all reaction are numbered.

"US imperialism is trying hard to find a way out by launching a world war. We must take this seriously. The focal point of the present struggle lies in Vietnam. We have made every preparation. Not flinching from maximum national sacrifices, we are determined to give firm support to the fraternal Vietnamese people in carrying the war of resistance against US aggression and for national salvation through to the end. Imperialism headed by the United States and modern revisionism with the leadership of the CPSU as its centre are colluding and actively plotting peace talk swindles for the purpose of stamping out the raging flames of the Vietnamese people's national revolutionary war against US aggression, of the national revolutionary struggles in Asian, African and Latin American countries and of world revolution. They will not succeed in their schemes so long as the people of the whole world keep their eyes wide open.

"Twenty years ago, Chairman Mao said that the people of the whole world must form a united front against US imperialism so as to defeat it. The revolutionary people of all countries are now advancing along this road.

"Chairman Mao has said, 'People of the world, be courageous, dare to fight, defy difficulties and advance wave upon wave. Then the whole world will belong to the people. Monsters of all kinds shall be destroyed.' Such is the inevitable future of the world.

"The Chinese people will continue to hold high the banner of Marxism-Leninism and the banner of proletarian internationalism and, together with the Marxist-Leninists of the whole world and the revolutionary people of all countries, carry the struggle against US imperialism and its lackeys and the struggle against modern revisionism with the leadership of the CPSU as its centre through to the end!

"Comrades and friends!

"All our achievements and successes have been scored under the wise leadership of Chairman Mao and represent the victory of Mao Tse-tung's thought. We must use Mao Tse-tung's thought to unify the thinking of the whole Party and the thinking of the people of the whole country. We must hold high the great red banner of Mao Tse-tung's thought and further unfold the mass movement for the creative study and application of Chairman Mao's works throughout the country. We must turn the whole country into a great school of Mao Tse-tung's thought. We must build our great motherland into a more powerful and prosperous country. This is the demand of the Chinese people as well as the hope placed on us by the people of all countries."

(Reproduced from NCNA English service dated October 1, 1966)

*   *   *

In a speech at the fifth mass Peking rally on November 3, 1966, Lin Piao said:

"The present situation of the Great Proletarian Cultural Revolution is excellent! With each passing day, the gigantic, vigorous mass movement is developing in depth. A tremendous change has taken place in the whole face of society and the mental outlook of the people. The great thought of Mao Tse-tung has become more extensively disseminated and it has gone deeper into the hearts of the people. As a result of Chairman Mao's call to take firm hold of the revolution and stimulate production, the great cultural revolution has been promoting the revolutionisation of people's thinking and spurring very rapid development in industry and agriculture and in science and technology. The recent successful test in the launching of a guided missile with a nuclear warhead is a great victory for Mao Tse-tung's thought, a great victory for the proletarian cultural revolution!

"The 11th plenary session of the 8th CCP Central Committee announced the victory of the proletarian revolutionary line represented by Chairman Mao and the bankruptcy of the bourgeois reactionary line. In the past two months, the correct line of Chairman Mao has been put before the broad masses and has been grasped by them, and criticisms have been made of the erroneous line. The broad masses have really translated into action Chairman Mao's call to 'concern yourselves with affairs of State.' This is an extremely fine thing. It is an important guarantee that the Great Proletarian Cultural Revolution will be carried through to the end.

"Chairman Mao Tse-tung's line is one of letting the masses educate themselves and emancipate themselves. It is the line of putting 'daring' above everything else and of daring to trust the masses, daring to rely on them and daring boldly to mobilise them. It is the application and a new development in the great cultural revolution of the Party's mass line. It is the line of the Great Proletarian Cultural Revolution.

"The bourgeois line is one of opposing the mass line, of opposing the education and emancipation of the masses by themselves, of repressing the masses and opposing the revolution. This bourgeois reactionary line does not direct the spearhead of its struggle against the small handful of persons within the Party who are in authority and are taking the capitalist road, and all the monsters and demons in society, but against the revolutionary masses. It uses various ways and means to incite one group among the masses to struggle against another group, and incite one set of students to struggle against another set.

"The proletarian revolutionary line of Chairman Mao Tse-tung is as incompatible with the bourgeois reactionary line as fire is to water. Only by thoroughly criticising the bourgeois reactionary line and eradicating its influence can the line of Chairman Mao Tse-tung be carried out correctly, completely and thoroughly.

"Under the guidance of Chairman Mao's correct line, the broad revolutionary masses of our country have created the new experience of developing extensive democracy under the dictatorship of the proletariat. By this extensive democracy, the Party is fearlessly permitting the broad masses to use the media of free airing of views, big-character posters, great debates and extensive contacts, to criticise and supervise the Party and Government leading institutions and leaders at all levels. At the same time, it is providing the people with full democratic rights along the principles of the Paris Commune. Without such extensive democracy, it would be impossible to initiate a genuine Great Proletarian Cultural Revolution, stage a great revolution in the depths of people's souls, carry out the Great Proletarian Cultural Revolution thoroughly and completely, eradicate the roots of revisionism, consolidate the dictatorship of the proletariat and guarantee the advance of our country along the road of socialism and communism. This extensive democracy is a new form of combining Mao Tse-tung's thought with the broad masses, a new form of mass self-education. It is a new contribution by Chairman Mao to Marxist-Leninist theory on proletarian revolution and the dictatorship of the proletariat.

"International historical experience of the dictatorship of the proletariat has demonstrated that without carrying out a thorough-going, Great Proletarian Cultural Revolution of this kind, without practising such extensive democracy, the dictatorship of the proletariat grows weaker and degenerates, capitalism uses various forms to stage a come-back and the exploiting classes once again ride on the backs of the people.

"It is not only essential to practise such extensive democracy thoroughly as between the leadership and the masses, but it is also absolutely necessary to carry it out thoroughly among the masses themselves and between all sections of the masses. Unless there is such extensive democracy among the masses themselves, unless they become good at mutual consultation, unless they become good at listening to dissenting views, unless they become good at presenting facts and reasoning things out, unless they become good at using their brains and pondering over problems, the masses cannot possibly educate and emancipate themselves, achieve the purpose of developing the ranks of the Left, uniting the great majority and isolating the handful of bourgeois rightists, and carry out to the full the line of the Great Proletarian Cultural Revolution put forward by our great teacher, Chairman Mao."

(Reproduced from NCNA English service dated November 3, 1966)

Lin Piao's Directive on Army Work for 1966

Lin Piao's five-point directive on how the armed forces can be brought to a higher ideological level calls for putting politics first at all times as a means of "revolutionising" the People's Liberation Army, heightening its combat-readiness, combating the rise of modern revisionism and putting politics before professionalism in the army.—Ed.

PLA Conference on Political Work

The General Political Department of the Chinese People's Liberation Army concluded its conference on political work in the army on January 18, 1966 in Peking.

During its twenty days of meetings the conference made a serious study of the important instructions given by the Central Committee of the Communist Party and Chairman Mao Tse-tung on building up the army and on its political work; there were discussions on implementation of the five-point principle[1] advanced by Comrade Lin Piao to keep on putting politics first; the experience gained in political work in the past two years was summed up and arrangements for political work in 1966 were decided upon.

The conference called on all commanders and fighters of the PLA to rally closely around the Central Committee of the Party and Chairman Mao Tse-tung, to hold still higher the great red banner of Mao Tse-tung's thought, to continue to put politics first and resolutely apply the five-point principle in this connection, and to heighten combat-readiness and be prepared at all times to smash US imperialist aggression.

The conference agreed that there was a new mass upsurge in the creative study and application of Mao Tse-tung's works throughout the army since Comrade Lin Piao's instructions on putting politics first were implemented. It was noted that the broad masses of cadres and fighters showed a deeper class feeling towards Mao Tse-tung's thinking and greater political consciousness in remoulding their ideology and directing their activities in accordance with the guidance given by Chairman Mao Tse-tung. Great numbers of fine people like Lei Feng and Wang Chieh had come forward, and they had good deeds to their credit. There were new developments in the campaign to produce outstanding companies. There were remarkable achievements in fighting, training and the fulfilment of various other tasks.

The consensus at the conference was that the principle of putting politics first formulated by Comrade Lin Piao conforms with what Chairman Mao Tse-tung has always taught us; it was put forward in accordance with the historical experience of the Chinese people's armed forces and the present situation, in accordance with the laws of development and the economic basis of socialist society, and with the fact that classes and class struggle still exist in socialist society. This principle is the foundation on which to strengthen the revolutionisation and modernisation of the army, to make good preparations for the smashing of the US imperialist war of aggression and to combat and prevent the rise of modern revisionism, and ensure that the army never degenerates. Comrade Lin Piao's five-point principle which calls for putting politics first not only serves as the general principle and task for all army work in 1966 but is the guiding policy in army building for all the years to come.

"Putting politics first" means putting Mao Tse-tung's thinking first, said the conference. It means regarding Chairman Mao Tse-tung's works as the highest instructions on all aspects of the work of the whole army, and putting Mao Tse-tung's thinking in command of everything. Chairman Mao Tse-tung's instructions are the criterion for all work. All his instructions must be resolutely supported and carried out, even if their accomplishment involves "climbing a mountain of swords and crossing an ocean of flames." Whatever runs counter to his instructions must be rejected and firmly opposed.

The conference called for the creative study and application of Chairman Mao Tse-tung's works and, in particular, for the utmost effort in applying them. Whether Mao Tse-tung's thinking has been really mastered must be judged above all by its application after study. In assessing anyone, hear what he says and see what he does, with emphasis on the latter. It is incumbent not only on the soldiers and cadres at grass-root levels, but even more on the senior cadres, to read Chairman Mao Tse-tung's works, follow his teachings, act in accordance with his instructions and be a good soldier of Chairman Mao Tse-tung. One must make the study of Chairman Mao's works and the remoulding of one's ideology a life-time endeavour if one is to devote one's life to the revolution.

The conference decided that in order to put politics first and resolutely carry out the five-point principle, the whole army must hold still higher the great red banner of Mao Tse-tung's thought, and stimulate a new upsurge in the creative study and application of Mao Tse-tung's works on an even wider scale and in still greater depth.

Consistent adherence to the mass line and the continued practice of democracy in political, military and economic affairs were stressed at the conference. The instructions of Chairman Mao Tse-tung, the principles and policies of the Central Committee of the Communist Party and the directives issued by the Party's Military Commission and Comrade Lin Piao must be made known directly to the broad masses of cadres and fighters and translated into the conscious action of the masses.

It was important to encourage all cadres and fighters to do political and ideological work, including the political, military and other cadres, declared the conference. Ideological work must penetrate the heart and mind of every fighter. Army units should do their administrative and educational work by means of political work and by the method of persuasion and education.

The conference stressed that the decisive factor in putting politics first was Party leadership. The principle that military affairs should be run by the whole Party must be adhered to. The system of dual leadership by the military command and the local Party committee under the unified leadership of the Party's Central Committee must be resolutely enforced. The army must come under the absolute leadership of the Party and the supervision of the masses in order to ensure that the line, principles and policies of the Party are resolutely implemented in the army.

The conference pointed out that Chairman Mao Tse-tung's ideas on Party building must be followed in order to strengthen the work of building the Party organisation in the army, and strengthen collective leadership by the Party committees. Democratic centralism must be adhered to and there must be a vigorous inner-Party life, criticism and self-criticism, and democracy, so that military work will be done well by concerted efforts.

The conference particularly emphasised that it was necessary to keep firmly in mind Chairman Mao Tse-tung's teaching that "modesty makes one progress, whereas conceit makes one lag behind" and be modest, prudent, and honest in word and deed at all times.

The conference called on all members of the army to sharpen their vigilance a hundred-fold and work earnestly to increase their combat-readiness.

It noted that US imperialism was now shifting the focus of its strategy to Asia. It was frenziedly enlarging its war of aggression in Vietnam and directing the spearhead of its aggression against China. At the same time the modern revisionists were working even more shamelessly in the service of US imperialism, thereby aggravating the danger of war.

The conference declared: "All members of the army must know that the root cause of war will remain until imperialism is overthrown and capitalism is eliminated. US imperialism has obstinately set itself against the Chinese people, and against the people of all countries. It has always wanted to impose war on the Chinese people and have a contest of strength with us. Therefore, to increase our combat-readiness is not a temporary measure but a long-term strategic task.

"We will not only defend our motherland and be ready at any moment to smash aggression by US imperialism. We will also resolutely support and help the people of other countries in their struggle against US imperialism. This is our bounden internationalist duty.

"We must make full preparations against the war of aggression which US imperialism may launch at an early date, on a large scale, with nuclear or other weapons, and on several fronts. All our work must be put on a footing of readiness to fight."

In conclusion the conference declared: "We are convinced that we will be invincible provided we put politics first, maintain an atmosphere of keen study of Mao Tse-tung's thought and foster a high level of proletarian consciousness, high morale, solid unity and deep hatred for the enemy, and a spirit of revolutionary heroism, the spirit of daring to make revolution and daring to struggle, fearing neither war nor sacrifice."

Should US imperialism dare to attack China, "our army, like a steel hammer, will crush anything it hits. Armed with the thinking of Mao Tse-tung, closely linked with the people throughout the country, and closely linked with the people throughout the world, we shall be more than a match for such a thing as US imperialism, and final victory will certainly be ours."

Lin Piao's Message on Study of

Mao Tse - tung's Works

— NCNA, Peking, June 19, 1966

The industrial and communications departments have laid stress on putting politics in command and keeping politics in the fore. It is very good to do so. It is very helpful for raising the level of political consciousness of the working class and for strengthening our socialist construction. It will increase the initiative and creativeness of the working class and make our socialist cause flourish more.

You are putting energetic study of Chairman Mao's works as the first item in all your work policies for the industrial and communications departments. That is very good.

China is a great socialist State of the dictatorship of the proletariat and has a population of 700 million. It needs unified thinking, revolutionary thinking, correct thinking. That is Mao Tse-tung's thinking. With it, and in no other way, we can maintain vigorous revolutionary enthusiasm and a firm and correct political orientation.

Mao Tse-tung's thought reflects the objective laws of the domestic and international class struggle; it reflects the fundamental interests of the proletariat, of the working people. Mao Tse-tung's thought has not grown spontaneously from among the working people; rather it is the result of Chairman Mao's inheriting and developing in a talented way the ideas of Marxism-Leninism on the basis of great revolutionary practice. It has summed up the new experiences of the international communist movement and carried Marxism-Leninism forward to a new stage.

Therefore, it is essential to imbue the workers and peasants with Chairman Mao's ideas through the living study and application of his works. Only so can the mental outlook of the working people be changed and the forces of the spirit transformed into tremendous material strength.

The industrial and communications departments have started acting in this way in the last few years. At their current meeting these departments have now summed up their experience and put forward new measures. They will certainly achieve fresh results.

Lin Piao

March 11, 1966

CHAPTER IV

Documents Proclaiming the Great Proletarian Cultural Revolution

The "Decision Concerning the Great Proletarian Cultural Revolution," drawn up under the personal direction of Mao Tse-tung at the 11th plenary session of the 8th CCP Central Committee which took place during the first twelve days of August, 1966, gives detailed guidance on how the current cultural revolution should be carried out.

The 16-point decision is described in official releases reproduced in this section as the programme of the GPCR, a document which applies in the main what is called the mass line of "from the masses and to the masses."

In theory and in practice, this mass line is espoused by Mao Tse-tung in launching the GPCR as he did in previous revolutions. It is the line of any revolutionary movement in China to get the masses fully aroused and organised. It is the line of mass campaigns of criticism and struggle

*against old ways of doing things
through the extensive use of "big-
character posters" in the course
of the GPCR so the revolution
may be kept alive.*

*This is essentially what Mao
Tse-tung's 16-point decision seeks
to achieve—an illusion of providing a popular basis for the revolution and making it more readily
acceptable to the masses. — Ed.*

A revolution is not a dinner
party... it cannot be so refined, so
leisurely and gentle, so temperate,
kind, courteous, restrained and magnanimous.

A revolution is an insurrection,
an act of violence by which one class
overthrows another.

— Mao Tse-tung

*(Report on an Investiga-
tion of the Peasant Movement
in Hunan, March 1927)*

CCP Central Committee's Decision on the Great Proletarian Cultural Revolution

(Adopted on August 8, 1966)

1. A New Stage in the Socialist Revolution

The Great Proletarian Cultural Revolution now unfolding is a great revolution that touches people to their very souls and constitutes a new stage in the development of the socialist revolution in our country, a stage which is both broader and deeper.

At the 10th Plenary Session of the 8th Central Committee of the Party, Comrade Mao Tse-tung said: "To overthrow a political power, it is always necessary first of all to create public opinion, to do work in the ideological sphere. This is true for the revolutionary class as well as for the counter-revolutionary class." This thesis of Comrade Mao Tse-tung's has been proved entirely correct in practice.

Although the bourgeoisie has been overthrown, it is still trying to use the old ideas, culture, customs and habits of the exploiting classes to corrupt the masses, capture their minds and endeavour to stage a come-back. The proletariat must do the exact opposite: it must meet head-on every challenge of the bourgeoisie in the ideological field and use the new ideas, culture, customs and habits of the proletariat to change the mental outlook of the whole of society. At present, our objective is to struggle against and overthrow those persons in authority who are taking the capitalist road, to criticise and repudiate the reactionary bourgeois academic "authorities" and the ideology of the bourgeoisie and all other exploiting classes and to transform education, literature and art and all other parts of the superstructure not in correspondence with the socialist economic base, so as to facilitate the consolidation and development of the socialist system.

2. The Main Current and the Twists and Turns

The masses of the workers, peasants, soldiers, revolutionary intellectuals and revolutionary cadres form the main force in this great cultural revolution. Large numbers of revolutionary young people, previously unknown, have become courageous and daring pathbreakers. They are vigorous in action and intelligent. Through the media of big-character posters and great debates, they argue things out, expose and criticise thoroughly, and launch resolute attacks on the open and hidden representatives of the bourgeoisie. In such a great revolutionary movement, it is hardly avoidable that they should show shortcomings of one kind or another; however, their general revolutionary orientation has been correct from the beginning. This is the main current in the Great Proletarian Cultural Revolution. It is the general direction along which this revolution continues to advance.

Since the cultural revolution is a revolution, it inevitably meets with resistance. This resistance comes chiefly from those in authority who have wormed their way into the Party and are taking the capitalist road. It also comes from the force of habits from the old society. At present, this resistance is still fairly strong and stubborn. But after all, the Great Proletarian Cultural Revolution is an irresistible general trend. There is abundant evidence that such resistance will be quickly broken down once the masses become fully aroused.

Because the resistance is fairly strong, there will be reversals and even repeated reversals in this struggle. There is no harm in this. It tempers the proletariat and other working people, and especially the younger generation, teaches them lessons and gives them experience, and helps them to understand that the revolutionary road zigzags and does not run smoothly.

3. Put Daring Above Everything Else and Boldly Arouse the Masses

The outcome of this great cultural revolution will be determined by whether or not the Party leadership dares boldly to arouse the masses.

Currently, there are four different situations with regard to the leadership being given to the movement of cultural revolution by Party organisations at various levels:

1. There is the situation in which the persons in charge of Party organisations stand in the van of the movement and dare to arouse the masses boldly. They put daring above everything else, they are dauntless Communist fighters and good pupils of Chairman Mao. They advocate the big-character posters and great debates. They encourage the masses to expose every kind of ghost and monster and also to criticise the shortcomings and errors in the work of the persons in charge. This correct kind of leadership is the result of putting proletarian politics in the forefront and Mao Tse-tung's thought in the lead.

2. In many units, the persons in charge have a very poor understanding of the task of leadership in this great struggle, their leadership is far from being conscientious and effective, and they accordingly find themselves incompetent and in a weak position. They put fear above everything else, stick to outmoded ways and regulations, and are unwilling to break away from conventional practices and move ahead. They have been taken unawares by the new order of things, the revolutionary order of the masses, with the result that their leadership lags behind the situation, lags behind the masses.

3. In some units, the persons in charge, who made mistakes of one kind or another in the past, are even more prone to put fear above everything else, being afraid that the masses will catch them out. Actually, if they make serious self-criticism and accept the criticism of the masses, the Party and the masses will make allowances for their mistakes. But if the persons in charge don't, they will continue to make mistakes and become obstacles to the mass movement.

4. Some units are controlled by those who have wormed their way into the Party and are taking the capitalist road. Such persons in authority are extremely afraid of being exposed by the masses and therefore seek every possible pretext to suppress the mass movement. They resort to such tactics as shifting the targets for attack and turning black into white in an attempt to lead the movement astray. When they find themselves very isolated and no longer able to carry on as before, they resort still more to intrigues, stabbing people in the back, spreading rumours, and blurring the distinction between revolution and counter-revolution as much as they can, all for the purpose of attacking the revolutionaries.

What the Central Committee of the Party demands of the Party

397

committees at all levels is that they persevere in giving correct leadership, put daring above everything else, boldly arouse the masses, change the state of weakness and incompetence where it exists, encourage those comrades who have made mistakes but are willing to correct them to cast off their mental burdens and join in the struggle, and dismiss from their leading posts all those in authority who are taking the capitalist road and so make possible the recapture of the leadership for the proletarian revolutionaries.

4. Let The Masses Educate Themselves in the Movement

In the Great Proletarian Cultural Revolution, the only method is for the masses to liberate themselves, and any method of doing things in their stead must not be used.

Trust the masses, rely on them and respect their initiative. Cast out fear. Don't be afraid of disturbances. Chairman Mao has often told us that revolution cannot be so very refined, so gentle, so temperate, kind, courteous, restrained and magnanimous. Let the masses educate themselves in this great revolutionary movement and learn to distinguish between right and wrong and between correct and incorrect ways of doing things.

Make the fullest use of big-character posters and great debates to argue matters out, so that the masses can clarify the correct views, criticise the wrong views and expose all the ghosts and monsters. In this way the masses will be able to raise their political consciousness in the course of the struggle, enhance their abilities and talents, distinguish right from wrong and draw a clear line between ourselves and the enemy.

5. Firmly Apply the Class Line of the Party

Who are our enemies? Who are our friends? This is a question of the first importance for the revolution and it is likewise a question of the first importance for the great cultural revolution.

Party leadership should be good at discovering the Left and developing and strengthening the ranks of the Left; it should firmly rely on the revolutionary Left. During the movement this is the only way to isolate the most reactionary rightists thoroughly, win over the middle and unite with the great majority so that by the end of the movement we shall achieve the unity of more than 95 per cent of the cadres and more than 95 per cent of the masses.

Concentrate all forces to strike at the handful of ultra-reactionary bourgeois rightists and counter-revolutionary revisionists, and expose and criticise to the full their crimes against the Party, against socialism and against Mao Tse-tung's thought so as to isolate them to the maximum.

The main target of the present movement is those within the Party who are in authority and are taking the capitalist road.

The strictest care should be taken to distinguish between the anti-Party, anti-socialist rightists and those who support the Party and socialism but have said or done something wrong or have written some bad articles or other works.

The strictest care should be taken to distinguish between the reactionary bourgeois scholar despots and "authorities" on the one hand and people who have the ordinary bourgeois academic ideas on the other.

6. Correctly Handle Contradictions among the People

A strict distinction must be made between the two different types of contradictions: those among the people and those between ourselves and the enemy. Contradictions among the people must not be made into contradictions between ourselves and the enemy; nor must contradictions between ourselves and the enemy be regarded as contradictions among the people.

It is normal for the masses to hold different views. Contention between different views is unavoidable, necessary and beneficial. In the course of normal and full debate, the masses will affirm what is right, correct what is wrong and gradually reach unanimity.

The method to be used in debates is to present the facts, reason things out, and persuade through reasoning. Any method of forcing a minority holding different views to submit is impermissible. The minority should be protected, because sometimes the truth is with the minority. Even if the minority is wrong, they should still be allowed to argue their case and reserve their views.

When there is a debate, it should be conducted by reasoning, not by coercion or force.

In the course of debate, every revolutionary should be good at thinking things out for himself and should develop the Communist spirit of daring to think, daring to speak and daring to act. On the premise that they have the same general orientation, revolutionary comrades should, for the sake of strengthening unity, avoid endless debate over side issues.

7. Be on Guard against Those Who Brand the Revolutionary Masses As "Counter-Revolutionaries"

In certain schools, units, and work teams of the cultural revolution, some of the persons in charge have organised counter-attacks against the masses who put up big-character posters criticising them. These people have even advanced such slogans as: opposition to the leaders of a unit or a work team means opposition to the Central Committee of the Party, means opposition to the Party and socialism, means counter-revolution. In this way it is inevitable that their blows will fall on some really revolutionary activists. This is an error on matters of orientation, an error of line, and is absolutely impermissible.

A number of persons who suffer from serious ideological errors, and particularly some of the anti-Party and anti-socialist rightists, are taking advantage of certain shortcomings and mistakes in the mass movement to spread rumours and gossip, and engage in agitation, deliberately branding some of the masses as "counter-revolutionaries." It is necessary to beware of such "pick-pockets" and expose their tricks in good time.

In the course of the movement, with the exception of cases of active counter-revolutionaries where there is clear evidence of crimes such as murder, arson, poisoning, sabotage or theft of State secrets, which should be handled in accordance with the law, no measures should be taken against students at universities, colleges, middle schools and primary schools because of problems that arise in the movement. To prevent the struggle from being diverted from its main target, it is not allowed, under whatever pretext, to incite the masses or the students to struggle against each other. Even proven rightists should be dealt with on the merits of each case at a later stage of the movement.

8. The Question of Cadres

The cadres fall roughly into the following four categories:
(1) good;

(2)   comparatively good;

(3)   those who have made serious mistakes but have not become anti-Party, anti-socialist rightists;

(4)   the small number of anti-Party, anti-socialist rightists.

In ordinary situations, the first two categories (good and comparatively good) are the great majority.

The anti-Party, anti-socialist rightists must be fully exposed, refuted, overthrown and completely discredited and their influence eliminated.   At the same time, they should be given a chance to turn over a new leaf.

9.   Cultural Revolutionary Groups, Committees and Congresses

Many new things have begun to emerge in the Great Proletarian Cultural Revolution.   The cultural revolutionary groups, committees and other organisational forms created by the masses in many schools and units are something new and of great historic importance.

These cultural revolutionary groups, committees and congresses are excellent new forms of organisation whereby the masses educate themselves under the leadership of the Communist Party.   They are an excellent bridge to keep our Party in close contact with the masses. They are organs of power of the proletarian cultural revolution.

The struggle of the proletariat against the old ideas, culture, customs and habits left over by all the exploiting classes over thousands of years will necessarily take a very, very long time.   Therefore, the cultural revolutionary groups, committees and congresses should not be temporary organisations but permanent, standing mass organisations.   They are suitable not only for colleges, schools and government and other organisations, but generally also for factories, mines, other enterprises, urban districts and villages.

It is necessary to institute a system of general elections, like that of the Paris Commune, for electing members to the cultural revolutionary groups and committees and delegates to the cultural revolutionary congresses.   The lists of candidates should be put forward by the revolutionary masses after full discussion, and the elections should be held after the masses have discussed the lists over and over again.

The masses are entitled at any time to criticise members of the cultural revolutionary groups and committees and delegates elected to the cultural revolutionary congresses. If these members or delegates prove incompetent, they can be replaced through election or recalled by the masses after discussion.

The cultural revolutionary groups, committees and congresses in colleges and schools should consist mainly of representatives of the revolutionary students. At the same time, they should have a certain number of representatives of the revolutionary teaching and administrative staff and workers.

10. Educational Reform

In the Great Proletarian Cultural Revolution a most important task is to transform the old educational system and the old principles and methods of teaching.

In this great cultural revolution, the phenomenon of our schools being dominated by bourgeois intellectuals must be completely changed.

In every kind of school we must apply thoroughly the policy advanced by Comrade Mao Tse-tung of education serving proletarian politics and education being combined with productive labour, so as to enable those receiving an education to develop morally, intellectually and physically and to become labourers with socialist consciousness and culture.

The period of schooling should be shortened. Courses should be fewer and better. The teaching material should be thoroughly transformed, in some cases beginning with simplifying complicated material. While their main task is to study, students should also learn other things. That is to say, in addition to their studies they should also learn industrial work, farming and military affairs, and take part in the struggles of the cultural revolution to criticise the bourgeoisie as these struggles occur.

11. The Question of Criticising by Name in the Press

In the course of the mass movement of the cultural revolution, the criticism of bourgeois and feudal ideology should be well combined with the dissemination of the proletarian world outlook and of Marxism-Leninism, Mao Tse-tung's thought.

Criticism should be organised of typical bourgeois representatives who have wormed their way into the Party and typical reactionary

402

bourgeois academic "authorities," and this should include criticism of various kinds of reactionary views in philosophy, history, political economy and education, in works and theories of literature and art, in theories of natural science, and in other fields.

Criticism of anyone by name in the press should be decided after discussion by the Party committee at the same level, and in some cases submitted to the Party committee at a higher level for approval.

12. Policy Towards Scientists, Technicians and Ordinary Members of Working Staffs

As regards scientists, technicians and ordinary members of working staffs, as long as they are patriotic, work energetically, are not against the Party and socialism, and maintain no illicit relations with any foreign country, we should in the present movement continue to apply the policy of "unity, criticism, unity."† Special care should be taken of those scientists and scientific and technical personnel who have made contributions. Efforts should be made to help them gradually transform their world outlook and their style of work.

13. The Question of Arrangements for Integration with the Socialist Education Movement in City and Countryside

The cultural and educational units and leading organs of the Party and government in the large and medium cities are the points of concentration of the present proletarian cultural revolution.

The great cultural revolution has enriched the socialist education movement in both city and countryside and raised it to a higher level. Efforts should be made to conduct these two movements in close combination. Arrangements to this effect may be made by various regions and departments in the light of the specific conditions.

The socialist education movement now going on in the countryside and in enterprises in the cities should not be upset where the original arrangements are appropriate and the movement is going well, but should continue in accordance with the original arrangements. However, the questions that are arising in the present Great Proletarian Cultural Revolution should be put to the masses for discussion at the proper time, so as to further foster vigorously proletarian ideology and eradicate

403

bourgeois ideology.

In some places, the Great Proletarian Cultural Revolution is being used as the focus in order to add momentum to the socialist education movement and clean things up in the fields of politics, ideology, organisation and economy. This may be done where the local Party committee thinks it appropriate.

14. Take Firm Hold of the Revolution and Stimulate Production

The aim of the Great Proletarian Cultural Revolution is to revolutionise people's ideology and as a consequence to achieve greater, faster, better and more economical results in all fields of work. If the masses are fully aroused and proper arrangements are made, it is possible to carry on both the cultural revolution and production without one hampering the other, while guaranteeing high quality in all our work.

The Great Proletarian Cultural Revolution is a powerful motive force for the development of the social productive forces in our country. Any idea of counterposing the great cultural revolution to the development of production is incorrect.

15. The Armed Forces

In the armed forces, the cultural revolution and the socialist education movement should be carried out in accordance with the instructions of the Military Commission of the Central Committee of the Party and the General Political Department of the People's Liberation Army.

16. Mao Tse-tung's Thought Is the Guide to Action in the Great Proletarian Cultural Revolution

In the Great Proletarian Cultural Revolution, it is imperative to hold aloft the great red banner of Mao Tse-tung's thought and put proletarian politics in command. The movement for the creative study and application of Chairman Mao Tse-tung's works should be carried forward among the masses of the workers, peasants and soldiers, the cadres and the intellectuals, and Mao Tse-tung's thought should be taken as the guide to action in the cultural revolution.

In this complex great cultural revolution, Party committees at all

404

levels must study and apply Chairman Mao's works all the more conscientiously and in a creative way. In particular, they must study over and over again Chairman Mao's writings on the cultural revolution and on the Party's methods of leadership, such as "On New Democracy," "Talks at the Yenan Forum on Literature and Art," "On the Correct Handling of Contradictions Among the People," "Speech at the Chinese Communist Party's National Conference on Propaganda Work," "Some Questions Concerning Methods of Leadership" and "Methods of Work of Party Committees."

Party committees at all levels must abide by the directions given by Chairman Mao over the years, namely that they should thoroughly apply the mass line of "from the masses, to the masses" and that they should be pupils before they become teachers. They should try to avoid being one-sided or narrow. They should foster materialist dialectics and oppose metaphysics and scholasticism.

The Great Proletarian Cultural Revolution is bound to achieve brilliant victory under the leadership of the Central Committee of the Party headed by Comrade Mao Tse-tung.

(NCNA English service dated August 8, 1966)

Communique of the CCP Central Committee

(Adopted on August 12, 1966)

The 11th Plenary Session of the 8th Central Committee of the Communist Party of China was held in Peking from August 1 to 12, 1966.

The 11th Plenary Session was presided over by Comrade Mao Tse-tung. Members and Alternate Members of the Central Committee attended. Also present were comrades from the regional bureaus of the Central Committee and from the provincial, municipal and autonomous region Party committees; members of the cultural revolution group of the Central Committee; comrades from the relevant departments of the Central Committee and the Government; and representatives of revolutionary teachers and students from institutions of higher learning in Peking.

The 11th Plenary Session after discussion adopts the Decision of the Central Committee of the Chinese Communist Party Concerning the Great Proletarian Cultural Revolution.

The Plenary Session after discussion approves the important policy decisions and measures concerning domestic and international questions adopted by the Political Bureau of the Central Committee since the 10th Plenary Session of the 8th Central Committee in September 1962.

Domestic Situation

At the 10th Plenary Session of the 8th Central Committee, Comrade Mao Tse-tung made a correct analysis of the situation at that time and once again stressed the theory of contradictions, classes and class struggle in socialist society. This is the guide for the socialist

406

revolution and socialist construction in our country. Under the leadership of the Chinese Communist Party headed by Comrade Mao Tsetung and under the guidance of the Party's general line of going all out, aiming high and achieving greater, faster, better and more economical results in building socialism, the people of our country have in the past four years unfolded the three great revolutionary movements of class struggle, the struggle for production and scientific experimentation, and have won great victories. The people's communes have been further consolidated and developed. An invigorating revolutionary atmosphere prevails in the whole country and the situation is one in which a new all-round leap forward is emerging.

The national economy of our country is developing steadily and soundly. The policy of readjustment, consolidation, filling out and raising of standards advanced by the Party's Central Committee has already been successfully carried out. The 3rd Five-Year Plan started this year. On the industrial front, not only have big increases been registered in the output and variety of products, but their quality has also greatly improved. On the agricultural front, there have been good harvests for four successive years. The market is thriving and prices are stable. The success of the three nuclear tests is a concentrated expression of the new level reached in the development of China's science, technology and industry.

During the past few years, an extensive socialist education movement has unfolded in the rural areas, the cities and the army. At present, a great proletarian cultural revolution unprecedented in history is developing in our country. The mass movement in which workers, peasants, soldiers, revolutionary intellectuals and cadres creatively study and apply Comrade Mao Tse-tung's works has ushered in a new era of direct mastery and application of Marxism-Leninism by the labouring people.

The Plenary Session fully approves the May 20, 1963 Decision of the Central Committee of the Chinese Communist Party on Some Problems in Current Rural Work (Draft). It fully approves the January 14, 1965 summary minutes of discussion at the National Working Conference called by the Political Bureau of the Central Committee of the Chinese Communist Party: Some Current Problems Raised in the Socialist Education Movement in the Rural Areas, that is, the 23-article document. These two documents were drawn up under the personal leadership of Comrade Mao Tse-tung and have been our people's powerful ideological weapon in carrying out the socialist revolution. We should continue to act in accordance with the two above-mentioned documents and, in combination with the Great Proletarian Cultural Revolution, carry through to the end the "four clean-ups" movement in both rural and urban areas, that is, the socialist education movement to clean up politics, ideology, organisation and economy.

The Plenary Session fully approves the series of brilliant policies of decisive and fundamental importance put forward by Comrade Mao Tse-tung over the past four years. These policies consist mainly of the following:

On the question of applying the principle of democratic centralism and carrying forward and developing the revolutionary tradition of the mass line;

On the question of raising and training successors in the proletarian revolutionary cause;

On the call for industrial enterprises to learn from the Tach'ing Oilfield, for agricultural units to learn from the Tachai Production Brigade, for the whole country to learn from the People's Liberation Army, and for strengthening political and ideological work;

On the strategic principle of preparedness against war, preparedness against natural calamities and everything for the people;

On the question of breaking down foreign conventions and following our own road of industrial development;

On the question of system and deployment in economic construction and national defence construction;

On the call for the whole Party to grasp military affairs and for everybody to be a soldier;

On the question of planning and arrangements for the gradual mechanisation of agriculture; and

On the call for the People's Liberation Army and all factories, villages, schools, commercial departments, service trades and Party and government organisations to become great schools of revolution.

The Plenary Session stresses that the series of directives by Comrade Mao Tse-tung concerning the Great Proletarian Cultural Revolution are the guide to action in our country's present cultural revolution; they constitute an important development of Marxism-Leninism.

The Plenary Session holds that the key to the success of this great cultural revolution is to have faith in the masses, rely on them, boldly arouse them and respect their initiative. It is therefore imperative

408

to persevere in the line of "from the masses, to the masses." Be pupils of the masses before becoming their teachers. Dare to make revolution and be good at making revolution. Don't be afraid of disturbances. Oppose the taking of the bourgeois stand, the shielding of rightists, attacks on the Left and repression of the Great Proletarian Cultural Revolution. Oppose the creation of a lot of restrictions to tie the hands of the masses. Don't be overlords or stand above the masses, blindly ordering them about.

Give enthusiastic support to the revolutionary Left, take care to strive and unite with all those who can be united and concentrate our forces to strike at the handful of anti-Party, anti-socialist bourgeois rightists.

The Plenary Session holds that the series of questions advanced by Comrade Mao Tse-tung over the past four years concerning socialist revolution and socialist construction have greatly accelerated the development and success of the socialist cause in our country. These questions are of most profound and far-reaching significance for consolidating the dictatorship of the proletariat and the socialist system in our country, for preventing revisionist usurpation of the Party and State leadership, for preventing the restoration of capitalism, for ensuring that our country adheres to proletarian internationalism and actively supports the revolutionary struggles of the peoples of the world and for ensuring our country's gradual transition to communism in the future.

International Situation

The 11th Plenary Session of the 8th Central Committee holds that the present situation as regards the struggle of Marxist-Leninists and revolutionary people throughout the world against imperialism, reaction and modern revisionism is excellent. We are now in a new era of world revolution. All political forces are undergoing a process of great upheaval, great division and great reorganisation. The revolutionary movement of the people in all countries, and particularly in Asia, Africa and Latin America, is surging vigorously forward. Despite the inevitable zigzags and reversals in the development of the international situation, the general trend of imperialism heading for total collapse and socialism advancing to world-wide victory is unalterable. US imperialism and its lackeys in various countries cannot avert their doom by brutally suppressing and wildly attacking the masses of the revolutionary people, or by bribing and deceiving them. On the contrary, this only serves to give further impetus to the revolutionary awakening of all peoples. The activities of US imperialism and its stooges in various countries against the people and against revolution are giving impetus to the revolutionary activities of all peoples. US imperialism and its stooges in various countries appear to be powerful but are actually very weak. Taking the long view, they are all paper tigers.

The new leading group of the Communist Party of the Soviet Union has inherited Khrushchev's mantle and is practising Khrushchev revisionism without Khrushchev. Their line is one of safeguarding imperialist and colonialist domination in the capitalist world and restoring capitalism in the socialist world. The leading group of the CPSU has betrayed Marxism-Leninism, betrayed the great Lenin, betrayed the road of the Great October Revolution, betrayed proletarian internationalism, betrayed the revolutionary cause of the international proletariat and of the oppressed peoples and oppressed nations, and betrayed the interests of the great Soviet people and the people of the socialist countries. They revile the Communist Party of China as being "dogmatic," "sectarian" and "Left adventurist." In fact, what they are attacking is Marxism-Leninism itself. They are uniting with imperialism headed by the United States and the reactionaries of various countries and forming a new "Holy Alliance" against communism, the people, revolution and China. But this counter-revolutionary "Holy Alliance" is doomed to bankruptcy and is already in the process of disintegration.

The Plenary Session holds that our Party's comprehensive public criticisms of Khrushchev revisionism over the last few years have been entirely correct and necessary. The Proposal Concerning the General Line of the International Communist Movement advanced by the Central Committee of the Communist Party of China on June 14, 1963 is a programmatic document. This document drawn up under the personal leadership of Comrade Mao Tse-tung and the nine comments by the Editorial Departments of *Jen-min Jih-pao* and *Hung-ch'i* on the open letter of the Central Committee of the CPSU, the article "A Comment on the March Moscow Meeting," Comrade Lin Piao's "Long Live the Victory of People's War," etc., give scientific Marxist-Leninist analyses of a series of important questions concerning the world revolution of our time and are powerful ideological weapons against imperialism and modern revisionism.

The Plenary Session maintains that to oppose imperialism, it is imperative to oppose modern revisionism. There is no middle road whatsoever in the struggle between Marxism-Leninism and modern revisionism. A clear line of demarcation must be drawn with respect to the modern revisionist groups whose centre is the leadership of the CPSU, and it is imperative resolutely to expose their true features as scabs. It is impossible to have "united action" with them.

The Plenary Session points out that proletarian internationalism is the supreme principle guiding China's foreign policy. The Session warmly supports the just struggle of the Asian, African and Latin American peoples against imperialism headed by the United States and its stooges and also supports the revolutionary struggles of the people of all countries.

The Plenary Session most strongly condemns US imperialism for its crime of widening its war of aggression against Vietnam. The Session most warmly and most resolutely supports the Appeal to the People of the Whole Country issued by Comrade Ho Chi Minh, President of the Democratic Republic of Vietnam, and firmly supports the Vietnamese people in fighting to the end until final victory is achieved in their war against US aggression and for national salvation. The Plenary Session fully agrees to all the measures already taken and all actions to be taken as decided upon by the Central Committee of the Party and the Government in consultation with the Vietnamese side concerning aid to Vietnam for resisting US aggression.

The Plenary Session severely denounces the Soviet revisionist leading group for its counter-revolutionary two-faced policy of sham support but real betrayal on the question of Vietnam's resistance to US aggression.

The Plenary Session holds that US imperialism is the most ferocious common enemy of the peoples of the whole world. In order to isolate US imperialism to the maximum and deal it blows, the broadest possible international united front must be established against US imperialism and its lackeys. The Soviet revisionist leading group is pursuing a policy of Soviet-US collaboration for world domination and has been actively serving US imperialism by conducting splittist, disruptive and subversive activities within the international communist movement and the national liberation movement. They cannot of course be included in this united front.

We must unite with all the people in the world who are against imperialism and colonialism, and carry the struggle against US

411

imperialism and its lackeys through to the end.

Together with all the revolutionary Marxist-Leninists of the world, we must carry the struggle against modern revisionism through to the end and push forward the revolutionary cause of the international proletariat and the people of the world.

Combat Revisionism by Upholding Mao Tse-tung's Thought

The 11th Plenary Session of the 8th Central Committee emphasises that the intensive study of Comrade Mao Tse-tung's works by the whole Party and the whole nation is an important event of historic significance. Comrade Mao Tse-tung is the greatest Marxist-Leninist of our era. Comrade Mao Tse-tung has inherited, defended and developed Marxism-Leninism with genius, creatively and in an all-round way, and has raised it to a completely new stage. Mao Tse-tung's thought is Marxism-Leninism of the era in which imperialism is heading for total collapse and socialism is advancing to world-wide victory. It is the guiding principle for all the work of our Party and country. The Plenary Session holds that Comrade Lin Piao's call on the People's Liberation Army to launch a mass movement in the army to study Comrade Mao Tse-tung's works has set a brilliant example for the whole Party and the whole nation. The most reliable and fundamental guarantee against revisionism and the restoration of capitalism and for the victory of our socialist and Communist cause is to arm the masses of workers, peasants, soldiers, revolutionary intellectuals and cadres with Mao Tse-tung's thought and to promote the revolutionising of people's ideology. The method of studying Comrade Mao Tse-tung's works with problems in mind, studying and applying his works in a creative way, combining study with practice, studying first what is urgently needed so as to get quick results, and of making great efforts in applying what one studies has proved effective and universally suitable and should be further popularised throughout the Party and the country.

The Communist Party of China is a great, glorious and correct Party. Founded and fostered by Comrade Mao Tse-tung, ours is a Party armed with Marxism-Leninism, with Mao Tse-tung's thought. Our Party is a proletarian vanguard that integrates theory with practice, forges close links with the masses of the people and has the spirit of earnest self-criticism. It is a proletarian revolutionary Party which has gone through the most fierce, the most arduous, the longest and the most complex struggles in history. Our people is a great people. Our country is a great country. Our army is a great army. We firmly believe that under the leadership of our great leader, Comrade Mao Tse-tung, and the Communist Party of China, the armymen and civilians of the whole country, relying on their own efforts and working energetically, will surely be able to surmount all difficulties and obstacles and fulfil the mission given by history, and will surely not disappoint the expectations of the revolutionary people of the world.

The 11th Plenary Session of the 8th Central Committee calls on all the workers, people's commune members, commanders and fighters of the People's Liberation Army, revolutionary cadres, revolutionary intellectuals, revolutionary teachers and students and scientific and technical personnel of the country to raise still higher the great red banner of Mao Tse-tung's thought, unite with all those who can be united, surmount the resistance coming from various directions, from the counter-revolutionary revisionists and the "Left" and Right opportunists, overcome difficulties, shortcomings and mistakes, cleanse the dark spots in the Party and society, carry the Great Proletarian Cultural Revolution through to the end, carry the socialist revolution through to the end, and strive to fulfil the 3rd Five-Year Plan and build China into a powerful socialist country.

We must be fired with great, lofty proletarian aspirations and dare to break paths unexplored by people before and scale heights yet unclimbed. We must do a good job of building a socialist China, which has a quarter of the world's population, and make it an impregnable State of the proletariat that will never change its colour. We must liberate Taiwan. We must heighten our vigilance a hundredfold and guard against surprise attacks from US imperialism and its accomplices. Should they dare to impose war on us, the 700 million Chinese people under the leadership of Comrade Mao Tse-tung and the Communist Party of China will certainly break the backs of the aggressors and wipe them out resolutely, thoroughly, totally and completely.

(NCNA English service dated August 12, 1966)

413

Other Decisions of the CCP Central Committee

Decision on Reorganisation of CCP Peking Municipal Committee

The Central Committee of the Chinese Communist Party has decided that Comrade Li Hsüeh-feng, First Secretary of the North China Bureau of the Party's Central Committee, be appointed concurrently First Secretary of the Peking Municipal Party Committee, and that Comrade Wu Teh, First Secretary of the Kirin Provincial Party Commi tee, be transferred to the post of Second Secretary of the Peking Municipal Party Committee to reorganise it.

Comrades Li Hsüeh-feng and Wu Teh are already at work at their new posts. The new Peking Municipal Party Committee will directly lead the great socialist cultural revolution in Peking.

(Jen-min Jih-pao, June 4, 1966)

*　　　*　　　*

Decision on Reform of Existing Educational System

Considering that the great cultural revolution is only now developing in the colleges, universities and senior middle schools, a certain period of time will be needed in order to carry this movement through thoroughly and successfully. Bourgeois domination is still deeply rooted and the struggle between the proletariat and the bourgeoisie is very acute in quite a number of universities, colleges and middle schools. A thoroughgoing cultural revolution movement in the higher educational institutions and senior middle schools will have most far-reaching effects on school education in the future. Meanwhile, though it has been constantly improved since liberation, the method of examination and enrolment for the higher educational institutions has failed, in the main, to free itself from the set pattern of the bourgeois system of examination; and such a method is harmful to the implementation of the guiding policy on education formulated by the Central Committee of the Party and Chairman Mao, and to absorption into the higher educational institutions of a still greater number of revolutionary young people from among the workers, peasants and soldiers. This system of examination must be completely reformed. Therefore, time is also needed to study and work out new methods of enrolment.

In view of the above-mentioned situation, the Central Committee of the Chinese Communist Party and the State Council have decided to postpone for half a year the 1966 enrolment into the higher educational institutions so that, on the one hand, they and the senior middle schools will have enough time to carry out the cultural revolution thoroughly and successfully and, on the other hand, there will be adequate time for making all preparations for the implementation of a new method of enrolment.

In order that enrolment and the opening of a new semester in the senior middle schools shall not be affected, the students graduating from senior middle schools this term in schools where the cultural revolution is still under way should be properly accommodated and their time-table arranged by the school authorities so that the movement may be carried out thoroughly and successfully; in the case of students in schools where the movement is completed before enrolment into the higher educational institutions has begun, their schools should organise them to participate in productive labour in the countryside or in the factories.

(*Jen-min Jih-pao*, June 13, 1966)

*　　　*　　　*

Decision on Large-scale Publication of Mao Tse-tung's Works

The Central Committee of the Chinese Communist Party has decided to speed up the large-scale publication of Chairman Mao Tse-tung's works in order to meet the urgent needs of the broad masses of

415

the people in studying Mao Tse-tung's thought. It has called on the broad masses of cadres and workers and staff members of publication, printing and distribution departments throughout the country to mobilise immediately, make all-out efforts and take the publication and distribution of Chairman Mao's works as their foremost task. Following the speed-up in the mass printing of Chairman Mao's works this year and next, these works, for which there has been a pressing demand by the broad masses, will gradually come to be in plentiful supply throughout the country.

Recently the Ministry of Culture, in accordance with the directive of the Party's Central Committee, convened a national conference on the work of printing and distributing Chairman Mao's works, at which concrete plans for their large-scale printing and plans for their distribution were mapped out. Thirty-five million sets of the *Selected Works of Mao Tse-tung* will be printed and distributed this year and next. The collections A and B of *Selected Readings From Mao Tse-tung's Works,* and Chairman Mao's works in pamphlet form will in general be printed in the provinces, municipalities and autonomous regions so that gradually, over this year and next year, they will fully meet the needs of the broad masses.

That the Central Committee of the Chinese Communist Party has decided to speed up the large-scale publication and distribution of Chairman Mao's works is an event of tremendous historic significance in China's political life, an event bringing great joy to the people of the whole country, and yet another victory for the current great proletarion cultural revolutionary movement.

(*Jen-min Jih-pao,* August 8, 1966)

CHAPTER V

The Group in Charge of the Cultural Revolution

On July 10, 1966 the New China · News Agency, reporting those present at a banquet given at the end of the Afro-Asian Writers' Emergency Meeting the previous day, referred to Ch'en Po-ta as the "leader of the group in charge of the cultural revolution under the Party's Central Committee." This was the first indication of the formation of the Party's Cultural Revolution Group and of the importance of Ch'en Po-ta's role in organising and directing the revolution.

In this section basic biographic information on the key members of the Cultural Revolution Group is provided and speeches by Ch'en Po-ta and Chiang Ch'ing at the "cultural revolution rally of revolutionary literary and art workers" are included to throw light on the part played by the Central Committee's steering group for the GPCR.
—Ed.

417

The cultural revolution groups...
are excellent new forms of organisation
whereby the masses educate themselves
under the leadership of the Communist
Party. They are organs of power of
the proletarian cultural revolution.

*(Decision of the CCP
Central Committee Concerning
the Great Proletarian Cultural
Revolution, August 8, 1966.)*

Cultural Revolution Group Named

The composition of the CCP Central Committee's Cultural Revolution Group, not officially announced but reported by the Peking correspondent of *Asahi Shimbun*, throws important light on the rapid rise of four leading members of the steering Cultural Revolution Group in the Party hierarchy during the current Great Proletarian Cultural Revolution.

The inclusion of a Deputy Propaganda Director of the Central Committee and the editorial staff of its theoretical journal in the steering group for the GPCR indicates a bid to control the Party's mass-media machinery in uniting the masses in support of the GPCR.

The formation of the Cultural Revolution Group, described in official releases as "an organ of power of the cultural revolution," provided the GPCR with formal leadership within the framework of Party organisation and thus brought order at a time when the "cultural revolution" in many aspects appeared to have got out of hand.—Ed.

The wall posters put up on the streets of Peking on November 22, 1966 introduced for the first time the names of 17 members of the group in charge of the cultural revolution under the CCP Central Committee.

Reporting this, the Asahi Shimbun of November 23, 1966 disclosed that most of the editors of *Hung-ch'i,* the CCP Central Committee's theoretical journal, and people related to the People's Liberation Army, in addition to the secretaries of various regional bureaus of the CCP Central Committee, were part of this group.

The names of the 17 members of the Cultural Revolution Group are as follows:

Head of the Group	Ch'en Po-ta
First deputy head of the Group	Chiang Ch'ing
Adviser	T'ao Chu
Adviser	K'ang Sheng
Deputy head of the Group	Wang Jen-chung
Deputy head of the Group	Liu Chih-chien

419

Deputy head of the Group .. .. .. Chang Ch'un-ch'iao
The following ten persons are all ordinary members:

Chang P'ing-hua

Wang Li

Kuan Feng

Ch'i Pen-yü

Mu Hsin

Yao Wen-yüan

Hsieh Ch'ang-hou

Liu Wei-chen

Cheng Chi-ch'iao

Yang Chih-lin

Ch'en Po-ta (陳伯達)

Standing Committee member, Political Bureau, CCP Central Committee; deputy director, Propaganda Department, CCP Central Committee; member, Political Bureau, CCP Central Committee; vice-chairman, State Planning Commission; chief editor, *Hung-ch'i*; member, Standing Committee, 4th Chinese People's Political Consultative Conference; vice-president, Chinese Academy of Sciences.

A Party theoretician of long standing, Ch'en Po-ta joined the Chinese Communist Party in 1927 and shortly afterwards went to Moscow, where he studied at the Sun Yat-Sen University. In the early 1930s he returned to Peking, where he studied Communist theories and taught history at the China University. With the outbreak of the Sino-Japanese war in 1937 he went to Yenan, where he worked for the CCP Central Committee as lecturer in the Party school and chief of the Chinese Problem Research Office, besides being political secretary to Mao Tse-tung himself.

When the Communists took over China in October, 1949, Ch'en was made deputy director of the Propaganda Department of the CCP Central Committee and a vice-president of the Peking Institute of Marxism-Leninism. In 1956 he was elected an alternate member of the Political Bureau of the CCP Central Committee and in 1958 when *Hung-ch'i*, the CCP Central Committee's theoretical journal, was founded, he was named its chief editor.

During the thirties and early forties Ch'en wrote a number of widely-read propaganda works and since 1949 he has published several important theoretical items which examine the characteristics of the Chinese Revolution and the originality of Mao Tse-tung's philosophy. His works include: "The Thought of Mao Tse-tung;" "The Pursuit of Truth;" "On the Cultural Front;" "How to Study Intelligently" and "Mao Tse-tung on the Chinese Revolution."

Ch'en has been closely associated with Mao Tse-tung since the early days in Yenan. He was a member of the entourage when Mao Tse-tung went to Moscow to negotiate the Sino-Soviet Friendship Treaty (December, 1949 — February, 1950). In 1955-56, Ch'en was Mao Tse-tung's spokesman during the drive to accelerate the collectivisation of agriculture. He has also through the years represented the Party line among scientists and social scientists in the CCP Central Committee.

The Introduction to the first issue of *Hung-ch'i* (June 1, 1958) noted that in the transition of capitalism to socialism, the main struggle in the country was one between the proletariat and the bourgeoisie and between socialist and capitalist roads.

To win a total victory in this struggle, the introductory statement declared, the proletariat had to wage a struggle fully, comprehensively and deeply on the ideological front...

"Comrade Mao Tse-tung has constantly taught the whole Party to be good at making close contact with the masses as Lenin did,... resolutely breaking with revisionism and all ideas that deviate from the orbit of Marxism..."

When Chou Yang and Lin Mo-han, deputy directors of the CCP Central Committee's Propaganda Department, were publicly attacked in June, 1966, they were accused of "usurping the leadership of literary and art circles" and "stubbornly insisting on carrying through their bourgeois line on literature and art which is against the Party, against socialism and against Mao Tse-tung's thought." This accusation occurred in the July 1, 1966 issue of *Hung-ch'i,* which reprinted Mao Tse-tung's "Talks at the Yenan Forum on Literature and Art" with an editorial note.

As chief editor of *Hung-ch'i,* Ch'en Po-ta would have had a hand in this attack on his colleagues in the Party's Propaganda Department, for the same *Hung-ch'i* article stressed that "the question of whether one supports or opposes Comrade Mao Tse-tung's line on literature and art establishes the line of demarcation between Marxism-Leninism and revisionism and between revolution and counter-revolution."

The No. 15, 1966 issue of *Hung-ch'i,* edited by Ch'en Po-ta, warned that adherents of the "bourgeois reactionary line," meaning factory workers and trade unions controlled by an unidentified "group of persons in the Party who are in authority and taking the capitalist road," were using force or other means to torpedo the Great Proletarian Cultural Revolution.

Unless "revolutionary workers" joined forces with "revolutionary students" in pushing the GPCR to a new stage of violence, the article cautioned, victories for Mao Tse-tung's "correct proletarian revolutionary line" could hardly be wrested from the opposition.

Chiang Ch'ing (江青)

First deputy head, CCP Central Committee's Cultural Revolution Group.

Chiang Ch'ing (Madame Mao Tse-tung) was present on the rostrum along with leaders of Party and State and leading members of various departments during the rally on August 18, 1966, and was reported by the New China News Agency as saying to representatives of the Red Guards: "You must unite with the revolutionary Left and further develop the Red Guard organisation." This was the first time that she was known to speak on political matters in public.

On August 31, the occasion of a large rally of revolutionary students and teachers held to express loyalty to Mao Tse-tung and discuss the progress of the cultural revolution, Chiang Ch'ing rode in the second car in the procession immediately behind Mao Tse-tung and she opened the rally, giving what NCNA described as "a proletarian revolutionary salute." She was at this point described as Deputy Head of the Cultural Revolution Group under the Central Committee, and the following day NCNA issued a correction giving her position as the First Deputy Head of the Group.

Until now Chiang Ch'ing has lived by all accounts a modest family life out of the limelight. In 1963 Edgar Snow reported that she had been in poor health for a long time. Visitors have described the simplicity of Mao Tse-tung's home life and have mentioned that his immediate family consisted of two daughters by his present wife and a grown-up son, who is said to work as an engineer in the provinces. In 1958 a nephew, the son of Mao Tse-tung's younger brother Mao Tse-min who was killed in the 1920's by the Kuomintang, was living with the family.

T'ao Chu (陶鑄)

Member, Standing Committee, CCP Central Committee; director, Propaganda Department, CCP Central Committee.

Rising rapidly in the Party hierarchy during the Great Proletarian Cultural Revolution, T'ao Chu attended a mass rally of one million people at Tienanmen Square, Peking, on August 18, 1966 in celebration of the GPCR.

T'ao was listed fourth in the Party hierarchy immediately after Mao Tse-tung, Lin Piao and Chou En-lai since the Red Guard rallies began. He ranked 95th in the CCP Central Committee list issued after the last Party congress eight years ago.

Before June, 1966 T'ao was first secretary of the Central-South Bureau of the CCP Central Committee. He has through the years back to 1958 supported Mao Tse-tung's commune policies. Even in 1960, when stricter commune policies were being relaxed, he criticised those commune cadres who were not following the Party's mass line. In February 1964 an article by him appeared in *Hung-ch'i* on the people's communes, and later on that year he wrote a pamphlet on the people's communes in Kwangtung Province.

In August 1965 T'ao Chu made a speech at the drama festival in Canton declaring that traditional opera should give place to operas on contemporary, revolutionary themes.

Early in 1965 T'ao Chu became a vice-premier of the State Council. He has had little foreign experience during his career, the only known trip abroad being to Moscow for the 22nd Congress of the Communist Party of the Soviet Union in 1961 in the delegation headed by Premier Chou En-lai.

On July 9, 1966 the New China News Agency referred to T'ao as a member of the Secretariat of the CCP Central Committee and as director of its Propaganda Department.

K'ang Sheng (康生)

Member, Political Bureau, CCP Central Committee and its Standing Committee; member, Secretariat, CCP Central Committee; adviser, CCP Central Committee's Cultural Revolution Group; vice-chairman, NPC.

K'ang Sheng, leader of the Chinese delegation to the Albanian Party Congress in November, 1966, has rapidly come into prominence since the GPCR was launched. Before his emergence as a member of the Mao-Lin group, he devoted most of his energies to handling the CCP's relations with foreign communist parties.

423

As an ideologist specialising in dealing with communist parties in other countries, K'ang's activities in that area brought him into contact with communists from Ceylon, Australia, France and Italy.

Addressing a meeting of teachers of Marxism-Leninism and Party propaganda workers on August 17, 1957, K'ang stressed that it was "our honour to guard the doctrine of Marxism-Leninism and the doctrine of the Communist Party." He urged teachers to be clear-headed and overcome the "ideological obstruction" of "demanding that Marxism-Leninism serve their personal interest." Except towards a few rightists, he said, the guiding principle of "unity-criticism-unity"† should be implemented in order to "attain the goal of solving ideological problems."

At the Albanian Party Congress held on November 2, 1966, K'ang was the first foreign delegate to address the meeting.

On China's Great Proletarian Cultural Revolution, he said that "all parts of the superstructure not in correspondence with the socialist economic base are being transformed." He meant that steps had been taken to criticise and repudiate those intellectuals in China who had not followed Mao Tse-tung's teaching that "socialist literature and art should first of all serve the workers, peasants and soldiers."

"All genuine revolutionary Marxist-Leninists must carry the struggle against modern revisionism through to the end," he said.

K'ang praised the Red Guards as "courageous and daring path-breakers," calling the "victory of the GPCR a great victory for Mao Tse-tung's thought."

K'ang's speech was given prominence in the *Jen-min Jih-pao* of November 3, 1966 and in Peking Radio broadcasts.

Wang Jen-chung (王任重), a deputy head of the Cultural Revolution Group, is first secretary of the Central-South Bureau of the CCP Central Committee and councurrently first secretary of the CCP Hunan Provincial Committee.

Liu Chih-chien (劉志堅), another deputy head of the Cultural Revolution Group, holds the office of Deputy Director of PLA's General Political Department.

Chang Ch'un-ch'iao (張春橋), the fourth deputy head of the Cultural Revolution Group, is secretary of the East China Bureau of the CCP Central Committee and concurrently secretary of the CCP Shanghai Municipal Committee.

Members of the Cultural Revolution Group, in the order given in wall posters put up in Peking, include:

- **Chang P'ing-hua** (張平化), Deputy Director of the CCP Central Committee's Propaganda Department.
- **Wang Li** (王力), assistant chief editor of *Hung-ch'i*, theoretical journal of the CCP Central Committee.
- **Kuan Feng** (關鋒), chief editor of *Hung-ch'i*.
- **Ch'i Pen-yu** (戚本禹), chief editor of *Hung-ch'i* and former chief editor of *Wen-hui Pao* of Shanghai which published the article "On the New Historical Play 'Hai Jui Dismissed from Office.'" Publication of this article in a way signalled the official start of the "great socialist cultural revolution."
- **Mu Hsin** (穆欣), chief editor of *Kuang-ming Jih-pao*, Peking.
- **Yao Wen-yüan** (姚文元), Director of the Propaganda Department of the CCP Shanghai Municipal Committee and concurrently chief editor of *Chieh-fang Jih-pao* of Shanghai. Speaking at a meeting in memory of Lu Hsün, called "the great standard-bearer of the proletarian cultural front," on October 31, 1966, Yao said that the GPCR was a continuation of the struggle between the proletarian line for literature and art and the bourgeois line for literature and art of the 1930's represented by Chou Yang. Yao recalled that in February last Lin Piao asked Chiang Ch'ing to conduct a forum on literary and art work in the PLA in order to uphold Mao Tse-tung's thought and defend the Maoist line for literature and art.
- **Hsieh Ch'ang-hou** (謝長厚), Deputy Director of PLA's General Political Department.
- **Liu Wei-chen** (劉維眞), Director of the Propaganda Department of the Southwest Bureau of the CCP Central Committee.
- **Cheng Chi-ch'iao** (鄭季翹), secretary of the Northeast Bureau of the CCP Central Committee.
- **Yang Chih-lin** (楊植霖), secretary of the Southwest Bureau of the CCP Central Committee and concurrently first secretary of the CCP Chinghai Provincial Committee.

Ch'en Po-ta, Chiang Ch'ing Address Cultural Revolution Rally

Speeches given by Ch'en Po-ta and Chiang Ch'ing at the rally of "revolutionary literary and art workers," excerpts of which are reproduced below, hailed the victory won by the Maoist line for the Great Proletarian Cultural Revolution.

These victories, according to the speakers, were seized only after strong resistance to the reform of literary works in general and Peking opera in particular was overcome. The former Propaganda Department of the CCP Central Committee and former officials of the Ministry of Culture were denounced by the speakers for opposing a "revolution" in the fields of literature and stage art.

The cultural revolution rally was a signal for what was called a "general offensive" against the opponents of the Maoist line for literature and art.

In this rally, Ch'en Po-ta was officially listed as one of seven Standing Committee members of the ruling Political Bureau of the CCP Central Committee, replacing one of the three ousted office-holders of the Political Bureau, namely Liu Shao-ch'i, Ch'en Yün and Chu Teh. — Ed.

Literary and Art Workers Hold Cultural Revolution Rally

More than 20,000 revolutionary militants in the field of literature and the arts, from Peking and other parts of China, held a rally on the Great Proletarian Cultural Revolution in the magnificent Great Hall of the People in Peking on the evening of November 28.

It took place in the midst of the excellent situation, immediately following the review of over 11 million members of the mighty army of the cultural revolution, received on eight consecutive occasions, by Chairman Mao Tse-tung, the great teacher, great leader, great supreme commander and great helmsman of the Chinese people, at a time when tremendous victories had been won by the proletarian revolutionary line represented by Chairman Mao.

Comrade Chou En-lai, Standing Committee member of the Political

426

Bureau of the Central Committee of the Chinese Communist Party and Premier of the State Council; Comrade Ch'en Po-ta, Standing Committee member of the Political Bureau and leader of the Cultural Revolution Group under the Party's Central Committee; and Comrade Chiang Ch'ing, first deputy leader of the Cultural Revolution Group under the Party's Central Committee and adviser on cultural work to the Chinese People's Liberation Army, attended the rally and made important speeches. The speeches were warmly applauded.

The rally became a pledge of a general offensive by China's mighty revolutionary contingents in literature and art against the handful of people in authority in literary and art circles who took the capitalist road and against the counter-revolutionary revisionist line in literature and art which they represented.

It is bound to push the Great Proletarian Cultural Revolution forward in the world of literature and art with great vigour and guide the victorious advance of the mighty revolutionary contingents in literature and art throughout China in the direction indicated by Chairman Mao Tse-tung.

Comrade Ch'en Po-ta presided over the rally and delivered an opening address. He was followed by Comrade Chiang Ch'ing.

The rally was also addressed by Hsieh T'ang-chung, head of the Cultural Department of the General Political Department of the Chinese People's Liberation Army. He announced the incorporation into the Chinese People's Liberation Army of the No. 1 Peking Opera Company of Peking (including the Red Guards troupe of the Peking Opera School which took part in the National Day performances), the National Peking Opera Theatre (including the Red Guards troupe of the Chinese Opera School which took part in the National Day performances), the Central Philharmonic Society, and the ballet troupe and the orchestra of the Central Song and Dance Ensemble, and their organisation as constituent parts of the army for political and literary and art work, in accordance with the directive of the Military Commission of the Central Committee of the Party and the decision of the Cultural Revolution Group under the Party Central Committee.

He extended an enthusiastic welcome to all the comrades in these units on behalf of the General Political Department of the PLA, all the commanders and fighters and all the army workers in literature and art.

*   *   *

427

Chiang Ch'ing Named PLA's Cultural Adviser

Comrade Hsieh T'ang-chung also announced the good news of the appointment of Comrade Chiang Ching by the Military Commission of the Party's Central Committee as adviser on cultural work to the Chinese People's Liberation Army. He said: "This decision reflects the great interest in the cultural work of our army taken by our most respected, beloved and great leader Chairman Mao and his close comrade-in-arms, Vice Chairman Lin Piao. Comrade Chiang Ch'ing is an excellent student of Mao Tse-tung's thought, understands it profoundly and has been applying it with great persistence and creativeness. Her appointment is an important decision for strengthening the revolution-isation of our army's cultural work and for making it more militant."

In conclusion, Comrade Hsieh T'ang-chung called on all literary and art workers in the army to study Comrade Chiang Ch'ing's speech conscientiously, apply the proletarian revolutionary line represented by Chairman Mao resolutely and thoroughly and, in accordance with the directives of the Military Commission of the Party's Central Committee and the General Political Department of the PLA, carry the Great Proletarian Cultural Revolution through to the end.

*   *   *

Ch'en Po-ta Speaks at the Rally

In his opening address, Comrade Ch'en Po-ta said:

"Today's meeting is one of great significance. Cultural revolutions in history, in most cases, begin in the field of literature and art. This is true as well of the Great Proletarian Cultural Revolution we are carrying out.

"Mao Tse-tung's thought is the guide for China's Great Proletarian Cultural Revolution. Comrade Mao Tse-tung has creatively developed the Marxist-Leninist theory of literature and art. Using the proletarian world outlook, he has systematically and thoroughly solved the problems on our literary and art front. At the same time, he has systematically and thoroughly blazed a completely new trail for us for the proletarian cultural revolution.

"At the 10th plenary session of the 8th Central Committee of the Chinese Communist Party in 1962, Chairman Mao Tse-tung called for taking a firm hold of the class struggle in the ideological field.

"Following this great call and under the direct guidance of Mao Tse-tung's thought, there was an upsurge in reforming Peking opera, symphonic music, ballet and other art forms— revolutionary reforms designed to make the ancient serve the present, to make the foreign serve China and to weed through the old to create the new. Peking opera and other art forms were used to portray the epic of the heroic struggles of the masses led by the Chinese proletariat.

"This new advance has given Peking opera, ballet, symphonic music and other art forms a new lease of life, making them not only completely new in content but considerably improved in form and different in appearance.

"Plays on contemporary revolutionary themes have appeared on the stage everywhere. This new proletarian literature and art has an unprecedented appeal for the masses.

"The reactionaries and counter-revolutionary revisionists, however, bitterly hate and revile this new literature and art solely because it will greatly enhance the people's political consciousness and greatly strengthen the dictatorship of the proletariat and the socialist system in our country.

"I want to say here that, among the comrades who have persisted in this policy of revolution in literature and art and waged unremitting struggles against the reactionaries and counter-revolutionary revisionists, Comrade Chiang Ch'ing has made outstanding contributions.

"History has blown sky high the dream of the reactionaries and counter-revolutionary revisionists. After the 10th plenary session of the 8th Central Committee of the Party, the revolution in literature and art became the real beginning of our country's Great Proletarian Cultural Revolution.

"The history of literature and art is full of sharp conflicts. The conflicts between the new and the old, between the modern and the ancient, are reflections of the class struggle in society. The bourgeoisie in the period of its revolution used the new literature and art of the time as an important weapon in destroying feudalism.

"Likewise, the proletariat today must use its own new literature and art serving the workers, peasants and soldiers as its weapon in destroying the bourgeoisie and all other exploiting classes.

"After the conquest of political power by the proletariat, the bourgeoisie is not reconciled to quitting the stage of history. Chairman

Mao often points out to us that the overthrown bourgeoisie is trying, by any and all methods, to use the position of literature and art as a seed-bed for corrupting the masses and preparing for the restoration of capitalism. Therefore, our tasks in literature and art are not lighter but heavier. Our leadership on the literary and art front should not be weakened but, on the contrary, strengthened. In order to fulfil their glorious tasks, our revolutionary literary and art organisations must carry the Great Proletarian Cultural Revolution through to the end!"

* * *

Chiang Ch'ing Speaks at the Rally

Comrade Chiang Ch'ing received a thunderous ovation from the entire rally when she went forward to speak. Greeting all comrades and friends in literary and art circles and young Red Guard fighters present, she extended to them proletarian revolutionary salutations.

She described the background which helped her to understand the importance of the Great Proletarian Cultural Revolution. Comrade Chiang said:

"A few years ago, when my fairly systematic contact with certain sections of literature and art began, the first question that arose in my mind was why were plays about ghosts being staged in socialist China? Then also, I was very surprised how insensitive Peking opera was as a means of reflecting reality. But then came "Hai Jui Dismissed from Office," "Li Hui-niang" and other plays showing seriously reactionary political tendencies. And under the fine pretext of 'rediscovering tradition,' many works were written portraying monarchs and officials, scholars and beautiful women. There was great talk throughout the literary and art world about 'famous plays,' 'foreign plays' and 'ancient plays' and it went out of its way to present them. The atmosphere was choked with emphasis on the ancient as against the contemporary, with worship of the foreign and scorn for the Chinese, with praise for the dead and contempt for the living. I began to feel that if our literature and art could not correspond to the socialist economic base, they would inevitably wreck it."

Comrade Chiang went on:

"In the wake of the changing struggle between the new and the old in the political and economic fields over a number of years, new literature and art, countering the old, have also made their appearance. New items have been created even in Peking opera, formerly considered the most difficult to reform. As you all know, Lu Hsün was the great standard-bearer leading the cultural revolution over 30 years ago. More than 20 years ago, Chairman Mao defined the orientation for literature and art as service to the workers, peasants and soldiers and he posed the question of developing the new through critical assimilation of the old.

"To develop the new through critical assimilation of the old means to develop new content which meets the needs of the masses and popular national forms loved by the people. As far as content is concerned, it is in many cases out of the question to weed through the old to let the new emerge. How can we critically assimilate ghosts, gods and religion? I hold it is impossible, because we are atheists and Communists. We do not believe in ghosts and gods at all. Again, for instance, the feudal moral precepts of the landlord class and the moral precepts of the capitalist class, which they considered to be indisputable, were used to oppress and exploit the people. Can we critically assimilate things which were used to oppress and exploit the people? I hold it is impossible, because ours is a country of the dictatorship of the proletariat. We want to build socialism. Our economic base is public ownership. We firmly oppose the system of private ownership whereby people are oppressed and exploited. To sweep away all remnants of the system of exploitation and the old ideas, culture, customs and habits of all the exploiting classes is an important aspect of our Great Proletarian Cultural Revolution.

"As for the old forms of art, our attitude can neither be nihilist nor one of total acceptance. A nation must have its own forms of art, its own artistic characteristics. It is wrong to be nihilist and not take over, in a critical way, the best there is in the art forms and artistic characteristics of our country. On the other hand, it is also wrong to take everything as positive and not develop new things through critical assimilation of the old. As to the outstanding forms of art of the various nations throughout the world, we must act in accordance with Chairman Mao's instructions about 'making foreign things serve China' and work at developing the new through critical assimilation of the old.

"Imperialism is moribund capitalism, parasitic and rotten. Modern revisionism is a product of imperialist policies and a variety of capitalism.

431

They cannot produce any works that are good. Capitalism has a history of several centuries; nevertheless, it has only a pitiful number of 'classics.' They have created some works modelled after the 'classics,' but these are stereotyped and no longer appeal to the people, and are therefore completely on the decline. On the other hand, there are some things that really flood the market, such as rock-and-roll, jazz, strip tease, impressionism, symbolism, abstractionism, fauvism, modernism—there's no end to them—all of which are intended to poison and paralyse the minds of the people. In a word, there is decadence and obscenity to poison and paralyse the minds of the people.

"I'd like to ask: Isn't it necessary to make a revolution and introduce changes if the old literature and art do not correspond to the socialist economic base and the classical artistic forms do not entirely fit the socialist ideological content? (Shouts of Yes! Yes! from the audience) I am sure most comrades and friends will agree it is necessary, while conceding that this involves serious class struggle and is a very painstaking and fairly difficult job. Fear of the difficulties involved was greater than it need have been among people in general because for a long time, the anti-Party, anti-socialist leadership of the old Propaganda Department of the Party Central Committee and the old Ministry of Culture thought up many 'reasons' for opposing this revolution and undermining the changes. There was also another handful of people with ulterior motives who attempted to undermine the revolution and oppose change. The reform of Peking opera, the ballet and symphony music was brought about only after breaking through these difficulties and obstacles."

Comrade Chiang pointed out that the nationwide Great Proletarian Cultural Revolution China had moved into since last May had affected almost the whole sphere of ideology. She touched on the question of the sending of cultural revolution work teams to various organisations and said this was an error in the Great Proletarian Cultural Revolution. And what these work teams had done in the course of their work was still more erroneous! Instead of directing the spearhead against the handful of people in authority within the Party who were taking the capitalist road and against the reactionary academic "authorities," they turned the spearhead against the revolutionary students. The question of what the spearhead of the struggle be directed against was a cardinal question of right and wrong, one of principles of Marxism-Leninism, of Mao Tse-tung's thought. As early as June this year our Chairman Mao made the point that work teams should not be sent out hastily, but a few comrades sent out work teams hastily without asking Chairman Mao's permission.

She added: "But it is necessary to point out that the question at issue is not one of form, of the work team, but one of principles and policy which it follows. In some units no work teams were sent in and the original persons in charge were relied upon to conduct the work, yet mistakes were made there nevertheless. On the other hand, some work teams followed correct principles and policy and did not make mistakes. This helps to illustrate the real question at issue."

Comrade Chiang said: "Chairman Mao received a million revolutionary youngsters on August 18. How well he respected the initiative of the masses, trusted them and cared for them! I felt I had learnt far from enough. Then, afterwards, the young Red Guard fighters turned outward to society and vigorously began destroying the old ideas, culture, customs and habits. We, the comrades of the Cultural Revolution Group under the Party Central Committee, rejoiced. But a few days later, new problems cropped up. We immediately gathered the facts and investigated and were therefore able to keep up with the constantly developing revolutionary situation. This is what I have described as striving to follow Mao Tse-tung's thought closely on the one hand, and striving to catch up with the spirit of daring and courage, the revolutionary rebel spirit, of the young revolutionaries on the other."

Comrade Chiang then concentrated on the great cultural revolution in the No. 1 Peking Opera Company of Peking. She said that this company was the first unit in Peking to undertake the glorious task of reforming Peking opera. Directly addressing the opera company, she said: "Guided by Mao Tse-tung's thought, in a matter of a few years you have indeed achieved good results in the work of creating operas on contemporary revolutionary themes, and you have thus set an example to the whole country in the reform of Peking opera."

She said: "In order to enable plays on contemporary revolutionary themes to be presented at the National Day celebrations, we had many discussions and we supported your performances and opposed the wrong views by which attempts were made to negate your achievements in revolution. We did a certain amount of explanatory work in various circles to enable you to present your 'Sha Chia Pang' (a Peking opera on a contemporary revolutionary theme) and to get on to the stage the

433

Peking operas 'The Red Lantern,' 'Taking the Bandits' Stronghold,' 'Sea Harbour,' and 'Raid on the White Tiger Regiment,' the ballets 'The Red Detachment of Women' and 'The White-Haired Girl,' and the symphony 'Sha Chia Pang.' "

"We explained that these creative works were an important triumph of the Great Proletarian Cultural Revolution and of Chairman Mao's ideas on literature and art in the service of the workers, peasants and soldiers. And, as facts have proved, the broad masses have recognised our achievements. The revolutionary Marxist-Leninists and the revolutionary people all over the world have placed a high evaluation on them. Chairman Mao and his close comrade-in-arms Comrade Lin Piao, Comrade Chou En-lai, Comrade Ch'en Po-ta, Comrade K'ang Sheng and many other comrades have affirmed our achievements and given us great support and encouragement."

She said: "I hope that after we have gone through the struggle and tempering in this Great Proletarian Cultural Revolution, we will continue ceaselessly to integrate ourselves with the workers, peasants and soldiers. In this way, we will surely be able to gain new achievements in the reform of Peking opera and other branches of literature and art! Our task is difficult. But we must bravely shoulder this glorious, but arduous, revolutionary task."

Comrade Chiang said that in the Great Proletarian Cultural Revolution in the No. 1 Peking Opera Company of Peking there was a very sharp and very complicated class struggle, a struggle for power between the proletariat and the bourgeoisie. "You have as yet not exposed and criticised the counter-revolutionary revisionist line of the former Peking Municipal Party Committee in a really penetrating and extensive way," she declared.

"Here it is necessary in all seriousness to point out," she went on, "that certain leading members of the No. 1 Peking Opera Company of Peking have not yet seriously drawn a clear-cut line between themselves and the former Peking Municipal Party Committee. They have neither exposed the crimes of the former Peking Municipal Party Committee in a penetrating way nor made a serious criticism of their own mistakes. They implemented the counter-revolutionary revisionist line of the former Peking Municipal Party Committee. Resorting to double dealing, and by either soft or tough methods, they resisted Chairman Mao's instructions, and by double-faced tactics carried out all kinds of obstruction and sabotage to undermine the reform of Peking opera.

434

They played many infamous tricks in their attacks both on you and on us.

"The heinous crimes in which the former Peking Municipal Party Committee, the old Propaganda Department of the Party's Central Committee and the old Ministry of Culture colluded against the Party and the people must be exposed and liquidated in a thorough-going way. Likewise, the bourgeois reactionary line within our Party which opposes the proletarian revolutionary line of the Party's Central Committee headed by Chairman Mao must be exposed and criticised in a thorough-going way. Otherwise, it will be impossible to safeguard the fruits of our successful revolution.

"Some leading members of the No. 1 Peking Opera Company of Peking must make a clean breast of what they have done and reveal what the others have done in a thorough-going way. This is the only way, and there is no other way out. If they really do so after full criticism by the masses, if they 'repent genuinely and make a fresh start,' they will still be able to take part in the revolution. If they really try to correct their errors and begin anew, if they return to the correct road of the Party, it is still possible for them to strive to become good cadres."

She said: "Since the counter-revolutionary revisionist line of the former Peking Municipal Communist Party Committee, the old Propaganda Department of the Party's Central Committee and the old Ministry of Culture has not yet been thoroughly criticised and repudiated, and since the effects of this counter-revolutionary revisionist line on your company have not yet been wiped out, it is impossible for the Great Proletarian Cultural Revolution to be conducted thoroughly in your company. And there is the possibility that the movement in your company may go astray and certain people with ulterior motives may usurp the leadership. This would have very harmful effects on the future development of your company."

She added: "It is not the case in your company that all the cadres, Party members and Youth League members have made mistakes, or that all the cadres have made the same kind of mistakes. They have to be treated differently, by presenting the facts and reasoning things out, with the attitude of 'learning from past mistakes and avoiding future ones and curing the sickness to save the patient.' They should be allowed to correct their mistakes and devote themselves to the revolution."

She emphasised that in the Great Proletarian Cultural Revolution, the struggle had to be conducted by reasoning and not by coercion or force. There must be no beating of people. "Struggle by coercion or by force can only touch the skin and flesh while struggle by reasoning can touch the soul."

She said: "I suggest that you hold fast to the general orientation in the struggle, to the correct principles and policy formulated by the Central Committee of the Party and Chairman Mao, oppose the handful of people in authority who are taking the capitalist road, gradually expand and strengthen the ranks of the Left in the course of the struggle, and unite with the overwhelming majority, including those who have been misled, and help them on to the correct road."

Referring to the question of "minority" and "majority," Comrade Chiang said one could not talk about a "minority" or "majority" independently of class viewpoint. "It is necessary to see who has grasped the truth of Marxism-Leninism, of Mao Tse-tung's thought, who is really maintaining a proletarian revolutionary stand, who is genuinely carrying out the correct line of Chairman Mao. Separate and concrete analysis should be made with regard to each separate unit."

In conclusion Comrade Chiang said: "I hope that all comrades in the company will raise still higher the great red banner of Mao Tse-tung's thought, put proletarian politics in the forefront, resolutely carry out the proletarian revolutionary line represented by Chairman Mao and thoroughly criticise and repudiate the bourgeois reactionary line, unite on the principled basis of Marxism-Leninism, of Mao Tse-tung's thought, and complete the three tasks — first, of struggling against and crushing those in authority who are taking the capitalist road; second, of criticising and repudiating the reactionary bourgeois academic 'authorities' and bourgeois and all other exploiting class ideology; and third, of transforming education, literature and art and all other parts of the superstructure that do not correspond to the socialist economic base — and that you will make the No. 1 Peking Opera Company of Peking an exemplary revolutionary company which is truly proletarianised and militant!"

(NCNA English releases, December 3, 1966)

CHAPTER VI

The
Birth
of
the
Red
Guards

*The first major rally of "revo-
lutionary students and teachers"
held in Peking on August 18,
1966 to celebrate the Great
Proletarian Cultural Revolution
brought the Red Guards to the
attention of the outside world for
the first time.*

*In this chapter the New
China News Agency, giving the
first official account of the appearance of the Red Guards on
the rostrum of Peking's Tienanmen Square, describes the young
militants as a new "vanguard of
the Great Proletarian Cultural
Revolution." It is followed by an
excerpt from Anna Louise Strong's
"Letter from China," in which the
writer tells of the formation of
the first Red Guard organisation
set up at the end of May 1966 by
the "Left-wing students" of the
middle school attached to Tsinghua
University.—Ed.*

437

There may be thousands of principles of Marxism but in the final analysis they can be summed up in one sentence: Rebellion is justified.

—Mao Tse-tung

(Speech at a Yenan rally celebrating Stalin's 60th birthday, December 1939)

Red Guards Appear at First Mass Peking Rally

In the official account reproduced below, the Red Guards were described as "revolutionary mass organisations" set up by college and secondary school students in Peking to spearhead the Great Proletarian Cultural Revolution.

The mobilisation of a million-strong army of the "revolutionary masses" with Mao Tse-tung's approval, the NCNA report reveals, marked the beginning of a new stage in the mass "cultural revolution" movement that was to engulf the greater part of the country. It was also a signal for turning loose hordes of teenage Red Guards to "smash the old world to smithereens."

In pledging themselves to carry the Great Proletarian Cultural Revolution through to the end, the Red Guards in effect pledged their resolve to answer Lin Piao's call to "sweep away all vermin and remove all obstacles."—Ed.

On August 18, 1966, at a mass rally to celebrate the Great Proletarian Cultural Revolution, Chairman Mao Tse-tung, our great leader, great supreme commander and great helmsman, joined one million revolutionary people from Peking and other parts of the country in the magnificent Tienanmen Square in Peking, the centre of the proletarian revolution and the capital of our great motherland.

At five o'clock in the morning when the sun had just risen above the eastern horizon and had begun shedding its brilliant rays, Chairman Mao arrived at Tienanmen Square which was covered by a vast sea of people and a forest of red flags. There he met the revolutionary people, who even earlier had converged on the square from all sides. He was clad in an olive cotton military uniform, and a red star sparkled on his cap. He walked across Chinshui Bridge in front of Tienanmen Gate into the midst of the masses, firmly shook hands with many of them and waved to all the revolutionary masses in the square.

The square was seething with excitement. People raised their hands overhead and, turning towards Chairman Mao, they jumped up, cheered and clapped. Many clapped so hard their palms became red while many shed tears of joy. Elated, they exclaimed: "Chairman Mao is here! Chairman Mao has come among us!" The multitude in the square shouted at the top of their voice: "Long live, long live Chairman Mao!" The crescendo of cheers shook the sky over the capital.

Our great leader Chairman Mao spent more than six hours with the one million members of the revolutionary masses that morning. He stood side by side with Comrade Lin Piao and reviewed the parade of the one million-strong army of the proletarian cultural revolution. Watching the magnificant march-past, he remarked with gratification to Comrade Lin Piao: "This is a movement of a momentous scale. It has indeed mobilised the masses. It is of very great significance to the revolutionisation of the thinking of the people throughout the country."

Tens of thousands of "Red Guards," wearing red arm bands and brimming over with high spirit and vigour, caught the eye of all present. The "Red Guards" are revolutionary mass organisations set up in the Great Proletarian Cultural Revolution by the capital's college and middle school students. Members pledge that they will remain red vanguards defending Chairman Mao, the Chinese Communist Party and their motherland all their lives. Representatives of the "Red Guards" filled the rostrum on Tienanmen Gate and the reviewing stands on both sides of the gate. Everywhere, on the rostrum, in the square, and on the boulevard running through the square, spirited "Red Guards" kept order at the rally.

During the rally, a "Red Guard" from the Girls' Middle School attached to Peking Normal University mounted the rostrum and put a red arm band of the "Red Guards" on Chairman Mao. The Chairman cordially shook hands with her. "Red Guards" on and off the rostrum were beside themselves with joy. Some of them jumped a foot in the air and exclaimed with great excitement: "Chairman Mao is our supreme commander and we are his soldiers." Some said: "Chairman Mao joins our 'Red Guards.' This is the greatest support and inspiration to us. With Chairman Mao's backing, we have nothing to fear."

One thousand and five hundred student representatives mounted the rostrum to attend the rally together with Party and Government leaders. Chairman Mao and Comrades Lin Piao, Chou En-lai and Chiang Ch'ing received them in groups, talked with them and had pictures taken together with them. When Chairman Mao received them, the students excitedly crowded around him and kept shouting "Long live Chairman Mao!"

The rally began at 7.30 in the morning. As the band played "The East Is Red," Chairman Mao appeared on the rostrum together

440

with Lin Piao and other comrades.   The crowd leapt with joy.   A great many hands, holding "Quotations from Chairman Mao Tse-tung" covered with red plastic jackets, stretched towards Tienanmen Gate.   A million warm hearts flew out to Chairman Mao and a million pairs of eyes sparkling with revolutionary fervour were turned on him.   The crowd became even more excited when they noticed that their respected and beloved leader was clad in a plain cotton uniform.   They said: "We feel Chairman Mao is even closer to us in military uniform.   Chairman Mao always fights together with us."   Some remarked: "We are boundlessly happy to have such a supreme commander as Chairman Mao.   We will always be his good fighters, follow him and make revolution for the rest of our lives."

The rally was presided over by Ch'en Po-ta, member of the Political Bureau of the Central Committee of the Chinese Communist Party and leader of the group in charge of the cultural revolution under the Party's Central Committee.   In this opening address, he said: "Our great leader, great teacher and great helmsman, Chairman Mao, is here today to greet you.   (The crowd cheered Chairman Mao enthusiastically.) Chairman Mao is always with the masses.   His heart is always turned towards them.   Our present Great Proletarian Cultural Revolution is led by Chairman Mao himself.   Today, he has come to meet us.   This is a great inspiration for us.   It will give a tremendous impetus to the great cultural revolution."

Comrade Lin Piao spoke amid stormy applause.   He was followed with a speech by Comrade Chou En-lai.

In the course of the speeches of Comrades Lin Piao and Chou En-lai, the crowd of one million in the square repeatedly raised their arms and shouted: "Long live the Great Proletarian Cultural Revolution!" "Long live the great Chinese Communist Party!" "Long live the great thought of Mao Tse-tung!" and "Long live, long live the great leader Chairman Mao!"

Nieh Yüan-tzu, representative of Peking University, and college and middle school students from Peking, Harbin, Changsha and Nanking also spoke at the rally.   With boundless, profound and sincere feeling for their great leader Chairman Mao and expressing the iron will of millions upon millions of revolutionary teachers and students throughout the country to carry the Great Proletarian Cultural Revolution through to the end and master Mao Tse-tung's thought and hand it on so as to ensure that our impregnable socialist State will never change colour,

441

they declared:

"A Great Proletarian Cultural Revolution without parallel in history is being carried out in our country under the leadership of our great leader Chairman Mao. This is a revolution of world significance. We will smash the old world to smithereens, create a new world and carry the Great Proletarian Cultural Revolution through to the end.

"Sailing the seas depends on the helmsman, the growth of everything depends on the sun, and making revolution depends on Mao Tse-tung's thought. We heartily wish long life to our most respected and beloved great leader Chairman Mao. We shall follow Chairman Mao's teachings, pay attention to State affairs and carry the Great Proletarian Cultural Revolution through to the end. We will certainly follow Chairman Mao's teachings, face the world and brave the storms, and become most reliable successors to the revolutionary cause of the proletariat.

"Chairman Mao is the reddest sun in our hearts. The Chinese people's revolution has never been all tranquil without storms and waves. We shall bear Chairman Mao's teachings firmly in mind, and temper and test ourselves in great storms and stresses. We will defy death to defend the Party's Central Committee and Chairman Mao. We face a mountain of swords and a sea of flames, but we also have a bright beacon light — Mao Tse-tung's thought which will surely guide us to victory.

"Chairman Mao stands among us. This is the happiest and most important moment in our lives. We'll read his works, follow his teachings, act according to his instructions and be his good pupils for the rest of our lives."

(NCNA English release, August 18, 1966)

A Visit to Red Guards' Central Headquarters

In the excerpt from *"Letter from China"* reproduced below, Anna Louise Strong, an American writer now residing in Peking, told of her first-hand impressions of the Red Guards and how Red Guard organisations of "revolutionary students" and students of the "five red categories" came to be formed.

In that article, the writer who visited Yenan in August 1946 on her fifth trip through China, revealed that the Red Guards burst forth and spread all over the country after a big mass rally was held in Peking on August 18, 1966 to review a million-strong army of "proletarian cultural revolutionaries." It was on this occasion that Mao Tse-tung put on the red arm band of the Red Guards, becoming in a symbolic sense their supreme commander.

Mao Tse-tung, according to the writer, defined the future role of the Red Guards as that of a "revolutionary youth organisation legal under the dictatorship of the proletariat" and armed with the thought of Mao Tse-tung. — Ed.

"I Join the Red Guards"

I hadn't the slightest idea that I was going to crash the Red Guards' central headquarters and be admitted to their organisation when I went with Sidney Rittenberg to Tienanmen Square on September 12 in the afternoon. We knew that hundreds of thousands of Red Guards from all over China were pouring into Peking. I saw them in quantities on streets; I heard the sounds of their marching from my quarters in the Peace Committee Compound. I had scores of anecdotes of their achievements and I had also read the slanders in the Western press.

Tienanmen Square was, one heard, a good place to meet them. They all went there to see it and often to be photographed. One might hope to find them in moments of relaxation and pick them up for talk. Sid talks Chinese, and I asked him to go with me. Neither of us dreamed we would visit any kind of headquarters; none had been announced and we didn't know that one existed.

When we reached the square we saw a throng with red arm bands moving into the archway of the Workers' Cultural Palace, part of the old imperial palace with many courtyards. It consisted of youth of both sexes and of ages from 14 upwards in miscellaneous clothing, much of which verged on olive drab in colour and some of which seemed to be old army uniforms borrowed from parents. Several of the tallest walked with more decision than others and appeared to be the new "Red Guard Patrols" which some districts had organised to bring about a common discipline and to expel "fake Red Guards" who secured arm bands for purposes of vandalism.

We joined the throng and entered the long arched passage. As two obvious foreigners with Chao Feng-feng, my interpreter, we were clearly under interested scrutiny of everyone but nobody tried to halt us till we came to a second gate. Here we were at once barred by several persons who had authority; we turned to leave. As we went out Sid suddenly said: "Don't hurry. Somebody has recognised you and they are whispering along the line that you are 'Sze Te-long' to whom Mao gave the interview about the paper tiger.[1] We might get in yet."

Before we reached the Tienanmen gate on our exit, eight or ten Red Patrols came hurrying after us and invited our return. Since the entrance corridor was crowded, they made a wedge to open our way, not barking orders but waving their hands and saying quietly: "Please don't crowd but let the comrades through." Sid noted their "excellent style of work."

We were ushered through one large courtyard after another, all paved with spotlessly swept cement, pleasant with shade trees and lavish with well kept beds of brilliant flowers. Thick fibre mats were stacked about; it seemed a lot of out-of-town guests were sleeping in the courts. One patrol asked: "Shall we go to the reception hall?" Another said: "Shall we go to the reading room; it has plenty of chairs?" I wondered how many buildings they had. But a firm voice replied: "We go to the centre." Sid told me later this made him think we might see Chou En-lai or T'ao Chu, "somebody in command."

In the fourth or fifth courtyard they brought us to a high-roofed structure whose ornate architecture indicated a reception hall of the old palace. In the large inside space a group of young people were having a meeting, that broke up as we appeared. We were received by a young woman whose serious but hospitable manner showed her as one of the experienced leaders. She had a rather chunky figure in a suit that might have once been khaki, now faded to a paler tan. She invited me to sit down next to her; the others quickly rearranged chairs in a circle which, at the end where I sat, soon became four or five chairs deep.

444

There were no upholstered chairs and coffee tables such as are common to reception rooms; these were plain, hard folding cane chairs of which they had a large pile. Instead of a table for the inevitable hospitality of tea, two extra cane chairs were opened in front of us and small white mugs without handles were set upon them and filled with hot water. Clearly they were treating us not as "foreign guests" but as comrades without protocol. So I asked for the name of the place we had entered and of the young people receiving us. They answered these and other questions frankly and with ease.

The place, they said, was the "Liaison Centre" for the Red Guards of middle schools and colleges in all Peking. It was not a "command centre" and had no power to give orders but was a "service centre" to make connections and exchange ideas. It had been set up August 27 on advice of Premier Chou En-lai at a mass meeting attended by 2,000 representatives of the Red Guard organisations all over the city. It had also become a centre to help handle the hundreds of thousands of Red Guards who were flocking to visit Peking from all over the country. It had five departments: propaganda, organisation, supply, protection and a secretariat, with nearly 200 full-time working personnel.

"We are elected by our school organisations and expect to serve a certain time and then be replaced by others, so that more people get the experience," they said.

The young woman who was taking charge said she was deputy head of propaganda, and that the Workers' Cultural Palace had been assigned by the Peking Municipality to their use and added with a touch of pride: "This is all now our territory." She herself was 18 years old, a student in the Drama School which had sent her to the Liaison Centre. Her surname was Hsu, and her given names had been "Ya-ya," meaning "Elegant," but she had changed them to "Chan-hong," or "Fighting Red," as "more suitable to the times."

Others of those who sat nearest were quickly introduced: a youth from the Aviation College, a girl from a part-work, part-study school run by the food trades, and young people of both sexes from various middle schools designated by numbers and from one with a revolutionary name, "Red Crag Middle School." Two stated that they had changed their personal names. A girl named Tsao with the given names of "Fragrant Celery" had changed them to "Look up to Mao." One of the Red Patrols who escorted us in said that his parents had named him "Always Lucky," but he had changed this to "Wen-ke," an abbreviation for "Cultural Revolution."

I asked "Fighting Red" how these names were changed; did they have to register them formally. She replied: "Each one can make his own rebellion about his name."

Our talk proceeded informally and yet with a certain natural order. All of the 30 or 40 young people in our circle were part of the working personnel of the Centre and occasionally one of them volunteered an answer, but most of the replies were channelled through Fighting Red to whom they came up and whispered with some frequency. Early in the talk a small group got up and left the hall and I asked where they were going. "They have to catch a train to Kwangsi" was the casual reply. Since Kwangsi is a province at least two days' distant by rail this seemed worth further comment. So I asked who determined their departure and how many went. Fighting Red replied that Kwangsi Red Guards had asked for people from Peking. "Also we all like to get experience of other provinces." The Liaison Centre had picked out the 59 representatives who were leaving by the express that goes several times a week.

I asked if anyone had any estimate of the number of Red Guards who had come to visit Peking. One of the group guessed: "Probably 600,000." This was interrupted by a youth who sat a little behind me and who flatly announced that there had been 470,000 such visitors. I asked whether this was an estimate or a statistic. He replied that he was the "data man" and he had to meet the visiting groups and help with their supplies. "It's not our own supplies," he volunteered. "The city gives them." (It was clear that 470,000 was a "statistic" but covering only those who contacted the centre from Aug. 27 to Sept. 12.)

"They all want first to see Chairman Mao," he added, "most of them say they won't leave Peking till they see him. They next want to see Peking and the Cultural Revolution in our schools and to exchange experiences."

My request for a brief history of how the Red Guards began was met by considerable data. They began as a movement of Left-wing students to protect themselves against "reactionary" school authorities; they were not at first considered legal but quickly won student support by their daring and the justice of their criticisms. The first organisation is considered to have been that of the middle school attached to Tsinghua University. It began at the end of May but was "under cover" until the new Municipal Party Committee sent a "Work Team" to

446

investigate the situation at the school. Then the Red Guards came out in the open on June 6.

Several other schools were also organising at about the same time under various names: "Red Guards, Red Eagles, Red Banners, Red Flag." Often there were several organisations in the same school with different names and somewhat different ideas. They debated hotly through posters and leaflets. They all tried to promote the Cultural Revolution and the study of Mao's works, so in general they try to get united. However differences still exist in methods and even in ideas. At first none of the organisations was recognised by the school authorities who sometimes even tried to suppress them.

"The big change," said Fighting Red, "was when Chairman Mao had the big August 18 Rally in Tienanmen Square and said he was joining the Red Guards and let us put the arm band on him. We all said Chairman Mao is our Red Commander-in-Chief. Then the Red Guards burst their dykes and spread all over the country. People of all ages want to join, even children and old people."

At first the Red Guards had limited themselves to "students of the five red categories," that is, those whose parents were workers, poor or lower-middle peasants, Liberation Armymen, revolutionary cadres (Party members before 1945), and revolutionary martyrs. This was to guarantee a class basis of a revolutionary type. Later they accepted other members who were personally considered revolutionary. Recently "Red Guards" have been organised in primary schools and also in adult organisations, but the Liaison Centre concerns itself only with student organisations in higher and middle schools.

These organisations also have widened, not by any planning from above but by combinations made by the lower groups for purposes of joint action. No city-wide organisation competent to make plans and issue instructions yet exists, as of September 12. Some organisational unity has been reached at district level in Peking's eight districts, some of which have Red Guard newspapers and Red Patrols. Otherwise their "orders" are given by newspaper editorial and occasional Party decisions, especially the now-famous "16-Points Decision of the CCP Central Committee," all of which the Red Guards study with thoroughness.

All of them take Mao's works as their basic authority and feel at liberty to write to Chairman Mao about their problems. "We wrote from the Drama School to Chairman Mao," Red told me, "and said we didn't want to spend seven years behind closed doors studying drama.

We want to go out to the hard places of our country, to see the needs of the people and to fit our dramas to those needs." In point of fact, many of Mao's recent decisions have been responses to some suggestion made by "revolutionary students" even before the Red Guards organised. (Such as the abolition of examinations for university entrance and the suggestion that graduates of middle schools go first to work in industry or farming.)

I asked Red what sort of things they had done so far and on what basis they proceeded. She replied that the Red Guards came as a new force to sweep out old ideas, customs and habits and to root the thought of Chairman Mao deep among the people. Many of the things they did were small but they added up to a considerable change in the face of the city. She mentioned the changing of names on shops and an incident in which she had taken part.

The Handley Watch Shop, she said, had been originally named for its foreign capitalist owner, but he was dead for many years and it had long been State-owned. Its workers had twice sent formal requests to the former Municipal Party Committee to remove this dead name, but they got no reply so the shop still bore the Handley name above it in heavy iron letters. Some Red Guards came on a Sunday, talked with the workers and then with their aid and applause climbed ladders and removed the old name, renaming the place together with its workers as "Capital Watch Shop."

"We thought that iron name would be hard to remove," said Red, "but the workers gave us tools and when we hit the iron with their heavy mallets it cracked very easily. It was just another paper tiger." Red thought this important because it broke a symbol of capitalist ownership.

Red said that in all such actions the Red Guards consulted the workers and usually found that they had already wanted a change but did not know how to do it. So the Red Guards took the responsibility and did it to applause.

When it came to the question of searching private houses, they consulted not only the local street committee and the local police but also "the neighbours round about." These were generally "very enthusiastic" in pointing out the places where "the class enemy" had long been evading or flouting the law. So this kind of search generally went very fast and had been basically finished in many parts of Peking but not in all. Quantities of gold and silver bars and "shoes" (the form in which these metals were formerly cast for hoarding), had been discovered and were on exhibition, together with many land deeds of property long since redistributed in the "land reform" and quantities of Chiang Kai-shek's former money. Also quite a lot of illegally held arms.

"It was clear enough what side these people were on," she said, "and what they intended to do if anything gave them the chance." She added that all this gold and silver was quite a revelation and an education for the Red Guards, for they had never seen such things and didn't at first know what they were. "When we saw all that Chiang Kai-shek's money, some thought it was tin."

I asked whether the "refugee landlords," all of whom were illegally in Peking and have been ordered by a city regulation over two years ago to go back to their villages of origin where their history was known and where they could redeem themselves by work, had been given any date limit for remaining in Peking. She replied that different Red Guard units had set such dates but none of them were binding; it was a matter on which "the competent city authorities" had to act. However, many such landlords left anyway because of the Red Guards.

In all this direct action Fighting Red remarked that some Red Guards had gone too far at first. "In any mass movement that attacks abuses, there is bound to be an over-correction at the start." She thought they had guarded against mistakes by mutual criticism and by frequent summing-up and discussion of their actions. It was now understood that it was not proper to hit people and that one should act "by reasoning and not by coercion." They were also learning how to co-operate with the authorities.

What she meant by this was clear from what had happened in connection with the renaming of streets. Many streets had been renamed by local Red Guard units and in some cases these names had actually been painted, and the old names had been removed. This caused confusion, especially when different Red Guard units gave different names to the same street or when a lot of streets were named "Anti-Imperialist" or "The East Is Red." So now big posters had been put up all over town signed by a committee made up of representatives of the Liaison Centre of the Red Guards and also of the various municipal departments, the posts, the transport, the City Planning, and other municipal departments that were concerned with names. These posters showed big maps of Peking and the suggested changes and asked all citizens who had any opinions to send these in at once.

"The final naming of these streets," said Red, "will be determined by these municipal departments in consultation with the Red Guards." Because of their initiative it would clearly be done much faster than usual.

The Red Guards' future, in Fighting Red's view, lies not with grammar grades or miscellaneous adult organisations but with youth of secondary school and college age, especially but not exclusively with students. It will be patterned after the Liberation Army and become a reserve for the army. She added that Chairman Mao had defined their future as an armed revolutionary youth organisation, legal under the dictatorship of the proletariat. The others all nodded.

"But you haven't any arms," I protested.

"Not yet," they said.

Sid intervened: "O, yes you have," and he held aloft the little red volume of quotations from Mao which all of them carry. They burst into loud applause.

Red continued: "So if Chairman Mao is our Red Commander-in-Chief and we are his red soldiers, who can stop us? First we will make China red from inside out and then we will help the working people of other countries make the whole world red." As if this were not enough she added: "And then the whole universe." She retreated from the universe to the United States, saying: "Some day you'll be putting up your own posters on the streets of New York."

"I'll invite you over on that fine day," I replied and they all applauded.

For some time a discussion in whispers had been going on between Fighting Red and the 15-year-old who sat on the other side of her and who looked even younger than her age. Later Sid told me about it. Red had a plan to give me a Red Guard arm band, the 15-year-old was protesting. "Don't be silly," said Red, "she's an international comrade and we can make her an honorary member." "It's you that is silly," retorted the 15-year-old. "People have to volunteer and she hasn't applied." Red was taken aback but soon found an answer: "She hasn't thought of it and she doesn't know the rules."

I heard the whispering only as a vague interruption. When Fighting Red gave me the red arm band I accepted it. She pinned it on, saying: "You were the first foreign comrade to talk to Chairman Mao about the paper tiger, and now you are the first to be admitted to the Red Guards." This also brought applause.

"Now we have answered your questions," Red continued, "so it is your turn. What are your instructions to us?"

I made a short speech about how the Red Guards looked to me,

I said three things.

"Yours is the generation that Secretary Rusk and the American reactionaries have been counting on. They said that the present leaders in China and the next ones after them are hopeless, but the third generation might turn away from Mao Tse-tung so China might gradually change colour as Moscow's leaders did. But now Chairman Mao has reached out and grabbed you; you are his successors. You will make it certain that Mao's thought, expressed through the Red Guards, will guide China for at least fifty years. You may become the reddest generation China has ever known." At this they all applauded very much. I went on:

"Next, **if** the US imperialists should attack China tomorrow or in a year or two, you have already given this country the best dress-rehearsal for defence that any country ever had. You have moved perhaps a million people across the country from end to end, quickly and without advance notice. You have shown that it is possible to concentrate and disperse population quickly and widely, if everyone travels light, with a minimum of food and clothing. You have also shown that, if the imperialists attack, the PLA is free to be busy where it wishes, because the Red Guards can manage the cities, helping the police.

"Third, you are beginning to work out a new system of education. The world has never had a really good system of education. Always the dead hand of the past has used education to try to dominate the future through the youth. The divorce between theory and practice has never been overcome. As for socialist education, it has not yet existed and nobody yet knows what it is. It is for you to work that out in the coming months. For the chance is opened by the Cultural Revolution now."

Their agreement was expressed in applause that almost tore down the house. Fighting Red asked: "May one kiss?" Several ones did.

After we left and began to get our breath back, Sid said: "I was thinking of John Reed in Leningrad and the 'Ten Days that Shook the World.' He talked with the Red Guards there and they accepted him as a fellow revolutionary from America. These Red Guards are international too. The youngest revolutionaries of China have given a membership to the oldest revolutionary from the United States."

Two days later I sat on my porch in the afternoon with a friend from Latin America watching the sunset through the trees and listening to the singing and the roars of cheers that came from another million-strong Red Guard rally on the Tienanmen Square three blocks away.

451

He said: "I am glad to have had these weeks in China. I am glad of the news that I am taking back to our difficult fight at home. Without China, without this Cultural Revolution, mankind would face the dark night of reactionary rule perhaps for centuries. No other nation has succeeded in marrying a socialist superstructure to the socialist economic base; failing that, they drift back towards capitalism. But now that I have seen China's Cultural Revolution and its Red Guards, I know that one-fourth of mankind is marching on."

Another roar of cheers louder than any yet swept over the trees from the Square, and seemed to fill the sky and the earth. It went on and on. We knew then that Mao had arrived.

(Reproduced from "Letter from China,"
No. 41, September 20, 1966)

NOTES

1. Referring to Mao Tse-tung's theory that imperialism and all reactionaries are papes tigers.

Appendix I

GLOSSARY

Ch'a-Hung-Ch'i (插紅旗)

"Hoist a red flag"

The red flag has become a symbol of advancement. Hoisting a red flag at a certain unit is a form of praise for advanced achievement.

Chan-Lioh-Shang-Miao-Shih-Ti-Jen; Chan-Shu-Shang-Chung-Shih-Ti-Jen (戰略上藐視敵人；戰術上重視敵人)

"Slight the enemy strategically; take full account of him tactically"

What Mao Tse-tung meant by this oft-quoted statement of his was that the people of China should never fear to match their strength with that of their enemy. On the contrary, when they deal with a particular situation or wage a specific struggle, they must never slight him but take full account of him and devote all their efforts to overthrow him.

This statement was intended also to apply to the overcoming of difficulties that may come up in the fulfilment of daily work or assigned tasks. Mao Tse-tung has been quoted as saying: "We should scorn difficulties strategically but pay full attention to them tactically."

Chan-Tou-Jen-Wu (戰鬥任務)

"A militant task"

This term refers to certain work which has to be done in a hurry.

Chao-Ch'a-Chu (找差距)

"Look for gaps"

This phrase is often used in connection with the campaign to emulate, learn from, catch up with the advanced, help the backward and

453

overtake the advanced. Disparities in ideology, knowledge, ability or achievements, once known to the less advanced or backward, will help him to realise that he has to double his efforts at learning and emulation.

Ch'ao-Chieh-Chi (超階級)

"Above class"

This term is often used to repudiate the theory that certain people are above class. Lenin, for instance, is quoted as saying that no one while living can stand aloof from one class or another.

Chen-Ti (陣地)

"Battle ground"

This term is used in a broad sense, covering nearly every field of work. For instance, trade unions and rural clubs are referred to as excellent "battle grounds" for ideological work. Such terms as "socialist battle ground," "cultural battle ground" have often appeared in the press.

Cheng-Chih-Kua-Shuai (政治掛帥)

"Politics takes command"

Politics refers to the leadership of the Chinese Communist Party. All work in China should pivot upon Party leadership. Politics therefore commands everybody and everything in China. Similar phrases with a similar meaning have been adopted. They are: (政治是靈魂，是統帥) meaning "politics is the soul, the commander," and (突出政治) meaning "give prominence to politics."

Cheng-Feng-Yun-Tung (整風運動)

"Rectification campaign"

This campaign is carried out in China to "enhance the people's consciousness of socialism so as to conform with the requirements in

454

consolidating the socialist system and further developing production."
The method used in the campaign is "criticism and self-criticism."

The campaign was first launched among CCP members to rectify
their working style and test their loyalty to the Party. The first campaign took place in 1942. Similar campaigns have taken place since.

Ch'eng-Sheng-Ch'ien-Chin (乘勝前進)

"Advance in the wake of victory"

This old phrase is commonly used to exhort workers and peasants
not to rest on their laurels after achieving success but to continue
striving for new successes.

Chi-Chi-Fen-Tzu (積極份子)

"Activists"

They are enthusiasts eager to carry out Party policies.

Chi-T'i-So-Yu-Chih (集體所有制)

"Collective ownership"

This is a form of socialist system of public ownership, differing
from the ownership by all people in that the principal means of production belong to the collectives.

The system of collective ownership features the right of the collective to distribute its output.

Chieh-Chi-Chiao-Yu (階級教育)

"Class education"

It refers to education conducted among the people to make them
understand the significance of class struggle — a revolution or an act
of violence by which one class overthrows another—and the method of
class analysis.

Chieh-Chi-Fen-Hsi (階級分析)

"Class analysis"

Class analysis means more than division of the people into classes. It means that the proletarians should always remember their own class and deal with persons or things from the standpoint of a proletarian. For instance, when food shortage was acute, the peasants and workers were not supposed to complain because in the old society, they are told, they had even less to eat.

Chieh-Chi-Lu-Hsien (階級路線)

"Class line"

This term means that Party policy must be carried out according to the Party's division of classes. In organising agricultural co-operatives and communes, for instance, Party cadres were told to rely on poor and lower-middle peasants and unite with middle peasants.

Chieh-Chi-Tou-Cheng (階級鬥爭)

"Class struggle"

This refers to the struggle of one class against another in a socialist society which is not a classless society. Hence the proletariat should always be on the alert against corrosion by bourgeois influences. They should wage constant struggle against the bourgeoisie.

Chieh-Fang-Chan-Cheng (解放戰爭)

"The War of Liberation"

It is also called "the Third Revolutionary War," referring to the Communist revolution against the Nationalist Government in 1946-1949. The "First and Second Revolutionary Civil Wars" were the Northern Expedition in 1926-1927, led by the Nationalists in co-operation with the Communists and the Communist revolution from 1927

456

to 1936. The war in 1937-1945 is referred to as the "War of Resistance against Japan."

Chieh-Kai-Tzu (揭盖子)

"Remove the lid"

The term "lid" was first used by certain intellectuals during the "hundred flowers blooming" period of 1957. These intellectuals were later denounced as "rightists" in the rectification campaign. "The lid" denotes any hindrance to progress.

Anything that hampers thought reform is referred to as (思想蓋子) meaning "an ideological lid."

Chien-Tuan (尖端)

"Tip-top"

This means pioneering or advanced science, for instance.

Chih-Lao-Hu (紙老虎)

"Paper tiger"

According to a Chinese saying, any person who is fierce outwardly but weak inwardly is called "paper tiger." Mao Tse-tung uses this as a phrase to scorn "imperialism" (the United States) and all reactionaries.

Ching-Chi-Chu-I (經濟主義)

"Economism"

This refers to the practice of using wage increases and other material benefits to undermine the "revolutionary fervour" of the working people and lure them away from the Maoist line—meaning the "proletarian revolutionary line represented by Chairman Mao."

Chua-Hao-Liang-T'ou (抓好兩頭)

"Grasp both ends well"

The "two ends" mean the upper and lower levels. The upper level refers to Party policy; the lower level to the actual conditions of a work unit or an enterprise. In implementing a Party policy, consideration must be given to local conditions. The whole phrase means to link the Party line with local needs or to link theory with practice.

Chuan-Chia-Lu-Hsien (專家路線)

"Expert line"

In designing a public building, a factory or a mechanical device, the Chinese practice is to advocate combining the efforts of three parties, namely, the leading cadres, the masses and the experts. They oppose relying on experts alone or the "expert line" because in their opinion experts are liable to emphasise grandeur in their designs. Grandeur would cause waste of money, materials and time.

Ch'uan-Chu-Kuan-Tien (全局觀點)

"Overall viewpoint"

Everyone in China today is expected to work hard to fulfil his assigned task while keeping the interests of the whole constantly in view. This is emphasised especially in planning.

Ch'uan-Min-So-Yu-Chih (全民所有制)

"Ownership by all people"

Since the State represents the people, ownership by all people denotes ownership by the State, or the highest form of public ownership of the socialist system. All State-owned enterprises using State property as means of production come under this form of ownership.

458

Ch'uang-Tsao-Ching-Yen (創造經驗)

"Create experience"

It means gaining experience. After one has gained experience, one is supposed to share it with others. Hence the phrase (推廣經驗) meaning "popularise experience."

Ch'ün-Chung-Lu-Hsien (群衆路線)

"Mass line"

Chinese Communist Party policies are supposed to be formulated on the opinions of the great majority of the people, made known to the masses through propaganda and carried out by them through persuasion. Hence the phrase (從群衆中來，到群衆中去), meaning "from the masses, to the masses."

Chung-Nung (中農)

"Middle peasants"

Peasants who possessed a fair amount of producer goods but did not "exploit" others. They were in three classes: (上中農), the upper-middle peasants referred to as the well-to-do middle peasants, (中農), the middle peasants, and (下中農), the lower-middle peasants.

In carrying out land reform in 1950-1952, China adopted the policy of waging struggles against landlords and rich peasants, uniting middle peasants and relying on poor peasants and farm hands. The present policy is to rely on poor and lower-middle peasants against upper-middle peasants, leaving the middle peasants alone.

Fan-Mien-Chiao-Yü (反面教育)

"Negative education"

This means teaching by a negative example to show what undesirable consequences would follow if a bad habit is not corrected. This

459

contrasts with (正面教育), meaning "positive education"—teaching by a positive example.

Fan-Shen (翻身)

"Turn the table over"

This term was used extensively during the early years of the Chinese Communist Party's rule to impress workers that through the help of the Communists they have turned the tables on capitalists and become masters of their own houses.

Fen-Lieh-Chu-I (分裂主義)

"Splittism"

China accuses Soviet leaders of disrupting the unity of the international Communist movement and calls them "splitters" (refer to the Comment on the Open Letter of the Central Committee of the CPSU (VII) published by the Editorial Departments of *Jen-min Jih-pao* and *Hung-ch'i* on 4 February, 1964).

Fen-San-Chu-I (分散主義)

"Dispersionism"

This denotes selfishness of the cadres of various work units without regard to the whole situation.

Fu-Nung (富農)

"Rich peasants"

These were peasants who possessed comparatively good means of production and some working capital and "exploited" others by hiring farm hands or lending money to others at high rates of interest.

Hei-Hsien (黑線)

"Black line"

In the present "cultural revolution" movement, the term, "black line" is used to condemn the so-called "anti-Party and anti-socialist" ideas that are reflected in works of literature and art.

Hsia-Fang (下放)

This term means "send down," "give to lower units," or "de-centralise." For example, (幹部下放) means "cadres are sent to farms or factories;" (資本下放), "capital is given to lower units;" and (權力下放), "decentralisation of power."

Hsiang-Feng (香風)

"Fragrant breeze"

This refers to the bourgeois way of life. The term has been used in describing fashionable dresses, facial make-up and stylish hair-styles found among women from Hong Kong visiting the Chinese mainland.

Hsieh-Chi-Wai-Feng (邪氣歪風)

"Ill or Evil Wind"

This refers to "pernicious influences spread by bad elements and bad customs."

Hsien-Chin-Ching-Yen (先進經驗)

"Advanced experience"

This is the experience acquired by a worker who has advanced in production technique and production. (先進份子) "advanced element" refers to a worker who overtakes another in production.

461

Hsing-Wu-Mieh-Tzu (興無滅資)

"Promote proletarian and eradicate bourgeois ideology"

Hsiu-Cheng-Chu-I (修正主義)

"Revisionism"

Any modification of orthodox Marxist-Leninist theory or the method of carrying out the theory is branded as "revisionism" and condemned in China.

Hsüeh-Hsi-Lei-Feng-Yun-Tung (學習雷鋒運動)

"Learn-from-Lei-Feng Campaign"

Lei Feng was an ordinary young soldier who died on duty. He was said to have left a diary in which he recorded his thoughts and also his efforts to learn from Mao Tse-tung's works. He has been hailed as a model young man for the youth in China to learn from and emulate.

Hsüeh-Wang-Chieh (學王杰)

"Learn from Wang Chieh"

Wang Chieh is the name of a hero lauded in China as one who embodied all those virtues every young man, young soldiers in particular, should possess. A campaign to "learn from Wang Chieh," similar to the one to learn from Lei Feng, was launched in the latter part of 1965. The campaign was to promote application of Mao Tse-tung's thinking, obedience to the Chinese Communist Party, dedication to the cause of revolution and sacrifice for the country and for the countrymen.

Wang Chieh was a squad leader of the first engineering company of a PLA armoured unit stationed in Tsinan, Shantung Province. He was sent to Changlo People's Commune in P'i County, Kiangsu Province to help train the local militia. On July 14, 1965, a package of explosives was accidentally set off, while Wang was at training work.

462

To save the lives of 12 militiamen and cadres standing by, he reportedly threw himself on the explosives and died.

Hung-Ch'i-Tan-Wei (紅旗單位)

"Red banner unit"

This term is often used in emulation drives. A production team of a commune or a workshop of a factory, which achieves a better output than others, is called a "red banner unit".

Hung-Se-Chieh-Pan-Jen (紅色接班人)

"Red successors"

They usually refer to children, the "Young Pioneers" in particular, who are politically oriented and reliable.

Hung-Yu-Chuan (紅與專)

"Red and expert"

"Red" means indoctrinated to become politically firm and reliable and "expert," well trained in some branch of knowledge. An expert who is not socialist-minded and absolutely obedient to the Party cannot be completely trusted. "Redness" therefore precedes "expertness" in importance.

Huo-Hsüeh-Huo-Yung (活學活用)

"Creative learning and application" [of such things as Mao Tse-tung's writings or People's Liberation Army's political and ideological work]

Individuals, enterprises and work units in China are urged to learn from Mao Tse-tung's written work or PLA's way of doing things in order to lay a firm grip on its essential spirit but apply it to each individual case as they see fit.

I-Fen-Wei-Erh (一分爲二)

"One divided into two"

This refers to a "Marxist method of dialectical analysis." According to Chinese interpretation, it means that one must look at a person or work from two sides: the good features and the defects, positive and negative factors. Struggle of one against the other brings about progress in a person and uninterrupted development in work. One is supposed to see more of others' abilities and attainments and less of their shortcomings and failures, so that one knows what one lacks and then tries to catch up with the advanced.

I-Hsiao-Ts'o (一小撮)

"A handful"

This is an expression used in a contemptuous sense to mean that there is only a handful of people opposed to the Chinese Communist Party. More recently, it is often used in the phrase, "A handful of anti-Party, anti-socialist elements."

I-Ku-Szu-Tien (憶苦思甜)

"Remember bitterness and think of sweetness"

The people in China are constantly reminded of the sufferings they or their fellow-countrymen have gone through and what the Chinese Communist Party has done to relieve them. This is also a part of class education.

I-Li-Chien (一厘錢)

"One tenth of one cent"

One cent is the smallest denomination of Chinese currency. In the economy drive, this phrase was used to emphasise that in production any material worth a fraction of one cent should be saved. The

464

socalled (一厘錢) spirit has been promoted in connection with the campaign for increasing production and practising economy.

I-Pang-I; I-Tui-Hung (一幫一；一對紅)

"With one assisting another; a pair will become 'red'"

With one who is "red" assisting another who is not, both will be "red." The underlying idea is for the "progressive" to help the "backward," so that everybody will be progressive.

"Red" denotes politically oriented and reliable.

I-Tien-Tai-Mien (以點帶面)

"Let selected points guide larger areas"

This is a call for one advanced unit (production brigade or team) to help backward ones to catch up with its own level of efficiency.

I-Tou, Erh-Pi, San-Kai (一鬥、二批、三改)

"Firstly, to struggle against...; secondly, to criticise and repudiate...; thirdly, to transform..."

The 16-Point Decision of the CCP Central Committee adopted on August 8, 1966, set the tasks for the Great Proletarian Cultural Revoluton as: Firstly, to struggle against and crush those in authority who are taking the capitalist road; secondly, to criticise and repudiate the reactionary bourgeois academic "authorities" and the ideology of the bourgeoisie and all other exploiting classes; and thirdly, to transform education, literature and art and all other parts of the superstructure that do not correspond to the socialist economic base.

Jen-Min-Kung-She (人民公社)

"People's Commune"

The people's commune is a mass organisation of peasants, consisting of 5,000 households on an average, which carried out farm work

465

as well as rural government work when it started in 1958. Each commune was formed by combining many agricultural producers' co-operatives. There were 26,000 communes formed from 740,000 such cooperatives in December, 1958. Failing in its objectives, the commune gradually lost its governmental functions and diminished in size. Each commune was later split into production brigades and again into production teams under production brigades.

There were 74,000 communes in 1963, according to an article written by Liao Lu-yen, Minister of Agriculture for *Cuba Socialista* of Cuba and reproduced in English in Peking Review, No. 44, November 1, 1963.

Jen-Min-Min-Chu-Chuan-Cheng (人民民主專政)

"People's democratic dictatorship"

It has been proclaimed that the government system of the People's Republic of China is based on the principle of "democracy among the people and dictatorship over the 'people's enemy'."

Ju-Tzu-Niu (孺子牛)

"Children's ox"

Lu Hsün, a leftist writer who died in 1936, described a revolutionary as one who would "raise his eyebrows and coolly defy a thousand pointing fingers, but would bow to children and willingly serve them like an ox." The Chinese quote Lu Hsün's words to illustrate that a revolutionary is as obedient as an ox in serving the people, while he calmly defies the enemy.

Kan-Pu-Hsia-Fang (幹部下放)

"Cadres sent to lower-level units"

This was a slogan put forward in 1956-1957, calling on Party and government organisations to send cadres (officials) to basic-level units, factories or farms to do physical labour as a part of training.

Ko-Chin-So-Neng, An-Lao-Fen-P'ei (各盡所能，按勞分配)

"From each according to his ability and to each according to his work"

This is the underlying socialist principle.

The second half of the phrase, "to each according to his work," which appeared originally in Stalin's Works was first translated into (各取所值) or to each according to his worth. The translation was wrong; it misinterpreted the meaning of the text in Russian and German, said Chang Chung-shih, Deputy Director of the CCP Central Committee's Compilation and Translation Bureau of the Works of Marx, Engels, Lenin and Stalin, in his article entitled "Concerning 'To Each According to His Work' and 'To Each According to His Needs'" [*Jen-min Jih-pao*, December 20, 1958].

The standard translation above was adopted at the 6th Plenary Session of the 8th CCP Central Committee, held at Wuchang from November 28 to December 10, 1958. It replaced all the three previous translations and emphasised the point that the peasants and workers of the socialist society are to get what is distributed to them. They are thus denied the right to claim compensation for their labour.

Ko-Chin-So-Neng, An-Hsü-Fen-P'ei (各盡所能，按需分配)

"From each according to his ability and to each according to his needs"

This is the communist principle.

The standard translation of this phrase from Russian and German was also adopted at the 6th Plenary Session of the 8th CCP Central Committee. It replaced the first translation, (各取所需) or to take what each needs, which was wrong because it implied that each person could take anything and any quantity of it from a warehouse, pointed out Chang Chung-shih.

The standard translation indicates that even in a communist society each will have to work as hard as he or she can and take only what is distributed.

Ko-Jen-Ying-Hsiung-Chu-I (個人英雄主義)

"Vainglorious individualism"

This refers to cadres who like to boast of their revolutionary deeds.

K'ou-Mao-Tzu (扣帽子)

"Put a label on a person"

This phrase is used in a figurative sense to label an opponent "reactionary," "rightist," etc.

Kuan-Liao-Chu-I (官僚主義)

"Bureaucratism"

It refers to officials who sit at office desk without making on-the-spot inspections and who put on airs in dealing with people.

Kuan-Liao-Tzu-Pen-Chu-I (官僚資本主義)

"Bureaucratic capitalism"

Former Nationalist officials who ran private enterprises while holding government posts were labelled "bureaucratic capitalists." Bureaucratic capitalism refers to such practices.

Kuo-Kuan (過關)

"Jump over the passes"

Many "passes" have been invented for the people and particularly for youth, to "jump over." These include the "political pass," "family pass," "livelihood pass," "the pass of conceit." A "political pass" refers to the conflict between socialism and capitalism. The "pass of conceit" refers to complacent attitudes.

Kuo-Te-Ying (過得硬)

"Live toughly"

The People's Liberation Army has been hailed for its "tough-living spirit," which is a "revolutionary quality." Lin Piao called on officers and men to be "tough in thinking, tough in their working style and tough in learning techniques." The soldiers of the "Good 8th Company on Nanking Road" are said to have "lived toughly" in political ideology by resisting the attractions of city life over a period of 15 years while they were stationed in Shanghai.

Lao San P'ien (老三篇)

"Three much-read articles" or "Three good old articles"

Among the articles in *Selected Works of Mao Tse-tung,* there are three entitled, "In Memory of Norman Bethune" (written on December 21, 1939), "Serve the People" (September 8, 1944) and "The Foolish Old Man Who Removed the Mountains" (June 11, 1945). During the socialist cultural revolution, a campaign to study these three articles was launched first in the PLA and later among workers in other fields in China. These three articles, old as though they are, are regarded as the indispensable guide in remoulding one's world outlook and the most powerful weapon to break bureaucratic habits.

Lao-Ta-Nan-Wen-T'i (老大難問題)

"Old, great and difficult problems"

This phrase refers to important problems which have remained unsolved for a long time. The Chinese use these three words jointly to emphasise the difficulty of solving them.

Lao-Tung-Kai-Tsao (勞動改造)

"Correction through labour"

It is generally known as "corrective labour," a form of punishment meted out for "counter-revolutionaries," robbers, thieves and corrupt officials.

Li-Kan-Chien-Ying (立竿見影)

"A pole casts a shadow as soon as it is set up"

This is an old phrase to illustrate immediate effect from prompt action.

Liang-T'iao-Tao-Lu-Ti-Tou-Cheng (兩條道路的鬥爭)

"Struggle between two roads"

The two roads refer to capitalism and socialism. This phrase was frequently used during the "anti-rightist" campaign in 1957.

Liang-T'iao-T'ui-Tsou-Lu (兩條腿走路)

"Walking on two legs"

This refers to Mao Tse-tung's policy of adopting both modern and primitive methods of production at the same time in order to increase output. The attempt at speeding up steel production in 1958 by using indigenous furnaces to smelt steel, which ended in a disastrous failure, was a typical example of this theory.

Liang-T'ou-Mao-Chien (兩頭冒尖)

"Double-ended prominence"

This term refers to the "two ends" of technical achievement and ideological backwardness.

This term appeared in an article in the *Chieh-fang-chün Pao* of May 20, 1966. It was intended to emphasise the theory that unless one first places politics in command, that is, imbibe the proletarian ideology, one's outstanding technical achievement will not benefit the proletariat. On the contrary it may serve the bourgeoisie. One's ideological backwardness is said to be projecting when one's ideological work is neglected.

Lo-Hu (落戶)

"Make a home" or "settle down permanently"

This phrase was first used in connection with the drive to send educated youth to villages and mountains and persuade them to settle down there for life. Now, it is used in a broader sense. For instance, (思想落戶), meaning to let an idea settle deeply in one's mind.

Lo-Shih (落實)

"Put into full effect"

This phrase is extensively used in the Chinese press. It means to realise or carry out. Example: "Let the 'four firsts' and 'three-eight working style' lo-shih (be fully implemented) in public health work, or in production." The two words are also used as a noun: hence (三落實), meaning that work has been properly carried out in three aspects.

Mang-Mu-Lo-Kuan (盲目樂觀)

"Blindly optimistic"

This term is often translated as "recklessly optimistic." It is used to blame cadres for or warn them against taking an optimistic attitude without reasonable assurance of success.

Ming-Fang (鳴放)

"Contending and blooming"

These two words stand for the old phrase (百家爭鳴，百花齊放), meaning, "One hundred schools of thought contend, and one hundred flowers bloom." A campaign of "letting different schools of thought contend (freely air views on academic theories) and hundred flowers bloom (freely create arts, especially plays and dramas)" was launched towards the end of 1956 and in the first part of 1957. Many people, especially members of the so-called democratic parties, thought that they were given freedom to air their views and began to criticise the policies of the Chinese Communist Party. As a result, they were attacked and down-graded by the Party.

Ming-Ling-Chu-I (命令主義)

"Commandism"

It means doing things by issuing orders without explanation.

Mo-Ti (摸底)

"Touch the bottom"

It means finding out all the facts. For example, a factory manager should find out how many workers there are, how much raw material is available and how much the factory can produce. In this way, he has a grasp of the situation and knows what to do.

Nan-Ching-Lu-Shang-Hao-Pa-Lien (南京路上好八連)

"The Good Company on Nanking Road"

This refers to a company of soldiers of the People's Liberation Army, stationed on Nanking Road in Shanghai since May, 1949. This company has been hailed as an exemplary army unit "successfully withstanding the quintessence of bourgeois corruption and decadence" from the old world-known cosmopolitan city in China. The whole nation has been called on to learn from this army unit as a "glorious example of Party discipline."

Nan-Ni-Wan-Ching-Shen (南泥灣精神)

"The Nanniwan Spirit"

It refers to the spirit of the 8th Route Army in facing hardships when they were engaged in land reclamation in Nanniwan, Shensi. This phrase has been used to illustrate a dauntless spirit in tackling arduous tasks.

Niu-Kuei-She-Shen (牛鬼蛇神)

"Ghosts and monsters"

Ghosts and monsters refer to all "ugly beings" who oppose the Chinese Communist Party, socialism and the thought of Mao Tse-tung.

P'a-Chan-Pien (怕沾邊)

"Afraid of being involved"

This means that workers are afraid of being accused of associating with capitalists.

Pa-Chia-T'ing-Kuan (把家庭關)

"Guard the family pass"

This phrase was used often at a time. Youths who had grown up in the socialist society but in "exploiting families" were warned against the corrosive influences of their parents and other relatives. Many youths who had been sent to the country to do farm labour were asked by their parents to return home. The parents may go to farms to vistit their sons and daughters and bring them better food to eat. Such parental care was frowned upon as a corrosive influence.

Pa-Kuan (把關)

"Hold the pass"

This was an old military tactical term. The Chinese believe that that breaking through a "pass" is easier than holding it against enemy's attempt to recapture it. They believe that to win a battle against bourgeois ideology takes effort but to guard it demands constant and unremitting vigilance.

Pa-Tzu-Hsien-Fa (八字憲法)

"Eight-character code"

The eight characters constitute a code for agricultural development. They mean irrigation, fertiliser, soil improvement, seeds, close planting, crop protection, reform of farm tools and field management.

P'an-Teng-Kao-Feng (攀登高峰)

"Scale the summit"

This phrase is a call for mastery of skills and techniques. It generally applies to achievements in science and technology.

Pao Huang T'ang (保皇黨)

"Royalists"

This refers to Chinese Communist Party and government officials supporting a handful of people in power who follow the capitalist road.

P'ei-To-Fei-Chü-Lo-Pu (裴多非俱樂部)

"Petofi Club"

This refers to the Petofi Circle, named for the Hungarian poet and patriot killed in the revolt of 1948-49. It was formed in 1955 to encourage free debate among students and intellectuals. The Hungarian uprising occurred a year later.

Pen-Wei-Chu-I (本位主義)

"Departmentalism"

It denotes care for the interests of one's own unit regardless of those of other units.

Pi-Hsüeh-Kan-Pang-Ch'ao-Yün-Tung (比學趕幫超運動)

"Campaign to compare with, learn from, catch up with, help [the less advanced and each other] and overtake [the advanced]"

This is a nation-wide drive to spur the peasants, factory workers and employees, miners, government and Party cadres and the personnel of every work unit to greater "revolutionary zeal" for production and fulfilment of assigned tasks. The campaign started with the first four characters. P'eng Chen, member of the CCP Central Committee, and former Mayor of Peking added the fifth to make the campaign as it is known nowadays.

P'i-P'ing-Yu-Tzu-Ngo-P'i-P'ing (批評與自我批評)

"Criticism and self-criticism"

Criticising others and oneself was a method used in rectification campaigns. Self-criticism is admission of one's own wrongs: it is tantamount to confession.

Piao-Ping (標兵)

"Standard bearers or pace-setters"

They are model workers for their fellow workers to emulate.

P'in-Nung (貧農)

"Poor peasants"

Peasants who had incomplete producer goods, paid high rents and interest and received low wages when working for rich peasants.

It is the poor peasants who have been regarded, together with the lower-middle peasants, by the Chinese Communist Party as a "reliable" class of people.

The foregoing classification of peasants was contained in a decision on the division of rural classes, adopted by the Chinese Government on August 4, 1950.

P'ing-Chün-Chu-I (平均主義)

"Equalitarianism"

It means equal distribution of everything such as equal pay for different kinds of work and equal distribution of raw materials among factories. Equalitarianism is rejected in theory in China.

San-Chia-Ts'un (三家村)

"Three-Family Village"

This refers to an "anti-Party and anti-socialist clique" comprising Teng T'o, a former member of the Secretariat of the Peking Municipal Party Committee; Wu Han, ex-vice mayor of Peking; and Liao Mo-sha, former director of the United Front Department of the Peking Municipal Party Committee.

San-Chieh-Ho (三結合)

"Triple combination"

The three (parties) are the leading cadres (officials), experts and the masses (workers). To make a success of an innovation, the Chinese advocate, the three parties must pool their ideas and strength; the leading cadres are to provide political guidance, the experts, the technical know-how and the masses, their collective wisdom and determination to carry out the innovation.

San-Fan (三反)

"Three antis"

The three antis were anti-corruption, anti-waste and anti-bureaucracy. Early in 1952, a nation-wide campaign was launched to stop corruption and bureaucracy and tendency towards waste among the Chinese Communist Party and government officials.

San-Ho-I-Shao (三和一少)

"Three reconciliations and one reduction"

A phrase used by Premier Chou En-lai in his report on government work at the 1st Session of the 3rd National People's Congress on December 22, 1964, revealed for the first time that during the period from 1959 to 1962 a political view and an open demand prevailed both outside and in the Chinese Communist Party to make peace with "imperialists," with reactionaries and with "modern revisionists" and reduce aid to other peoples in their revolts either to replace one government with another sympathetic to the cause of communism or to gain independence.

San-Kao-Cheng-Ts'e (三高政策)

"Three-high policy"

This means high salaries, high writing fees and high cash awards.

San-Mien-Hung-Ch'i (三面紅旗)

"Three red banners"

Red banner is a symbol of victory. The three red banners represent the general line for building socialism, the great leap forward and the people's commune.

San-Ming-Chu-I (三名主義)

"Three-famous principle"

This is a phrase referring to famous writers, famous directors and famous actors.

San-Pa-Tso-Feng (三八作風)

"Three-eight working style"

This refers to the three phrases and eight characters written by Mao Tse-tung to describe the working style that officers and men were exhorted to adopt.

The three phrases are: correct political direction, a simple and arduous working style, and flexible strategy and tactics. The eight characters mean, "united, tense, stern and lively."

San-Shih (三史)

"Three histories"

In the case of peasants, the "three histories" refer to those of families, villages and communes. In the case of workers, they denote those of families, factories (mines), and revolutionary struggles. Writing "three histories" is to reveal how poor peasants and workers suffered before liberation. Many school children have been organised to inquire into the histories as a part of class education.

San-Ta-Ke-Ming-Yün-Tung (三大革命運動)

"Three great revolutionary movements"

The three great revolutionary movements are the class struggle, the struggle for production, and scientific experimentation.

San-Ta-Kuan-Tien (三大觀點)

"Three great viewpoints"

They are the political viewpoint, production viewpoint and mass viewpoint.

San-Tso-Ta-Shan (三座大山)

"Three big mountains"

The three big mountains referred to in Mao Tse-tung's writings mean "imperialism, feudalism and bureaucratic capitalism" which are said to have oppressed the Chinese people like mountains.

San-Tzu-I-Pao (三自一包)

"Three freedoms and one contract"

The three freedoms refer to extension of plots of land for private production, free markets and increase of private enterprises. One contract means allowing each household to assume a contractual obligation towards the State for producing a fixed quantity of grain.

Sha-Wen-Chu-I (沙文主義)

This is a transliteration of chauvinism, meaning "narrow nationalism."

Shan-Feng-Tien-Huo (扇風點火)

"Fan wind and light fires"

This is a phrase which means attempts at provoking incendiary acts. For instance, persons identified as "counter-revolutionaries" in China are often accused of instigating others to carry out sabotage activities or acts detrimental to the cause of socialism.

Shang-Ts'eng-Chien-Chu (上層建築)

"Superstructure"

It refers to social and political organisations, while economic system is considered their base.

She-Lai-She-Ch'ü (社來社去)

"From communes; back to communes"

The whole phrase, meaning "coming from communes and returning to communes," first appeared in 1962 when the agricultural middle schools decided to enrol students from among young commune members and return them, upon graduation, to the communes to carry on productive labour. The same phrase came into prominence again in July and August 1965 in connection with a nation-wide drive to train some young commune members into part-time doctors or spare-time health workers and mid-wives by giving them short-term courses in medical schools and returning them to the communes to practise their newly-acquired professions.

Shih-Yen-T'ien (試驗田)

"Experimental plot"

It refers to parcels of land, cultivated by new techniques such as close planting or deep ploughing to attain high yields.   The present-day term for an experimental plot to demonstrate the superiority of a new technique is (樣板田) or "demonstration field".

Shuo-Fu-Chiao-Yü (說服教育)

"Education by persuasion"

This is a common way of reasoning with political dissenters. Cadres (officials) in China persist in "persuading" until one admits one's fault or wrong view and accepts the Communist view or doctrine.

Szu-Ch'ing Yün-tung (四清運動)

"Four clean-up movement"

This campaign, referred to on December 26, 1964 as Szu-Ch'ing (four clean-up) in the *Nan-fang Jih-pao,* was described by Premier Chou En-lai in his Report on the Work of the Government a few days previously as being of "great revolutionary and historic signficance... In this movement it is necessary to carry out a cleaning up and capital construction in the political, economic, ideological and organisational fields in accordance with the socialist principle of thorough-going revolution and to condnct a profound class education and socialist education among the masses of the people so as to promote proletarian and eradicate bourgeois ideology."

In practice, this meant to tidy up the local party organisation, screen and re-educate basic-level cadres and clean up the financial, operational and management systems in the people's communes.

Szu-Chiu (四舊)

"Four-olds"

It refers to old ideas, old culture, old customs and old habits. In China's great socialist cultural revolution, teen-age students were organised for the first time on August 18, 1966 in Peking, as "Red Guards" to eradicate old ideas, culture, customs and habits of "all the exploiting classes."

Szu-Hao-Lien-Tui (四好連隊)

"Four-good company (of the Liberation Army)"

This refers to companies of soldiers who were good in political ideology, good in three-eight working style (San-Pa-Tso-Feng, see above), good in military training, and good in management of the living conditions of men.

Szu-Ko-Ti-I (四個第一)

"Four firsts"

This refers to Lin Piao's concept on the relationships between men and weapons, political and other work, all aspects of political work and ideological work, and books and living ideas. He made the oft-quoted statement, "Human factor is first, political work first, ideological work first and living ideas first."

Szu-T'ung (四同)

"Four togethers" or *"four-togetherness"*

Cadres sent to farms or factories to do productive labour are not supposed to remain aloof from farmers or workers; they are required to eat together, live together, toil together and consult together with farmers or workers.

Ta-Chai-Ching-Shen (大寨精神)

"Tachai spirit"

"Tachai" is a production brigade of Tachai Commune in a poverty-stricken district of Shansi Province. It is a national model for the spirit of self-reliance. It is said that by dogged effort, the peasants of Tachai during the past decade have transformed their barren rocky hillsides into fertile terraces.

All production brigades and teams throughout the country are told to "learn from the Tachai spirit." A National Agricultural Exhibition was opened in Peking on November 1, 1965, featuring the "achievements" of the Tachai Brigade.

Ta-Ch'ien-Mieh-Chan (打殲滅戰)

"Carry out a campaign of annihilation"

The whole phrase implies concentration of all forces to complete a job thoroughly and quickly.

Ta-Ch'ing-Ching-Shen (大慶精神)

"Tach'ing spirit"

Tach'ing is the name of a large oil field in North China. Its exact location has never been made public. The term is intended to typify the hard-working spirit of workers in China.

Ta-Hsüeh-Ta-Pi (大學大比)

"Learn and emulate energetically"

The Chinese Communist Party declared in 1964 that the year was to be a year for everyone to learn and emulate vigorously.

Ta-Min-Chu (大民主)

"Extensive democracy"

According to an explanation given by Lin Piao, to practise "extensive democracy" is to permit the broad masses to use the media of free airing of views, big-character posters, great debates and extensive contacts, to criticise and supervise the Party and government leading institutions and leaders at all levels.

482

Ta-P'o-Chiu-K'uang-K'uang (打破舊框框)

"Smash the old frames"

"Old frames" refer to standards and records set previously. Certain workers and athletes are content when they have come up to the records and standards set in the past. They are exhorted to surpass them, to "smash the frames" that have confined their vision.

Ta-Tzu-Pao (大字報)

"Big-character posters"

These are propaganda posters written in big characters, stuck on walls or boards. These posters were widely used during the 1957 "anti-rightist" campaign and the 1958 commune movement. They are even more extensively used in the present "cultural revolution."

Ta-Yo-Chin (大躍進)

"Great leap forward"

Liu Shao-ch'i made reference to this term in his report to the 2nd Session of the 8th CCP Central Committee. The term was used to describe the development of production in the years 1956, 1957 and 1958 in the form of a leap forward. It was on the basis of the Great Leap Forward that the 1958 campaign for smelting steel in indigenous furnaces in order to reach the target of 10,700,000 tons of steel production for the year was launched. This ambitious target was raised from that of 8,000,000-8,600,000 tons which was fixed at an enlarged meeting of the CCP Central Committee's Political Bureau, held at Peitaiho from August 17 to 30, 1958.

T'an-Chia-Shih (談家史)

"Relate family history"

Family histories [of poor peasants' or workers'] are related in meetings to arouse class hatred among the youth as a part of the class education.

Tan-Shun-Yeh-Wu-Kuan-Tien (單純業務觀點)

"Purely business point of view"

Many industrial and trading units have been blamed for "losing sight of the collective interest as a whole" and caring only for the profit and loss of their own units.

Tou-Tao, Tou-Ch'ou, Tou-K'ua (鬥倒、鬥臭、鬥垮)

"Struggle... down, stink and collapse"

This refers to the "thoroughgoing revolutionary method" of waging struggle against the opponents and hitting them hard until they are pulled down and completely discredited.

Tso-Ch'ing-Fen-Tzu (左傾份子)

"Left deviationists"

It refers to those who think that the Chinese Communist Party is too conservative.

Tso-Hao-Jen-Ti-Kung-Tso (做好人的工作)

"Make a success of the work of dealing with men"

The work of dealing with men refers to the handling of relationships between men and matters, men and their fellow men, individuals and the collective. The Chinese Communist Party holds that each person can be made into a fighter with nigh consciousness and a strict sense of organisation and discipline on a production front or on a battleground; so can a group of persons.

Tsu-Ch'eng-Pu-Fen (組成部份)

"A component part"

A part of the whole is referred to as "a component part." A member of a team or party, for brevity, is called a Ch'eng-Yüan (成員).

Tsun-Tien (蹲點)

"Stay at fixed spots"

This phrase refers to cases in which a cadre is sent to a selected place or organisation to study conditions or solve problems and is expected to stay there for a certain length of time. It contrasts with the old Chinese phrase, 走馬看花, meaning "looking at wayside flowers from a galloping horse," which is used to describe a superficial and hasty investigation of conditions or study of problems by cadres.

Tsung-Lu-Hsien (總路線)

"General line"

This phrase was originally a slogan coined by Mao Tse-tung to urge the people to catch up with and surpass the United Kingdom in industrial production. It was adopted as the general line for building socialism at the 2nd Session of the 8th CCP Central Committee, held from May 5 to 23, 1958 in Peking.

The general line is to "build socialism by exerting the utmost efforts and pressing forward consistently to achieve greater, faster, better and more economical results."

T'u-Chi-Tui (突擊隊)

"Shock brigade"

This refers to a body of workers drafted or volunteering for some specially arduous task. Such task is called 突擊任務, "an emergency task."

T'u-Ch'u-Cheng-Chih (突出政治)

"Give prominence to politics"

One of the oft-repeated slogans in China is, "Politics is primary, the soul, the commander." This slogan has been used to remind workers and peasants that political studies—the study of Mao Tse-tung's writings—precedes work in importance. Workers and peasants often say that politics should give way to work when they are extremely busy.

485

Cadres in charge of political indoctrination retort, however, that politics is primary. Workers are required to attend classes or meetings held for political studies even when they are hard pressed to fulfil their tasks during busy seasons.

The phrase that politics is primary is stressed particularly in the armed services.

Tu-Ts'ao (毒草)

"Poisonous Weed"

All those literary and art works—books, articles, films, stage plays, songs, paintings, etc.—which are considered by the Maoists as against the interests of the Party and socialism and the thought of Mao Tse-tung, are "poisonous weeds." A variation of this is Tu-Chien (毒箭), meaning "poisoned arrow."

T'uan-Chieh-P'i-P'ing-T'uan-Chieh (團結 - 批評 - 團結)

"Unity-criticism-unity"

This phrase refers to the formula set forth by Mao Tse-tung of "starting from the desire for unity, distinguishing between right and wrong through criticism or struggle and arriving at a new unity on a new basis."

In other words, it is a method of conducting ideological struggles within the ranks of the Chinese Communist Party. To overcome Party members' objections to Party policies, leading Party cadres were told to criticise Party dissidents from the standpoint of a desire for unity and make them change their opinions so as to attain final unity among themselves.

A different phrase, "unity-struggle-unity," is used to underline the Party policy on Party dealings with its opponents.

T'ung-Chan-Pu (統戰部)

Abbreviation of the "United Front Work Department" of the Chinese Communist Party, whose function is to unite intellectuals, former industrialists and merchants, and members of satellite political parties — to enlist their support through indoctrination.

486

Tung-Feng-Ya-Tao-Hsi-Feng (東風壓倒西風)

"East wind prevails over West wind"

This was a phrase used by Mao Tse-tung to say that the forces of Communism are growing stronger than those of the Western countries. Mao referred to this phrase for the first time in his speech to the Chinese students in Moscow on November 17, 1957.

Tzu-Ch'an-Chieh-Chi-Chih-Shih-Fen-Tzu (資產階級智識份子)

"Bourgeois intellectuals"

This refers to those born in so-called bourgeois families or those who had received "bourgeois education," having imbibed "bourgeois ideas."

Tzu-Fa-Ch'u-Shih (自發趨勢)

"Spontaneous tendency"

When peasants like to earn interest from loans made to others or to make profit from trading in subsidiary farm products, they are described as having a "spontaneous tendency toward capitalism."

Tzu-Jan-Hung (自然紅)

"Becoming 'red' naturally"

Many young workers and peasants in China think that they do not have to go through ideological reform to become "red" because they were "born in the new society and have grown under the 'red flag'." Rebutting the view, the Chinese authorities allege that to become "red" one must constantly steel oneself and remould one's mind.

Tzu-Li-Keng-Sheng (自力更生)

"To survive by relying on one's own efforts"

This phrase, generally translated as "self-reliance," has come into more extensive use since the Soviet Union withdrew her experts and aid in 1960.

487

Wang-Ming-T'ou-Hsiang-Lu-Hsien (王明投降路綫)

"Wang Ming capitulationist line"

Wang Ming, pseudonym for Ch'en Shao-yü, studied at the Sun Yat-sen University in Moscow in 1925. He was one of the two leading figures among the "Twenty-eight Bolsheviks"—young men who had no revolutionary experience but were imbued with the view prevailing in Moscow that a good grounding in Leninist theory was far more important. Joining the Communist Party in 1927 in Moscow, Wang pursued a policy now identified as the capitulationist line — a policy which disclaims the leadership of the proletariat but stresses the common interests of all the people while advocating class harmony and class capitulationism.

Wang-Wo-Lao-Tung (忘我勞動)

"Selfless labour"

This was a slogan put forward in 1958, calling on workers and peasants to work hard regardless of remuneration.

Wen-Tou-Wu-Tou (文鬥武鬥)

"Struggle conducted by reasoning, struggle conducted by coercion or force"

In a decision adopted by the CCP Central Committee on August 8, 1966 concerning the Great Proletarian Cultural Revolution, people are called upon to conduct the struggle by reasoning and not by coercion or force.

Wu-Hao-Chan-Shih (五好戰士)

"Five-good soldiers"

This refers to the training of young soldiers to be good in political ideology, good in military techniques, good in the "three-eight working

488

style," good in carrying out assigned tasks, and good in physical training.

Wu-Lan-Mu-Ch'i (烏蘭牧騎)

"Ulanmuchi" or "red cultural team"

"Ulanmuchi" is a "form of team formed by artists and writers of Inner Mongolia. Each team consists of a dozen performers, each of whom is a specialist in one field — music or singing, acting or dancing — but all of whom are versatile all-rounders. The team travel the year round by horse or cart with light stage props to serve the herdsmen."

"Ulanmuchi" has become a term to describe a cultural troupe which roves in the countryside to perform for villagers.

Wu-Lei-Fen-Tzu (五類份子)

"Five-category elements"

These are landlords, rich peasants, counter-revolutionaries, bad elements and rightists.

Wu-Nien-Shih-Yen, Shih-Nien-T'ui-Kuang (五年試驗十年推廣)

"Five years to try it; ten years to popularise it"

This phrase came into prominence in a *Jen-min Jih-pao* editorial of December 11, 1965, showing the Chinese spirit of persistence, caution and patience toward the enforcement of the half-work and half-study education system. Cadres in charge of education say they are prepared to try the system for five years and popularise it for ten years.

Wu-Shih (五史)

"Five histories"

The so-called "five histories" refer to family history, personal history, history of the Party, history of the PLA and history of world revolutionary struggle.

Wu-Szu-Yüan-Chu (無私援助)

"Selfless aid"

This referred to Soviet aid which the Chinese Government proclaimed to be without selfish motives while they were leaning "one-sidedly" towards Soviet Russia.

Ying-Ku-Tou-Liu-Lien (硬骨頭六連)

"Hard-bone 6th Company"

This is another army unit, whose "stiff" combat-readiness, battle style, military techniques and military and political discipline are praised throughout the People's Liberation Army. All PLA units are called on to learn from the "Hard-bone 6th Company spirit."

Yu-Ch'ing-Fen-Tzu (右傾份子)

"Right deviationists"

It refers to those who think that the Chinese Communist Party policy is too radical or impracticable.

Yü-Kung-Ching-Shen (愚公精神)

"The Yü Kung spirit"

According to a Chinese fable, a grand old man known as "Yü [meaning foolish] Kung" decided to level two mountains in front of his house. He said that if he could not finish the job in his life time, his sons, grandsons, or great grandsons would do it. The fable is used to describe a spirit of determination and persistency in fulfilling an assigned task. Mao Tse-tung recommended this spirit to Party members in his address at the close of the 7th CCP Central Committee session on June 11, 1945.

Index to Glossary

491

492

Appendix II

CHRONOLOGY

(November 1965 — November 1966)

November 10   *Wen-hui Pao* of Shanghai published an article by Yao Wen-yüan criticising the historical drama "Hai Jui Dismissed from Office." The article pointed out that the drama, written by Wu Han, Vice Mayor of Peking, was a big "anti-Party poisonous weed."

November 25   Lin Piao, Vice-Chairman of the Military Commission of CCP Central Committee and Defence Minister, issued instructions on the work of the PLA in 1966, stressing the importance of giving prominence to politics and of creatively studying and applying Mao Tse-tung's thought.

December 30   *Jen-min Jih-pao* published an article by Wu Han criticising his own writings. He admitted his mistake in falsifying the character of Hai Jui.

February 1   *Jen-min Jih-pao* published an article criticising the stage play "Hsieh Yao-huan," written by T'ien Han, Chairman of the Union of Chinese Drama Workers and Vice-Chairman of the All-China Federation of Literary and Art Circles. The play was described as a "big poisonous weed."

March 11   *Kuang-ming Jih-pao* of Peking published an article attacking the book *Collected Works on Motion Pictures* written by Hsia Yen, Vice-Chairman of All-China Federation of Literary and Art Circles. This was followed by another article on March 12 criticising Hsia Yen's play, "Sai Chin Hua."

April 14   *Jen-min Jih-pao* published an editorial entitled "Politics Must Take Command over Work," which stressed that in all fields of work, politics must be given top priority and that Mao Tse-tung's thinking must be taken as the guide for doing things.

April 14   At the 20th meeting of the Standing Committee of the National People's Congress, Kuo Mo-jo, Vice-President of the NPC Standing Committee and President of the China Academy of Sciences, criticised himself for not having been reformed ideologically according to the thought of Mao Tse-tung.

April 16   *Pei-ching Jih-pao* published a lengthy article denouncing the anti-Party, anti-socialist works carried in the magazine *Ch'ien Hsien* under the column "Notes from Three-Family Village" and in the newspaper *Pei-ching Wan-pao* under the column "Evening Chats at Yenshan." The articles of the "Three-Family Village" series were attributed to Wu Han, Teng T'o and Liao Mo-sha and those of the "Evening Chats" series to Teng T'o.

April 18   *Chieh-fang-chün Pao* published an editorial under the title of "Hold High the Great Red Banner of Mao Tse-tung's Thought and Actively Participate in the Great Socialist Cultural Revolution." The editorial called on literary and art workers of the armed forces to take an active part in the revolution to eliminate old bourgeois ideas on literature and art and usher in a new epoch of socialist, proletarian art and literature.

May   4   In an editorial entitled "Never Forget Class Struggle" *Chieh-fang-Chün Pao* warned the members of the PLA against "unarmed enemies" who were described as being more dangerous than open enemies. The editorial called on members of the PLA to resolutely fight the "anti-Party, anti-socialist black line" of the bourgeoisie and modern revisionism.

May   10   Shanghai's *Chieh-fang Jih-pao* and *Wen-hui Pao* simultaneously published an article by Yao Wen-yüan, editor in chief of the *Chieh-fang Jih-pao* and a member of the Cultural Revolution Group of the CCP Central Committee, which exposed the reactionary nature of "Evening Talks at Yenshan" and "Notes from Three-Family Village." The article pointed out that Teng T'o, author of "Evening Talks at Yenshan," and his cronies of Three-Family Village made *Ch'ien Hsien,* the *Pei-ching Jih-pao* and *Pei-ching Wan-pao* instruments for opposing the Party and socialism.

May   25   The newly reorganised CCP Peking Municpal Committee decided to dismiss the previous editorial board of *Pei-ching Jih-pao* and *Pei-ching Wan-pao* and Fan Chin, their director, and set up a new editorial board. It also decided to dismiss the editorial board of the fortnightly *Ch'ien Hsien* and to temporarily suspend publication of the journal pending reorganisation.

May   25   A "big-character poster" appeared in Peking University denouncing Sung Shuo, deputy director of the department in charge of university affairs under the CCP Peking Municipal Committee, Lu P'ing, president of the University and 1st secretary of its Party Committee, and P'eng P'ei-yun, deputy secretary of the Peking University Party Committee. The three were charged with sabotaging the cultural revolution at Peking University.

June   1   *Jen-min Jih-pao* carried an editorial entitled "Sweep Away All Monsters" which pointed out that in the last few months, in response to the militant call of the CCP Central Committee and Chairman Mao, hundreds of millions of workers, peasants and soldiers and vast numbers of revolutionary cadres and intellectuals, all armed with Mao Tse-tung's thought, had been sweeping away a horde of monsters that had entrenched themselves in ideological and cultural positions. It further stated that the great and unparalleled proletarian cultural revolution was sounding the death knell not only for the remnant capitalist forces on Chinese soil, but for imperialism, modern revisionism and all reactionaires.

June   2   A commentary in *Jen-min Jih-pao* hailed the "big-character poster" put up by Nieh Yüan-tzu and six others of the Philosophy Department of Peking University on May 25, as the first Marxist-Leninist poster in the whole country. The poster was reproduced in full by the paper.
An editorial entitled "A Great Revolution That Touches the People to Their Very Souls," appeared in the *Jen-min Jih-pao.* It held that the Great Proletarian Cultural Revolution was a struggle between the antagonistic world outlook of the proletariat and the bourgeoisie, which invariably resulted in one vanquishing the other.

This revolution, it declared, was a sharp struggle to shatter all schemes for the ideological restoration of capitalism. The revolution also had to dig out the ideological roots of revisionism, as well as struggle to strengthen the dictatorship of the proletariat and defend Mao Tse-tung's thought.

June	3	The CCP Central Committee decided that Li Hsüeh-feng, 1st secretary of the North China Bureau of the CCP Central Committee, be appointed 1st secretary of the CCP Peking Municipal Committee, and that Wu Teh, 1st secretary of the CCP Kirin Provincial Committee, be transferred to the post of 2nd secretary of the CCP Peking Municipal Committee to reorganise it.
June	4	*Jen-min Jih-pao* reported that the newly reorganised CCP Peking Municipal Committee decided to dismiss Lu P'ing, president of Peking University and 1st secretary of the University Party Committee, and P'eng P'ei-yun, university vice-president and deputy secretary of the University Party Committee, from all their posts and that the University's Party Committee be reorganised. Both Lu and P'eng were accused of having committed anti-Party and anti-socialist crimes.
June	4	In its editorial "Tear Aside the Bourgeois Mask of 'Liberty, Equality and Fraternity'," the *Jen-min Jih-pao* charged that a handful of representatives of the bourgeoisie who wormed their way into the Party hoisted aloft the black bourgeois banner of "liberty, equality and fraternity" in opposition to the line of the proletarian cultural revolution advanced by the CCP Central Committee headed by Mao Tse-tung. Pointing out that the enemy holding a red flag is more dangerous than the enemy with a white flag, it declared, "We shall smash anyone who tries to oppose the Party and socialism, to oppose the dictatorship of the proletariat and oppose Mao Tse-tung's thought. No matter what his authority, no matter how high his post, the whole nation and the whole Party will rise to denounce him... In dealing with the enemy of revolution, we cannot rely on persuasion but on struggle."
June	6	*Chieh-fang-chün Pao* published the esessential points for propaganda and education in connection with the great cultural revolution under the title "Raise High the Great Red Banner of Mao Tse-tung's Thought and Carry the Great Proletarian Cultural Revolution through to the End."
June	7	*Chieh-fang-chün Pao* carried an editorial entitled "Mao Tse-tung's Thought Is the Telescope and Microscope of Our Revolutionary Cause." It pointed out that Mao Tse-tung's thought was the most powerful ideological weaopn with which to sweep away all monsters and that it was the ideological and political telescope and microscope for observing and analysing all things. The paper further asserted that in this great cultural revolution, Mao Tse-tung's thought should be put in command of everything.
June	8	China's broad masses of workers, peasants, soldiers, revolutionary cadres and revolutionary intellectuals, using as their weapon the thought of Mao Tse-tung, started to criticise the old world, old things and old thinking on an unprecedented scale, *Jen-min Jih-pao* declared in its editorial, "We Are Critics of the Old World."

June	13	The CCP Central Committee and the State Council announced their decision to change the old system of entrance examinations and enrolment of students in higher educational institutions and to postpone 1966 enrolment of new students in colleges and universities for half a year.
June	15	The Central Committee of the Chinese Communist Youth League announced its decision to reorganise the League's Peking Municipal Committee and to dismiss Wang Chia-liu, deputy secretary of the CYL Peking Municipal Committee, from all her posts.
June	17	Premier Chou En-lai, in a speech at the banquet given by the Central Committee of the Rumanian Communist Party and the Rumanian Council of Ministers in Bucharest declared that the Great Proletarian Cultural Revolution in China is a question affecting the destiny and future of the Chinese Communist Party and the State. The spearhead of this revolution, he said, was directed against a small handful of anti-communist villains who donned the cloak of communism and a small handful of anti-Party, anti-socialist and counter-revolutionary bourgeois intellectuals.
June	17	Ch'en Ch'i-t'ung, deputy director of both the Culture and Propaganda Departments of the General Political Department of the PLA, was denounced in a *Jen-min Jih-pao* article for his work, *A Searching Anatomy,* in which he was alleged to have spread capitalist and revisionist ideas on art and literature and proposed a reactionary programme for drama that ran counter to the line presented by the Party and Mao Tse-tung.
June	17	Ch'in Mu, editor of *Yang-ch'eng Wan-pao,* Canton, and a well-known writer, was denounced as an "extremely reactionary rightist" by workers in Canton. He was alleged to have said that the Communist cadres cared only for themselves and were arrogant and ruthless.
June	19	In a letter, printed in the *Jen-min Jih-pao* and all other Peking newspapers, which dealt with the creative study and application of Mao Tse-tung's works on the industrial and communications fronts, Lin Piao said it was a very good thing that the industrial and communications departments stressed putting politics in command and putting politics first.
June	20	In an editorial entitled "Revolutionary Big-Character Posters Are Magic Mirrors That Show Up All Monsters," *Jen-min Jih-pao* encouraged the masses to write "big-character posters" to express their views fully and frankly, expose all the representatives of the bourgeoisie who oppose the Communist Party, socialism and Mao Tse-tung's thought, expose all the monsters and, one by one, smash to pieces the reactionary bastions of the bourgeoisie.
June	27	In a speech at a mass rally in Tirana during an official visit to Albania, Premier Chou En-lai stated that in the last analysis, the present class struggle in China was a struggle between attempts at staging a capitalist come-back and efforts to thwart such attempts. This struggle to dig out the roots of revisionism, he said, will further consolidate the dictatorship of the proletariat in China, including the dictatorship in all cultural spheres.

June	29	The All-Army Conference on Creative Art and Literature was summoned by the General Political Department of the PLA, and Liu Chih-chien, deputy director of the PLA General Political Department, stressed that the main task of the literary and art workers of the PLA was to publicise and defend the thought of Mao Tse-tung, make thoroughgoing criticism of bourgeois ideology, and wage a resolute struggle against all bourgeois, revisionist ideology.
July	1	In its editorial "Long Live Mao Tse-tung's Thought" which commemorated the 45th anniversary of the founding of the Chinese Communist Party, *Jen-min Jih-pao* pointed out that the great thought of Mao Tse-tung was the biggest barrier to the schemes of all anti-Party cliques trying to stage a counter-revolutionary coup d'etat. It warned that anyone who opposed Mao Tse-tung's thought, now or in the future, would be a mortal enemy of the revolution and the people, and would be condemned by the whole Party and denounced by the whole nation.
July	1	*Hung-ch'i*, the theoretical organ of the CCP Central Committee, published an editorial in the No. 9 issue of 1966 entitled "Thoroughly Criticise and Repudiate the Revisionist Line of Some of the Principal Leading Members of the Former Peking Municipal Party Committee." The editorial made ten charges against the former CCP Peking Municipal Committee led by P'eng Chen, and labelled it "an insidious anti-Party and anti-socialist clique." The same issue of *Hung-chi* also carried an editorial note on the reprinting of Mao Tse-tung's "Talks at the Yenan Forum on Literature and Art," which was published in May 1942. It pointed out that the talks of Comrade Mao Tse-tung made a systematic criticism of the bourgeois line on the literature and art of the 1930s which was represented by Chou Yang. However, for 24 years, Chou Yang and Company consistently refused to carry out Mao's line on literature and art and stubbornly adhered to the bourgeois, revisionist black line on literature and art. It said further that under the control and influence of this black line, came a spate of absurd theories and a profusion of "poisonous weeds," creating a miasma in literary and art circles.
July	10	While reporting those present at a banquet given at the end of the Afro-Asian Writers' Emergency Meeting on July 9, the New China News Agency referred to Ch'en Po-ta, member of the Political Bureau of the CCP Central Committee and Chief Editor of the Central Committee's theoretical journal, *Hung-ch'i*, as the "leader of the group in charge of the cultural revolution under the Party's Central Committee." This was the first indication of the formation of the Party's Cultural Revolution Group as a steering organ of the cultural revolution. (*NCNA* reported on August 31 that Chiang Ch'ing [Madame Mao Tse-tung] is First Deputy Leader of the Group.)
July	11	Furthering the attack launched by *Hung-ch'i* on July 1, the Chinese press opened an all-out campaign against Chou Yang, alternate member of the CCP Central Committee and deputy director of the Department of Propaganda, CCP Central Committee. *Chieh-fang-chün Pao* published an article entitled "Chou Yang the Planner and Concocter of the Anti-Party Play 'Hai Jui'." This article pointed out that Chou was the behind-the-scenes commander responsible for the production of the play "Hai Jui's Memorial to the Emperor," which it described as a "poisoned arrow" directed at the Party, socialism and the thought of Mao Tse-tung.

July	16	Chairman Mao Tse-tung once again swam in the Yangtse River. In 65 minutes his swim took him from near the mouth of the Wuch'ang dykes to a place near the Wuhan Iron and Steel Company, and covered a distance of almost 15 kilometres.
July	17	*Jen-min Jih-pao* said in its editorial "A New Stage of the Socialist Revolution in China" that the Great Proletarian Cultural Revolution had pushed China's socialist revolution to a new, deeper and broader stage. The aim of the current revolution, the editorial pointed out, was to solve the question of who will win out in the ideological struggle, socialism or capitalism.
July	21	The *Jen-min Jih-pao* declared in an editorial entitled "From the Masses, to the Masses," that every Communist Party member must be tested in the Great Proletarian Cultural Revolution, in the flame of the mass struggle. It asserted that "they must prove by their actions that they are the faithful servants of the masses, and that they really take Comrade Mao Tse-tung's teachings as the supreme guide in all their actions." The paper charged that a handful of people have adopted the attidtude of bureaucratic overlords towards the masses and had taken reltaliatory actions against the masses who criticised them. The paper warned that if they acted in this way, they would be discarded by the masses.
July	26	Chairman Mao's swim in the Yangtze River on July 11 was hailed by *Chieh-fang-chün Pao* in its editorial "Valiantly Forge Ahead along the Revolutionary Course Charted by Chairman Mao." Simultaneously, NCNA reported that people all over the country had expressed their joy over the news of Chairman Mao's swim in the Yangtze, and had pledged to follow him closely in forging ahead in the teeth of the storms of class struggle.
August	1	*Chieh-fang-chün Pao* published an editorial entitled "Turn Our Army into a Great School of Mao Tse-tung's Thought," in commemoration of the 39th anniversary of the founding of the Chinese People's Liberation Army. The editorial referred to a call issued by Mao that the PLA should be turned into a great school and that military men should get into politics, run farms and medium or small factories and do mass work besides their regular duties.
August	1	The 8th Central Committee of the Chinese Communist Party held its 11th Plenary Session in Peking with Mao Tse-tung, Chairman of the Central Committee, presiding., It was the first plenary session of the 8th Central Committee in four years. The 10th plenary session was held in September, 1962.
August	7	The Central Committee of the Chinese Communist Party announced its decision to speed up the mass publication of Mao Tse-tung's works in order to meet the urgent needs of the people in studying Mao Tse-tung's thought. It directed the publication, printing and distribution departments throughout the country to make all-out efforts to make the publishing and distributing of Chairman Mao's works their foremost task.
August	8	The Central Committee of the Chinese Communist Party adopted a 16-point decision concerning the Great Proletarian Cultural Revolution. The resolution was drawn up under the personal direction of Mao Tse-tung.

498

August	10	Chairman Mao Tse-tung this evening met Peking's revolutionary masses at the reception centre near the headquarters of the CCP Central Committee, who gathered to celebrate the Central Committee's decision concerning the Great Proletarian Cultural Revolution. Speaking to the crowd, Mao said, "You should pay attention to State affairs and carry the Great Proletarian Cultural Revolution through to the end!"
August	11	In an editorial entitled "Master the Ideological Weapon of the Great Cultural Revolution," the *Jen-min Jih-pao* urged all the people in China to earnestly study the decision of the CCP Central Committee concerning the Great Proletarian Cultural Revolution, and to put this decision into effect. Noting that resistance to the cultural revolution was great and stubborn, it called on the people to master the powerful ideological weapon of the decision of the Central Committee, to knock down those in power within the Party who take the capitalist road, and sweep away all freaks and monsters."
August	12	The 11th Plenary Session of the 8th Central Committee of the Chinese Communist Party issued a communique announcing its approval of the 16-point decision concerning the Great Proletarian Cultural Revolution adopted by the Central Committee on August 8, as well as the important policy decisions and measures concerning domestic and international questions adopted by the Political Bureau of the Central Committee since the 10th Plenary Session of the 8th Central Committee in September. 1962.
August	18	Chairman Mao Tse-tung attended a mass rally of one million revolutionary people at the Tienanmen Square in Peking, to celebrate the Great Proletarian Cultural Revolution. Dressed in an army uniform, he reviewed a parade of the one million revolutionaries with Defence Minister Lin Piao beside him.

Speaking at the rally, Lin Piao declared, "The Great Proletarian Cultural Revolution is aimed precisely at eliminating bourgeois ideology, establishing proletarian ideology, remoulding people's souls, revolutionising their ideology, digging out the roots of revisionism, and consolidating and developing the socialist system. Under the leadership of Chairman Mao, we must launch fierce attacks on bourgeois ideology, old customs and old force of habit! We must thoroughly topple, smash and discredit the counter-revolutionary revisionists, bourgeois rightists and reactionary bourgeois authorities, and they must never be allowed to rise again!"

Other speakers at the rally included Premier Chou En-lai, Ch'en Po-ta, member of the Politburo of the CCP Central Committee and leader of the group in charge of the cultural revolution under the CCP Central Committee, and Nieh Yüan-tzu, a representative of Peking University.

Among the million people attending the rally were tens of thousands of Red Guards, from the capital's colleges and middle schools, all wearing red arm bands. During the rally, a Red Guard mounted the rostrum and put the arm band of the Red Guards on Mao, amid the cheers of the Red Guards who exclaimed, "Chairman Mao has joined our Red Guards. This is the greatest support and inspiration to us. With Chairman Mao's backing, we have nothing to fear!"

August	20	An editorial in *Chieh-fang-chün Pao,* the organ of the army, called on all members of the PLA to follow Lin Piao's instructions to creatively study and apply Mao's works and make a great effort to apply them. It said that in the final analysis the Great Proletarian Cultural Revolution aimed at establishing the complete ascendancy of Mao Tse-tung's thought. It also aimed at using Mao Tse-tung's thought to change the mental outlook of the whole society and to turn its great spiritual force into a great material force.
August	22	NCNA reported that since August 20th, the Red Guards in Peking had been taken to the streets and had launched a fierce attack against bourgeois customs and habits, all old ideas and culture. They changed street names and shop signs which had "feudal, capitalist and revisionist" connotations, and proposed that barbers, tailors and book-sellers never again give outlandish haircuts, make outlandish clothing, and sell or rent out decadent books or magazines.
August	23	*Chieh-fang-chün Pao* and *Jen-min Jih-pao* simultaneously praised in their editorials the "proletarian revolutionary rebel spirit" of the Red Guards in Peking. *Jen-min Jih-pao* also called upon the workers, peasants and soldiers to give resolute support to the revolutionary students.
August	26	The Peking Municipal People's Council, at the demand of Peking's Red Guards and revolutionary masses, announced the banning of *Franciscaines Missionaires de Marie* and the taking over of *L'Ecole Sacre-Coeur,* a school run by the mission. It also decided to deport the eight foreign nuns of the mission who were charged with "counter-revolutionary" activities.
August	28	A call for the Red Guards to learn from the PLA was made by *Jen-min Jih-pao* in its editorial entitled "Revolutionary Young People Should Learn from the Chinese People's Liberation Army." The editorial stated that they (the Red Guards) should always be loyal to the Party and to Mao Tse-tung, and resolutely observe the "Three Main Rules of Discipline" and "Eight Points for Attention" laid down by Mao for the PLA.
August	29	In its editorial "Salute to Our Red Guards," *Jen-min Jih-pao* praised the Red Guards for their meritorious deeds in dragging out the "blood-suckers," by taking out their concealed gold, silver, valuables and other treasures as well as secret accounts and various kinds of murderous weapons, and showing them to the public. It further stated that the Red Guards were playing the role of a shock force of the culutral revolution, sweeping away the old customs and habits of all the exploiting classes.
August	31	Chairman Mao Tse-tung with his "close comrade-in-arms" Lin Piao and other Party leaders received half a million Red Guards and revolutionary students and teachers at Tienanmen Square in Peking. During the rally, the Red Guards and revolutionary teachers and students who came from various parts of the country pledged themselves to follow the Party and Mao forever and carry the proletarian cultural revolution through to the end.

Speaking at the rally, Lin Piao emphatically declared that the main targets of the revolutionary struggle were those persons in authority who wormed their way into the Party and took the capitalist

500

road. He urged the Red Guards to carry out the struggle by reasoning and not by coercion or force.

Also speaking at the rally, Premier Chou En-lai stressed that the Red Guards must be built into a highly organised and disciplined militant army with a high level of political consciousness and become the reliable reserve force of the PLA. He announced that the Party's Central Committee had decided that all college students and representatives of middle school students in the other parts of the country should come to Peking, group after group, at different times, to exchange revolutionary experiences with their counterparts in the capital.

September 5
The *Jen-min Jih-pao* stated in an editorial, "Struggle by reasoning instead of by coercion or force is an important policy of the Party in the Great Proletarian Cultural Revolution. We must persist in this policy, abide by it and implement it."

September 7
The editorial of the *Jen-min Jih-pao* urged the Red Guards and revolutionary teachers and students to organise themselves and go to the countryside to take part in manual labour, help with the autumn harvest and learn from poor and lower-middle peasants their diligence, revolutionary enthusiasm and other fine qualities they possessed as working people. It stressed that the important tasks before the whole Party and the entire people were to take a firm hold of the revolution and stimulate production.

September 15
Chairman Mao Tse-tung again received a million Red Guards and revolutionary teachers and students in Peking's Tienanmen Square. Addressing the rally, Lin Piao, while reiterating that the main targets of attack in the cultural revolution movement were those in the Party who were in power and were taking the capitalist road, noted that some people were going against Mao's instructions and the 16-point decision of the CCP Central Committee. Lin further stated that they were creating antagonism between the masses of workers and peasants and the revolutionary students and were inciting the former to struggle against the latter. He called upon the masses of workers, peasants, soldiers, revolutionary students and revolutionary comrades to unite and carry the revolution through to the end.

In his speech, Chou En-lai stressed the importance of promoting production and urged the revolutionaries to respond to Mao's call to take a firm hold of the revolution with one hand and spur production on with the other. Specifically, he advised the Red Guards and revolutionary students not to go to the factories and enterprises, to Party, government and public organisations of county level or below, or people's communes in the rural areas to establish revolutionary ties, because factories and rural areas could not take time off like the schools and stop production to make revolution. He further stated that the Red Guards and revolutionary teachers and students should organise themselves and go and work in the countryside, help bring in the autumn harvest and learn from the poor and lower-middle peasants.

September 15
Today's *Jen-min Jih-pao* emphasized that production on industrial and agricultural fronts must not be interrupted by the cultural revolution. The paper asserted that the "four clean-up" movement would be temporarily suspended in the rural areas, during the busy

period of the autumn harvest and that it was not necessary for the Red Guards and revolutionary teachers and students to go to factories and rural areas to exchange revolutionary experience and interfere with the arrangements there.

October 1   China marked its National Day with a mammoth rally and parade of 1.5 million people in Peking's Tienanmen Square. Chairman Mao Tse-tung together with other Party and State leaders including Lin Piao, Liu Shao-ch'i and Chou En-lai reviewed the parade from the rostrum. Speaking at the rally, Lin Piao declared that in the current Great Proletarian Cultural Revolution, hundreds of millions of Chinese people had been aroused, and that the reactionary bourgeoisie had been completely discredited and the corner-stone of victory laid.

October 1   The editorial of *Hung-ch'i* No. 13, 1966 noted that the struggle of the two lines within the Party had not yet come to an end; and that in some places and units, it was still very acute and complicated. Some people, it alleged, adopted new forms to deceive the masses and acted against the 16-point decision of the Central Committee, stubbornly persisting in the bourgeois reactionary line and inciting the masses to struggle against each other.

October 9   *NCNA* reported that Lin Piao recently gave extemely important directions on the study of Mao Tse-tung's works in the PLA. The directions, which were communicated to a meeting of Air Force cadres by Hsiao Hua, Director of the General Political Department of the PLA, called on the entire army to carry forward to a new stage the mass drive for the creative study and application of Mao Tse-tung's works. Lin Piao asserted that every comrade in the army must raise higher than ever before the great red banner of Mao Tse-tung's thought and do his utmost truly to grasp Mao's thought and truly to master it.

October 18   Chairman Mao Tse-tung, accompanied by Lin Piao and other leaders of the Party centre, received for the fifth time 1.5 million Red Guards and revolutionary teachers and students who had come to Peking from various parts of China to establish revolutionary ties. Dressed in military uniforms the CCP leaders, riding in nine open cars, with Mao standing in the first one, reviewed the young revolutionaries lining both sides of the boulevards running into Tienanmen Square.

October 19   *Jen-min Jih-pao* commemorated the 30th anniversary of the death of Lu Hsün, a noted leftist writer, by publishing an editorial entitled "Learn from Lu Hsün's Revolutionary Spirit of Unyielding Integrity." The editorial called on the revolutionary people to carry forward Lu Hsün's spirit of "beating a dog in the water" and never to become soft-hearted or show any kindness to the enemy. The editorial further stated, "We must resolutely hit hard, pull down and completely discredit, without exception, the handful of persons within the Party who are in authority and are taking the capitalist road, the counter-revolutionary revisionists and all ghosts and monsters, so that they can never get up again."

October 20   *Jen-min Jih-pao* editorially praised as a significant pioneering action the 15-member "Long March Detachment" of Red Guards of Dairen Mercantile Marine Institute who walked all the way from Dairen to Peking to establish revolutionary ties, and covered a distance of

502

1,000 kilometres within a month.   While calling on other revolutionary students to do the same if they wish to, conditions permitting, the editorial noted that people who had no intention of undertaking hard struggle can never become genuine revolutionaries.   It cautioned, "Whoever imagines that he will make a revolution in comfort will likely effect a comfortable peaceful evolution in himself and slide down into the quagmire of revisionism."

October   31   Speaking at a mass meeting to commemorate the 30th anniversary of the death of the noted leftist writer Lu Hsün, Ch'en Po-ta, head of the Culturual Revolution Group under the CCP Central Committee, recalled a statement made by Lu Hsün on the eve of his death, "Never mix with people who injure others yet oppose revenge and advocate tolerance."   This, he said, contained some penetrating remarks which were worthy of deep thought even today.

November   3   More than two million people were reported to have taken part in a mammoth rally in Peking's Tienanmen Square when Chairman Mao Tse-tung, accompanied by his close comrade-in-arms Lin Piao, received for the sixth time revolutionary teachers and students and Red Guards from all parts of the country.   Addressing the rally, Lin Piao pointed out: "Under the guidance of Chairman Mao's correct line, the broad revolutionary masses have created the new experience of developing extensive democracy under the dictatorship of the proletariat.   By this extensive democracy, the broad masses are allowed to use the media of free airing of views, big-character posters, great debates and extensive exchange of revolutionary experience to criticise and supervise the Party and government leading institutions and leaders at all levels.   At the same time, the people's democratic rights are being fully realised in accordance with the principles of the Paris Commune."

November 10-11   Chairman Mao Tse-tung received and reviewed for the seventh time some two million Red Guards and revolutionary teachers and students in Peking's Tienanmen Square.   The young revolutionaries rode in 6,000 motor vehicles, waving the "red book"—"Quotations from Chairman Mao Tse-tung" — as their cars drove past the rostrum. The review lasted more than six hours, during which time Mao was reported to have said to some "leading comrades" on the rostrum: "You should put politics in command, go to the masses and be one with them and carry on the Great Proletarian Cultural Revolution even better."

November 15   Premier Chou En-lai and other Communist leaders received some thirty "Long March Detachments" of Red Guards who travelled on foot from various provinces to Peking to establish revolutionary ties with the Capital's Red Guards.

November 24   A *China News Service* report stated that over nine million revolutionary teachers and students had come to Peking to "exchange revolutionary experiences" since August 1966.

November 25-26   Chairman Mao Tse-tung again received two and a half million revolutionary teachers and students and Red Guards in Peking's Tienanmen Square, this being his eighth reception of the revolutionaries since August 18, and also the last one until next spring, *NCNA* announced.   The news agency estimated that in three months

503

and more, Mao had received altogether 11 million revolutionary teachers and students and Red Guards from all parts of the country.

November 28 More than 20,000 revolutionary militants in the field of literature and art from Peking and other parts of China held a rally for the Great Proletarian Cultural Revolution in the People's Hall in Peking. Premier Chou En-lai, Ch'en Po-ta and Chiang Ch'ing, leader and first deputy leader respectively of the Cultural Revolution Group under the CCP Central Committee, made important speeches at the rally. They called upon the revolutionary fighters in literature and art throughout the country to hold high the great red banner of Mao Tse-tung's thought, give prominence to proletarian politics, resolutely implement the proletarian revolutionary line represented by Chairman Mao, thoroughly criticise and repudiate the bourgeois reactionary line, unite on the basis of the principles of Marxism-Leninism and Mao Tse-tung's thought, complete the tasks of struggle, criticism and transformation and strive to create the most splendid new proletarian literature and art in human history.

Hsieh T'ang-chung, head of the Cultural Department of the PLA General Political Department, announced at the rally the appointment of Chiang Ch'ing (Madame Mao Tse-tung), by the Military Commission of the CCP Central Committee, as adviser on cultural work to the Chinese People's Liberation Army. He also announced the Military Commission's decision to incorporate the No. 1 Peking Opera Company of Peking, the National Peking Opera Theatre, the Central Philharmonic Society, the ballet troupe and the orchestra of the Central Song and Dance Ensemble into the PLA as constituent parts of the army for political and literary and art work.

BIBLIOGRAPHY

Newspapers

An-hui Jih-pao (安徽日報) [Anhwei Daily], Hofei, Anhwei Province
An-shan Jih Pao (鞍山日報) [Anshan Daily], Anshan, Liaoning Province
Chang-chia-k'ou Jih-pao (張家口日報) [Changchiakou Daily], Kalgan
Ch'ang-ch'un Jih-pao (長春日報) [Changchun Daily], Changchun, Kirin Province
Ch'ang-sha Jih Pao (長沙日報) [Changsha Daily], Changsha, Hunan Province
Che-chiang Jih-pao (浙江日報) [Chekiang Daily], Hangchow, Chekiang Province
Cheng-chou Jih-pao (鄭州日報) [Chengchow Daily], Chengchow, Honan Province
Ch'eng-tu Jih-pao (成都日報) [Chengtu Daily], Chengtu, Szechwan Province
Ch'i-ch'i-ha-erh Jih-pao (齊齊哈爾日報) [Tsitsihar Daily], Tsitsihar, Heilungkiang Province
Chi-lin Jih-pao (吉林日報) [Kirin Daily], Changchun, Kirin Province
Chi-nan Jih-pao (濟南日報) [Tsinan Daily], Tsinan, Shantung Province
Chiang-hsi Jih-pao (江西日報) [Kiangsi Daily], Nanchang, Kiangsi Province
Chieh-fang-chün Pao (解放軍報) [Liberation Army Daily], Peking
Chieh-fang Jih-pao (解放日報) [Liberation Daily], Shanghai
Ch'ien-hsien Pao (前綫報) [Front Line Press], replacing Ta-kung Daily, published every two days, Peking
Chin-chou Jih-pao (錦州日報) [Chinchow Daily], Liaoning Province
Ch'ing-hai Jih-pao (青海日報) [Chinghai Daily], Sining, Chinghai Province
Ch'ing-tao Jih-pao (青島日報) [Tsingtao Daily], Tsingtao, Shantung Province
Ch'ung-ch'ing Jih-pao (重慶日報) [Chungking Daily], Szechwan Province
Chung-kuo Ch'ing-nien Pao (中國青年報) [China Youth Daily], Peking
Fu-chien Jih-pao (福建日報) [Fukien Daily], Foochow, Fukien Province
Fu-shun Jih-pao (撫順日報) [Fushun Daily], Fushun, Liaoinng Province
Ha-erh-pin Jih-pao (哈爾濱日報) [Harbin Daily], Harbin, Kirin Province
Hang-chou Jih-pao (杭州日報) [Hangchow Daily], Hangchow, Chekiang Province
Hei-lung-chiang Jih-pao (黑龍江日報) [Heilungkiang Daily], Harbin, Kirin Province
Ho-nan Jih-pao (河南日報) [Honan Daily], Chengchow, Honan Province
Ho-pei Jih-pao (河北日報) [Hopeh Daily], Paoting, Hopeh Province
Hsi-an Jih-pao (西安日報) [Sian Daily], Sian, Shensi Province
Hsi-tsang Jih-pao (西藏日報) [Tibet Daily], Lhasa, Tibet
Hsia-men Jih-pao (厦門日報) [Amoy Daily], Amoy, Fukien Province
Hsin-chiang Jih-pao (新疆日報) [Sinkiang Daily], Urumchi, Sinkiang Province
Hsin-hua Jih-pao (新華日報) [New China Daily], Nanking, Kiangsu Province

505

Hsinhua Daily News Release (新華社電訊稿) (English and Chinese Editions), Peking
Hsü-chou Jih-pao (徐州日報) [Hsuchow Daily], Hsuchow, Kiangsu Province
Hu-pei Jih-pao (湖北日報) [Hupeh Daily], Wuhan, Hupeh Province
Hung-wei Pao (紅衛報) [Red Guard Daily], (replacing *Yang-ch'eng Wan-pao,* (羊城晚報)
　　　　　　　　　　　[Yang Cheng Evening News], Canton, Kwangtung Province
Jen-min Jih-pao (人民日報) [People's Daily], Peking
Kan-su Jih-pao (甘肅日報) [Kansu Daily], Lanchow, Kansu Province
Kuang-chou Jih-pao (廣州日報) [Canton Daily], Canton, Kwangtung Province
Kuang-si Jih-pao (廣西日報) [Kwangsi Daily], Nanning, Kwangsi Province
Kuang-ming Jih-pao (光明日報) [Kuangming Daily], Peking
Kuei-chou Jih-pao (貴州日報), [Kweichow Daily], Kweiyang, Kweichow Province
Kuei-lin Jih-pao (桂林日報) [Kweilin Daily], Kweilin, Kwangsi Province
Kung-jen Jih-pao (工人日報) [Workers' Daily], Peking
Liao-ning Jih-pao (遼寧日報), [Liaoning Daily), Mukden, Liaoning Province
Lu-ta Jih-pao (旅大日報) [Lushun-Dairen Daily], Dairen, Liaoning Province
Nan-ch'ang Wan-pao (南昌晚報) [Nanchang Evening News], Nanchang, Hunan Province
Nan-fang Jih-pao (南方日報) [Nanfang Daily], Canton, Kwangtung Province
Nan-ning Jih-pao (南寧日報) [Nanning Daily], Nanning, Kwangsi Province
Nei-meng-ku Jih-pao (內蒙古日報) [Inner Mongolia Daily], Huhehot, Inner Mongloia
Ning-hsia Jih-pao (寧夏日報) [Ningsia Daily], Yinchuan, Ningsia Autonomous Region
Pei-ching Jih-pao (北京日報) [Peking Daily], Peking
Pei-ching Wan-pao (北京晚報) [Peking Evening News], Peking
Shan-si Jih-pao (山西日報) [Shansi Daily], Taiyuan, Shansi Province
Shen-si Jih-pao (陝西日報) [Shensi Daily], Sian, Shensi Province
Shen-yang Jih-pao (瀋陽日報) [Mukden Daily], Mukden, Liaoning Province
Shen-yang Wan-pao (瀋陽晚報) [Mukden Evening News], Mukden, Liaoning Province
Szu-ch'uan Jih-pao (四川日報) [Szechwan Daily], Chengtu, Szechwan Province
Ta-chung Jih-pao (大衆日報) [Tachung Daily], Tsinan, Shantung Province
Ta-kung Pao (大公報) [Takung Daily], Peking
T'ien-chin Jih-pao (天津日報) [Tientsin Daily], Tientsin, Hopeh Province
T'ien-chin Wan-pao (天津晚報) [Tientsin Evening News], Tientsin, Hopeh Province
Wen-hui Pao (文滙報) [Wenhui Daily], Shanghai
Yun-nan Jih-pao (雲南日報) [Yunnan Daily], Kunming, Yunnan Province

Periodicals

Chiao-hsueh Yu Yen-chiu (教學與研究) [Teaching and Research], monthly, Peking
Chieh-fang-chün Chan-shih (解放軍戰士) [Liberation Army Fighters], semi-monthly,
　　　　　　　　　　　　　　　　　　　　　　　　　　　　Peking
Chieh-fang-chün Hua-pao (解放軍畫報) [Liberation Army Pictorial], monthly, Peking
Chieh-fang-chün Wen-i (解放軍文藝) [Liberation Army Literature], monthly, Peking
Ch'ien-hsien (前線) [Front Line], semi-monthly, Peking
Ch'ü-i (曲藝) [Song Art], bi-monthly, Peking

506

Chü-pen (劇本) [Book of Drama], monthly, Peking
Chung-kuo Chien-she (中國建設) [China Reconstructs], English, monthly, Peking
Chung-kuo Ch'ing-nien (中國青年) [Chinese Youth], semi-monthly, Peking
Chung-kuo Fu-nü (中國婦女) [Women of China], monthly, Peking
Chung-kuo Wen-hsüeh (中國文學) [Chinese Literature], English, monthly, Peking
Hsi-chü Pao (戲劇報) [Drama News], semi-monthly, Peking
Hsin Chien-she (新建設) [New Construction], monthly, Peking
Hsin-hwa Yueh-pao (新華月報) [New China Monthly], Peking
Hsin Kuan-ch'a (新觀察) [New Observer], semi-monthly, Peking
Hsüeh-shu Yüeh-k'an (學術月刊) [Arts Monthly], monthly, Shanghai
Hung-ch'i (紅旗) [Red Flag], semi-monthly, Peking
Jen-min Wen-hsüeh (人民文學) [People's Literature], monthly, Peking
Jen-min Hua-pao (人民畫報) [China Pictorial), monthly, Chinese and English, Peking
Jen-min Yin-hsüeh (人民音樂) [People's Music], monthly, Peking
Ko-ch'ü (歌曲) [Songs], monthly, Peking
Mei-shu (美術) [Fine Arts], monthly, Peking
Min-chien Wen-hsüeh (民間文學) [Folklore], monthly, Peking
Min-tsu Hua-pao (民族畫報) [Minorities Pictorial] bi-monthly, Peking
Pei-ching Chou-pao (北京週報) [Peking Review], English, weekly, Peking
Pei-ching Ta-hsüeh Hsüeh-pao (北京大學學報) [Peking University Journal] quarterly,
                    Peking, reported to have been renamed *Hsin Pei-ta*
                    (新北大)
Pei-ching Wen-i (北京文藝) [Peking Literature], monthly, Peking
Shang-hai Chiao-yü (上海教育) [Shanghai Education], monthly, Shanghai
Shang-hai Hsi-chü (上海戲劇) [Shanghai Drama], monthly, Shanghai
Shang-hai Wen-i (上海文藝) [Shanghai Literature], monthly, Shanghai
Shih-chieh Chih-shih (世界知識) [World Knowledge], semi-monthly, Peking
Shih-shih Shou-t'se (時事手冊) [Current Events Handbook], semi-monthly, Peking
Ta-chung Tien-ying (大衆電影) [Popular Cinema], monthly, Shanghai
Ta-chung Yen-ch'ang (大衆演唱) [Popular Acting and Singing], monthly, Chekiang
Tien-ying Ch'uang-tso (電影創作) [Film Creation] bi-monthly, Peking
Tien-ying Wen-hsüeh (電影文學) [Film Literature], monthly, Changchun, Kirin Province
Tien-ying I-shu (電影藝術) [Film Arts], monthly, Peking
Wen-hsüeh Kai-k'e (文學改革) [Literary Reform], monthly, Peking
Wen-hsüeh P'ing-lun (文學評論) [Literary Review]. bi-monthly, Peking
Wen-hsüeh Yüeh-k'en (文學月刊) Literature Monthly], monthly, Mukden
Wen-i Hsüeh-hsi (文藝學習) [Literature and Study], monthly, Peking
Wen-i Pao [文藝報] [Literary Gazette], monthly, Peking